TORPEDO JUNCTION

WITH THE PACIFIC FLEET FROM PEARL HARBOR TO MIDWAY

By ROBERT J. CASEY

WAR

The Cannoneers Have Hairy Ears
I Can't Forget

MYSTERY

The Secret of No. 37 Hardy Street
The Secret of the Bungalow
Hot Ice
News Reel
The Third Owl

TRAVEL

Four Faces of Siva
Baghdad and Points East
Easter Island
The Land of Haunted Castles
The Lost Kingdom of Burgundy

ROMANCE

The Gentleman in Armor
Cambodian Quest

SATIRE

The Voice of the Lobster

TECHNICAL

Manual of Radio Interference

VERSE

The Vest Pocket Anthology

ROBERT J. CASEY

TORPEDO JUNCTION

25693

WITH THE PACIFIC FLEET FROM

PEARL HARBOR TO MIDWAY

By ROBERT J. CASEY

THE BOBBS-MERRILL COMPANY

INDIANAPOLIS   NEW YORK

BY THE CORNWALL PRESS, CORNWALL, N. Y.

TABLE OF CONTENTS

Book One
MURDER IN PARADISE

Book Two
THE MARSHALLS

Book Three

MARCUS

TABLE OF CONTENTS—*Continued*
Book Four
MYSTERY CRUISE

Book Five
CORAL SEA

Book Six
MIDWAY!

APPENDIX

LIST OF ILLUSTRATIONS

THE NAVY HAS A WORD FOR IT

Can or *Tin Can.* The familiar name for a destroyer.

Chicago Piano. Multiple pompom—a small-calibre (1.1 inch) rapid-fire cannon with four barrels used in antiaircraft fire.

Cincus, Cincpac, etc. Telegraph code for Commander in Chief Pacific Fleet, etc. *Cincus* for obvious reasons was later changed to *Cominch*.

C.P.O. Chief Petty Officer.

Donald Duck. The loud-speaker aboard ship, so-called because of its accent.

Flat-top. A term generally applied to a carrier but sometimes applied to a tanker.

Gee-Dunk. A double scoop of ice cream. Derivation unknown.

Greenhouse (or *Blister*). The transparent turret on a bomber.

Maru. A term of endearment hitched onto the names of Japanese merchant ships such as *Kitano Maru, Taiyo Maru,* etc. But in Navy slang any Japanese ship is now a *maru* unless it's a battleship when it's a *san*. Some U. S. ships are called *maru* by way of heavy humor—such as the *Swayback Maru*.

Nisei. Second generation (American-born) Japanese.

O.N.I. Office of Naval Intelligence.

Shangri-La. Your guess is as good as anybody's.

S.O.C. Scout Observation Curtis—a cruiser plane. Other Navy planes similarly titled are *T.B.D.* (Torpedo Bomber Douglas) and *S.B.D.* (Scout Bomber Douglas), and *PBY*, naval long-distance patrol bomber—the same flying boat which the British have labeled "Catalina."

Tail-End Charlie. Rear gunner on a bomber—in England he is called, impolitely, something else.

Tin Tub. The steel splinter screen around the ack-ack and secondary batteries.

BOOK ONE

MURDER IN PARADISE

Journey to the beginning of Night . . .

1

FORGET PEARL HARBOR

THE MARINES had gone into the Solomon Islands. Landing parties had made a wreck of Makin, in the Gilberts. And cautious now for the first time since the Japanese moved south like an epidemic last winter, Hirohito's fleet, beaten in a clash off Tulagi, had delayed battle, desperately anxious to knock out our land forces without being knocked out in turn. The Japanese anxiety was significant, but to a couple of us not entirely surprising.

There were four of us in the party—the Commander, an ensign, an Army aviator and myself—and if two of us as we read the stop-press bulletins in a Peoria newspaper could see the rainbow peaks of Malaita step back from the sea, if we could smell the Cape-jasmine bruised under Marine brogans and sense the hot moist calm of the jungle before the doomed Japanese began to run shrieking through its quiet, that wasn't because we were any closer to the scene than nine thousand miles. For two of us had been there in the days before the coming of the Japs. Twice, more recently, we had passed just over the rim of the world from this savage Paradise in ships that at the moment had no reason to make a landfall.

The aviator seemed to realize something of this. He was sympathetic as he spoke to the Commander.

"I suppose it breaks your heart to be out of that fight," he said. "It must be maddening to go through all that preparation and then lose your chance to help drive the Japs back. . . ."

The Commander looked at him for a moment, smiled and shook his head.

"You have it wrong, boy," he said. "I *was* in that fight. I was in the most important part of it—the part we fought at Midway on

13

June 4. And before you talk to anybody else, let me tell you that I fought in all the future battles for the Pacific and all of them at the same time and in the same place."

There wasn't any argument about that because all four of us, unlike a majority of the people of the United States, knew some of the facts and implications of the battle the Commander was talking about. And all of us, including the aviator who probably had meant something else by his question, realized the effect it must have on Japan's sea strategy forever. . . . The bulk of her carriers sunk, a vast assemblage of her best aviators, sailors and marines drowned, her dry docks filled with smashed and burned-out ships (if indeed she got any home to put into dry dock). Japan can no longer take risks like that of the June drive on Hawaii. And the technique of Pearl Harbor, based on the supposition that the American people would be gullible and their armed forces asleep, probably can't be worked again. . . .

"I am thinking of a new motto for the new U. S. fighting forces," said the Commander. "It goes like this: 'Forget Pearl Harbor.' "

And we all understood that, too.

Let us not toy with the fact that the most outstanding surprise of this war to quite a lot of us has been the discovery that the Navy is really as good as we used to think it was on, say, December 6. Those of us who were forced to make contact with its reluctant representatives may be excused the pained skepticism that came to us a day later. The ungodly grist of Navy moving pictures, through which we had learned that a battleship is a cross between bedlam and a night club, was still too generally in circulation to let us doubt the physical evidence of a Pearl Harbor.

To those of us who were in France before the cataclysm and after, there was a sickening similarity between the attitude of our peevish suppressionists and that of their opposite numbers on the staff of Darlan at Maintenon or in the squirrel wheels of Hôtel Continental in Paris. When we came to Honolulu after the Japs, most of us were of two minds as to whether we were looking at the beginning of a war or its finish. We stayed to find out.

And those of us who survived, who clung on for six months in the rarefied atmosphere of Honolulu and acclimated ourselves to an attitude that varied between mistrust and downright antagonism, were recompensed. We saw one of the most tremendous melodramas in the record of great military institutions unfold itself, scene by scene, act by act, in strict conformity to the rules of unity and plot. We saw the Navy—flattened not only by the Pearl Harbor tragedy but by the global war that grew out of it—suddenly setting out to do whatever could be done with what materials happened to lie at hand, going ahead with ever-increasing momentum, gathering up material and men as it moved and fought, outguessing Admiral Yamamoto and his talented knifemen with something of the traditional American brilliance, striking cautiously at first, then with daring—through the Marshalls and Gilberts and Wake and Marcus to the ornate shambles of the Coral Sea. And finally, outnumbered and outgunned, to the incredible victory of Midway.

This is a saga to which some future historian may give proper place. . . . For he will get an attentive audience among people far enough away from this fantastic affair to realize that in seven months the United States Navy had suffered one of the most complete and most humiliating defeats ever sustained by a first-class naval power and had won what may possibly be classified as the greatest naval battle of all time. And he will point out in a footnote somewhere that the test of the United States itself was in that battle—not particularly in the physical aspects of the outnumbered fleet, but in the psychological elements involved in it which we consider so peculiarly our own: fearlessness, strength in defeat, perseverance, endurance, initiative and above all resilience. If the Navy had refused battle with the Japanese that June day, refused to fight against such desperate odds, then what is left of the world would have known that it wasn't the Navy that got smashed at Pearl Harbor but the country. And he will point out also that had we been defeated at Midway, even though we might have displayed all the courage and skill and endurance of American naval tradition, we'd have been virtually out of the Pacific save for our own home waters, our ships—a great number of them—sunk irretrievably, our strategists unable any longer to choose the time and place for battle, unable to think of fighting anywhere much at any considerable distance away from West Coast ports. In other words, the historian will say, we should have been in much the same position in which

Japan found herself after inventory on the afternoon of June 6, 1942.

Well, there it is. The grand dukes and mystic potentates of the Navy were right and the talented press observers were wrong. . . . Or were they? Is it possible that the shock of finding out that you aren't so good as you thought you were might spur you to deeds of unbelievable valor and brilliance and make a miracle-worker out of you in no time at all? So far as the country is concerned, it really doesn't matter. One does not go about looking gift miracles in the mouth.

Those of us who lived with the fleet in those dark days of re-construction know it was no miracle—whatever we might say on the subject to the brass hats. It's no accident, spiritual, supernatural or otherwise, when your gun crews work like the gears of a metro-nome and your ship moves into battle as easily as she might slip up to a dock. It's no accident when you can sink a ship with five shots.

As nearly as we can gather from official reports, something like fifty-three torpedo planes went out on the morning of June 4 to break up the Japanese carriers, and only five came back. In train-ing and experience, these men were the best qualified fliers in the Navy. So they were under no illusions about their prospects when they took off that morning. They knew more about their own job than anybody' else. And so they knew even before they got into their planes what percentage worked against them. They knew even then that their chances for getting back to dinner that night were just about five in fifty-three.

Somehow the fact that men with patriotism deep enough and courage great enough to start out on a mission like that should have broken the backbone of Yamamoto's fleet doesn't seem miraculous at all. From the moment they took off a new day was coming up over the Pacific—or at least it looked that way from where we sat. The Navy was definitely on its way to a new, interesting and prof-itable phase of accomplishment. Its past didn't seem to count any more. And maybe, you think looking back on it, the Commander was right—"Forget Pearl Harbor."

2

DESCENT INTO FEAR

THE Japs attacked Pearl Harbor on Sunday, December 7, and it appeared that they wrecked the place with frightful loss of life. Sitka had its third mysterious fire that night.

I went down to the office of the Chicago *Daily News* late in the afternoon and was assigned to Honolulu. I took the midnight plane to Washington.

That night in transit I got an inkling of how total war is going to act in a democracy. Plane traffic was more balled up than it has been since the Wrights left Kittyhawk. Every patriotic congressman in the country—particularly the lads caught out on their soapboxes at isolationist rallies in the Middle West—was exerting his influence. The government had served notice on the commercial lines that every facility must be given these statesmen to insure their presence in Washington on the morrow to cast a vote for a declaration of war. One shudders to think what might have happened to the country had they failed to arrive on time.

I was able to get a passage to Pittsburgh out of Chicago. From there I went to Cleveland. From Cleveland to New York. I came down in a very jittery Washington about 5:45 A.M. The capital was responding with fine hysteria to the alarm of war. Sandbags were being piled hastily on sidewalks and in front of public buildings and along the Potomac, and the area about the White House was sparkling with bayonets.

I went to the Lafayette Hotel where they refused to let me rent a room for longer than half a day—that seemed long enough for anybody to stay in Washington.

At 10:30 I went to the Navy Building. The taxi driver enlivened the trip over with a vocal think-piece on Washington's prospects of an imminent bombing. He thought they were pretty good. . . . If the Japs could get to Pearl Harbor, he said, why couldn't the Germans get to Washington?

I said I didn't know.

"But we're prepared," he said enthusiastically. "We're ready for them."

"Yes," I said. "So is all the rest of America. I found that out by listening to a lot of people talk on the radio."

"We're sure as hell in luck," he said.

While I was waiting to see Admiral Hepburn a dispatch came in to report another attack on Oahu. It was widely believed, even by men close to the best sources of information, that most of the fleet had been sunk and that Hirohito's landing parties could take over Hawaii when and if they pleased.

Admiral Hepburn told me that he would cable the admiral commanding the Pacific fleet and have me assigned to the fleet at Pearl Harbor. I took the 1:50 plane for Chicago and arrived about 7 P.M.

I spent the next day getting ready to pull out once more. Meantime there was more and more evidence that I mightn't have to go looking for the war—that it might very likely be on its way to me. New York went jittery when somebody reported enemy planes overhead. San Francisco had a blackout. Honolulu was still expecting invasion. Aside from that we had little news of what was happening out there. Somebody got word that a Seattle airplane plant had been blown up. Why go looking two thousand miles away for trouble when you could find so much of it at your door?

But I went. And had some more experience with wartime transport.

The plane which had started from New York didn't get to Chicago until 1:30 Wednesday morning. It sat down a couple of hours later at North Platte, Nebraska, and then reluctantly hopped from one anchorage to another until it came down in San Francisco at 9:30 P.M., local time. Upton Close was at the airport to meet Ken Fry of NBC who also had made the long and perilous trip from Chicago. Close said that an admiral had been killed in the raid on Hawaii and "we are losing the Philippines tonight."

I went to the Palace Hotel and to bed.

It was a fine night. We had one air-raid alarm indicated by fire engines which stood at suitable street corners and sounded their sirens. A little later we had a four-eleven fire somewhere with similar sound effects. I decided that it might be tough to live in this town. When the horn sounds you won't know whether to dive into the cyclone cellar or go to the fire.

I got a message from the office to report to naval authority which I did. I also applied for a passport—I'll never tell you why unless Hawaii is to be classed as a foreign territory.

The news of the day was more heartening: A Jap battleship down near Manila, a cruiser and a destroyer down near Wake. Later reports said that another enemy battleship had been set afire. There are indications that the second attack on Honolulu, Monday's attack (if it ever occurred at all), didn't add much to the casualty list.

I spent the evening looking at a very fine movie produced by R.A.F., *Targets for Tonight*, the simple record of how you dynamite a town. Went back to hotel about midnight. Found call from Navy telling me to collect my orders and get on my horse. . . . So I checked out.

About two o'clock Friday morning I came aboard a Navy supply vessel at Pier 36 where on another day I boarded the *Taiyo Maru* on her way to Yokohama. I was given a bunk in a cabin with Commander King who apparently in civil life is an electrical engineer.

Norman Alley was aboard, also Joe Rucker and Ralph Jordan of INS.

There were about a hundred passengers, mostly experts of one sort or another, dashing out to patch up the holes in Pearl Harbor. We were carrying stacks of mail—a hold full of mail—most of which probably would not be delivered. The ship was so new she still smelled of varnish. The meals were good.

I sat up quite late talking with Jordan and Alley. They, too, figured they're going to be away for a long time.

The next day we were rolling like hell but the trip wasn't uncomfortable. I came into the wardroom to find a lieutenant commander of submarines complaining to the chief engineer that our ship's stack was throwing sparks all night. At the moment it was belching smoke. The day was beautiful and visibility unlimited. The skipper, however, said that we were in no danger at all. He had a ouija board or something.

A couple of patrol planes passed over us shortly after noon. Everybody made snide remarks such as "Didn't know we had 'em."

Sunday came with sea rolling, weather clear.

We'd been getting some cheery news on the wireless. Wake was still holding out . . . also Midway. It became apparent that there had been no second raid on Oahu. Colonel Knox made a speech in Honolulu and indicated that previous reports of damage in Pearl Harbor had been exaggerated. He said that one battleship had been sunk and another damaged. Other ships of various classes would be repaired and put back into service in a matter of time ranging from a few days to several months.

The Japs, so the radio said, had so far been unable to get a foothold on Luzon. We weren't so sanguine.

That afternoon we came into the danger zone—the halfway mark. That we had come this far safely with a flaming stack by night and a plume of smoke by day was an indication, the sub-commander said, that there isn't a Japanese submarine in the Pacific.

Monday I got up late with terrific headache which might have been some form of sea-sickness. It was a fine day with a roll something like the crest of an Ohio river flood. The furniture was all braced to the walls with four-by-four timbers.

The trip was getting boresome in direct proportion to the increase in danger. We somehow lacked the element of dramatic suspense. We were carrying a load of steel and some spare cannon in the hold, a couple of nine-inch guns on deck and two launches aft and three sea-going tugs forward. It was odd to think that if the Japs should hit this crate she'd sink like a shot leaving five ships floating on the sea where one had been before—a weird surprise for the little nippers, eh wot?

There were some flares on the horizon astern that night. We

shall probably never know what they were . . . Jap decoys maybe. Or perhaps the signals of some ship whose stack flamed a trifle more brightly than ours.

Tuesday the ship was rolling twenty-seven degrees. We measured it with a pendulum and protractor in the wardroom, otherwise I might not have believed that we weren't completely capsized. The weather was getting hot—for one reason or another nobody got much sleep.

There was some gossip about the two ships Colonel Knox mentioned in his report. The *Arizona* and *Oklahoma* were in dry dock until recently because of a collision at sea three weeks ago. The *Oklahoma* was in turmoil because the ship's service-officer had skipped with $12,000. Troubles, somebody remarked, are an assembly-line product.

In the wardroom a medical captain talked of leprosy. A line captain, a hard old customer from the cruisers, seemed to know more about it than the doctor did.

Wednesday, December 17, was bright and clear and rolling as usual. The morning radio gave news of Japanese subs in area ahead of us. And we told each other that maybe this was the day. The navigator hadn't slept since we left San Francisco. The skipper hadn't been off the bridge.

Below decks the gobs—mostly an itinerant lot on their way to posts in Hawaiian waters—paid no attention to the seriousness if any of the present situation.

Conversation: "I'm glad they gave us a cargo we could put in the hold this time. . . . Usually we pile it on top." "Draw everything you've got coming from the paymaster. If we get dunked the records all get dunked too."

In the wardroom the younger officers amused themselves with a toy pistol and some tin targets. Some of the older ones howled complaints. The platform around the five-inch gun had been freshly painted the night before—also the B-deck toilet. Somebody seems quite certain that this voyage is going on as usual and that bathrooms after all are merely a conceit of the idle rich.

We got a priority dispatch that night—obviously something about how we were to proceed to get into Pearl Harbor. But when the boys had assembled all their code books and other paraphernalia in the wardroom they couldn't translate it. They had the wrong code. So we opened up our radio to explain. . . . We assumed that probably it made no difference. But we weren't very happy although we felt that if the Japs hadn't located us through our fireworks and smoke screen they weren't likely to locate us at all.

Japanese submarines were still reported off Honolulu. . . . A barge loaded with a million pounds of dynamite was adrift somewhere along our course. About that time—8:30 P.M.—everybody decided to stay up all night.

> 3:30 A.M. In the dead watches of the night one of the mess-boys played softly on his harmonica. . . . The burden of his song was "Swing Low Sweet Chariot."

By Thursday (December 18) we were well inside the sub zone heading for Honolulu. We finally got our instructions. Sparks explained the previous mix-up. He said that the sender had a code machine that he loved to use whether or not the receivers were able to translate it. The radio from Hawaii indicated that all was well, although the news from other spots was none too encouraging. The prospects for Hongkong and Singapore were bad. Elsewhere our side was holding its own with some difficulty. In the Philippines, for instance, and Wake and Midway. Russia had just begun an extensive counterattack, or so the story went. . . . Odd how skeptical you get when you try to piece together the fragments of news that reach you at sea.

At 8:30 P.M. they began to run the engines at critical speed to vibrate the muck out of the stack which was flaming brightly in an overcast night. There was a lot of phosphorescence in the water. All in all we looked very gay.

At midnight a couple of the boys came in with their code gadgets. Said one, "It's a priority message and they're shooting with real bullets now so we don't want to mess around with it." And when they had made some sense out of the message they told us: "Don't enter Pearl Harbor until 21:45 GMT." I was too tired to dope out what time it would be for us when it's 21:45 Greenwich time.

Anyway at 2 A.M. we began to near Honolulu through a murky night.

7 A.M. Got up. Island of Oahu dimly visible over port bow. We rendezvous at 8. The navigator is puzzled by the fact that the boys in Pearl Harbor seem to know exactly where we are.

8 A.M. Picked up four-stack destroyer.

9 A.M. Range of hazy pink and chocolate-colored mountains on starboard. Lots of gray and white warships still afloat are dashing about between us and the fantastic beach. Bright sun, brilliant cobalt sea with boas of white spume.

Noon. Pilot aboard. Entering Pearl Harbor. Hickam Field hangar frames rising rusty brown on our right. The Japs don't appear to have wasted a shot.

3

BOMBS AND STREETCAR TOKENS

WE STOOD on the dock for a while amid piles of burned and oily junk—gun mountings, ship fittings, cable, pipe and, well, just junk. We stepped aside now and then for traveling cranes and trucks that picked up oddments of this stuff and moved it away presumably to some larger and more complicated junk-pile without making any visible dent in this one. And as we leaned in the hot shadow of a warehouse looking with scorched eyeballs at this appalling activity we had plenty of time to think. We began to wonder, as many a person was wondering in Honolulu right at that time, if we weren't totting up the score for a war that had ended before it began.

Whatever may have been the official estimates of damage, however optimistically we might have read the communiqués, it was certain that this wreck of Pearl Harbor was startling, stupendous, and disgraceful. These wrecking crews, soiled and sweating and worn lean with hard labor, had been biting into the debris the Japs left for more than a week and they'd made hardly any progress at all. The aura of desolation was over everything along with the smell of burned oil and iron rust. The sense of an utter destruction was poignant and inescapable.

It wasn't only a few barge loads of knotted iron before your eyes or the slippery filth under your feet that made you wonder if you'd ever be able to sleep at night again. What you guessed of the job that the scavengers had before them was greater than what you actually saw. But there was nothing imaginary about the looks you saw on the faces of the dock wallopers. Their races varied from dim white to Chinese and their gifts as workmen were just as haphazardly assorted. But they were alike in one thing,

24

an attitude of aloofness approaching unfriendliness and the blank expressions of men coming out of the ether. We didn't have to be told that here were some more citizens who had believed the vast power of the United States unassailable and themselves secure, men who now believed Heaven knew what, with faith behind them, hope crumbling and despair not far ahead.

For this was the United States, whether we liked to think about it or not. The United States was right here in the ashes of Pearl Harbor, with its arrogance, its pride and its chances, if any, for salvation. Stars had fallen and the earth had trembled and the showdown was at hand—and the motley citizenry at the derricks and winches and scrap shovels knew that well enough, however incoherently they might have expressed it. The fact that we had been victims of incredible evil, of a trust betrayed, didn't seem to make much difference. There is the moment when the fine, altruistic, trusting humanitarian begins to look only dimly like an angel and quite definitely like a sap. And that moment seemed to have arrived, too.

It is significant that all that day—and all during many days to come—we heard no suggestion of what we might do to pay back some of this. Yesterday, the day of wrath, was still with us, and tomorrow unlikely ever to dawn. You got the impression that whatever the inventory of damage, the United States wasn't going to hit back because the United States couldn't hit back. What the United States was going to do was sit down and wait for the next attack. The general attitude was that this time they wouldn't take us by surprise—whether, completely aware and unsurprised, we might be able to do something about it was something that no unprejudiced observer was likely to bet on.

The banshees and little people were still abroad in the land that day although we had no way of finding out about it until considerably later. It wasn't yet to be admitted that the stupid Japanese had been able to sneak in here with a couple of carrier-loads of second-rate planes and bust up our version of the Maginot line at no great expense. There had to be some sort of black magic in it—a contention which one must admit seemed at the time very logical. And so by day one walked constantly under the scrutiny of unseen eyes . . . and by night shadowy creatures breathed hot down one's back. Aged Japanese aliens were just biding their time against the day when they could slip out of the woods and poison the water supply, or destroy the military oil dumps, or burn down Schofield barracks. Traitorous Nisei were calling their brothers to a race revolt that would make the rest of the Pearl Harbor business look like a wire-cutting raid. Hawaii was so hysterical that you momentarily expected the shrieks and tearing of hair—make no mistake about it.

The officers we met that day were far from panicky, grant them that. They were, like many another man with a front-line job before him, so completely taken over by their work that they'd no time to think about personal prospects or for that matter about the abstruse political philosophies that had contrived to bury them under so large a quantity of scrap iron in so short a time. But while they shared none of the general fear, they undoubtedly shared the belief in many of the local apocrypha.

"We brought it all on ourselves," said one lieutenant who had come with a station wagon to get us out of the way of the salvage trucks. "They tell me that all the Jap aviators shot down at Kaneohe were wearing McKinley High School rings. Not just one of them but all—and I've heard they got thirteen of them over there. It hurts to think that we brought those boys up to be good Americans. We educated them. We gave them citizenship and they went back to Japan and made ready for the day they could pay us back with this." He waved a hand vaguely in the direction of the junk piles and we excused his approach to the lyrical. "They had Honolulu streetcar-company tokens in their pockets and American watches on their wrists." The story up to this point had seemed all right and we'd been listening politely. After all we didn't know what odds and ends had been found on the corpses of Japanese pilots. Until that moment we hadn't heard that any Japs had been shot down. But there was something about the streetcar tokens that struck an incongruous note in the picture of battle. Ralph Jordan looked at the lieutenant squarely.

"Why the streetcar tokens?" he inquired. "Do you suppose they intended to take the bus in from Pearl Harbor?" But this, it seemed, was not the place for humor. It wasn't that levity was frowned upon exactly—rather it was not recognized.

THE U.S.S. "SHAW"

United States destroyer, shortly after Japanese aerial bomb made direct hit, Pearl Harbor, December 7, 1941.

MAGAZINE OF THE "SHAW" EXPLODES

This, one of the most remarkable combat photographs of all time, was made at the exact moment the destroyer blew up during Japanese attack on Pearl Harbor.

"It isn't enough to have to fight an enemy like the Japanese who come at you with planes and bombs," the lieutenant went on. "We have to fight the civilian population too, the people who are friendly to our faces and enemies behind our backs. They knew this was coming off and the way they kept the secret is something to frighten you. Not one peep did they let out. And yet they cut arrow-shaped swaths through the cane fields pointing to Pearl Harbor as guides to the bombers and they burned flares in the hills and they carried transmitters right onto the reservation at Bellows Field in milk cans. They smashed up their cars on the Pearl Harbor road on the morning of the seventh to block traffic. And they're arrogant about it. They laugh at us for a lot of suckers."

"They've got some reason to," remarked one of the cameramen. It seemed to have become twice as hot, if such a thing were possible. The sheds were quivering in a sort of violet light where the overhang of the roofs stuck out into the sun. The crane crew of the wrecking squad passed by shining with sweat. The lieutenant wiped his forehead and for a moment looked as if he wished we hadn't come to remind him of his troubles.

"Anyway they laugh at us," he said. "And I don't like it. One of those pilots who came down at Kaneohe wasn't hurt at all. He walked away from the wreck. And he was the cockiest SOB that ever came to Honolulu and that's saying a lot. He was one of our local products, a graduate of McKinley High School and the University of Hawaii. And he began to kid the guard who captured him. He said that he didn't expect to be a prisoner long, that other Japs were coming along behind him to take Hawaii and the Pacific coast and ram a peace down the President's throat in Washington.

"The guard didn't get sore at that. He thought it was any soldier's privilege to think his side was good. But then the Jap told him what a sucker he was, how a smart Japanese could outguess half a dozen brain trusts, how all Americans could do was bluff and brag and how they'd never been up against anybody who could fight until now. . . . So the guard put down his rifle and clipped him on the chin. . . . And he's going to be court-martialed for it . . . for putting down his rifle, I mean.

"They've got the Jap in the clink now. He's not talking much

except to say that it'll be a short war because we don't know anything about anything except conversation."

"Do you think the Japs will be back here again?" Jordan asked
him.

"No," he said with quiet positiveness. "I don't think they will.
They might've done pretty well if they'd followed up their attack.
But they've muffed the chance."

We nodded hopefully. But somehow as I piled my suitcase
and overcoat into the station wagon I kept hearing the voice not
of the lieutenant but of another optimist: "Hitler has missed the
bus."

It's an axiom, the truth of which any war correspondent will
attest, that the more jittery a town the more uncomfortable it is
to live in it. They used to call Honolulu "The Paradise of the
Pacific" but it wasn't any Paradise of the Pacific as we saw it then.
It was just the latest amateur to join the ranks of the blacked-out
cities and had already arrived at a state of regulation that left a Jap
concentration camp little to offer.

Dark comes quickly in this region in the so-called winter.
So lights went out at 6 P.M. and everybody was off the street at
6:30 or else. Whatever else you can say for the lads who ran
Honolulu in those days they had a good blackout—probably have
yet for that matter. They didn't know much about the business
except that the general object was to keep the lights turned out
and that they did. That they might have accomplished the same
result with quite a lot less hardship on the public was something
that seemed to be of secondary moment with them, as I guess it
should have been.

After all, the purposes of Honolulu's blackout were not to be
compared with, say, those of Paris or London. London's idea was
to keep so black that the Germans couldn't find the town as a
target. Paris apparently wanted to be dim enough to let people
know there was a war but not so dim that anybody, including the
Germans, might be seriously inconvenienced. Honolulu, unless
the signs are all wrong, wanted the kind of blackout that would
force the populace to go home and to bed.

There has been a lot written—ninety per cent of it in the local newspapers—about the vulnerability of Hawaii sitting out there all alone in the broad Pacific. But don't let that deceive you. If Hawaii doesn't know about the approach of planes or surface ships until the time when the blacking out of Honolulu is a factor, then it's too late to do anything about the attack. If one may be allowed to mention an example in point, there is Pearl Harbor. Furthermore if a lot of Jap navigators are good enough to pick up the island of Oahu after nightfall they can find Honolulu no matter how black it is with the lump of Diamond Head sticking into a frothy, not to say luminous sea at one end, and the trefoil of Pearl Harbor spread out amid the hills on the other.

But, like the lieutenant who had heard the weird stories of Japanese treachery, Honolulu recognized the danger of an attack from within. And the blackout and attendant curfew controlled that situation nicely.

At the last census there were 82,000 Japanese in Honolulu county, 32 per cent of the total population, a quarter of them aliens. Whether or not the some 60,000 citizens were going to remain loyal to the U. S. was then and is now a topic of conversation that will get you through many a long evening. There has been at this writing no indication that they aren't as good Americans as anybody else in the neighborhood. But there they were, an unknown quantity that the military government couldn't overlook. It wasn't considered good form—not at that time—to intern 60,-000 citizens out of a total of 231,000 merely because of their race. So they were allowed to circulate as usual and hold jobs everywhere but in Pearl Harbor and go anywhere they had a mind to between daybreak and 6 P.M. After 6:30 the buses had stopped running, all cars were off the streets—save those with military licenses—and the patrols were out. Conspiracy in the dark became definitely a hazardous occupation.

Come to think of it the police and the military seem to have been in fairly complete control of the interior situation from the very first. But we had no way of knowing that as a taxi brought us into town and deposited us at the hotel. All we could see was the fear in the faces of a lot of people who knew no more about what was going on than we did.

We discovered with no delay at all that blackout time in the new order of things in Honolulu was actually coincident with bedtime. The blackout had arrived on about ten hours' notice and nobody seems to have considered its possibility even remotely, any more than the brass hats had considered the possibility of Pearl Harbor. For a while after the blitz people did what business they had to do—including the eating of their dinner—during the brighter hours and sat in darkness after that until such time as it seemed possible to sleep. In a couple of weeks some of the brighter citizenry had realized that this foolishness had come to stay with them just like pineapples and the Matson Line. So they bought tar paper and black cloth and fixed up rooms in their homes where they could sit and read the newspapers for an hour or so after early dinner or listen to the radio trying to be cheerful about the situation in the Philippines. By the time of our arrival the hotel had got around to blacking out the lobby and dining room. So you could eat dinner as late as 6:30 and then you could sit in the lobby with a huddle of frightened, silent people, all of them with one ear uplifted to hear the first squall of the siren that would announce the return of the Japs.

An evening at home thus became something like a session in the common room of an institution for elderly mutes. There was no sound but the click of knitting needles or the tapping of an impatient foot on the marble floor. The vistas of the room were broad and empty as those of a railroad station save for the tight little group of worried old ladies—male and female. And the atmosphere was something straight out of Edgar Allan Poe. Out there in the blackness was Doom with nothing to stop his entry, probably, but an inexperienced ARP warden named Roger. Knit! Knit! Knit! while mysterious dangers walked with catsteps outside and almost any moment now a bomb was going to fall and bring the whole place down around your ears.

Somebody had brought a Christmas tree into this horrible place. It had been sprayed with salt to give it a glint of phony frost and tufts of cotton had been tastefully thrown at it. It was lighted by a couple of hundred electric lights—blue ones. The effect was something like a grand-opening celebration in a morgue.

I mentioned to Jordan that night that I'd never seen a blackout where the whole populace sat around in such a state of terror—in such a catastrophic hangover.

"Is it hangover," he wanted to know, "or is it intuition?"

I spent a lot of time in the wakeful hours that night, as the guard changed under my window and rifle shots spattered in the distance, wondering if that might be the answer.

This was certain, however fantastic might be the stories of the Jap pilots with streetcar tokens and McKinley High School rings, and of arrow-shaped swaths in the cane fields and transmitters in milk cans and all the rest, the yarns were dangerous symptoms in themselves. This community expected another attack—from without or within or perhaps both—and the community, to put it badly but accurately, figured that the United States of America, or more particularly the United States Navy, couldn't do anything about it.

4

"WHAT'S HAPPENED TO THE FLEET?"

THE leitmotif of the Honolulu vigil was given the next morning by one deaf old lady talking to another deaf old lady at break-fast. . . .

The blackout was finished and the morning sun was not yet high enough to make you hate to be alive. Wooden-faced Japanese waiters were going automatically through the only routine they knew, which at the moment produced quick and efficient service. The food was plentiful—and unspoiled. And there was something in the languorous air that made you remember Honolulu as it used to be when it was all leis and hibiscus blossoms and steel guitars. For a minute or two, if only for a minute or two, you could forget the war and you could set at the back of your mind the thirty-five hundred raw graves on the side of Red Hill. But only for a minute or two. The voice of the little old woman was shrill and penetrat-ing:

"When the Japanese come back I'm not going up into the hills. I'm going to stay right here. Because I haven't anybody to drive my car and anyway you wouldn't be safe up there. When they land they'll land all over the place . . . in parachutes . . ."

There it was! Her concern, and as it turned out the concern of thousands of others like her all over Oahu, was not conditional. She was making no plans for a situation that might occur IF the Japs should come back. There was no IF about it. She was already looking toward the day WHEN they'd be back and it was obvious she didn't think it far away.

Of course the war came back then. You realized that she might be right. You'd no evidence to the contrary . . . only the hope that seemed to have been knocked out of this place thoroughly when the smoke of the burning *Arizona* began to pour over the town on the morning of December 7. She and the other frightened people who filled the dining room had been living with this situation. Maybe they knew a lot of things that we newcomers might be slow in finding out.

"I tried to get a place on the clipper," said the other old lady. "But it's all filled up for goodness knows how long—that is if they ever start flying it again. But they say there'll be a ship in a few days. They think I can get on that. . . ."

There were some altered words in this recital . . . such things as "ships" and "clippers" hadn't been part of the original. But if you shut your eyes and made allowances you found yourself right back in Paris in the days when the Germans were roaring down through Flanders and the great exodus had begun. The French civilians, too, had been frightened before they ran away. They had come to the conclusion that their army was powerless and their leadership futile. And in making the terrible trek with them to the South you had learned to respect their judgment. The parallel was sickening.

"I wonder what's happened to the fleet," one of the old ladies murmured. And you wondered, too. You were to wonder many times in the next few weeks as the Japs asked it constantly and cockily in the English broadcasts from Tokio. You were to hear men of intelligence discuss it with outward calm as they might discuss any other mystery in which they had no personal interest. You were to mumble senseless explanations dozens of times when people asked you about it under the impression that you might know the answer.

"My daughter's husband says that the whole fleet's on the bottom——" This from the first old lady. "He says we've all got to get out of here and go to the Mainland . . . that we'll have to fight off the Japanese in the Sierras until we can build a new Navy. . . ."

I left my breakfast and went out to get a breath of fresh air in the thick mugginess of the street.

Probably there was good and sufficient reason for the long period of silent meditation that the censors enforced on the American reading public immediately after the attack. I have been informed on occasion that there was. And I've been in nobody's confidence regarding the press strategy of the two or three weeks after that. After all the disaster of Pearl Harbor must have presented just as many undreamed-of problems to the military publicitors (or whatever you call them) as it did to the strategists. Admittedly it would have taken a high-ranking professional press agent to have given a message of reassurance to the shocked electorate and made it sound convincing. There's no object in going into that. But, whatever the cause—or excuse—the situation looked to most of us just as it did to the Old Ladies of Honolulu. . . . "When the Japs come again . . ." "I've got a place on the next boat . . . " "Where is the fleet?"

And where *was* the fleet? The correspondents knew, of course, that the blasting of Pearl Harbor hadn't sunk the physical Navy. We felt even then that if the United States weren't indeed the shell it seemed to be, that if we hadn't completely lost the power and intent and skill to defend ourselves, we might speedily repair or replace everything we had lost save the lives of 3,500 men. But what had happened to the intangibles of the Navy—its morale and leadership—we couldn't tell from surface observations. We couldn't tell either from our contacts with a lot of vague young spokesmen who considered—perhaps rightly—that there was something shameful about the whole business and the less said about it the better. What some of us could do in the circumstances was to remember similar sources of information in the befuddled squirrel cage of Hôtel Continental in Paris and how we had assured ourselves that such wool-witted institutions were not typical of the management of the French army. . . . And weren't they!

We began to feel as the dismal weeks piled up in Honolulu that if the Navy ever got around to do anything in this war we were going to be pleasantly surprised.

Out there a couple of thousand miles west of us, the Marines were still holding Wake. Over in the Philippines MacArthur's Inconsequentials were still putting up a fight. And as Americans we got a bit of a thrill and plenty of consolation out of that. In a few outposts the United States of Valley Forge and The Wilderness and the Argonne was surviving and our ancient swaggering faith in ourselves and our Destiny didn't seem quite so ludicrous.

But the cheer came for the most part only as a contrast to deepening gloom. For we weren't doing anything about it. Apparently we weren't going to do anything about it. You were left to draw your own conclusions about what we might have done had we wanted to.

In a grandiose gesture the radio carried to Major Devereux, commanding at Wake, a message asking him if he wanted anything. Did he want anything? What did anybody suppose he wanted? And he knew all the answers as well as anybody else. He replied, "Send us more Japs." We hadn't much doubt about the quick granting of that request.

Then came to Honolulu the Roberts Commission to fix the responsibility for the chaos of December 7. We didn't meet the commissioners socially and they didn't discuss their affairs in public. But we didn't have to be told what sort of evidence they were getting. And, expectant of no miracles, we knew that eventually the commanding officers of the Army and Navy establishments in Hawaii would be held to blame: The total lack of co-operation between these men, as afterward revealed in the commission's report, was nothing that we hadn't guessed for ourselves. But for all that the investigation was a bit of routine proceeding toward a routine end, the presence of the commissioners did nothing to bring any cheer to Pearl Harbor or bestir the jittery public to a hope for better days.

The Roberts Commission wasn't asking as the would-be refugees were asking, "Where is the Navy?" They were asking rather, "Where was the Navy?" And to the lay mind the probable answers seemed interchangeable.

As a matter of fact, to anticipate the record somewhat, we know a little now about where the Navy was. We shall start out by admitting that the portion of the fleet inside the harbor while Kurusu and Nomura were concluding what the Japanese laughingly called their "peace mission" was caught unawares by a treacherous attack and temporarily at least put out of business. It wasn't mentioned in the dispatches that at the same time other large units of the fleet were loitering about in near-by portions of the Pacific, blacked out, alert, and ready for war at the blast of a bugle. Some of these units—among them Admiral Halsey's seagoing commandos—took on the job of plaguing the Japanese in their island bases for months. But even so, even though the bombing of Battleship Row produced only a small fraction of the chaos that the Japs might have wrought had they known how to use their opportunity, Yamamoto's coup had given him definite tactical advantage. The fleet, with its dispositions as they were, could not have retaliated then except at a disadvantage in numbers and it would have had to meet the Japs in a battle area and at a time of their choosing.

Despite the almost universal and justifiable belief that we hadn't known anything of what was going on in the Pacific, the Navy had not been entirely unaware of the possibility of war. We had a submarine screen operating far beyond the international date line in waters that Japan looked upon as her own. And so the admirals knew while bitter criticism was goading them to impossible action, that the bulk of Hirohito's fleet lay just beyond Wake Island preparing an ambush into which we were expected to throw ourselves in a blind and characteristic rage.

Maybe the marines on Wake knew that as they carried their fantastic fight to its inevitable finish. It would have made no difference, of course. They'd have gone on fighting anyway. But it might have made them feel better to know that they weren't being deserted merely because some brass hat couldn't make up his mind what to do next.

We learned later also some of the other unadvertised jobs of the supposedly inactive fleet.

As early as December 8 it had been no secret to anybody that travel and commerce between the United States and the Philippines by any direct route were ended. A few hours later, as the momentum of the Japanese southward sweep was realized, it became obvious that we were going to have to set up a front in Australia, right away. So, in addition to what work it might have to do avenging Pearl Harbor, the Navy suddenly found itself riding herd on a convoy line seven or eight thousand miles long—a tedious job and as the Japs moved on from island to island into the southwest Pacific, exceedingly dangerous. Leaving out the Atlantic and Hitler and his submarines, as we naturally did, it might have appeared to us that there weren't many fast cruisers or spare carriers available for any splendid but unprofitable gestures. It didn't of course. We thought much about the absence of the fleet during a long series of dark and steamy nights. We had little else to do. And we reached a lot of wrong but, I maintain, logical conclusions, which didn't help to make life more serene or bearable.

About the time Wake fell a couple of Filipino lads dared the blistering noonday sun to take down the festive Christmas lights from the long block of Bishop Street in front of the Young Hotel. They had quite a lot of work, for this gala display had run to thousands upon thousands of colored bulbs and long rosaries of wire hung with the local conception of ice and snow. There was a feeling among those who watched the removal process that the lights probably would have amounted to something if anybody could have turned them on. But of course nobody ever did turn them on. Few people noticed they were there until one of the perspiring Filipinos lost his balance on top of a ladder and smashed a few blue and red lamps on the pavement. The display was to have been turned on for a test on the night of Sunday, December 7. It had been just something else that you couldn't see in the blackout ever since.

Maybe the matter of blacked-out Christmas lights in view of the momentous happenings that were tearing the world apart elsewhere, was unimportant. But it didn't seem to be. It seemed so typical of local conditions that really weren't local at all but the affair and concern of thousands of unharried inland Americans who probably would never hear an air-raid siren or break their bones in a blackout. Wartime here, I began to believe, had many phases worthy of study by our kindred patriots on what I was already referring to as "the mainland." For Hawaii, advertised as a worry-free Paradise and an impregnable bastion, had been the first to take the rap for national unpreparedness, the first community in the union to find out that when the bombs are falling there is no safety in conversation. So what had happened to Hawaii seemed nothing more than what might happen to the rest of the United States should occasion arise. Pearl Harbor to a man in, say, Keokuk shouldn't be looked upon as a regrettable tragedy in the same class and of the same local significance as a flood on the Yangtze. It was something for the folks at home to remember in shame on the day

when the curfew should sound and they'd hurry in from the street
to keep from getting shot and they'd sit down in the dark to tell
their beads or learn how to read braille.

In the first place everybody in this community, setting the style
perhaps for every community between Dutch Harbor and the
Canal Zone—had to provide himself with a definite identification.
That meant he must be fingerprinted in triplicate—and the finger-
printing was thorough. It wasn't confined to the right hand as it
was in England and France when the aliens were being enrolled.
All your fingers were smudged out on the record sheets. Thus, if
a bomb took off your right hand, so the theory seemed to run,
you could prove you weren't an enemy alien by making smears
with your left. You could prove it here and also in Washington
where a set of prints went on file with the FBI. This permitted you
to get a police registry card. For another set of fingerprints and
a questionnaire provided at another office, you could get a territorial identification card. What that was for I never found out.

These preliminaries completed, the police would issue a receipt
for your fingerprints and you could then go home and wait for the
enumerators. The enumerators were like census takers only more
so. They found out all interesting particulars about yourself and
family and took a list of your personal property with emphasis on
such gadgets as radio sets, sewing machines, typewriters, tools and
such. Their work was independent of the work done by other
inspectors who made sure that you didn't show any lights by night
or take part in any subversive activities by day.

Until the glad Yuletide nobody in the territory was allowed to
buy a new radio set without a permit from the local office of the
U. S. Signal Corps. The order extended to phonographs and record
changers whose military uses were not divulged. This made matters
exceedingly tough for a lot of merchants who had stocked up on
four-tube super-bloopers for the giftie trade, and it did not affect
the market for communications receivers, sets of size, design, wave-
length range, etc., to make them suitable for something besides
broadcast reception—because the Signal Corps had requisitioned
all such sets in the first place. The impasse was broken by somebody just before Christmas. After that anybody could buy a radio

set who wanted to and spend the long dark evenings trying to hear something on it.

There wasn't a flashlight battery in town nor flashlight bulbs nor flashlights. You couldn't buy a spade or a can of red paint. The military government had frozen all professional photographic outfits and a long list of drugs. You still were allowed to buy aspirin, and needed it. As for the rest you probably fitted your disease to what you might be able to pick up in the way of a cure. Electric-light fixtures were off the market, and wire and fuses. Meat was scarce. So were most fruits except pineapples and papayas. In the sugar capital of the country, candy was hard to get. There wasn't much butter. On the other hand there wasn't any sugar ration—not likely.

You weren't allowed on the street after 6 o'clock without a pass and nobody seemed anxious to issue one. Navy credentials admitted us only to Pearl Harbor. Army passes of that period were useful only to get to headquarters or to show the engineer colonels who were eternally questioning your right to circulate. Chief of Police William Gabrielson finally assumed responsibility for us and gave us leave to be out after dark. Nobody questioned his judgment.

There was a ration of ten gallons of gasoline a month to ordinary citizens. War workers were given enough of a bonus to get them to and from work. No white or red flashlights were permitted—even in the hands of those privileged to go out of doors in the blackout. You weren't allowed to smoke cigarettes in the street. One guard in Bishop Street one night delivered a stern warning to the wearer of a wrist watch with a luminous dial.

The movies shut down somewhere around four-thirty in the afternoon at which time most of the stores closed. You could occupy yourself during the hour and a half remaining of daylight in marveling how the resilience of the great American people was equalled only by its complacency.

5

THE FESTIVAL OF THE RIFLES

It HAS been some time on the so-called Mainland since citizens harried by martial law had to worry about the jittery condition of a green militia. The jittery militia, if any, has long since been absorbed into the more serene and better-trained Army of the United States. But on the Mainland there haven't been any duplications of Pearl Harbor.

When—as Honolulu describes it—"the trouble came," it was obvious that something would have to be done to augment the city police force, and, with a major offensive threatening, it was equally obvious that no great strength of the military establishment could be detached for police duty. So the lads of the R.O.T.C. were called out of their trundle beds, slapped into their partly fitting uniforms, lined up in something approximating a column of squads and made a part of the Territorial Guard. They were given rifles and bayonets and quantities of ball ammunition, and their spirits were buoyed up with talks like Rockne's address to the Four Horsemen—talks in which it was represented to them that the air was filled with parachutists and the cane fields crawling with sudden death. To them, even more than to the rest of the populace, the war suddenly became real and deadly. When they went to guard their lonely posts in the depths of the blackout, every whispering leaf was a messenger of doom, every shadow was wrapped round an enemy.

It's said that they killed a few people, these boys, but that is just hearsay and possibly untrue. But it is certain that they wounded numerous stray citizens before they learned which comes first, the challenge or the trigger squeeze. They made a walk in the moonlight more hazardous than a swim in Pearl Harbor during a bomb-

40

ing attack. They, more than any other influence in Hawaii, popularized the idea of staying home nights. And—you may be surprised to learn—about sixty per cent of the members of this eager little group of deadshots were of Japanese extraction. Some of them, despite a painful process of education at McKinley High School (where the pilots' class pins were supposed to come from), spoke English with a definite accent or rather spoke a definite accent with a trace of English. But their language turned out to be good enough for their job. They said, "Halt!" And you halted. What might happen to you after you halted was something that had to be worked out on a ouija board.

On a typical night the din of them made life an interesting thing around the intersection of Hotel and Bishop Streets (the Alexander Young Hotel corner).... Vibrant challenges to unwary walkers—brave souls these walkers whoever they were, thus to venture abroad with their lives in their hands! Calls from one sentry to another in mushy vernacular about who was to take over from whom at the Number Two post in Bishop Street. The silence of a deep-sunk catacomb was over the town—silence so deep that you could hear the lapping of the surf against the blackness—but that had little effect toward soothing the noisy hysteria of the nervous pickets. . . . High-pitched conversations! Commands! Rifle shots!

"Lights! Put out that light! Got-tam-eet, put out that light!" How familiar it all sounded. I lay on my back staring at the unplumbed blackness beyond which somewhere hung the ceiling, and I thought of the night in the Argonne when Lieutenant Hudson had instructed Lieutenant Newman in the uses of the dark. "On a night like this, Newman," he had said, "even you could be a general officer." On a night like this the risk of being in Honolulu was about on a par with that of life in London in the blitz . . . and these guards who talked this odd English were no different from the kinky-haired mumblers who stood willing to bayonet any and all who might move in the shadows of blacked-out Lagos, Nigeria.

"Lights! Lights! Put out that light! ..." There was something of a convention down in the street under my window. Wearily but with an alacrity born of long experience, I rolled out of bed and flattened myself against the back wall. There I figured I'd be out of the way of the stray shots that might presently be coming if the boys should decide to shoot out a light on this side of the building. Then for a while there was silence . . . after that the tramping of feet in the corridor and a polyglot harangue outside my door.

"No light! It's the way moon hits on white window frame. Can't do anything about it." And then a loudly bawled assurance to marksmen in the street below. "Don't shoot. It's just reflection."

That too brought memories of the Argonne as I dusted myself off and crawled back into bed. "Put out that light or I'll shoot it out!" "Hell, that ain't no light. It's a white horse!"

And so it went, night after night, until your subconscious mind failed to react to any shooting outside your own block. But you slept fitfully nevertheless as did everybody else on the premises. It needed no rifle shots to apprise you of trouble close at hand. One of the photographers diagnosed the situation at breakfast one morning after a singularly boisterous row in the alley under his window.

"This town," he said, "is sitting right on the edge of its chair all ready to get up and run somewhere."

6

"THEY HAD US COLD . . . !"

ONE day as a variant to our routine of waiting for the Japs to come back, the Army took us to look at the wrecks of Hickam and Wheeler Fields.

It was a ghastly show, for the debris hadn't been cleaned up—wouldn't be cleaned up for many a day—and the spectacle of destruction was poignantly like other spectacles, the parallel between the lazy nation that had allowed this thing to happen and the France whose errors it was repeating vividly exemplified. Those piles of unsalvageable scrap that had been intricate motors, those twisted sheets that had been flying fortresses and P-40's, differed only in geographical location from the piles of Martin bombers pushed back from the pitted runways at Chartres. In looking at them here you seemed to be reliving a part—and a particularly unpleasant part—of your life. And you were conscious of a mounting rage, first against the innate evil of one people who could justify such treachery as had wrought this, secondly and perhaps more intensely against the stupidity of another people who lived in a world but were not of it, who had eyes and ears and never knew what was going on.

"They got us cold," said the quiet-voiced colonel at Wheeler. "They were on us before we knew they were coming and they'd smashed up our planes before we could get out to them."

"Before we knew they were coming!"

We hadn't heard then, though we were to learn later from the Roberts Report that the incoming Jap bombers had been picked up 150 miles at sea by a detector device whose operator couldn't get his superiors to believe what he had seen. But even so we knew that the colonel's comment was an epitomization of all that had

43

gone wrong that terrible morning. . . . We should have known but we hadn't.

The Japanese knew all right. We found evidence of that at Hickam. You could trace the progress of their first flight across the field by burned-out fires, machine-gun bullet holes, wreckage and craters.

"You've got to give them credit for a fine operation," our guide here said admiringly. "They knew what they were doing. They did it. They didn't waste a shot.

"They came in low, in formation from that lower end of the field, and they came right up the runways working on the hangars. They took one hangar past the administration building but skipped the last one. It was empty. Then they turned at right angles to the left and smashed up all the automobiles in the park and bombed the barracks as they left. They didn't touch the administration building or the church. They dropped a bomb on the corner of the canteen. I'd say their information was perfect."

There is no need to repeat again the technique of the Pearl Harbor attack save to mention that it had two phases—the first a strafing attack which put about ninety per cent of our air force out of business before it could get into the air, the second a dive-bombing and torpedo attack on the ships in the harbor. In both cases their information seemed perfect save for the fact that they mistook the old target ship *Utah* for a carrier. Only through perfect pre-knowledge of what they were going to do and perfect co-ordination in carrying out their plan were they able to keep an overwhelming air force from taking off against them. And only by maintaining their own air superiority were they able to complete their vicious attack against the warships. All the commentators agree that from the time the attack on the flying fields was finished until the slow-moving torpedo planes went out through the oil smoke homeward bound, the initiative, the method and timing of the blitz and the choice of targets rested entirely with the Japs. Save for sporadic and for the most part uncontrolled ack-ack we had no defense against anything that the invaders might have chosen to do. And that brings us to one of the great mysteries of this war:

Knowing as they did all details of our situation why did they make the sort of attack they made? Why, at the one moment when the gate stood wide open for them—the only moment of its kind they will ever see—did they fail to take advantage of their opportunity and seize the islands?

I heard a discussion of the matter some months later in the monastic uncomfort of a wardroom on a cruiser as we moved south for the big smash in the Marshalls—a discussion that began when someone idly asked why the Germans had let 350,000 English troops get away from Dunkirk. There had been no answer of course to a question that has remained dangling in air since it was first posed somewhere in July, 1940. But one of the aviators had mumbled something about mysteries having parallels. Germany at Dunkirk had a chance to cut the throat of England. Japan at Honolulu had a chance to take the Hawaiian Islands and establish a permanent menace to the Pacific coast. . . . Of course some men saw things and some didn't. Foch, for instance, had had a chance in another war to turn the flank of Von Kluck.

"I'll never make it out," said the lieutenant who had been in the intelligence. "We had done a lot of things wrong at Pearl Harbor in the placing of stores and the construction of buildings and the arrangement of protective batteries and all that. The Japs undoubtedly knew all about those mistakes before we did. So they had a chance on the morning of December 7 that they never in God's world will have again. They could have come in just as they did and they could have made a havoc of the harbor itself. They could have destroyed installations without which Pearl Harbor could no longer function as a base. They could have started a fire and undoubtedly would have destroyed more ships than they actually hit in their torpedo attack. And with Pearl Harbor out of business what would have happened to our task forces at sea all over the Pacific? Dead in the water, adrift, derelict, they would have waited until the Japanese could get around to pick them off one at a time."

The Marine captain took a long pull at his pipe and contemplated the blue ocean framed in the doorway.

"Somebody suggested," he said, "that they didn't want to start fires because the wind was the wrong way and the smoke would have covered the harbor and prevented their working on the target. . . ."

The lieutenant shook his head.

"I don't think that's the explanation," he said. "This bombing was a highly complex affair. It embraced many simultaneous actions of different natures and at different places. But it was one of the most beautifully carried out maneuvers of this or any other war. It's an old story how they worked on the important points first to forestall opposition. And it's known to everybody that their principal objectives, the one they never forgot, was the destruction of battleships. It is not so generally known that on the photographs of our capital ships which they were carrying with them—copies of which were later taken out of their wrecked planes—they had marked the most effective points at which to send torpedoes, the spots where armor was thinnest or where magazines might be reached. . . . No, it might have been good policy for a less well organized force to subordinate everything to the main attack. But there was nothing in the actions of these men to indicate that had it been part of their plan they mightn't have burned up the whole place including oil stores as a final gesture. . . . No, the only explanation that occurs to me is that they saved the physical establishment of Pearl Harbor because they intended to take it for themselves."

"That makes a little sense," admitted the navigator.

"Except," commented the marine, "that it merely brings us back to the point we started from. Why didn't they come back?"

"Well," the lieutenant said, scratching his head, "I'm beginning to think I don't know. It's another of your mysteries: Why didn't the Confederates go on to Washington after Bull Run? Why didn't the Germans go ahead when they'd broken through on the Somme? Why did the British quit the Dardanelles just when they'd flattened the Turks? Not to mention the obvious one somebody cited a minute ago, the fantastic business of Dunkirk.

"We expected an attack. The signs were obvious but we didn't take them on faith. We checked up. We didn't overlook that destruction of the installations might have been left to some civilian sabotage agency that had failed to work. We found there was no truth in reports that marine guards had shot down half a dozen Japs armed with hand grenades in the vicinity of fuel tanks. We established that only two parachutists had landed on Oahu and neither of these was a parachute jumper. We were able to trace only one case of sabotage. . . . An aged Japanese laborer came out of his house with a pick and started to demolish the fire plug on the corner. It was his idea—not a bad one—that water pressure would be needed to fight the fires at the naval base. So, in his simple way, he tried to reduce the pressure a bit. He was put into the local clink not as a saboteur but as a nuisance. There's a law about destroying city property. . . .

"I believe, despite everything, that the Japanese American in Honolulu is quite likely to remain American, and a good law-abiding American, as long as it suits his policy to be American. War or no war, we have a lot of Japanese on the islands who wouldn't want to be dumped back into Tokio to earn a living. They don't have to be told that they are sitting prettier under the present regime than they'll ever be under the glorious new deal that Japan is trying to dump upon the world. Down in their hearts they have deep racial affiliations and yet they don't want Japan to win this war. The successful Japanese, of course, is like the successful man of any other nation; he wants to hold on to what he's got and it's going to take a lot of convincing argument to make him trade his tangible effects for some abstruse philosophy of government.

"All of the important Japanese in the islands are actuated by some such motives. And their interest in the matter is interpreted in some fashion or other for the less favored people who work in cane fields or clean out the ponds in the fish hatcheries. The lowly, by some odd quirk of intellect which I am sure cannot be duplicated elsewhere in the world, take their cue from the comfortable rich who naturally couldn't have got rich and comfortable without first being careful and wise.

"In other words, with things as they are just now you don't have to worry a great deal about your Japanese population. They'll follow their leaders and their leaders will do what is best for their checkbooks. And that desirable situation will continue until the visiting Japanese make a definite threat to these islands with some prospect of success. When that happens fear may finish off a lot of what looked like loyalties when the boys and girls were in the grandstand last fall cheering for the McKinley High School football team.

"If the Japanese had gone on with the Pearl Harbor assault, if they had come back as we expected them to, if they had swept in when our guard was beaten down, and landed troops and had taken over the community by force, the local Japs might have had a change of heart, for their financial assets would automatically have become as good as nothing and their valuable hides would obviously have been endangered. As a realist I can't see any threatened Japanese defying these invaders of his own race because of any traditions of Bunker Hill and Lexington. . . . I can remember once I heard a Jap school kid reciting 'Barbara Frietchie' . . ."

An airplane came off the catapult and snapped past the screened windows. A yeoman came in with a message from radio— something about a merchant ship acting peculiarly over near Christmas Island. For the moment it was possible to realize that this war was not purely a localized phenomenon of Honolulu.

"It looks as if holding the islands would have to be a sort of inside-out job," commented the Marine captain when he could be heard over the tearing racket of the airplane motor. "Too bad, too. If we can't use the raw material on hand, we may have to import a lot of Americans for the next election."

"We shall see what we shall see," admitted the lieutenant. "It's just as well that we realized that our little brown brothers are nationally ambidexterous. Large numbers of them in Honolulu hold two passports. Some of the more modern and more practical have fixed up an identity card with the Japanese nationality attested at one end by the Mikado's consul general, and U. S. nationality, declared before the police, at the other. This ingenious gadget is made up of two cards pasted together and perforated so that the least useful half may be torn off and thrown away when the great day comes.

"If you have outgrown a belief in Santa Claus and the stork you don't suffer any increase in blood pressure from thinking about such a device. As a realist you are forced to admire it. It is patently the one arrangement best suited to the present emergency. Keep on being an American if the going is good but change over in a hurry when you have to. There is no guile about it. Just expediency and common sense.

"The Japanese government has always recognized the essential Japaneseness of Japs no matter where you find them. Irrespective of what country a Japanese might think he owes allegiance to, regardless of what he has to say about it in any language, he has always been a Japanese in the eyes of the paternal foreign office. And if he had children, they too were Japanese, a fact which the framers of our Oriental exclusion act seem to have recognized. Some years ago Japan, keeping step with the rest of the world, agreed to relinquish all claim to any child of Japanese parents born in a foreign country who, before reaching the age of sixteen years, should file with a Japanese consul notice of intent to become a citizen of that country. Nothing more came of this than might have been expected inasmuch as not many children are instructed in the problems of citizenship before reaching the age of sixteen.

"Just before the present dustup the foreign office relented a bit further. It was announced that any Japanese could become a citizen of another country—another country besides Japan—by filing a declaration with a Japanese consul. A couple of hundred Honolulu Japs took advantage of this boon, and I should say that of all the Japs in Hawaii who want to see the United States win, these belated Americans are the most eager. For something happened to their applications. They got no farewell notes or certificates of release from the consulate that they might present to the police as evidence of right thinking, good faith and loyal Americanism. On the other hand the consulate got a pretty fair list of the more lukewarm Japanese patriots on the island of Oahu."

7

THE RETURN OF THE WHIRLING DERVISHES

IN THIS business you get fairly used to coincidences and after running into Lee Stowe in the Grand Hotel in Lagos, Nigeria, I was prepared to have anybody I'd ever heard of show up in Honolulu to tell me how small the world was getting. But even at that I wasn't quite prepared to see Tom Yarbrough of the A.P. The first time I ever saw him was when he alighted from an airplane on the North rim of the Grand Canyon to cover the ascent of a mesa called "The Temple of Shiva." The last time I had seen him was in Dublin as I put him aboard a bus for Kerry. Yes, I guess as everybody remarks with such originality it *is* a small world.

On the hot bright morning of Saturday I went to a press conference at Pearl Harbor. I didn't expect much of it because nothing in my long and reasonably accurate memory has ever come out of one. But I went. At press conferences you meet a lot of interesting people.

At this one there turned up Joe Harsche of the *Christian Science Monitor*. . . . The last I saw of him was in Jim Kilgallen's room in the hotel Nakotosh at Natchitoches. And there came also Bill Doherty who was working for INS at Asheville at the time the wandering Raymond Robbins regained his memory and a position in a society that he may have found amusing.

We were led to the meeting by Sam Riddick, public-relations officer for the fourteenth naval district, formerly a Washington press agent. And, in the officers' club at the submarine base, we were given seats at a long table while some of the surviving officers of the December seventh fiasco passed in review. These men we were told could not be mentioned by name. Their ships were also wrapped in quiet.

Some of the boys of the intelligence section tried to talk us out of a conviction that all press releases to date have been stupidly misleading. In this brave but futile effort they got a little help from officers of the fleet public-relations department—laughingly so called—Lieutenant Commander Waldo Drake and Lieutenant Jim Bassett. Commander Drake was once a ship-news reporter in Los Angeles and presumably knew something about the newspaper business. That put him one up on everybody in the neighborhood.

The officers told interesting stories—particularly a lieutenant who apparently had been the only line officer aboard his ship. He tried to get her out into the channel but was ordered not to leave the harbor. So with torpedoes popping down below, he nosed her into the mud, flooded her forward magazine and beached her. It was an exciting story and filled with pathetic incident—but mostly useless to us. It's hard to describe the heroic conduct of men aboard a ship that mustn't be mentioned in the dispatches.

It was obvious, too, that we were due to have a little trouble with the censors. Mr. Drake, quite obviously, thought that the job belonged to him. Mr. Riddick was just as obdurate.

Never before now did it ever occur to me that somebody might actually want to be a censor. And here were two candidates. Not only did each of them want to be censor. He was prepared to fight for the privilege. . . . Well! Well!

Without writing anything about the things that we had heard in the press conference and then were advised to forget, I went away from Pearl Harbor a bit exhausted. There was something about this incipient bedlam that recalled the whirling dervishes of the Hôtel Continental in Paris. And there was something terrifying in the memory of what that connoted. We had been wont to console ourselves in the early days of the Sitzkrieg with the thought that France had a dual personality—that the dazed ones who ran the Continental, with its bureaus of circulation and public relations and censorship and intelligence and its eternal atmosphere of befuddlement, were quite different from the intelligent, selfless and patriotic men who ran the army. And when we discovered that they were all of the same pattern it was too late for us to do anything about it except strike out for the Spanish border. We had come out of the screaming shambles of Bordeaux with the fixed idea that a nation can't be dim-brained in the upper end of its directives without being dim-brained all the way. And here, unless the signs were all wrong, was a brand new Continental. One hesitated to draw the obvious conclusions.

The day after the conference I walked purposelessly about the town until 10 A.M. when the theaters opened and then went in to see a tripeful offering called *Suez*. It depicted a world in which Ferdinand DeLesseps was in love with the Empress Eugenie—but withal no more unreal or cockeyed a world than the one I stepped out into when I decided I wouldn't stay to see how the movie ended.

I wrote a few hundred words about life in Honolulu and took the copy over to Riddick's office. There I met Bill Ewing, a lieutenant, who was formerly A.P. correspondent here. I was away from the place and the copy on its way to some mysterious bourne out of my reach when I learned that this was a blind censorship. You threw the copy in and if it came out or not you'd find out only when somebody at home raised a howl. I announced then to all and sundry that I should certainly not stay here and try to work under such a system.

All the bars were closed. One mentions it almost regretfully.

I spent the next afternoon working up a blood pressure with Mr. Riddick over his blind censorship. He promised to tell us if he cut anything out of our copy or held it up. It wasn't much of a concession but anyway a beginning.

One bit of the unpleasantness deserves a note. I had told Mr. Riddick that even the English had not subjected us to a blind censorship and Mr. Riddick replied: "You're not in England now, Mr. Casey. You're in the United States. And we'll do this job the American way."

So I told him I thought the point was well taken. It is the American way, I told him, to go blunderingly ahead, taking advice from nobody and reading no signs and portents until of our own untutored contriving we arrive at something like a Pearl Harbor. I suggested that maybe if some doctor in London developed a new technique in appendectomy it might not be considered too un-

American of a doctor on this side of the Atlantic to take advantage of his discoveries. At the risk of being counted a screwball if not a traitor I hinted that we, starting off from scratch in this war, might learn something from people who'd been working at it diligently and to the exclusion of all other interests for a couple of years.

When I left the wrangle seemed to have ended in a tie. But I don't know.

8

ONE-MAN BATTLE OF NIIHAU

ALL in all there was little to brighten our lives in those days save that one morning they brought a large Hawaiian gentleman to a Honolulu hospital and we heard about the invasion of the island of Niihau and a few details of its heroic defense. A two-man putsch it was and a one-man, one-woman counterattack, and like everything else that the coming of the Japs precipitated it was wholly fantastic and incredible.

Niihau is a small island off Kauai. It is owned by one of the missionary families but it has never been exploited. On the contrary it has been maintained for many years as a last refuge for natives who want to live their lives in their own way—as they did before the White Man came with his manifold blessings. No boats touch at Niihau. No tourists or other curious visitors are allowed to land. No regular inhabitants are allowed to leave for anything longer than a fishing trip unless they wish to stay away for good. For they won't be allowed back.

This control of the itching foot is possible because all ownership of the land is vested in the family which makes the rules and there isn't any room for argument about it. If a native is content to live in the simple old way without any yearning for the movies and streetcars and quick lunchrooms and similar delights of Honolulu every facility is given him. He is allotted a parcel of land. What he raises on it is his own. He doesn't have to worry about white men's laws except insofar perhaps as they may have to do with murder and such. He finds redress from grievances in palaver with his own people. And in most respects he lives a calm, beautiful, idyllic life unbothered by wars that may affect other worlds and other islands. Well, there you have the scene.

Into this paradise about noon on the day of the bombing a Jap aviator fell with his plane for lack of fuel.

The aviator crawled out of the cockpit, found himself not seriously hurt and began to look about the island. Presently he came upon another Japanese, which even in Niihau doesn't seem to have been difficult.

This part of the plan comes to light only through deduction, but skipping the reconstruction process it seems that the pilot, far from figuring that he had crashed himself into a hot spot, saw an opportunity to make a one-man conquest of the island. It would be simple to hold the place in subjection, he thought, if he could contrive to keep the simple natives from getting out word to the rest of the world that he had arrived. Otherwise it seemed likely that the U. S. Marines or somebody would be along looking for him. And he feared for the worst.

The sympathetic Jap farmer entered into the spirit of the thing. The pair of them took what arms there were in the plane, including the machine gun, and then went out to round up the other inhabitants of the island.

All went unbelievably well with this venture, largely because there were few shacks close together. The surprised populace was coralled family by family and marched along in a group for internment at a point which the Japanese had not yet determined. But just as they were assured of success they ventured to collect a previously good-natured Hawaiian who in company with his wife was eating poi in his little grass shack. He objected to the interruption. He got up and started after the pilot who shot him three times with the machine gun. The pilot paused after that burst waiting to see him fall down. But he kept coming and before there was a chance for another trigger squeeze, the Hawaiian picked the Jap up and battered his brains out against a stone wall. His wife in the meantime charged the Jap farmer, knocked the gun out of his hand with a club and routed him. The farmer went home and committed hara-kiri. It seemed like a good time for it.

It turned out then that the roundup of the natives hadn't been complete. Some of them had sneaked away from the procession and started for Kauai in a fishing boat. They were intercepted by a patrol boat, taken ashore and given a chance to relate their story to the Army. An expeditionary force was assembled at once and an hour later made a landing, complete with jeeps, foot and artillery. The rescuers found the situation well in hand.

The Hawaiian was taken to Honolulu and given treatment for sundry serious and painful wounds. He issued a statement to the press to the effect that the Jap pilot had oversold his case.

"When he shot me the first time I saw there wasn't any good making a fuss about it," this sturdy householder said, presumably in Hawaiian. "But when he shot me the second time it seemed to me like he was doing it just to make a foolishness and I got sore. And when he shot me the third time it looked like he was going to kill me no matter what I did. So I smashed his head. I'm going to move away from Niihau if they're going to let people like that land on it."

9

CHRISTMAS ON A STEEL HARP

DECEMBER 24, *Tuesday*. Honolulu. " 'Twas the night before Christmas . . ." A beautiful hot day. Stymied in my attempt to buy tar paper or similar stuff I collected a lot of photograph-album filler-sheets at the ten-cent store and pasted them together for blackout material. Then I moved out to the Moana Seaside Bungalows.

The night presented only one surprise—a call from Frank Smothers. He had arrived during the evening, he said, with H. R. Knickerbocker and Ed Angly.

December 25, Thursday. Honolulu. Merry Christmas! Got routed out early today for jaunt to navy yard which produced practically nothing. We saw Admiral Leary aboard the cruiser *Honolulu* in dry dock and he said he thought it was going to be a long war. So did I.

Luncheon at Royal Hawaiian. Spent afternoon with Knick, Angly, Yarbrough and others at home of Riley Allen, editor of the *Star Bulletin*, a Shangri-La sort of place up on the hill behind the punch bowl. Had dinner at Royal Hawaiian with Frank Smothers, et al. Thence to bed in my bungalow. Hawaiian music doesn't fit in very well with Christmas—even a hot Christmas.

"God rest ye merry, Gentlemen, Aloha!"

A couple of days after Christmas we went with the Navy to look at Kaneohe air base over beyond the Pali. We had a nice ride but got no information. The keynote of the Navy air force is "We wish they'd try it again." It's beginning to sound like a popular song. We saw piles of junked airplanes and banks of replacements. But we heard few words that we could add up to make any sense. Some civilian employee out here was probably the first guy to discover that the Japs were attacking. So he called up Wheeler and Hickam Fields and tried to tell whoever he got on the phone. They hung up on him.

I sat up until about 10 P.M., talking with Knick and Angly about Egypt, Ethiopia and the smell of Nigeria.

At church the next day I ran into Jim Kilgallen who seems to have arrived when I wasn't looking. The beauty of wars, if any, is that you meet everybody you ever knew in them. We had luncheon at the Young. After that I went back to the beach. Some survivors of a sunken freighter got into town. Otherwise there wasn't much doing.

Dinner at Royal Hawaiian. Afterward I listened to the broadcast in English from Tokio. I heard quite a harangue about *Bushido*, the noble code of the warrior. It seems that the English were careless of precious Chinese lives in the defense of Hongkong and that American sportsmen raised hell with the good old Japanese nationals in Davao. Also, the orator announced, it was just nonsense to suggest that the chivalrous warriors of Japan had bombed any churches or schools in Manila.

The musical program that followed was also bad.

Monday, December 29, is memorable because it was cool. There was nothing much in the day's news except the bombing of Manila and the sinking of about two of the eighty Japanese transports approaching the Philippines. I went into town and bought this typewriter for twenty-five dollars. I saw *The Wizard of Oz* and an even more fantastic reel of Art Menken in Hawaii. Part of Menken's act was in collaboration with Admiral Kimmel about whose program of "constant vigilance" he made suitable remarks.

I tried to buy a strap but couldn't get any. There are no harness shops because there are no horses.

The Jap radio that evening explained why Manila couldn't be considered an open city. But you gathered that it didn't make any difference anyway because all the fires had been started by undisciplined U. S. troops in cowardly retreat. The Jap radio is the funniest diversion that the war so far has provided.

Newspapers that day made much of the appearance of U. S.

planes in the Philippines—apparently enough of a novelty to be news.

I went shopping during the afternoon to pick up some sort of phonograph and a couple of files of Gilbert and Sullivan records. It occurred to me that Pearl Harbor might see something ironic in a suggestion that *Pinafore* and *The Mikado* ought to be played out there at least once a day.

Wednesday, December 31, was of course the day before New Year's and many of us I dare say recalled other, wetter holidays. But memory did us no good. The town was really dry ... with such penalties as a five-hundred-dollar fine for being adjudged drunk and ten years in the penitentiary for dealing in hooch. . . . Not that I cared. I was beginning to see some of the advantages of being on the wagon.

We went over to Pearl Harbor this afternoon and met Admiral Chester Nimitz, the new commander of the Pacific fleet. He was reasonably frank about saying nothing. He wouldn't forecast any action by the U. S. Navy but freely prophesied what the Japs are going to do. Most probably, he said, their submarines will raise hell with the Pacific coast towns of the mainland. The agile censors changed "probably" to "possibly" before the copy was released.

Maui and Hawaii were bombarded by a Jap sub during the night. The Army released the story but the Navy censor killed it. There was a good Navy release on a PBY crew that landed on a rough sea, rescued eight Army fliers, and got off again—a miracle of the first order.

Thursday, January 1. Honolulu. Clear, cool. I went to town to nine o'clock Mass and there discovered that all the boys were howling bloody murder because their stories on the shelling of Kauai have been held up by the Navy despite Army release. I also learned that all correspondents were barred from the cemetery on Red Hill for no stated reason. Foster Hailey of the New York *Times* made the point that if the cemetery is only a cemetery it isn't a source of news that might give aid and comfort to the enemy. On the other hand, he says, if guns are hidden there it's no place for a cemetery. . . .

10

RAW MATERIAL FOR PANIC

CONSIDERING that for quite a long time the Hawaiian Islands were America's front line in this war it isn't remarkable that Honolulu's state of flutter turned out to have many lasting qualities. After while people began to go swimming in the surf again if always with an ear cocked for machine-gun fire. But the barbed wire continued to make a fine hazard of Waikiki. You still had trouble finding anything to eat after 5:30 at night. You still couldn't get into Pearl Harbor without an armed guard no matter how many sets of your fingerprints happened to be on file. You still heard forecasts of the wrath to come.

There was something of the atmosphere of embattled Paris about Honolulu then, something of the atmosphere of Cairo, Illinois, when the Ohio River was beginning to lap the top of the wall— a sense of fear plus a sense of helplessness. But save in the rush for outbound boats, the surrender to doom that you got in conversation with the old-timers, and the unbelievable rigor of the military law, there was little sign of panic. The town might gasp and die at six o'clock every night. But all day long it was more or less alive—dazed, perhaps, but alive. It went through the routine motions of business with convincing zeal—although as you looked on you may have remembered the lads who went on painting the ceiling of the pressroom in Tours when the Germans bombarded the city. Shops spread out an amazing lot of wares such as tapa-cloth souvenirs of Hawaii, fittings for sailboats, sportswear and sukiyaki and other stuff that nobody seemed likely to want ever again. The show of the shocked community bravely carrying on was impressive. But in three weeks you couldn't buy a suitcase or a trunk or a shawl strap anywhere between Pearl Harbor and

Diamond Head. Business may have had some of the symptoms of permanence but the populace certainly didn't.

In those days naturally you wondered how much of this resignation to a fate worse than death was based on a restricted diet and financial worry and how much on inside information. It was difficult to get much in the way of statistics on this. You could only keep your eyes open, read the newspapers, talk to such people as might want to talk to you and draw your own conclusions. You speedily got the idea that the jitters of the populace were due not to any inside revelations but to a conviction that lightning always strikes twice in the same place and with worse effect on the second visit.

The condition of American information services in the Hawaiian Islands at the time of the Japanese coup was just about what most of the newspapermen in the United States had expected it to be. In what sources were open to us at least there had never been any suggestion of parity between the information that Japan had gathered in and about the United States, and the information that the United States had gathered in and about Japan. As a sort of corollary it had been pretty generally felt by people who made a business of finding out such things that our spy system had no organized existence outside of J. Edgar Hoover's press releases, and that we got most of our intelligence on foreign affairs through the gentlemanly and discreet use of the crystal ball.

Army and Navy men used to laugh at the ingenuous activities of Japan's non-secret secret agents. One recalls the case of a naval officer who one sunny day pointed out a slant-eyed fisherman doing odd things with a vertical fish line close inshore.

"Look at him," the naval officer said cheerily. "He's going to all that trouble making soundings when he could go inshore and buy a geodetic survey map for fifty cents. . . ."

I mentioned that incident sometime later to a harried commander during a blackout in San Francisco.

"Probably the Japanese wanted better maps," he said.

Then there was the incident of the leading laundryman of Sitka. He died suddenly and the mourning customers who had admired him greatly turned out to do him final honors. They buried him in a quaint costume that they had found in a box under his bed. There seemed to be no reason why he should not wear it openly in death. No one would criticize him for it now. It was the uniform of a full commander in the Japanese navy.

And there was the related matter of the fires on the Sitka naval base—the dynamite explosions that occurred so mysteriously on three different occasions, putting numerous people in hospitals, wrecking great quantities of material and filling a few graves. The last of these spectacular blasts happened on the night of December 6 and until that time a large part of the American populace and a few American officials were unwilling to read a lesson in the law of averages and told themselves that Sitka was being visited by a lot of totally coincidental hard luck.

There were other signs and portents including our obvious lack of factual knowledge or even competent guesswork about what Japan might do, what naval strength she might be able to muster for a surprise blow. It is doubtful if, when we went to war, we knew for a certainty how many battleships of the line she had in commission, not to mention such items as submarines and destroyers. So there was reason for suspicion on December 6 or thereabouts that if we had any working intelligence system in the Hawaiian Islands, it was the only one we had anywhere. That supposition turned out to be right.

Whatever criticism has been given the Navy for its part in the Pearl Harbor fiasco, and whatever the Navy's delays in finding out what was going on, it must be said in all fairness that the fleet intelligence had made a start and a good one. Their trouble was that the start had been late and that progress was slow. . . . But at any rate there had been remarkable progress. Perhaps in the normal course of things it might not have taken a catastrophic visitation to bring action on their recommendations. But one remembers the Sitka fires and asks permission to doubt.

The Amy G2 had not been badly conducted in the Hawaiian establishment—so far as national policy would permit. The rule of rotation that has been applied to officers throughout the army moving them from post to post at regular intervals had been suspended here so that many remained in the service of intelligence for fifteen or twenty years. They came to know the country. They understood its economy and its politics. They felt after a while that they understood its people.

In a way they did understand the people. They certainly assembled a lot of facts about their culture, customs and attitude toward labor. But throughout the long period of their work they had been hampered by the same kindly, thoughtful Federal policy that had kept us from fortifying Guam or warning Japan off the Indo-Chinese islands. They hadn't been allowed to shadow suspects or to watch their homes or to ask them questions or, for that matter, to examine their friends. They must do their detective work—if you could call it that—by remote control a couple of times removed.

When crisis was dumped into their laps they discovered that most of what they actually knew could have been picked up out of travel books. A lot of their investigators found themselves in the position of a father who has just caught a delicate and rather effeminate son red-handed in murder. They knew the surfaces of these people, particularly of the Japanese people, but they were beginning to wonder if they really knew anything at all about the psychology that makes a Japanese a Japanese and not, for instance, a Shetland Islander.

And did they know how these people behaved themselves in the quiet of their homes away from occidental eyes? Did they know, really, where those homes were? Did they know whether Tanaka whose front porch overlooked Pearl Harbor wrote letters to the wrong people in Japan? Did he have a camera? Did he know how to make a map? Did he have means of transmitting information secretly? They began to wonder if the file couldn't have been more complete on subjects like this.

Frank Smothers, who was long Far Eastern correspondent for the Chicago *Daily News,* passed through Tokio on his way back to the United States after his recall from a wartime appointment to the Berlin office. During his stay in Germany his family had moved from Evanston, Illinois, a suburb of Chicago, to Wheaton, Illinois, another suburb. When he arrived in Japan in 1940 en route to Chicago he had never seen his new home and he wasn't certain about its location. He met no one in Japan to whom he so much as mentioned his change of address. When he left the Imperial Hotel in Tokio to catch a boat for home, he left no forwarding address. So he wasn't at all surprised six weeks later when he received a letter that had been addressed to him at the Imperial Hotel and forwarded by the Japanese postal authorities to his new address in Wheaton. He had expected that the Japanese would have information like that.

The failure of the intelligence workers in Hawaii to produce local dossiers as complete as those which the Japanese had prepared for Americans abroad was, under the existing rules, no fault of the personnel. They were uniformly intelligent and despite more than the ordinary term of years in the quieting atmosphere of Hawaii, reasonably energetic. They had scores of friends in Honolulu, Hilo, in the canebrakes, in the hill country. Their knowledge of general conditions was excellent. But they remained impersonal and therefore completely hamstrung by the headquarters decision that the private affairs of any American citizen were his own affair no matter what his color or racial extraction. They couldn't ask Yama San the name of his next-door neighbor and they couldn't ask the next-door neighbor whether or not Yama San had a transmitter in his attic. It is hardly remarkable that the Army's information about individuals within what were speedily to become its front lines were less complete than that in the files of a chain store's credit department.

The police, probably, are the greatest realists on the island of Oahu. They quite conceivably know more about what is going on than any other group in Hawaii. But spy hunting has never been a part of their curriculum. And while undoubtedly they are the best local authority on race loyalty, their own mixed origins make them to some extent part of the problem. From the beginning of the crisis, Chief Gabrielson placed little confidence in the Americanism of the home-grown Japanese whom he suspected of being, like many other members of the human race, inveterate opportunists. But he had no doubt about the Japanese boys on his force.

"The United States might possibly be a secondary thing to them," he said. "And Japan might be more important than it ought to be to a good American. But they have discipline and they have pride of service. And they'll stick no matter what comes."

One needs little more than a look at the disagreement between the police and G2 about the intentions of the civilian populace after the bombing to determine just what our inside information amounted to. Army officers who numbered hundreds of island-born Japanese among their friends were certain that this element would stand firm against the old country, particularly after the dishonorable features of the attack on Pearl Harbor had been given sufficient publicity.

"Ninety-eight per cent of them," said one officer who had spent fifteen years finding out, "are better citizens of the United States than we are."

"The Japanese are good, law-abiding people," said Chief Gabrielson. "And in a wrangle between the United States and Japan I wouldn't trust them for twenty-five seconds."

The Japanese bombers went away. Hundreds of horribly burned and wounded men stretched out on the docks of Pearl Harbor to die in peace. The smoke of the burning *Arizona* drifted in a black cloud out to sea. And presently darkness came to Hawaii and with it the most amazing exhibition of martial law ever seen on U. S. soil.

Followed then a sort of open-house week in bedlam. The authorities felt for a moment that they had succeeded in putting all the possible dynamiters under cover but they had no way of telling where the dynamite had been concealed. The curfew, perhaps, had stopped a race riot and massacre with frantic Filipinos leading the attack, and all Japanese, loyal or disloyal, well in the lead as prospective clinical material. On the other hand the curfew perhaps had merely postponed trouble. Who could be sure that murder was not at the very instant stalking cat-eyed through the darkness? Who could say that there was no well-organized, well-equipped sabotage unit that would presently strike? Was the Japanese attack finished? Were the islands safe against another surprise? All through the nights the authorities sat close to their telephones and lifted their ears through the silence of the dead town to catch a sound of airplane motors or the pounding feet of infantry or the screaming of whistle bombs. All night long the nervous guardsmen shot homing citizenry and stray dogs and one another—all night long—all week long.

The old standards were gone. Your neighbors were strangers. Your friends had turned into enemies ... or had they? It wasn't the bombs that had transformed Honolulu into the city of the dreadful night. It was the uncertainty of everything. That was the trouble. ... You didn't know. ... You couldn't know. ...

11

THE UNBELIEVABLE ADVENTURE

Save a place in history for Mr. Roy Vitousek who momentarily became the Albert-the-Aviator of the Pacific war and retired miraculously famous but even more miraculously alive. For it was Mr. Vitousek, a gifted amateur pilot, who, on the morning of December 7, found himself flying an outer wing guard for the Japanese bomber fleet, changed sides just for the expediency of the thing and presently became a discredited Paul Revere and the Number One victim of Pearl Harbor's goofy season. Mr. Vitousek is still just as incredible as he was that morning—more so, for the impossibility of the affair increases with each new whisper that comes over the glistening trefoil of the harbor. He might be a dubious legend by this time save for one thing: If you can believe the story of Pearl Harbor you can believe the story of Mr. Vitousek and vice versa.

Mr. Vitousek is a lawyer of calm demeanor and simple habits, one of those good solid American citizens who have made the much-advertised standards of the country really work. He has made quite a comfortable living out of his practice in Honolulu. He is active in civic affairs. He is a member of the police commission. Hawaii has treated him kindly and he has appreciated the treatment. He knows all the ways of gracious living. He is generous, kindly. You know him or his like. You will find his counterpart sometimes in a cultured, well-favored, American community.

It will be obvious to future historians who look into the Vitousek phenomenon as it is linked up with the bombing of Pearl Harbor that the quiet security of a life such as his, particularly against the background of the languorous islands, is hardly likely to be disrupted by any great amount of violence and excitement or seriously cluttered up with adventure.

Very likely the researchers, if they are interested, may discover that there are more frustrated Rembrandts, Napoleons, Captains Kidd and Babes Ruth among the well-to-do, comfortable, contented men of Mr. Vitousek's class than anywhere else in society. . . . Not that the defeated ones suffer much pain. (It must be reasonably easy to go on being a mute inglorious Milton as you sit in a shaded deck chair among the glorious hibiscus flowers and watch the surf spin its feather boas on the golden beach—the while you listen to the music of ice in tall glasses.) But it is axiomatic that nothing breeds discontent so quickly as contentment. And save for a certain heaven-sent inertia, the leisure class would certainly be the busiest exhibit in the human race. It makes little sense but that's how it is.

So it will surprise nobody very much to discover that Mr. Vitousek owned an airplane and knew how to fly it. He was one of the few of his kind who, having recognized the existence of a secret and overpowering yearning, have decided to do something about it, and, having decided to do something about it, have found themselves in a financial position to carry on the work. He bought a plane—an Aeronca. He learned to fly it. He got a license. He flew regularly and he flew well. He was close to fifty years old on the afternoon of December 7, 1941, but even so he was trying to make some sort of deal with either Army or Navy recruiting services whereby he would be allowed to pilot a combat airplane.

"Somebody told me a man's as young as his reflexes," said Mr. Vitousek. "And I had just found out that mine were pretty good. Anyway the wars ought to be fought by the older men. . . . Then so many manpower hours aren't wasted when they get killed."

It is not stated what he was thinking about the possible approach of war at daybreak on the morning of the seventh. But he had already made some tentative offers of his services even before that. . . . So maybe he shouldn't have been surprised.

He rose well before the dawn on that glorious morning. He roused his son, sat down with him at a brief breakfast, then drove out to John Rodgers airport which is so close to the Hickam Field of the Pearl Harbor establishment that a stranger pilot would have to look twice to tell one from the other. He rolled out his plane, motioned his son into the rear cockpit, put on his goggles and took off.

You have heard what kind of day it was. But nobody on our windy, snow-swept, winter-locked mainland could possibly envision the setting—air soft as that of a Georgia spring, filled with flower scents and the tang of the sea—a clear blue sky and a clear blue ocean—the island paradise stepping up through green cane fields and zones of croton, hydrangea, and bougainvillea to misty, mysterious mountain peaks. It was, as Mr. Vitousek said, a very nice time for flying and a very nice place. So he went up.

Mr. Vitousek climbed up over Pearl Harbor and lazily crawled southward above the Pacific. He turned along the beach toward Diamond Head, crossed it gaining altitude, and came back. Below him lay the city of Honolulu, blazing white in the morning sun, and he remarked its beauty and its emptiness. As in most tropical places, the lighting of Honolulu varies whimsically from hour to hour—that is why the brooding mountains are never the same two days in succession—that is why Honolulu rates as a modern Eden instead of a second-rate tropical seaport. Mr. Vitousek thought that he had never seen the tints of flower gardens and terraced parks so vivid against the brightness of the morning as they were just then. He passed over the Aloha Tower and gave an appreciative thought to the scintillant blue of the harbor. . . .

The harbor! In only a few weeks, now, it would be garlanded with leis of ginger blossom and gardenia, thrown from the decks of outbound steamships by travelers who wished to insure their return to the enchanted islands. The tourist season would be in full flower. Probably as gay and profitable as ever, it would be, for tourists were notoriously skeptical people who throughout the written history of man had never believed in "ancestral voices prophesying war." God was in his Heaven, and Mr. Vitousek was past the Aloha Tower and heading west and a little north toward Hickam Field at 7:55 A.M. Oh, singular and amazing moment!

It may have been the reflex of exhilaration that made him throw back his head just then. It may have been instinct. But at any rate he did look up and became aware that in some fashion he had got mixed up with a lot of airplanes—military airplanes. He recognized the lines and equipment at once. They were flying in close formation, a series of three V's with five planes to a V. And he was slightly to the rear and right of and almost a part of the leading V.

He was not alarmed. After all, this region was full of aircraft. As things were rated nowadays, perhaps Oahu's fields weren't over-crowded. . . . But anyway the local defense force was probably the biggest concentration of flying machines so far gathered up by the United States anywhere but in political harangues. There must be five hundred planes down there at Hickam and Wheeler Fields—five hundred planes that could actually fly and armed with guns that could actually shoot. No, it was not a matter of alarm for Mr. Vitousek to find the air filled with planes—fifteen here and some more coming in from the sea behind. But it was very surprising, Mr. Vitousek thought, for Mr. Vitousek hadn't lived in the island all these years without learning something of the social habits of the Army and Navy. This was Sunday morning, the time of all the week when in the normal course of events everybody would be asleep or trailing in to breakfast, and Mr. Vitousek and sundry other civilian amateurs could hope to have the free use of an uncrowded sky.

Fifteen planes up here in this flight . . . some more back there over the sea. . . . Something funny about them. . . . They were gleaming silver in the morning sunlight—the camouflage if any was different from any that Mr. Vitousek had ever seen on an American plane before. Some new idea, he supposed.

All of this thought took very little time but as he recalls, it rode idly through his consciousness. He was still virtually unconcerned with the planes except insofar as they were coming into his course. He toyed vaguely with the thought of closing in on the formation, attaching a sixth plane to the force of the first V. But he knew that somebody would get sore about that. The Army wouldn't like to be kidded.

Then a gun went off near his head and he heard two or three cracks loud enough to break through the roar of his engine. Even that didn't alarm him. A signal, he thought. Pity he couldn't catch the code. Maybe a wing commander was taking him into the game. Maybe he was signaling: "Come in here, you, and close up the for-mation," or something like that. Then came a couple more cracks and a piece of the cowl pushed back into his face.

He took a closer look, a more interested and more personal look, and saw a red disk on the wing of the plane nearest him. The Rising Sun! Japan! And may God have mercy on us!

In that same terrible instant Mr. Vitousek noticed that the flight, already at less than two hundred feet, was on its way down. He pulled back on the stick, opened the throttle wide and shot up as rapidly as the *chug chug* of his flying flivver would take him. At six hundred feet he leveled off and looked down. For a moment he thought that the visitors might overlook him because they had other plans. They had swooped down toward the runway along the hangars of Hickam and the lower air was crosshatched with the tracery of flaming bullets. The planes followed the hangar line to the end and swung left. The ghastly business of Pearl Harbor was well started.

Mr. Vitousek looked at this dazed and unbelieving but rapidly recovering his senses. He might not have realized at the moment that he had seen the beginning of the greatest naval disaster in American history, that he had witnessed the invasion of the United States for the first time since 1813, but he did realize all at once that he was definitely in a bad spot. Few civilian fliers have ever found themselves involved with enemy formations so there is no good precedent for conduct under such circumstances. Mr. Vitousek had to solve his problem in his own way.

As matters stood at the moment of the attack on Hickam Field, he didn't seem to have much choice. At least one plane of the first formation had peeled off to spray the personnel and hangars of John Rodgers airport with machine-gun slugs. It wasn't going to be safe to land at John Rodgers. On the other hand it was going to be unpleasant to hang in the air at six hundred feet above Hickam Field and that very presently. The planes he had noticed out over the sea were coming up rapidly.

However short might be Mr. Vitousek's qualifications as a combat pilot, he was well enough trained as a flier to know that he wasn't going to be able to outrun a military plane in an Aeronca.

"Well," he said afterward, "man's natural element is said to be the ground and probably I was stronger on instinct than on strategy. I saw that for the time being—just at that minute, I mean—nobody was bothering John Rodgers airport. So I went down."

Mr. Vitousek went into a power dive and flattened onto the runway in the best landing of a long and prideful flying career. He and his son were out of the plane simultaneously. Mr. Vitousek's first impression, as he recalls it now, was the indignant face of an officer of the civil aeronautics authority. He had come running out of a hangar, apparently under the impression that the Vitousek plane was part of the flight whose violent echoes were now coming back from the direction of Pearl Harbor. His head was lowered and he seemed unhappy. He recognized Mr. Vitousek with an expression of relief.

"I thought you were part of that crazy Army show," he said. "And I was going to tell you off. My God! What's the world coming to? We have to have an Army Air Force and we have to keep it trained and all that, but, dammit, what right have they got to get roaring drunk and go around killing people . . ."

"They're———" began Mr. Vitousek gasping for breath as he tried to make certain that he was really standing on solid ground and for the nonce alive.

"Look at this field," demanded the outraged inspector. "Look at those cars———" He pointed to a line of civilian cars, some of them afire, some scarred by dozens of bullet holes, and beyond them to the body of a sailor in fresh, new whites, the naval guard of the field.

"Dead!" raved the inspector. "Shot down just as you see him there by these crazy drunken idiots. What in the name of God is American aviation coming to?"

"That's not American aviation," said Mr. Vitousek who had just recovered his breath and realized what the inspector was talking about. "That's Japanese aviation."

"Good Heavens! No!" blurted the inspector. And he ran toward Hickam to tell somebody about it. Hickam was already in flames.

Young Vitousek discovered their car unhurt where they had left it at the end of the field. Without bothering to push the plane into the hangar, they got moving toward town. They turned into the Honolulu road which still lay virtually empty for seven miles, just as a second flight came over to splash incendiary bullets on what the first flight had missed and to kill the civil aeronautics inspector.

Mr. Vitousek stopped at a filling station a mile or so along the road and began to telephone his news to the folks at home. His first effort brought the ear of somebody in the office of the chief of police.

"What you say?" inquired this person.

"The Japs," said Mr. Vitousek. "I said that the Japs have started to bomb Pearl Harbor. They're over in force—hundreds of planes."

"Brother," said the policeman patiently, "either you're drunk or I am. It sounds as if you was saying that the Japs are bombing Pearl Harbor." He hung up.

By turns Mr. Vitousek called city officials, police officials, judges, and such members of the Army and Navy as he thought might be in town. Until 9:30 that morning it was the unanimous opinion among Mr. Vitousek's friends that he was probably the least convincing practical joker in the community.

"They called me names," he recalls somewhat bitterly. "I couldn't get anybody to listen to me . . . least of all the people with authority to do something about it. And for the time I was sore. I couldn't see how people could go on making such fools of themselves. They just wanted to go on lying in bed even after I had told them what was going on.

"And then in the afternoon when the smoke was rolling over the town and the panic was on, I got to thinking it over. Would I have believed that the Japs were attacking Pearl Harbor if I had called up and told myself so? I didn't think so. I remembered how hard it was for me to figure out what was happening even after they'd taken a couple of shots at me and I could see the rising sun on their wings. . . .

"I suppose it was what you could call a novel experience and I know that whatever happens to me I've got a copyright on it for this war. They aren't going to let amateur planes fly any more. It'll be a long time before I can see the island again as it looked that morning. Unless they give me a job with the Army I'll just have to sit here and wait, I suppose. Too bad."

The end of this story, of course, will be found in the footnotes of the historians who assemble the source material for an account of what happened at Pearl Harbor. Mr. Vitousek's name unquestioningly will go into the school histories of the United States to remain forever alongside that of Paul Revere who got a better audience-response to the same dramatic technique. For, however you may read it, Mr. Roy Vitousek is the first man in history to go blithely sailing into a murderous enemy-plane formation. And, moreover, he was the first man on the island who knew that the *dolce far niente* was over.

Perhaps the sequel may show that he went back unprotesting from the wrecked hangars of John Rodgers airport to the grassy terrace of his home, the shaded deck chair, the pleasant communion with stirring memory as the hasty twilight goes and the blackout begins. Perhaps it may show that he was willing to accept the old comfortable, contented, soporific life against which his flying in the dawn on Sunday mornings was a gesture of revolt. . . . After all there are few dwellers in the scented islands to whom adventure really comes, no matter how steadily they may dream of it. To no man in all the world has ever come an experience like his. After all, when a man has one moment like that, no matter what he does for the rest of his existence it must seem pretty flat to him. And he'll never have another such experience. The impossible happens only once.

12

THE BELT OF A THOUSAND STITCHES

On the hill behind the opal bay of Kaneohe they buried K. Hurushi, the Japanese ex-ace, with full military honors. The work that Hurushi and his suicidal companions had done before his plane went out of control and crashed against the rocky uplift lived after him—smashed hangars, burned planes, a scattering of American graves. But they buried him properly, nonetheless, with a bugler and a firing squad and a bit of flag at the end of his coffin. It was an impressive performance.

After the funeral there was a sort of survey at Number One hangar—an inquest in a way because it had to do with how the dead pilot came to his fortunate end, but the subject of the inquiry was not so much Hurushi San as his recent plane, pieces of which were laid out where interested technicians might take a close look at them.

"I wonder how much of my old Ford went into that," mentioned a lieutenant commander who had something to do with ordnance.

"We've all probably contributed something to it in our lives," admitted the flying officer who was running the show. "Fitting, isn't it, that it should come back to us here in its original form—junk!"

"But who made it junk?" the commander pursued. "Did it come that way or did we break it up? What made it come down?"

The flying officer's answer was unexpected.

"The belt of a thousand stitches," he said. "That's what made it come down."

"The what?" inquired the commander.

"The belt of a thousand stitches," said the flying officer. "It's

75

standard equipment in the Japanese air force and also in the Japanese army. In a way it's the most remarkable invention that has come out of the war. You wouldn't think to look at it that it is a better protection against machine-gun bullets than armor plate, would you, now?"

"No, I wouldn't," said the commander a little peevishly. "When do I laugh?"

"I'm perfectly serious about this," the flying officer said. "Here is the thing I am talking about. We took it off the body of Hurushi San. I'm not sure we shouldn't have buried it with him. Maybe his soul is restless and defenseless without it. . . ." He held up a sort of cummerbund of dark cloth roughly edged with a buttonhole stitching of red. The band was rumpled and torn in two or three places. One end of it was bloodstained.

"Wonderful," conceded the commandant without putting a hand out to take it. "And how is it supposed to work?"

"It is motivated by love, right thinking, and good wishes," explained the flying officer. "That's what makes it so superior to material things like bullets. You see the idea is that bullets can't work without an impetus of hate. And love conquers hate."

"You've got something there," said the commander, "and it's wrong."

"I'm beginning to feel that way about it myself," said the aviator. "I have made a deep study of the belt of the thousand stitches and I was just about at the conclusion that there must be something in it. So many million people can't be wrong. . . . Long before there was any hint of this war—that we had heard about—long before Saburo Kurusu came over to teach us the beauties of peace, Japanese thinkers had discovered the incontrovertible truth that if you can immobilize enemy bullets you won't need so many of your own. . . .

"You might make a nice little legend of what happened then— how they wandered about Japan looking for somebody who would provide the mechanism to put the idea into effect. The ordnance people said that a steel plate was the best amulet they could think of. The old soothsayers had only the old sooth that they used to employ against long swords and short arrows. The *camoufleurs* and diverters and deceptors of the army who had worked on the similar plan of turning aside yourself rather than the bullet were willing to co-operate but had nothing to offer, as recent reports from China tended to show. In fact the search looked pretty hopeless until a committee of influential Buddhists and some Shinto priests went back into Japanese history and literature and dug out the belt of a thousand stitches.

"Of course everybody in Japan knew that was the answer to everything. You didn't need any expert help to make belts of a thousand stitches. You didn't need any factories or blast furnaces or material priorities. Furthermore you didn't need any manpower because it was essential that the work on the belt, including the fundamental juju, be put into it by a woman.

"There was an immediate popular response—as we were informed by our military attachés while the cables were still working. All the women of the empire started making the thousand-stitch belts. They stood in long queues every morning at a central distributing depot which handed out materials for such things. They stood in longer queues every evening at the receiving window in the same depot returning their handiwork. It must have been something like the epidemic of knitting that seized upon the United States during the last war except that this was more widespread. Not every woman could knit or find enough wool for knitting. But every woman in Japan was able to sew a couple of buttonhole stitches and the government furnished the material.

"The manufacturing process is as simple as it is touching and effective. Each woman sews not more than two stitches in the belt—which means that at least five hundred have had a hand in the work before the finished product is turned over to the quartermaster's department. Each woman as she puts her stitches in makes a suitable wish: 'May all the gods preserve the man who will wear this in our emperor's service. May this belt, the token of our love for him, bring him back safely when his work is done.' Pretty, isn't it?"

"And as you have mentioned," observed the commander, "it works."

"It must work," replied the aviator. "Just look at the number of Japanese who are still alive."

"The lad who wore this one—Mr. Itchimitchi or whatever

his name was—he isn't alive. What do you suppose happened?"

"Hard to say," admitted the aviator after some thought. "Maybe somebody dropped a stitch or maybe the juju on the pompom that got him was a little stronger than love."

"Maybe," agreed the commander.

The commander, having made a report that everything in the wreckage of Mr. Hurushi's plane—except the belt of a thousand stitches—was copied from an American naval craft of recent vintage, went home. He has had, since the coming of the fleet to Pearl Harbor, a modest bungalow in town. And for the same length of time an important part of his domestic establishment has been Mai Su, housekeeper, maid and cook.

She was putting some iced drinks on the coffee table of the living room when the commander began to tell his wife about what he had done that day. And Mai Su stopped fascinated in the kitchen door and listened to the remarks about the belt of the thousand stitches. Then, with the familiarity of an old retainer, she came back into the living room and took part in the conversation.

"It is all true, this about the belt of the thousand stitches," she said. "It is all true and terrible and nothing to make fun about."

"I assure you——" began the commander apologetically.

"It is nothing," said Mai Su. "It is nothing because you do not know. But for me it is a great thing that you have said. This nasty dog of a Japanese pilot wears this charm, this belt of a thousand stitches, and he comes down and he is dead and that is good. But do not think the charm is not good because of that. The charm is strong. It never fails. I could tell you better in Korean but you do not speak Korean. . . ."

"No, but I've been listening to double talk all day," said the commander.

"Well, I can try in English although I am not so good at that now as I was when I was at school here many years ago. I went back to Korea with my people when I was sixteen years old—that was ten years ago. I have not talked much English since. I was in Korea when the Japanese started this war in China. Soon after that we began to hear about this belt of a thousand stitches. We knew all about it of course. My mother told me about it when I was a little girl. It is a story that you will hear in all oriental countries. But we didn't know that it was a true story. Nobody knew that except the Japanese. So pretty soon all the Japanese women were making these belts. They tried to get us to help them but we wouldn't. We told them it was all nonsense, and we didn't want to save the lives of any Japanese anyway. It looked like very uninteresting work putting a couple of stitches in a piece of cloth and making a couple of good wishes and then making a couple more stitches in another piece of cloth and so on. . . . And it *was* uninteresting work. We found that out later.

"All the Japanese women in Korea were working on belts and so, I guess, were all the women in Japan. But the army wasn't getting belts fast enough. The captains up at the front couldn't find enough to go around even by taking belts off the men who had been killed. So an order was put out that all the women of Korea whether they were Japanese or not would have to help make these belts.

"They came to my mother's house and got me. They took me to a sewing place where there were two hundred other Korean girls. They gave us needles and thread and materials and little slips of paper marked with the wishes we were to wish as we sewed our stitches into the belts. Then they went away. They never watched us. They were interested only in having the belts finished at night. If we didn't have the required number we got punished. So we discovered that we didn't have to make the wishes they had put on the paper. We thought up other wishes and we sewed these into the belts.

"We wished: 'May the dog who wears this fall out of the sky in flames and may other dogs refuse to eat him.' That is what we wished. . . ."

The commander started to say something but didn't. Somehow he couldn't think of anything appropriate. Mai Su, however, supplied that.

"I suppose the belt this foul Japanese was wearing was one of ours," she said with great satisfaction. "So you see, what I have said is right. The talisman of the belt is a great and terrible talisman. It has come out of the ancient wisdom and it is very good. . . ."

"But the man died," broke in the commander. "And he wore the belt to keep him alive. . . ."

"What he thought does not matter," declared Mai Su in what may have been the manner of the Cumaean sybil. "It is the good wish that gets into the sewing that is the important thing. And in this case the good wish was that he break his useless neck. It must have been so, because he died, didn't he? It is really quite simple. . . ."

"I see," said the commander.

13

LIFE IN WONDERLAND

EVERY day we saw the dour old lads of Roosevelt's investigating committee filing into the Royal Hawaiian dining room for their meals—Justice Roberts, Admiral Standley, Admiral Reeves, General McCoy, General McNarney.

Not that it has any bearing on this war . . . the chief of police and other residents have recently made interesting comment on the status of women hereabouts, unblacked-out or otherwise. One Mr. Bishop, a local writer with leanings to the labor movement, says that most of them except the Hawaiians and the Koreans are essentially cold-blooded. We'll take his word for it.

Another of our spies narrates that most of the brothels are owned by Japanese—not a startling indictment as the Japanese seem to own most of the business enterprises on the island. These interesting institutions once operated in the middle of town until popular indignation, abetted no doubt by the travel bureau of the Chamber of Commerce, got large enough or loud enough to make a difference. So they moved a couple of blocks toward the canal and there they are now practicing their vice if any in broad daylight, virtue returning as it were with the darkness when the customers have to go home.

A lot of professionals of Caucasian tinge appear to have been removed under the guise of refugees along with Navy wives, missionary spouses, Doris Duke Cromwell, etc. A group of semi-professionals is still in town, easily recognizable in the restaurants, moving-picture lobbies and similar haunts of vice. These cuties came over ostensibly as clerks, stenographers and the like, to assist in the great work that used to be called defense. They didn't seem to be working at the jobs they came over here to do. But then maybe the whole defense theory had gone as cockeyed as the ambitions of the girl office help. There was talk of sending them home to regions where what they call defense work was being done in restricted areas and under police supervision.

Assistant Chief of Police Kennedy took Smothers and me for a ride over the Pali and around the shore via Koko head and the Diamond Head road. Coming back he pointed to the Girls' Industrial School, a large, modern installation set back under the broken edge of a lava apron. I said that it was pretty large for a female reformatory and Kennedy said with the air of explaining the whole business in simple language, that it was occupied chiefly by oversexed young women.

"They have been very well behaved since the bombing," he added cryptically.

I said that the connection was not immediately clear.

"Well," he said, "since the bombing, the town has been under martial law and the provost marshal has more to do than think about coddling Honolulu's hot-panted minority. So when girls are captured who have escaped from here they are not sent back. They are slapped into the common jail to live as common prisoners for the duration. Most of them know what the county jail is like so they are willing to stay where they are.

"Of course a few of them get over the fence now and then. You can't blame them, poor girls. They sit around thinking of the day when romance will come to them—real romance, you know, no bull—and they'll have a Filipino to take care of them."

And we wanted to know the why of the Filipino.

"Filipinos are ideal husbands," said the chief. "They are not disturbed at having to earn the living for the family. They expect to do it. Then they bring all of their money home to the woman. And in addition to that they do all the housework. The lady of the house doesn't have to do anything but nurse the baby. It's an ideal existence—or so I have been told."

On January 2 we received news of the fall of Manila. The official press releases apparently were trying to dress it up as a blessing in disguise . . . and I began to wonder if we'd ever learn.

There was no indication in any of the local departments of signs and portents that the great U. S. was ever going to do anything about anything. Everybody in the neighborhood was expecting a bombing or worse. Only martial law kept the ingredients of panic from mixing.

Along with the fall of Manila the newspapers printed the day's prize story—that of a sleuth from the Signal Corps who got arrested for speeding as he was trying to make a re-section on an illegal short-wave transmitter. It was said that plenty of wildcat stations were still in operation, but there had been no active sabotage of any sort.

The local ARP director issued advice to householders to keep the bathtub filled with water for use against incendiary bombs.

"But I can't," wrote the commentator in the *Morning Advertiser*. "My bathtub is full of gin."

Corregidor was bombed for five hours on Saturday, January 3. Wavell was put in command of the allied land forces. Hart was chosen to run the combined navies—U. S., British, Dutch, Australian—in oriental waters. This would seem to give the British our Philippine Army remnant in exchange for H.M.S. *Warspite* which is now in a U. S. repair yard.

I don't know whether I have noted it so often that I seem to be mumbling, but the censorship business was still very bad. "The American Way," as Buck Riddick called it, had done the Navy no good with the visiting correspondents. All of them were sore—just as they used to be in Cairo before they had the standard of the Riddick-U. S. method of censorship to show them how well off they were.

Angly told us at dinner that Knickerbocker had just had a run-in with that part of O.N.I. that looks after the press. Knick had called his wife over long distance and in the course of conversation asked her if an automobile he had ordered for her as a Christmas present had been equipped with radio. One Lieutenant Butler had questioned him about this. Why did Knick ask questions about a radio? he wanted to know. Because Knick had paid for one that the dealer was dubious about being able to deliver, Knick replied. And why, Mr. Knickerbocker inquired, did Mr. Butler want to know about all this? Mr. Butler, very aloof, said in effect: You are a newspaperman and we know that all you newspapermen will try to put things over on us. We know you'll do it if you can. We just want you to know that we know it and that we'll act accordingly.

This observation explains many things.

On Monday, January 5, a hot, muggy winter day, we were called out to Pearl Harbor for what we figured might be a tour of the islands via cruiser or destroyer. It turned out that our advance information was wrong. The fleet, we were told, was going to take the correspondents, photographers, etc., on some jaunts with task forces. The arrangements were to be just about what we had with the British—two men to a ship. We drew straws to see who would go on the first trip. Foster Hailey won and was the only reporter aside from the agency men to qualify for a ride. I couldn't see that made much difference. I didn't mind waiting now that there were signs that the so-called fleet actually existed.

There was some news in the *Star-Bulletin* to indicate that Corregidor was still holding out. Tokio's news commentator stated flatly that the fires in Manila had been started by retreating Americans who also, one supposes, bombed the Cathedral and the odd little houses of the *intra muros*.

I left this interesting harangue to go to a party given at the Young Hotel in honor of the visiting newspapermen by Chief of Police Gabrielson, Police Commissioner Sumner and Police Commissioner Roy Vitousek. Colonel Green, the provost marshal, was an honored guest. It was a very interesting evening.

I started home about 10:30 pervaded by a sense of well-being and discovered that I had been given a ticket for parking without lights in the blackout. . . . Am I awake or have I never left Paris?

The next day I got up betimes and went to the police station to pay my fine for illegal parking. The cops settled for a dollar and I felt deeply grieved. I had been with the chief of police, two commissioners, and the provost marshal, so I had a reasonably good start toward a fix. And there I go and get myself pinched for an offense so cheap that I haven't the crust to bother anybody about it.

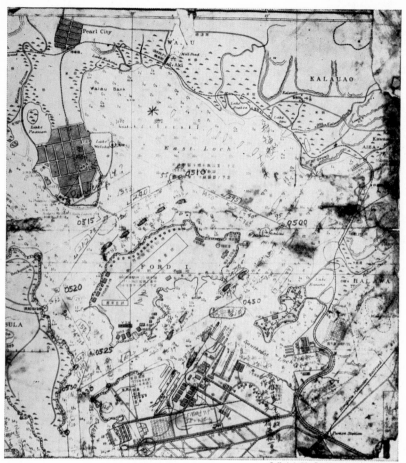

CHART OF PEARL HARBOR FOUND IN CAPTURED JAP SUBMARINE
Japanese symbols drawn on the chart indicate the anchorage of ships
and details of military establishments around the inner harbor of Pearl
Harbor U. S. Naval Base, in Hawaii. Note misspelling of "Southeast
Loch" (lower right). See references to this map on page 88.

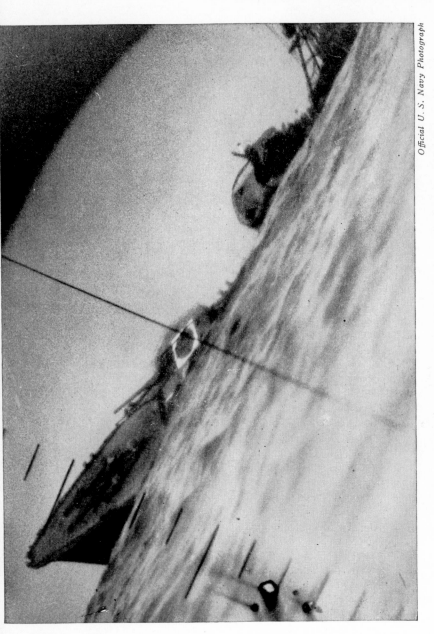

AN AMERICAN SUB'S EYE VIEW OF THE SINKING OF A JAPANESE DESTROYER

This remarkable photograph, the first combat action photograph taken through the periscope of an American submarine, shows an enemy destroyer of one of the latest and largest types after it had been struck by two torpedoes launched by the submarine from which the picture was taken. The destroyer sank in nine minutes. Note the Rising Sun insignia on top of the turret to the left which serves as an

Spent the morning with Frank Smothers who was trying to get out of Honolulu for Australia. Never before now did I realize the extent to which the communications of the world have been snarled up. To get to Batavia you have to travel about 20,000 miles if you can find anything to travel in.

As we were leaving luncheon we came upon Admiral Husband Kimmel who had been chief of the Pacific fleet in the days when it was proud and magnificent. Admiral Kimmel was on his way up-stairs to testify before the Roberts Commission. And while—literally—his chin was up, he was a pathetic figure. . . .

"Can you tell us, Admiral, just what part of the grand strategy of defense it was to have all those battleships nose to nose at anchor in Pearl Harbor?" "Will you explain to us, Admiral, why so few ranking officers were present when the bombs began to drop. . . . Why so few were later added up in the casualty lists?" "Will you tell us, Admiral?" "Is it your opinion, Admiral?" "Do you think, Admiral?"

Only a month ago Kimmel appears to have been the stiffest, most opinionated, most self-sufficient, most unapproachable, most arrogant old man in the naval service. Now he didn't need any examining board to identify him as the commanding officer of the U. S. fleet in its most thorough and senseless defeat.

None of us spoke to him. He hadn't noticed us. And to force our way into his attention probably would have added to his present difficulties. So we watched him into the elevator and went away, realizing that we had witnessed the beginning of a terrific melodrama—a melodrama no less stupendous in its plot and implications because its principal moments were to be acted out before a group of eminent sourpusses in the privacy of a swank hotel bridal suite.

It probably should be mentioned for the purpose of record here that Admiral Nimitz and Secretary Knox, acting in long-distance accord, jettisoned the Riddick American way of censorship just about then. It was arranged that we'd have one censor—a fleet appointee—and that he would give each correspondent a copy of all censored material. We were quite cheered about it.

On Monday afternoon we went out to Fort Shafter and met Lieutenant General Emmons. It was a pleasant afternoon though not particularly instructive. Emmons is young as generals go. But he seemed alert and friendly and a free talker.

He said among other things that Japan was quite likely to attack Hawaii, that the loss of these islands would be a desperate threat to Alaska, the Pacific coast, and the canal. He said with emphasis that he had enough men and equipment to defend the position successfully even should Japan come in with all her air force and fleet.

Like everyone else in the place it was obvious that he expected Hawaii to be attacked soon. But anyway he's one person on the premises who doesn't look rattled.

Harry Lang of the Chicago *Sun* announced next day that he had had enough of everything and was going home Wednesday on the clipper. Everybody seemed to be trying to get him to carry a few letters—presumably to managing editors.

The evening radio reported that there had been some earthquakes in Honolulu during the morning. I confess I didn't notice any. What's an earthquake in Honolulu?

The announcer finished his discussion of seismology with a bit of advice that may be one of the prize bits of conversation of this war: "Don't get that blackout look!"

I'm trying hard not to.

14

THE COMICAL JAP SPY

EVERYBODY in the United States except one or two die-hards learned that in the business of war as in other activities, comedy and tragedy are twins never far apart. We used to laugh heartily at those energetic and futile little creatures, the Japanese. We thought they were funny. And maybe they were. Maybe they still are.

"He jests at scars that never felt a wound," or as Joe, the Chief Pharmacist's Mate, says: "The biggest laugh I ever saw was on the mug of a guy full of strychnine. . . ."

Whether or not our intelligence in Japan was worth anything —and one doubts that it was—very few Americans were under any delusions about the extent of the Japanese secret service in the United States. The Jap spy was a commonplace in the comic strips and the peacetime blackouts of musical comedy. The Jap with his camera was a more familiar sight at Army posts, aviation meets, naval bases and the like than the officer of the day. And nobody thought he was taking pictures of places like Sparta, Wisconsin, and Fort Meade, South Dakota, because of his feeling for art. There were so many of these eager and tireless workmen on the national horizon that we came to think of all Japanese as spies—and maybe we weren't so far wrong about that.

So logically we get this one:

Sometime during the morning of December 7, 1941, a two-man submarine came up against a reef that Jap fishermen had probably failed to report, and so, presently, was cast up like a dead whale on the beach near Bellows Field. The commander opened the manhole at the top of the thing, disentangled himself from an amazing complication of wires and pipes, and stepped ashore with his co-pilot to surrender.

87

There was no terrific heat of battle at Bellows Field just then. There had been some machine gunning but no such havoc as was later to be inventoried at Hickam Field and Pearl Harbor. The guards knew that a fight was going on somewhere, but they had not yet seen enough of blood and death to experience any violent reaction. So curiosity rather than resentment greeted the sub commander when he came out of the water. A number of men looked over him as they might have studied a strange fish. And their attitude angered him. It was disrespectful. It was out of keeping with his rank and importance, and what was worse it was indifferent.

"I am Japanese officer," he announced in pretty good English. "Shoot me intimately."

"With pleasure," said the sergeant of the guard. "But take your time."

So the skipper and his aide were taken before the commandant of the field and after that turned over to naval intelligence. And that as you might say was the finish of the incident save for one thing. Intelligence men got into the submarine and they took out numerous interesting things including a photograph of the harbor to the bottom of which a chart had been pasted. And on the chart were sundry notations. The ink in which they were written was not yet dry. And this they showed:

At four o'clock in the morning of December 7, 1941, Commander What's-his-name San of the two-man submarine Number X-O had slipped into the main channel at Pearl Harbor. No nets or booms or alarm devices had barred his way to a rendezvous with the fleet which for months had been theoretically on the alert and at the moment was awaiting only the technical collapse of a doomed peace conference to get on with a war.

Nothing stood in the commander's way and he picked out a slow course toward the first of the berths shown on his picture. He nosed into it and made a notation: 04:00 arrived berth A, occupied. And he went on quickly. 04:30 arrived berth B, occupied; 04:50 arrived berth C, occupied. . . .

Two or three cruisers, a carrier and some destroyers were out on a mission. His chart indicated that he had made a painstaking round of their anchorages and noted their absence. He rode into slips, along wharves, under the fins of battleships and the keels of destroyers. And no sounding device had betrayed him, no detector had brought the depth charges tumbling down on top of him. Perhaps nobody was looking at the dials or listening to the sounders.

At a few minutes past six he was out of the harbor and traveling along the beach toward the reef that was to trip him up. The sun had not yet appeared and the dark cloud of invading planes had not yet lifted above the horizon.

But the lads in the submarine were able and ready to give the invaders operational data and map corrections as of 6 A.M. on the day of the attack. The mission of at least one of the two-man subs had been accomplished with efficiency and dispatch. There remained for the commander only to lie off shore somewhere and transmit the information, which, presumably, he did.

The planes came and they knew where their targets were. The commander proceeded along shore until the sub's belly scraped.

Then he stood up to meet his doom. Soldiers of a nation outraged and betrayed were waiting for him on the glittering sand. And it did not occur to him that their knowledge of what was going on was less than his own. He needed no eyes to see Pearl Harbor and the raining torpedoes and the flaming powder magazines and the crumpling battleships. He did not need to count the dead. He knew all of these things in the tradition of the ancient musical-comedy favorite—the Jap with the camera.

BOOK TWO

THE MARSHALLS

"Set Condition One . . ."

15

AND SO TO WAR

It seems that in time there must be an end to everything. So it had been with the Hôtel Continental in Paris, so it was with the squirrel cage of Honolulu. There came, one day, a telephone call from Lieutenant Commander Drake suggesting that I get out to Pearl Harbor and go to sea. I said that I would, that it seemed like a better plan for covering the war than I'd been following to date.

So I went out to the Royal Hawaiian for a farewell luncheon with Smothers and discovered a flock of Hawaiian minstrels and hula dancers tossing leis about the necks of the Roberts committee and wishing them well. Justice Roberts looked particularly lovely in his decoration. I wondered if these old boys would toss the wreaths overboard from the clipper as they flew across the reef on their way home, and if so, would the leis float ashore and would the committee live long enough to come back here and make the old superstition come true.

As for my boat ride, here is the written record:

January 10, Saturday. Honolulu. At 3:30 P.M. I locked my door and started for Pearl Harbor leaving my rented automobile with its owner en route. I arrived via taxi at the dock in front of the C. in C.'s headquarters at 4:30 and half an hour later was ferried out with Bob Landry of *Life* magazine to a heavy cruiser the name of which may be announced after the war.

The ship is a treaty cruiser with a theoretical displacement of 10,000 tons and a dead weight of something more than 15,000. The treaty cruisers have changed a lot since the day of their design.

This ship was laid down in 1930. She has a fine equipment of Chicago pianos (1.1-inch fore and 20-mm. aft), five-inch all-purpose batteries and eight-inch guns said to outrange Jap guns of a similar type. The officers we met at dinner were a pleasant, eager crowd, similar to the lads who used to run the *Valiant* in the Mediterranean.

The wardroom like all other wardrooms looked like the wreck of a garage—bare girders, pipe and iron bulkheads. . . . All superfluous furniture including the piano had been removed. Sleeping quarters on the ship, however, are singularly better than those on British ships in all classes.

There was a movie at 8 P.M. somewhere in the depths of the ship. I sat through five reels in steaming heat and gave it up. Every port in the ship of course has been shut up tight for the blackout— that seems to include the ventilators.

Later in the wardroom I sat for a time watching a tableful of white-coated officers censoring a pile of mail. The radio as we came in was playing gypsy music which seemed very popular with the wardroom audience. After that came the *Scheherezade Suite* by Rimski-Korsakov. . . . Surprisingly an aviation officer came in from the deck to listen. . . .

"Sounds like Stravinski," he said after a bit. "I thought it was *The Fire-Bird*. But that bit in there's *Scheherezade*. That's Rimski-Korsakov. . . ."

With hardly any treatment at all this wardroom might easily be the setting for another *Journey's End.*

I turned in at 11 P.M. in the bed of Lieut. Boland who is ashore for the night.

January 11, Sunday. At sea. Clear, hot. I was awakened by the arrival of my landlord quite early. So to breakfast where I ran into a new lot of officers all tremendously pleased at the prospect of going to the wars. . . . And that is what it seems to amount to. We get no details but the consensus is that we are going out somewhere to meet the Japs. Considering their ubiquity on this ocean that we used to call ours we oughtn't to have much trouble finding some of them.

After breakfast I went out to see the guns tested. I learned why naval guns need such short recoil mechanisms. They are fed compressed air from an external compressor. The glycerine buffer mixture is just about the same as it was when the 75 was considered a pretty good gun.

While we were looking at the quick skillful work of the mechanics on the guns there was a rush of unemployed gobs to the side of the ship. We saw then that a big barge laden with steel had overturned at the end of the dock. Three men had been aboard. Numerous rescuers were diving into the oily water from the dock but it seemed more than likely that the three sailors on the barge had been caught underneath. . . . A silly sort of accident. You felt yourself cursing bitterly the carelessness that could sacrifice even one more life needlessly in this cradle of carelessness.

Soon afterward I moved into the cabin of the navigating officer, Commander Church Allen Chappell. He will be staying on the bridge while we are at sea and I will be enjoying a fine corner room all to myself.

We sailed at 11 A.M.—a fine show with dozens of clean young sailors in white undershirts and shorts dashing about the deck with snakelike mooring lines and then standing at attention as we slipped from the entrance of the dry dock into the channel. With us go a big new carrier, heavy cruisers of a later model than ours, a cruiser of even more modern design, as well as destroyers and a tanker.

As we went out through the submarine net all hatches were closed and the watertight compartments sealed up as a precaution against mines that might have been sowed during the night. Once we hit the open sea and started south, things were opened up again and the loud-speaker announced another movie in the 'tween-decks broiler at two o'clock. The sea is pure cobalt and flat as a pan of gelatin. The horizon is cluttered up with warships including some four-pipers of the coastal patrol. Diamond Head is turning from green and gold to light chocolate and mauve in the distance behind the white wake of the ship.

In this force as we turned south were an imposing line of warcraft. Lacking battleships we are not so large a force as those that the British operate in the Mediterranean. Nevertheless this is a large collection of ships, the biggest, I guess that we have ever sent out in anger against anybody. The presence of the tanker in the convoy indicates that we are likely to be out a long time.

It is obvious that the crew know we are in a war. The men talk of Pearl Harbor as it looked wreck-strewn and still afire when they came in on the morning of December 8. They needed oil that day. So did the other task force abroad at the time. From their description it's easy to judge what might have happened if the Japs had put their minds to it—the harbor smashed, the planes down, the workable units of the fleet out of fuel. . . . What stood in the way of a landing? What was to prevent the firing of the oil storage and the utter destruction of Pearl Harbor as a base. . . .?

"We wouldn't believe it when we heard the radio reports," one CPO said. "Old officers laughed at the report that one battleship was upside down and another afire. We were still dubious when we got to Honolulu that morning and saw the destroyers running up and down outside. We eased into the channel expecting every minute to feel the bow coming up over a stray mine. But even then we didn't know what had happened.

"Then we got a sight of the Hickam hangars and the piles of burned planes and finally the *Arizona* still afire and the *Oklahoma* rump-up in the water. And as we came around Ford Island to the anchorage, there was the *Utah*—also bottom up. . . . Morale went to nothing just about then. We weren't frightened—or maybe we were. . . . But we certainly were sick and shocked. We couldn't believe that this had happened to us. Our only interest was to take on our oil and get away again to anywhere.

"That night there was an alarm. Somebody said that the Japs were landing at Fort DeRussey. It was a tense moment even though we knew the report must be the bunk. We knew it but then the report about Pearl Harbor had also seemed like the bunk.

"There was no reason why the Japs after a victorious onslaught on the harbor should pick DeRussey for a landing. There was no reason why they should have waited this long. But after seeing the wrecks over by Ford Island we were ready to believe anything.

"Tuesday we went out to look for submarines. We had a wild time of it for a couple of days. There seemed to be submarines everywhere—hundreds of submarines. Every now and then you'd see a destroyer dash over somewhere and sidle about. Then you'd see it start forward again full speed and the geysers of the depth charges would come blowing up behind it. We kept telling our-

selves how good we were and how high the score was. We estimated at the end of the week that we'd knocked off about twenty-
seven subs. But now I guess maybe we didn't. I recall a message
sent to the admiral by the commander of one of the cans: 'If floating
viscera of blackfish are any indication, our depth-bombing expedition has been eminently successful.'

"But we learned one thing from the expedition. We learned to
consider the enemy's presence more or less dispassionately. We
began to show a little discretion in our selection of targets and a
little more technical skill in handling the guns. We hadn't needed
guts very much but we had needed calm and detachment and
experience. And you get experience quickly when you need it. . . .

"We have quite a few officers and men aboard from the wrecked
battleships. The war is rather personal for them. . . ."

January 12, Monday. At sea bound southwest. The day is
beautiful, the sea a deep glistening blue feathered with downy little
whitecaps. Last night was very choppy. The ship rolled so that
virtually nobody got any sleep. I awoke with a violent headache
and have been seasick and miserable all day.

Landry and I had dinner last night with Capt. Zacharias (E. M.
Zacharias, Class of '12) in his cabin. With us was Lieut. Coggins
M.C. who is sailing more or less as we are as a passenger.

Capt. Zacharias is one of the most remarkable naval officers I
have ever met inasmuch as he has had plenty of duties apart from
the routine of naval stations and the social round of service home
ports. He was once in charge of press relations in San Diego where
apparently he found out something of the good as well as the bad
of the newspaper business. He has since had widespread and varying
jobs in naval intelligence that gave him a knowledge of the world
as it exists outside of Carmelite convents and the Navy. Capt.
Zacharias in other words has been about.

He was somewhat pained at the examples of what should and
should not be done with publicity in Pearl Harbor—particularly
the dignified silence of the Navy while the Army was making a
fine business of garrulity and miraculously getting its story over with
the press.

"Admitting that the whole affair was disgraceful and that some-

body must be severely punished for it," he said, "the fact remains
that the Army made no better showing, if no worse, than did the
Navy. There is no reason why the Navy, through its own unwill-
ingness to tell what happened, should take over the complete responsibility for it."

Hear! Hear!

Capt. Zacharias spent three years as a language student in Japan.
He is one man in the Navy who knows what the Japs are thinking
about and he has had singular success in his relationships with their
important people. He was a friend of Admiral Nomura and knew
Saburo Kurusu intimately. (Not so odd, that part of it. I did too.)
Just before Pearl Harbor blew up it was on the books that he should
be sent to Tokio as naval attaché.

He has many interesting theories about the relationship of the
Jap psychology to the prosecution of this war. And, considering the
way things happen, that may be one reason why he is at sea in a
battle command when, one might imagine, he would be of so much
more service at home. It is his idea that the Japanese are splendid sailors and military men but that they lack initiative. It is his
idea that if the Navy were to do things for which there are no ready-
made answers in the Japanese book, the high command in Tokio
would be sunk.

Lieut. Coggins, by profession a doctor, has made a long study
of intelligence methods and recently completed a work of seven
years in the compilation of a digest of Japanese source books on
the conduct of a possible war with the United States.

He made one interesting comment during the evening: (There
were dozens of others but this one stands out because it has to do
with that species of the obvious that everybody ought to grasp at
sight and so seldom does) "Unless you make it hard for a spy to get
information you'll never catch up with him. If it were possible for
instance for a man to sit in a New York apartment and get his information from a clipping bureau, there would be no possible way
in which we could come into contact with him. But if we cut off
the sources from the clipping bureaus as such, if we make it difficult
for him to get information, he will have to look for it in person. He
will have to go into forbidden areas. He will have to break some
minor law. He will eventually come into the hands of the police.
Then we are in contact with him."

We learned a little about our route. We are headed southwest toward Samoa where we will join another task force. After that our mission is a bit more nebulous but nothing that you mightn't piece together if you had a map and the inclination.

A lot of aircraft were out on scout duty today, including a brace of the four that we carry. I came to about four o'clock when the loud-speaker announced that they were returning. In spite of a hellish headache I went out onto the deck and saw quite an amazing sight.

The planes came back—ours and some more of a similar lot belonging to the other cruisers. They flew about for a good three-quarters of an hour before they showed any sign of coming down. About 5:15 we slackened speed to ten knots. The ship heeled over, leaving a broad slick in her wake. Out of the thickening dusk came the little plane landing astern in the slick and bumping up and down dangerously. In a few breathless seconds a cable had been hooked to it and the winches were hauling the plane to its cradle behind the catapult.

From the signal bridge the flag signal went up into the gloom: "Both aircraft recovered. Both returned with bombs."

Landry picked up some dope somewhere today that fifty-six merchant ships have been reported in these waters. That more or less bears out what we've heard about this expedition.

The more able portions of the intelligence section discount the widely circulated story that the Japs shot down about Pearl Harbor were wearing McKinley High School class rings. They don't think much of the theory that Hirohito's aviation corps trained locally for a suicidal return to the old alma mater. But they point out that a fine panorama photograph of Pearl Harbor was found in one of the two-man submarines chewed up in the harbor. This was traced to a Honolulu photographer who had taken it, on the occasion of the fleet's return some months ago, from the front steps of a prominent local Jap. He admitted that he had sold several hundred copies of it.

"I took it to Pearl Harbor," he said. "The officer told me that it mightn't be such a bright notion to publish it but that if I did, nothing could be done about it. And the officer over him said that it was a fine picture and he wanted one like it for himself."

There is something complex in that statement—something that

should be studied out in a twilight of a silent evening at a secluded spot such as the cemetery on Red Hill.

There was a neat piece in one of the Honolulu papers yesterday. Some genius going over the birth records found out that Hawaii just about four weeks at war had received an overwhelming majority of boy babies during the latter part of January. He commented that this was in accordance with a phenomenon observable in wars for hundreds of years, that boy babies were born in large numbers presumably to make up for the loss of males at the front. The Honolulu babies born yesterday, one gathers, were all conceived sometime after the bombing of Pearl Harbor.

The radio as we got it tonight was mostly phonograph music from Honolulu. . . . The Honolulu schools are still closed for fear of a renewed bombing attack. . . . General Emmons is conducting hearings on the relaxing of liquor regulations. Some folks apparently are in hope that something may come of it.

There has been much discussion as to the right of the Army to make rules governing Pearl Harbor. Why, they inquire, couldn't the Navy continue to have beer at its clubs and shore canteens? You wonder at the importance attached to this question just as you marvel at the unflinching dryness of the dry Navy. It's something worse than a court-martial offense to do any drinking aboard ship, it's a violation of good form.

They tried out the Chicago pianos this morning for the first time on this ship. It was also, so says an officer who ought to know, the first time they'd been fired even in practice.

There was no important news over the radio tonight. The fight for Kuala Lumpur goes on. The Dutch reported some success against the invasion of the Celebes. MacArthur's forces drove back an attack. But you get the impression that the Japs are resting. . . . There seems to be definite confirmation of the report that the Japs took an ungodly beating at Changsha. Also there is some casual mention that Admiral Rader may get the gate "for the failure of the submarine war in the Atlantic."

16

SUB CONTACT!

JANUARY 13, *Tuesday*. At sea. Beautiful weather, slightly rolling blue sea. The prospect all around is like that of the Mediterranean in the old days.

Table talk at noon ran to a variety of things between anti-amaryll shots to naval artillery—the easy, cheerful, interesting conversation of intelligent, well-educated men. After while it came to me that we were going out to battle in the proper American tradition though not, thank God, in the tradition of the American naval movies. We had quit boasting, apparently, on the morning of Dec. 7. We were content now to let somebody make an independent discovery of how good we are. We waved no flags. We sang no patriotic songs. On the verge of cataclysm we plied ourselves with chicken salad, potatoes gaufrette and custard and iced tea and we talked about the extent of the food rationing in England. We discussed the advisability of going to the movies below decks this afternoon—*The Shepherd of the Hills*, in technicolor. And yet there's nobody aboard who doesn't realize by this time that we're not out here to frighten the flying fish. We are looking for trouble in an area where it is most likely to be found. Quite conceivably a few hours may find us in the biggest naval engagement in American history since Dewey went into Manila Bay.

And it's quite within reason—although information in that respect is lacking—that we may be approaching a climax very close to that historic spot.

Sat up late (till 9:30) with a mob—mostly aviators—in the wardroom. They are spoiling for a fight—seem to feel that they're personally responsible for the vindication of their service. As is the case with the ship's line officers, there's no loud talking about this.

But you find that they spend a lot of time talking about the characteristics of Jap planes known to operate from carriers, the vulnerable spots in the armor of Japanese battleships and that sort of thing. You feel quite set up as you listen to them and also a little sad, for you know that these catapult fliers might well be classed as the suicide squadron of the fleet. Their planes are slow, hard to maneuver, and poorly armed. In ordinary warfare craft of this kind on a fire-spotting job might get some protection from the carrier fighters. But in this sort of combat—the sort task forces are designed to do at a considerable distance from the carrier—they themselves are fighter planes and they'll prove that or sink.

January 14, Wednesday. At sea. Somewhere near the equator. Hotter. Brighter. Calm. The sea is typically the Pacific—long deep swells with dazzling plumes of foam. The horizon is filled with destroyers tumbling like dolphins. Awoke late despite what seems to have been a noisy morning. Got a cotton issue for my ears. Now all I lack is a tin hat, flash suit, first aid kit, gas mask, identity tag and another tetanus shot.

Last night Dr. Coggins got a bit indignant over an aviation magazine—the leading popular publication of its kind in the United States. It was filled with pictures of every type of U. S. military plane now in use, with a couple of pages of information about experimental types that may be in use a couple of years from now. He mentioned that the intelligence had taken from a Honolulu agent a pamphlet of instructions outlining a number of things that the Japanese high command wanted to know about the U. S. military establishment. . . . "And I can assure you," he said, "that fifteen per cent of the things that our little brown brothers wanted to know about our aviation are to be found right here. This magazine costs fifty cents at a newsstand. It would cost a foreign G2 a million dollars not to mention invaluable time to duplicate its contents in the reports of hired spies."

I heard another odd story today from Captain Zacharias. The captain because of his schooling in Japan and subsequent assignment to jobs with visiting Jap notables has a wide and friendly acquaintance among the brass hats of the Mikado's naval staff. One day he asked a destroyer commander for the secret of the exemplary discipline of the Japanese sailor.

"We all know your men," Captain Zacharias said. "We know that they are sober, obedient, honest. How do you maintain that standard?"

"It is simple," the man replied. "If a sailor is brought before me I say to him, 'You have been most unruly on the following named occasions. But mind you I am not blaming you for that. The fault, of course, lies with me. It is my duty to inspire you to a proper mode of life and a high standard of thinking. In some way I have failed you. I have not properly inspired you. So inasmuch as punishment must be meted out for misdeeds and I have been remiss, I shall take the punishment for these bad acts you have performed. I shall deprive myself of leave from this ship for six weeks. And meanwhile I shall devote my enforced leisure to a study of how in the future I can better carry out my obligation to you. . . .'"

The captain says that the most remarkable thing about this fantasy is that the scheme works. The average Japanese sailor in such circumstances would feel that in forcing his commanding officer to take his punishment he had lost face. And rather than let the officer go through with it he would quite likely jump overboard.

There is another story about Z's Japanese connections. Some years ago he was assigned as naval aide to Prince Somethingorother, the Mikado's brother, who was visiting the United States with his wife. At a dinner in Washington Capt. Zach was seated between the Princess and the wife of a prominent senator. The senator's wife listened to him for a while as he talked Japanese to the Princess and seemed puzzled about something when a moment afterward he turned to her. It was not until near the end of dinner that she explained: "Captain Zacharias," she said gushingly, "I must congratulate you on your magnificent command of the English language."

There was a little to-do at lunchtime when the radio brought word of an air-raid alarm at Honolulu. It occasioned no qualms because we know that with the disposition of task forces hereabouts as it is, Japan would find herself in a bad pocket should she bring her carriers close enough to Hawaii for a new attack on Pearl. What the thing was we never got to know because the radio announced the all-clear almost at once.

It rained a little this afternoon. Bob Landry and I went up among the odd coops and bridges on the foremast looking for a suitable place from which to view the battle, if and when. We finally decided that a battle worth its keep may be properly viewed from almost any place.

Toward dusk I went out onto the deck to watch the planes coming back to the carrier. I was talking to Chief Quartermaster Peck when the ship suddenly heeled and a bomber went streaking over us.

"Something doing," said Peck and he lit out for the bridge. I moved to the starboard where a gob with a portable telephone outfit was giving information to one of the five-inch batteries. "One of the destroyers reports that a submarine went right across her bows," said the gob at the 'phone. Then we settled down for a long wait.

The first alarm had come about 5:15 and the tropical dusk was coming down fast. Planes began to buzz about overhead—three that had just come off the carrier, three homing SBD's that had been out all afternoon. They began to travel in broadening circles about the carrier. . . . After all that is the most vulnerable and the most important target in this expedition.

All of this, of course, looked like immediate action to our crew who took the business in stride. The five-inch guns swung down to horizontal. The covers came off. The gunners, in the stiff unlovely denim that serves for flash-suiting, clustered about the open sights just as they had done at drill an hour or two before.

The setting for all this was intensely dramatic—a gray-blue sea laced with white-gray wave-tops—a cloudy gray sky that was almost black at the zenith and lightened to a sort of mauve by reflected sunset at the horizon. Against that stood out the silhouettes of the fleet—really silhouettes—motionless, deep cuttings of gray mat pasted against the sky. Only the tremendous white waves looping their bows showed that they were moving.

All about us was a high, hissing spume as we drove into the rollers. The circling of the planes eventually narrowed to an area well off to starboard, taking in the carrier and four destroyers. So for another steadily darkening half hour. The quest became monotonous to the lookouts but increasingly thrilling to those who watched it. For it was obvious that the planes couldn't stay up there all night. Presently must come the moment when they would have to land—if they were to land at all—and then in that brief instant of unguarded twilight, the submarine if it were still traveling unseen in our company would have its chance.

"Touch and go," said the warrant officer at the five-inch battery. . . . "Touch and go. . . . If they touch us we go and vice versa."

It came to me that few men in any lifetime have a chance to look at such a spectacle as this. The ships of the fleet seemed everywhere on this dull and threatening ocean from horizon to horizon— twenty of them, just about as formidable a fleet as has operated in one unit since this war began. . . . They looked unreal. It was difficult to realize for instance that that cruiser back there and that further cardboard cutout that was another cruiser were teeming with eager young life just as this ship. But even as a two-dimensional fantasy they made one of the most convincing pictures of alert destruction that these tired eyes have seen.

It was about a quarter to six that the planes began to fall out of the sky onto the black deck of the distant carrier. The gunners put back the paulins over the breechblocks, capped the muzzles and swung the guns upward. The lights on the cruiser went out and the loud-speaker blatted a message about the setting of condition watches. The show was over.

The paymaster and a couple of lieutenants had gathered at the rail during the last ten minutes of our crazy course over the Pacific. "I wonder if Halsey liked our zigzag," the paymaster said. (Admiral Halsey is in command of the task force.) "I remember one night he got peevish. He gave us orders about interval and then we had a little engine trouble. In the meantime somebody got the message wrong by about a mile and with a combination of troubles we kept falling back. Then we got a second message: 'May I suggest that if at all convenient you get where you belong.'

"And right after that we got another one: 'Have you any officer aboard able to judge distance accurately within 6,000 yards?' "

So eventually to dinner and to converse on such subjects as shoes and ships and sealing wax—with little or no emphasis on the ships— until ten o'clock. Thence to my cabin where I am reading *Treasure Island*. The book is enjoying a fine wave of popularity aboard this ship.

January 15, Thursday. At sea. Warm, sunny. Not much roll. Awoke to hear the daybreak rush to general quarters. But did not hear the testing of the whistle (gas alarm) and bells (battle stations). Opened an eye when the navigator came in to use his shaving material. (Everybody in the Navy has an electric razor except me.) But I went back to sleep again until half past ten. I've had no reaction to my tetanus shot. No other qualms. I seem to be getting used to this life of blood and battle.

Went down to the wardroom, poured myself a cup of coffee and learned that we aren't going to have any Neptune Ceremony when we cross the equator. However we shall doubtless have the usual (so far as I am concerned) confusion when we cross the international date line.

There was quite a bit of general conversation about obscure details of the Pearl Harbor attack which, I daresay, will continue to be a principal topic of discussion in the Navy for many years to come. For instance there was the matter of fifteen-inch shells which the Japs used as bombs. They converted them to this use by screwing flimsy plywood fins onto their bases. Dr. Coggins suggested that this may have been the result of a plea to all patriotic Japanese to offer ideas for winning the war. One of the ideas, he said, is for a flash bomb of terrible candle power which the Tokio ARP authorities believe will blind an enemy aviator for an appreciable length of time. This device stems from a civilian suggestion that the entire populace enlist to repel daylight air raids by flashing mirrors skyward. On dull days probably they could go out and work cigarette lighters.

Some of the fifteen-inch wood-finned bombs were dropped where they could be examined. One, for instance, penetrated the forward turret of a battleship but did not explode. The TNT in the shells had been manufactured in 1902—two years before the Russo-Jap war—which may account for its lethargy in use. The metal was badly flawed and unevenly annealed. (Apparently a product of the pre-Bourcoud era.)

Officers who know something about Japanese psychology have discounted the theory of any wholesale suicide in the Pearl Harbor attack. For instance one plane dived a seaplane tender, failed to pull out of the dive and crashed on the deck with the bombs still

in the rack and the two aviators still in their seats. The crew of
the tender quickly cut the bombs loose and threw them overboard but not before discovering that the fuses had not been
armed. Here, then, was a perfect setup for heroic and devastating
suicide in everything except the intentions of the fliers. They hadn't
figured on sacrificing themselves or they would have armed the
fuses.

This brings us to the interesting subject of duds. Ffteen shells
were tossed onto Maui in the recent shelling of the island by a Jap
submarine. Of these seven were duds, probably for the reason that
the 1902 ammunition used at Pearl Harbor was not exceptional. The
Chinese dud ration of the Japs was said to have been 40 per cent.
The percentage seems to be holding up.

We are now somewhere below Christmas Island. Pretty soon,
now, we pick up another task force similar to our own. Our mission
as far as Samoa seems to embrace only the landing of mail.

We catapulted a couple of planes off this afternoon. The boys
aren't so badly off this trip because we are close to several groups
of islands. Even Tahiti isn't so far off.

The Japs sent out a radio communiqué about two o'clock announcing that the *Lexington* and the *Enterprise* have been sunk
"thus ending the danger of an attack by carrier planes along the
great circle route to Japan." The report is silly but it shows what
the Japs are worried about.

Evening. The weather is getting unbearably hot, the sea much
calmer. I went out after dinner to take the air and met a Marine
gunnery sergeant whose name turned out to be Tim O'Donoghue.
With him I went down to the CPO mess and passed a couple of
very enjoyable, and decidedly vocal, hours. Blundered back
through the darkness about ten and then sat up most of the night
reading the life of General Grant. (*A Man Named Grant*, by Helen
Todd.) It may or may not be part of the same psychology that
made me rate *Gone With the Wind* the world's greatest picture
because I saw it in Leicester Square during a first-class air raid, but
this book is fascinating. Grant and his badly disciplined but at
times suicidal army seem far from the book of the Prussians and

Hitler—yet not so far from Pearl Harbor. We seem to have been doing the same things in the sixties that we were doing before December 7, 1941.

America I suppose will always be prodigal of everything—money, conversation and life, until the day this tragi-comic tendency finishes us off.

17

BURIAL AT SEA

JANUARY 16, *Friday*. At sea. Bright, hot, calm. I woke up at eight o'clock to hear the general alarm sounding. Not the Donald Duck announcer but the gongs . . . and I had been told that the gongs weren't going to be rung for anything but the real thing.

I was still asleep—almost completely—when I hit the floor and began to blunder around for my clothes without thinking or bothering to turn on the light.

In the meantime the cruiser began to sound like old H.M.S. *Valiant*—shoes pounding on steel ladders, gunners dropping down from roosts aloft onto gun platforms, crash and clatter, smash and thump.

It was all over pretty quickly. By the time I had dissociated myself from my pajamas, acquired my pants and crawled up to the signal bridge, the bugle was blowing and everybody was going below to shed his life preserver.

We were naturally curious about this matter. But Donald Duck set us at rest almost immediately. The bridge had reported, "Cruiser firing on horizon, bearing 170 degrees." The cruiser was trying out some machine guns. But by the time the message went through a couple of relays it had become "enemy cruiser firing on horizon." *Und so weiter.*

Got little sleep during the morning. The ship was considerably keyed up, inclined to find a huge joke in anything that had happened when the alarm went but obviously trying to relax from what had been a pretty severe tension. . . . What I was doing when the alarm sounded . . . What I thought . . . What I said . . . What Joe said . . .

Four planes took off at 1:30. We are getting down among the islands and quite thoroughly into the danger zone.

Piecing together bits of information that come to you here
and there, you come to the conclusion that we're about two-thirds
of the way to Samoa. We ought to be making rendezvous in a
couple of days.

Studying the map and giving proper attention to the Jap bases
in the Carolines and other mandated islands you begin to get the idea
that maybe we're part of another Pearl Harbor business in reverse.
In that case this probably will turn out to be an air battle with us
sitting 200 miles back of the grandstand. Maybe we're on the
wrong ship.

Along about dusk we broke through an odd region of spotty
storms—lumpy puffballs of black cloud rolling out of skies brilliantly, spotlessly blue. There was warm drizzling rain about six as
the planes began to circle overhead for landing.

I was looking at the weird weather when I learned that one of
the planes from another of the cruisers had failed to come back. . . .

Failed to come back . . .

It's going to be hard to sleep tonight thinking of that lad out
there in the rain waiting for a slow but inevitable death. We
learned tonight that one of our boys had been crushed to death in a
powder hoist. Alongside the aviator still alive out there he seems
to have been lucky.

Night. The Southern Cross is out there if anybody wants to
risk breaking his neck in the blackout to look at it. The North Star
has dropped under the horizon. The equator is definitely behind us.

The Japs tonight announced that units of the U. S. fleet are
heading for Samoa. It's obvious of course that they're guessing but
remarkable how well they manage to guess.

January 17, Saturday. Calm. Cooler. All morning today we
refueled from the tanker.

The U. S. Navy is said to be the only one in the world that
does this thing. It's a fine piece of work. Inasmuch as we can load
up the tanks with only a small reduction from cruising speed this
process gives the fleet an unlimited range. Fuelling in motion does
away with the menace of subs, which would have to surface to keep
up. And we seem to have eliminated the old dangerous practice of

returning to a base for fuel. . . . This was definitely serious because a vessel virtually out of oil is not able to maneuver and defend herself.

I keep meeting all sorts of boys from Chicago. Odd how being one of a group of three million people makes you almost the favorite brother of some other member of the group of three million people when you meet in the middle of an ocean.

While we were at luncheon there was a rush to the deck. We got out just in time to see a plane which apparently had been trying to land on the carrier crash into the sea. In the roll of the ocean it sometimes rose so we could see all of it; sometimes it was hidden, as if submerged. But while we looked we could see the heads of both pilots rising up on the edge of the silhouette. Then with our eyes on it the plane, which had seemed likely to float forever, went down like a shot. We tried to follow the two heads. One disappeared with the plane. After that there was only one black spot on the water.

One of the destroyers picked up the survivor. Other destroyers circled around for a long time in a vain hunt for the other one. That makes three planes in two days. The one that didn't get back yesterday was off the carrier. Another we learn was smashed up in landing on the carrier's deck last night.

The tanker went around fuelling the three other cruisers and the carrier. Late in the afternoon we picked up some speed and got started on our work again.

The Night's News: New, fierce attack on MacArthur's army. Japs still advancing in Malaya. Chinese peevish, apparently with good reason, because the Allies are not making an all-out war on Japan. Carole Lombard's body was found in the wreck of a TWA plane. Thirty-nine Jap ships have been sunk in forty-two days. Churchill has returned to London.

There will be a funeral service tomorrow for a sailor who was killed in the powder hoist.

The captain says we'll be two more weeks on our mission unless we get sent to Australia. If that happens, he says, there's no telling when we'll get home.

January 18, Sunday. At sea. Calm. Hot. For a day now we've been circling around—as the executive says, "like a man lost in a wood." The fueling was resumed today after I had thought it finished. We apparently are on patrol duty at one end of the more or less immobilized fleet.

Sat up late in wardroom last night talking to officers who, like myself, were unable to get to sleep because of the heat. The paymaster's reason for wakefulness was different. "I can't sleep," he said, "because I keep thinking of those two kids we lost in the plane yesterday."

The chaplain persists in thinking that they will be recovered. The pilot sent a message, he says, that the plane was lost and that he had thirty minutes' supply of fuel left. The carrier broke radio silence with "put out the hayrake" and set the plane on its course, then turned on her deck lights. After twenty minutes the lights went out. The chaplain figures that if the plane hadn't returned the lights would have remained on the full thirty minutes.

Excerpt from the "Plan of the Day."

(1) The burial at sea will be conducted in the following manner:

Chaplain lay aft to well deck with remains accompanied by eight pallbearers and division officer.

Marine captain station Marine firing squad.

Bugler lay aft.

Boatswain sound "all hands lay aft to bury the dead."

March all hands to well deck.

Report "Ready" to bridge.

Lower flag to half mast.

Chaplain conduct service.

Bugler sound taps as ship stops for burial.

Marine squad fire volleys.

Ship under way.

Two block colors.

Captain Zach made a speech pointing out that the lad had died in line of duty, a phrasing that had more than ordinary significance to boys who saw Pearl Harbor the morning after.

He then stated without going into details that the task force was seeking out the Japanese and expected to close with them in an important engagement. He urged extra attentiveness at all look-out stations and offered prizes to men first reporting enemy craft. He urged constant attention to duties and constant review of work. . . . The busy man, he said, will have no time to become panic-stricken.

One bit of good advice he gave them had to do with the remote chance of their being captured alive. "Keep your mouth shut" was the gist of his message. "Under international law you are required to tell nothing but your name and rank. But if you have to talk . . . if you are made to talk, talk a lot. Talk of trivialities. Talk of home, of mother, of your stamp collection, of anything. Words are con-fusing to a Japanese especially when he gets the idea that they ought to mean something."

I went with Bob Landry to a stupendous turkey dinner in the chiefs' quarters. During the meal Marine First Sergt. Emmett Pat-rick Hughes reviewed the captain's offer of prizes. "It's fifteen dol-lars for a sub," he said. "Probably only twelve for a two-man sub. And for a battleship I guess about fifty cents."

One of the chiefs—a radio man—told us some more of the miss-ing aviators. They weren't landed on the carrier as the chaplain had hoped. The chief says that a destroyer went out to look for them. He says they have a better chance than one might suspect offhand. The other night he was on duty when he picked up a call from a plane belonging to one of the other cruisers. The pilot said: "If we don't get help soon, we're through. I've just about enough fuel to keep the radio going." The chief reported the call to the bridge which reported to the flagship and a destroyer was sent out after them. They were picked up in the morning.

It might be worth while sometime to remember the meal we had today. It is especially noteworthy inasmuch as within the next couple of days—perhaps tomorrow—we may be in a battle. I can't remember any other battles that I went into after a menu such as this: Soup, crabmeat cocktail, celery and olives, roast turkey, cran-berry sauce, chestnut dressing, candied sweet potatoes, mashed white potatoes, green peas, ice cream, blueberry pie, pink lemonade.

The mess steward came up to my cabin at 6 P.M. to make certain that I was coming down for my evening meal with the officers. He was under the impression that I hadn't eaten all day.

Six-thirty. Donald Duck sounded the routine call, all hands to battle stations. I went up onto the signal bridge and watched a magnificent tropical sunset. We were heading straight into it when darkness came.

January 19, Monday. At sea. Calm. Sunny. Perhaps a little cooler. Samoa was off the port bow briefly today. We are still heading southwest although I am told that we may be heading north in a couple of days.

I read Joseph Barber's *Hawaii: Restless Rampart* today. The conclusion you'd draw from it is that we ought to give Hawaii back to the Hawaiians only there aren't any.

18

LOST AVIATOR

JANUARY 20, *Tuesday*. At sea. Calm. It's a little cooler on deck. The sky is a bit gray with ranks of destroyers standing black against it. We're still dashing about off Samoa. A tanker came briefly over the horizon yesterday, looked at us and went away. We're both probably waiting for some unit that has work to do in Samoa.

Fifteen or twenty dive bombers cavorted in the air above us this morning—the porpoises of this trip. And while they performed, one of our aviators and I stood at the rail and dug up more odd bits about Pearl Harbor. The aviator said that the detectors picked up the Jap planes 130 miles out at sea. The operator reported it to proper authority and was ignored. The aviator says also that a Jap submarine surfaced in front of a destroyer about twenty-five miles off Honolulu the morning of the attack. The destroyer fired at once in accordance with a rule that visiting subs have responsibility for establishing their identity in advance. The sub dived. The destroyer dropped ash cans and smashed it up. The destroyer commander then went through the worst few minutes he will ever experience as he figured that while he had obeyed orders implicitly he had probably sunk one of our submarines—that 150 young American gobs had been sacrificed to the inflexible positivism of the brass hats. He was preparing his report and thinking up the wording of the speech he would deliver at his court-martial just before sentence. And just about that time somebody brought him news of what was going on in Pearl Harbor.

The further one goes into this thing, the more one is amazed.

As long as we stick around here I don't see much relief from the heat wave. There were two or three little short-weight rainbows in the patchy dark sky this morning, if that means anything.

115

It rained a little this afternoon. The air got heavier and hotter. Obviously we weren't going anywhere. The navigator got a dispatch about noon telling him to keep thirty miles away from land. From that it appears that we are still no great distance from Samoa. . . . Jaluit, don't be impatient!

Sunset as they call it came when the gray sky and the gray sea merged in black. The ocean was dead calm. Last visible on the afterdeck were members of the flight crew, bundled in life jackets awaiting the arrival of Ensign B. L. Davis, one of our aviators long overdue.

I went in to dinner and then sat around trying to get some news on the radio. No hope. Somebody was using an electric razor and the homemade static was enough to flag down the whole Japanese navy.

At 8:30 Captain E. E. Stone, the executive officer, came in obviously worried. I sat down at the table with him just for company's sake and didn't notice for some time that, as the labeled napkin ring in front of me indicated, this place had been reserved for Davis. I stayed anyway. He wouldn't be getting in right away.

Captain Stone said that Davis had radioed that he was nearly out of gas. He had asked permission to land someplace in Samoa. There had been an interchange of messages from Apia and Pago Pago—enough conversation to tip off the Japs that most of the navy must be down here. But Davis didn't answer.

The captain said he wasn't too upset about it because Davis had had experience operating tugs in Puget Sound and would know how to take care of himself, that he would probably land to conserve fuel and look for us in the morning. I confess I didn't see how anybody could do much about taking care of himself out there on the broad Pacific. But somehow I began to share the captain's hope. After all we had a fair idea of Davis' position and at the moment we weren't on a mission that would make us go away and leave him. He was getting a break that the two fliers in the carrier plane hadn't got.

At 8:45 W. J. Tate, Jr., another of the aviators, came in. He too had been on patrol and he had sighted a school of bonito that looked like the rendezvous of all the submarines in the world. He sat down and looked at the clock: 8:50.

"Davis is just about out of gas now," he said cheerily. "If he's going to get back now somebody else will have to do the job."

About ten o'clock we got some news. The bulletin about the sinking of Japanese ships was confirmed by the Navy. Forty-two Jap naval vessels—including transports but not freighters—had been sunk in forty-two days. A lieutenant J.G. named Bulkeley had taken a motorboat into Subic Bay, sunk a 5,000-ton ship and escaped through a terrific barrage. A cruiser and a tanker had been sunk by U. S. Army fliers. MacArthur had been pushed back again. Singapore was being threatened by a new and effective drive.

We are still waiting.

January 21, Wednesday. Gray, rainy, calm, hot. At daybreak today, or what passes for it on a day like this, we sent off a plane to look for Davis. In about half an hour we got a report that an SOC had been sighted in the water about thirty miles dead ahead. So with one destroyer we pulled out of the fleet, poured on the coal and went after him.

It was the biggest moment of the trip so far. Every sailor who could find an excuse to get out on deck crowded the tops, the gun positions, the open spaces on or under the turrets as we plowed into the murk.

At 8:30 we caught sight of the plane. Carrier planes maneuvering ahead of us and around us had previously signaled that it was squarely in front of us. The destroyer zigzagged as we approached on the supposition that a sub might be lying out there waiting for just such a moment as this. But there was no sub. We came up on the starboard side of the plane, passed it and started to swing around. At that the radioman in the cockpit began to signal us with a flashlight.

"We have gas," he signaled. "We'll come up. . . ." Then the propeller jerked and turned and spun and the plane began to make a little headway in the calm water. A minute later it was alongside and the tackle was hooked and it was being swung aboard. Davis slowly raised himself from his seat.

An ensign standing next to me broke a deep silence.

"He's okay," he said. "Did you notice how he looked up at the bridge? He's wondering what he's going to be hearing from the old man. . . ." We turned around and started back toward the fleet.

I went down onto the well deck and met the captain who seemed much cheered by the whole business as well he might be. We join our own task force shortly off Samoa, he said. There we meet another of the same size that has been landing some marines. After the rendezvous we turn toward Jaluit.

This fits in with some interesting scuttle butt that has been in circulation during the past few hours.

Radio news two nights ago mentioned the bombing of Rabaul by a force of 200 Jap planes. Well, if you know anything about the region—New Guinea, New Britain, the Solomons—it's hard to make any sense out of this. There is nothing in Rabaul except an active volcano, a mud geyser and a couple of reformed cannibals. But little by little gossip adds up to an interesting and convincing theory. We are informed by our informants that somebody, guess who, went over and bombed the island of Truk, near Guam, a Japanese sub-base. The Japs apparently figured out that the only place the attack could have come from was Rabaul. So they sent out a punitive force, apparently from Jaluit. Our best thought on the subject reaches the conclusion that we will arrive at Jaluit just in time to take on the returning expedition.

Crowley went ashore last night or yesterday with a message from the captain to the governor. The governor was requested to pick up the supercargo of the Matson Line suspected of being a news source for the Japs. It was suggested to him that he prepare for immediate attack. I don't know what that means or if it means anything.

Crowley may have added something to the worries of the Japs if they had any observers around. He wigwagged a message to the senior aviation officer of another cruiser: "Where did you put the keys to the rocket ship?" Everybody in the fleet is wondering about this breach of military secrecy—all but us. We know that the "rocket ship" is a palsied flivver owned jointly by Crowley and his colleague.

I heard another story apropos of the fresh-water crisis that occurred today. A sailor filled a bucket with water from the cold tap and carried it to the steam valve which on ships serves as a hot tap. (You run steam through the water to heat it.)

The steam had gone down, creating a vacuum in the pipe, so when the lad turned the faucet the water was sucked up out of his bucket into the pipe.

"Doggone," said the gob. "They give it to you and they take it away! The scientific sons-of-bitches."

More about the plane-radio conversation came to light at lunch. Howeth was almost raving. It seems that the carrier butted in with some talk after Davis had suggested that he land on a near-by island. That would have been all right but just then the carrier radio added: "All planes aloft, attack submarine bearing so and so." There was no submarine of course but the message went abroad. Howeth says that taking the most pessimistic view of the matter the Japs could now guess our whereabouts more or less concealed these ten days and might also guess that a carrier was with us. The pessimistic view he points out is the normal one these days.

There are numerous interceptor stations in the mandated islands—plenty of chances for the Japs to get a resection on us. Maybe our prospects have been altered considerably. Howeth, on the other hand, may be overconcerned about this; he is said to be a good communications officer.

Crowley got back in the midst of a glorious sunset. He said that he had met Knickerbocker and Harsche over in Samoa. They got transferred from the carrier via a destroyer and are going for reasons best known to themselves to Australia.

Crowley reported Scotch at $1.25 a bottle in town. But he didn't bring back any. Hooch has become the subject of a lot of wistful conversation aboard. One has only to close his eyes and drop off a lot of years and find himself at the beginning of the old prohibition era.

Landry and I went up and saw the sunset from the top. As dusk came thundering down the ship did a neat about-face and headed west.

This is the hottest night since hot nights were invented. The decks are covered with sleeping gobs.

19

CALL TO QUARTERS

January 22, *Thursday*. At sea. Calmer. Hotter. Who shot the albatross? I feel something like a corpse but warmer and sourer. Thank God the water's turned on this morning.

Despite last night's indications we seem to be still wandering around like the Flying Dutchman. Land off the port bow—probably the same land. All night we sail the ocean blue and in the morning we are thirty miles from Pago Pago. The trouble with this war is that it takes so long to get to it.

Joined the morning round table this morning at breakfast and heard some disparaging things about our big bombers—nothing however that I hadn't heard before. It looks for the nonce as if we could never hand out much to Japan without some bases nearer than those we have at present. Carriers are definitely in the picture now and maybe the Japs are right in thinking that battleships are still important.

I was standing on deck at 9 A.M. when general quarters sounded with the beating of gongs that certified it to be a McCoy alarm. I stood aside while the kids who had been sleeping or reading or leaning against the mast and looking out at the sea jumped up and began to tear for battle stations. They were up and away in a couple of minutes, a performance that might have astonished anybody who didn't know how often and how wearily they had been drilled in this sort of business. I stood aside from the general rush (1) for fear of being bowled over; (2) because I had looked at the calm unruffled sea and the clear empty sky and had noticed that the planes floating overhead were engaging in no dizzy maneuvers. Somebody, I thought, might have sighted another blackfish.

As soon as the ladders were clear I went up on top and saw

120

nothing in particular except the silhouette of Samoa in a blaze of sun off port. After ten or fifteen minutes Donald Duck announced that four ships had been sighted by somebody but that they had turned out to be our own.

I went back to the well deck. Our beat to and fro in front of the island continued. Several of the CPO's were on deck mumbling a little about the heat and the inertia. . . . "Why the delay?" was the burden of their song. "Let's get on with the war."

So through the dull and dreamy day. The heat remains virtually unbearable which is no wonder considering our more or less permanent berth here. After dinner I went out on deck to look at the sunset which as usual was terrific. For miles about us the ocean was clear, and straight above us the sky hadn't a wisp of vapor in it. The horizons were walled with dense cloud masses of varying color. To starboard—which is southwest—they were gray and black with rifts in them through which the sun glowed like a blast furnace in red and orange. Ahead of us a black destroyer sailed in the dead unrippled calm of a flawless sea. Above it floated a cloud, no bigger than the destroyer itself, brilliantly red.

After the sun had gone I stood around for a while talking to the doctor. The crew were making preparations at the rail that seemed to indicate we'd be giving fuel to one of the destroyers tomorrow.

That, of course, would mean that we're not going anywhere right now.

We sit around and wait, raising barnacles where once we raised callouses. I have contrived new methods for wasting my time. Yesterday afternoon I slept—and dreamed I was taking a boat ride.

January 23, Friday. At sea near Samoa. Calm. Cloudy. Got up early to see one of our destroyers, a new one, come alongside. By nine o'clock she had pulled away and we sat down to do nothing as usual.

The news today says that the Dutch got direct hits on two cruisers, two destroyers and two transports.

Shortly after noon we began to pick up a little more speed. The ship began to roll despite a calm sea and we held our fingers crossed as it began to look as if we might be on our way. The overcast became complete as the afternoon wore on—gray from horizon to horizon—but there was no rain. This would be delightful weather for an attack.

The fleet has been rearranged somehow. We have lost one heavy cruiser and a couple of destroyers. They've probably gone across the horizon to join our other force, no trace of which we've seen since we came here.

I met the chaplain on the deck and found that he takes an extremely practical view of the proceedings. "I wish I knew whether or not Sunday is going to be peaceable," he said. "If it is, I'm going to have to write a sermon."

With no effort at all you can find plenty of evidence that we must be on the verge of doing something. The flour supply is getting low. The ship's service store has sold all its canned sardines. One of the marine sergeants told me that the food lockers hadn't been loaded for any polar expedition. And there's verification of these signs and wonders in the scuttle butt. According to our best rumors we have still about 2,000 miles to go to our objective. We'll refuel in a couple of days when we catch up with our tanker which left us yesterday.

The news tonight about the Malaya situation is not encouraging. MacArthur is still holding out in the Philippines. Rabaul, on the other hand, has given up to the Japanese.

Well, anyway, we are moving away from Samoa.

20

NOTES ON THE ROBERTS REPORT

JANUARY 24, *Saturday*. At sea. Hot. Calm. Eastbound. I learned a little more about our trip today. Not too much. The captain is an ex-intelligence ace and a good magician never tells how he does his tricks.

But we know that sometime this evening we start north. We shall make a couple of miles and get oil for our dash to the mandated islands. At 500 miles a day we shall continue northeastward toward Jaluit, Truk and other points where the Japs have important bases. We should get to our objective about Tuesday morning if the refueling doesn't take too long. At present we have about 1,400 miles to go.

The captain told some of this to an assembly of officers in the wardroom before luncheon. He said that the patrol about the Samoan islands had been necessary to screen the planting of a large defense force. As a result of this rearmament, he said, Samoa is now strong enough to take care of any possible Jap attack.

He was not too definite about our target but he did say that we are going to seek out enemy strongholds and that he hoped for a bag of about twenty-five Jap ships. This work, he believed, would fall mostly to the aviators—but one never could tell.

He announced also the receipt of a dispatch telling of a scrap between four destroyers of the Asiatic fleet and a quantity of Japanese in the Straits of Macassar—between Borneo and the Celebes and north of Surabaya. The destroyers sank one large ship, blew up another and noted a severe list in a third. They made several hits on ships of the accompanying destroyer screen. Our casualties were four injured—the result of one hit.

The captain was very cheerful, eager and convincing and he

had an immediate effect on the morale. After all it's unexpected to find an abiding calm among the officers of this crate. Not one of them has ever heard a shot fired for business reasons. It all sounds simple as it has been put to us and as the commissioned personnel discusses it in the wardroom. We go in, we sink twenty-five Japanese ships. We come out. After hearing the talk I confess I too am inclined to believe it will happen just that way but in some of my quieter moments when the hypnosis wears off I wonder what we're going to run into while we're doing all this.

Our success if any in this enterprise will come from the element of surprise and at the present writing I don't think that amounts to much. We got a good start toward informing the Japs of our intentions the other night when the carrier talked with our missing plane. Then we paraded two days within sight of land in front of Samoa. Finally last night the other cruiser talked for twenty minutes trying to contact with a missing plane. . . . Eventually the plane broke silence with one brief message: "I'm all right!"

Oh well, maybe the Japs are deaf.

Evening. The zip of the ship has increased since the captain's announcement that we were on our way to more profitable fields. I won't say the morale has improved because morale is self-confidence and there never was any lack of that. But the sailormen are mostly kids and like other kids find no amusement in standing still.

Most of them are taking a hell of a beating from the heat but they don't complain about that.

Tonight we heard Bill Henry in Los Angeles reviewing the report of the Roberts investigation committee over the radio.

It's no whitewash. Admiral Kimmel and General Short get the blame. What few defense measures they took were taken independently. They don't seem to have been speaking to each other most of the time. It was verified that a sub was sunk outside the harbor at 6:30 A.M. Another was spotted inside the harbor at 7:20 and was destroyed at about 8:30 after the bombardment had begun.

The Jap planes were spotted 130 miles to the northwest by an amateur working a detector. (This device as a general rule was in use only about three hours a day.) The Army lieutenant who received this report had heard that some bombers were coming in from California. So he wasn't moved to any action.

Both Army and Navy had been warned repeatedly that an attack was imminent. But they didn't change their ways. The last warning which had to do with Pearl Harbor was to have reached Kimmel and Short at 6:30 A.M. But they never got it.

Planes had been grouped together so that they could be guarded against sabotage and this made them a setup for an air attack. The Air Corps had been notified to be in a state of alert—i.e. to be ready to take the air in four hours!

Not in the report as we heard it but possibly in the version submitted to the President was some news that subs had been sighted repeatedly in the defense zone days before the attack.

The destroyer that smashed up the submarine at 6:30 on the morning of the seventh was the *Ward*. The commander reported what he had done twice. Both times shore authorities told him to verify. Nobody did anything about it.

The pilot of a plane present at the spat between the sub and the *Ward* dropped a bomb and went back to report to his superior, a lieutenant commander. He was advised to keep quiet. "It's most likely one of our own submarines. . . ." And as perhaps I have noted before the farther you get into this business the more *Alice in Wonderland* looks like a book of sermons.

January 25, Sunday. At sea. Bright. Calm. Hot. Northbound.
Today we've been at sea two weeks. We've traveled about 5,000 miles as the crow flies and a couple of thousand more miles in a zigzag course. And still we are viewing the battle from afar off. According to the latest estimates we should arrive at Jaluit Wednesday morning and be on our way home or to the bottom by Wednesday evening.

Ted Kobey, the engineer officer, told us an interesting yarn about Pearl Harbor last night. I suppose there will never be an end to these anecdotes as long as American sailors have ships to sail in. It seems that a Commander Carroll had been ashore over the week end because of the illness of his wife. He was due to move his destroyer to a new berth at 6 A.M. Sunday. And to insure that the sick woman wouldn't be bothered during his absence, he took his six-year-old boy with him. He got permission to take the kid aboard, escorted him to the bridge where he would be out of harm's way and went about the business of pulling out. He was in mid-channel when the blitz came.

The destroyer shot out through the slot to chase submarines. The kid was transferred at sea to a coast-guard cutter, thence to another coast-guard cutter and finally brought ashore. The admiral's car was waiting to take him the rest of the way home.

The clock went back another hour last night. We aren't very far from the international date line, the zone of day-after-tomorrow or continuing today depending on your approach. That makes it appear that we might be a day too early in our attack and a day too late coming back.

The officers generally take the Roberts Commission's report with satisfaction and in the main are pleased with its frankness. The finding doesn't show the Navy in too bright a light. But on the other hand it slips a fair share of blame to the Army. It holds Kimmel and Short jointly responsible and hints that warnings of an inevitable and imminent crisis were not shared by these brass hats with their men or for that matter with each other. You realize as you hear the boys talking about it to one another that the Navy has been a lot lower in spirit than it let on. It has gone about, as it were, concealing a lot of justifiable humility under a highly polished armor of righteousness. With the appointment of some goats for the blood sacrifice, heads were lifting once more and the old spirit of importance and invincibility is coming back frayed but recognizable from the cold tomb. A good kick in the pratt is medicine for the soul.

Our friend young Ensign Blum is compiling some protractor gadgets locally known as ouija boards. There has been a suspicion that these devices were used in navigation by the aviators. This supposition probably arose from the fact that young Mr. Blum is a catapult officer. And he has been kidded in the wardroom with such cracks as "it's easy to see why the ocean is getting cluttered up with lost airplanes."

As a matter of fact, he explained today, the ouija boards are for the use of antiaircraft gunners firing at dive bombers. Maybe they'll work. But I doubt that the gunners who use them will live long enough to find out.

There was a bit of warlike conversation for the first time today at the luncheon table. Somebody wanted to know if the fuses of the one-one ack-ack guns would prime on a signal halyard. I know the answer to that one. They would and possibly will.

I learned yesterday evening that patrol planes yesterday evening spotted a submarine and bombed it. The sub crash-dived and got away. It was about sixty miles away from the fleet and angling on a course that would have brought it up even with us tomorrow morning. The navigator says we are just about within spitting distance of the sub playground.

News tonight is encouraging for a change. Our forces in the Philippines attacked successfully though possibly temporarily. Twenty-two of a convoy of twenty-five Jap ships were reported sunk by U. S. destroyers, Dutch and British planes in the Straits of Macassar. Also Malayan pressure continues. Siam has declared war on the United States but I suppose we'll try to bear up. The South American Conference goes on and on. Just one big happy family all of whom seem to be trying to decide whether they like us more or Hitler less.

Our casualties in the Macassar engagement are said to total four wounded. You get to reading communiqués with a certain aloofness today. Even your own. The Japs, one remembers, reported that they had taken Wake Island with the loss of one man. His name was probably Elmer.

January 26, Monday. At sea. Clear. Hot. Calm. The navigator was in this morning with some more news about Macassar which, for lack of anything else to make note of, I shall set down here. The latest bulletin puts the Jap losses at twenty-six ships, which out of an original total of twenty-five seems to be all anybody could ask.

Spent most of the morning gassing with the captain about our prospects and came away somewhat cheered. He says that the Japs apparently are following a schedule prepared well in advance of December 7. They had calculated on the immediate fall of the Philippines, a quicker collapse of the Malayan defense and no resistance from the Dutch. Now they are proceeding as if all these things had occurred. He says with things as they are he thinks we might well continue our mission on down toward Australia, cleaning up bases as we go.

Just before noon we learned that a U. S. submarine had torpedoed a Jap carrier of recent class—also in the the Straits of Macassar. One of our carriers has been reported hit north of Oahu but there's some confusion about the report and it may not be true. Inasmuch as the carrier isn't named it probably isn't.

We had a battle practice this afternoon with Donald Duck calling the shots of imaginary planes and announcing the untimely death of sundry gun crews. Nothing was very realistic about the business except the process of shutting up the watertight doors. I got caught down below and was parboiled for the hour and a half of our imprisonment. Our damage control squad did one bang-up job with an actual fire that had not been listed on the program—a cigarette butt in a waste basket.

The sea got choppy toward sunset and our four returning planes had to land in the rough. Despite that, they were hauled aboard fast enough to get a signal of good cheer from the Division Commander. These planes, old Curtisses, have plenty of stamina and whatever else they have somebody else will have to write about. The catapult which tosses them off accelerates them to sixty miles an hour in sixty feet of travel—literally shoots them out of a cannon. And when they come back they dunk their floats, their wings, and sometimes their engines, and bounce in the grip of serious cross strains. But they take the battering daily with little or no need for repair.

The aviators appreciate their durability but otherwise look at them askance. They have a fixed gun which is of no use because they can't catch anything. They carry two puny bombs. They wouldn't last two minutes against any other plane of the current vintage. "A plane strictly without a future," says Lieut. Crowley.

Somebody chided the paymaster today because the string on his dog tag is too loose. "You want it tight to keep it from slipping over your head," said Dr. Hays. "If it slips over my head it will make no difference to me and I won't worry about what difference it makes to anybody else," said the paymaster.

Dropped in to see the captain this afternoon. He knocked down a report that the Japanese have seventeen battleships. He figures that with one due in April they will have eleven. However nobody

hereabouts denies that Admiral King had to tell the Senate committee that he didn't know how many battleships Japan had.

The news tonight was hard to understand because of the static
but it seems that we are claiming to have sunk fifty-two ships since
the beginning of the war including a carrier torpedoed today—if it
should prove to have been sunk. The British are falling back in
Libya; the Cairo communiqué sounds just as stupid as it did a year
ago when the word was that "our troops are concentrating in areas
more suited to the plan of operation." The Australians are still
loudly calling for help. The situation in the Philippines and Malaya
is virtually unchanged.

We had a rabbit hunt around 5:30. One of the planes spotted a
blackfish or something and the destroyers chased out for a field day.
They retired without letting off a depth charge.

Bob Landry was asleep when the war drill started this afternoon.
He was awakened by Donald Duck announcing the approach of
enemy bombers. Then as he opened an eye he heard the announcer
say that No. 4 gun crew had been wiped out and that a fire was
raging in No. 2 turret. He got his life preserver and dashed to the
air, after having a hell of a time finding an open scuttle to crawl
through. He was easily the most impressed observer on the ship.

One of the officers told a story illustrating the odd life of the
Navy today. He had been in the service since boyhood and had
been stationed at many bases but he and his wife had never been
aboard an ocean liner. They took a cruise as a sort of busman's
holiday and their kids promptly got sick.

We are still headed for Jaluit with possible stops in the Marshalls.

21

"STEERING CASUALTY"

JANUARY 27, *Tuesday*. At sea. Hot. Calm. Sunny. I slept late for reasons I can't explain. The sounds of test firing of pompoms and machine guns and the usual clatter of rush to battle-stations in the early-morning drill never caused me to bat an eye. Someday they'll fight a first-class battle aboard this ship and I'll never know a thing about it.

I strolled down to the deck in something of a haze and found a scene of quiet detachment that might have been taken bodily out of *Outward Bound*. Everybody in sight was asleep except for a couple of officers visible through the open door of the wardroom who may or may not have been asleep. They were playing chess.

I found a spot to sit down and read an essay on Japan by James Young. He was quoting another newspaperman for the most part and the duet had a lot of sound sense in it. The theme of the piece was in itself familiar: that Japan, once she encounters a tool of war or twist of strategy for which she has not made long and studious preparation, will fold up. I hate forecasts in diaries which in their essence are mere echoes of past performance. But I am including this because it fits my own observation and beliefs: I can't see why a nation so gullible as Japan in peace should not remain gullible in war. Nor can I believe that a people who consistently manufacture the most worthless trash in all the world, who consistently filled orders with junk below the standards of the samples submitted, could fail to work the same processes of gyppery on themselves. Someday I expect to see a real test of Japanese war equipment in wholesale lots, and when I do I expect to see at least half of it fall apart of its own volition after the fashion of things made in Japan.

We got somebody's issue of news bulletins at noon and from

130

what the commentators tell us we are beginning to fit the action of the Macassar Straits into the list of the world's important naval engagements. There is no doubt that Japan has taken a terrific licking, even should the Dutch announcement that a battleship has been destroyed prove erroneous. According to the present score eleven ships are known to have been sunk, six probably sunk, and seventeen damaged more or less severely.

We crossed the equator last night and are back once more in north latitude. We are also so close to the international date line that I don't know whether it's yesterday or day after tomorrow.

The navigator came in late for luncheon and announced that we are running into a typhoon which lies about 100 miles ahead of us—just around the corner so to speak. We asked him how he knew about such things and he smilingly admitted that he didn't. Some aerologist traveling with one of the other ships had worked it out on his ouija board. Or perhaps some ship up there had sent us word. That, to a layman, seemed more likely. Up ahead of us somewhere—up there in the middle of the navigator's typhoon—must be the tanker which is theoretically going to give us oil tomorrow . . . if and when.

Drill began as usual after luncheon. Four planes were catapulted at one o'clock. There was no sign of storm in the air which was neither more hot nor more muggy than usual. But at 1:30 P.M. Donald Duck relayed an order that all ports of the ship would be secured against heavy weather.

It began to rain soon after that and when I went down the decks were wet and the crew had been forced down into the insufferable heat below. Our airplanes came back after a brief maneuver and were lashed up. Meantime the officers off watch had gathered in the wardroom to do nothing in particular.

"It's bad news for you," the doctor suggested, thinking probably of my talent for seasickness in odd forms. "But don't worry. If you get thrown out of your bunk and break your leg I'll be right there to carry on."

I left this cheerful atmosphere and paid a visit to the soda fountain. I couldn't get near to it. Yesterday was payday and today is the day after payday, hurricane or no hurricane. I went back to the cabin which, thanks to the rising wind, was beginning to cool off for the first time in two weeks. Commander Chappell was there writing some notes about something and we exchanged important ideas for the rest of the afternoon. The commander won the prize. He pointed out that the Japanese at Pearl Harbor in a few hours had changed over the U. S. naval force from a seventeen-knot fleet to a twenty-five-knot fleet. The thought is worth putting away for reference.

I contributed to the discussion only what I had heard in the wardroom where the officers were milling over the proposition of a unit command at Pearl Harbor. Somebody said that only God could take the job because only He could outrank Emmons in his present mood.

The thin rain was still slopping the deck when I went down to dinner and the wind had freshened a bit. But there was no sign yet of the typhoon. Commander Chappell says it will be around tomorrow when we start to fuel. It's sure to be here then.

We got an important dispatch this afternoon. It was secret so I didn't get the text. But the gist of it is that we have carte blanche to pursue our own destiny out here. Our mission is unchanged but we don't have to hurry back to Pearl Harbor or anywhere else. We are at liberty, these orders go, to look up more targets as long as we stay afloat. And I hope the beans hold out.

The breeze has penetrated the upper part of the ship and it's actually comfortable inside this cabin. I guess I made note of that before. But no matter. It's very important to me.

January 28, Wednesday. At sea. Weather report: Something happened to our typhoon. The ship rolled a little last night and there are some whitecaps and swells but no severe gale. The day is sunny and coolish.

I came down to meet a lot of officers peevish over a mix-up of orders. Their trouble is of no moment save for one lad's suggested solution of it. He said with all sincerity and it must be admitted with some sense that it would be a good idea to retire all admirals automatically at the beginning of war. You might lose a lot of good officers but, he said, the general increase in brains and initiative would compensate.

The radiomen brought in a sheet of news this morning. They've decided to get out the ship's paper (a mimeographed affair) one sheet at a time in numerous editions. There were two very interesting bits. One related to the reason for the flying visit of Hess to England. Churchill publicly said that Hess had wished to make a deal with the English appeasers to oust him (Churchill) and promote acceptance of Hitler's offer of "a magnanimous peace."

The other paragraph had less international significance but was more stirring to me. H.M.S. *Barham*, battleship of the *Warspite* class, had been sunk in the Mediterranean. That leaves only the *Valiant* of the Mediterranean fleet as I knew it. And maybe she's gone too.

A destroyer came alongside at 8:30. As on the occasion of her first visit the officers and crew spent about half their time looking at Bob Landry and me, apparently trying to make out the meaning of our civilian clothes. Landry says they'll probably think we're prisoners.

This destroyer, which apparently is our private and personal "can," is generally conceded to have done more damage to the enemy than any other craft in this war. Her specialty for the past month has been submarines and it is said that on her last arrival she came in covered with brooms. Hoisting of brooms is an old stunt in navies since old Admiral Van Tromp hung them out to celebrate his defeat of the British in the seventeenth century. The idea in his day meant, of course, that he had swept his enemy from the seas. The can's brooms probably were intended to mean the same thing although the spiteful marines say they really meant, "We have curried the blackfish."

Sometime after the destroyer had gone away we made an erratic turn and almost crashed another ship. As in all collisions and near-collisions at sea, it seemed to be wholly the other fellow's fault. The captain, however, said that it had been a steering "casualty." (At sea any accident to anything is a "casualty.") A lad named Lorisco in the steering engine room had noticed that the rudder wasn't answering the helm and had acted to avert a serious smash.

Lieutenant Brewer, referring to the failure of the electric steering apparatus, told the sad story of a destroyer captain who undertook to recommission a ship that had been laid up for some time and did all the wiring himself. Everything went all right until he sailed out to battle practice. At the proper moment he pushed the button to start the firing. Nothing happened except that a Filipino cabin boy popped into the cabin with a cup of coffee. Thereafter the skipper never dared push the cabin boy's button for fear . . .

22

DRESS REHEARSAL

JANUARY 29, *Thursday*. At sea. Slightly overcast, breezy, fairly cool. We seem now to be about 400 miles off the Marshall Islands.

There will be no battle today—at least none of our seeking. The fueling jamboree of yesterday took up a lot of time. That caused a delay while the carrier took on some oil last night. The delay has lengthened our schedule toward glory or the bottom by a full day or reasonable facsimile thereof. Somebody observed last night that it takes just about as long to get into battle now as it did in 1812.

Toward midnight Lieutenant Crowley came down to my cabin and called me out to look at what he called the most amazing exhibit he had ever seen. An albatross, tired from a long fishing trip, had come to roost on our yardarm and sat there in the moonlight unconcerned at the weird conduct of the shadows moving about on the gun decks below him. A flag was on the yard and the signalmen were careful to get it down without driving him into flight again. Word went around the ship and gobs came sleepily from their holes to see for themselves and check up on this evidence of the ship's luck. A very fine thing is the albatross when you're in the south seas on your way to a battle, although the fish probably think otherwise.

At dawn the bird took off and probably resumed his fishing. What concern of his a battle? But nobody cared as he sailed out into the sun. Nobody had shot him with a crossbow and he had stayed long enough to give the ship his accolade.

The news report at noon gives clearer picture of the battle of Macassar Straits than we have been able to piece together from broadcasts. There is no further mention of a second Jap carrier

135

presumed to have been sunk by Dutch or Australian airmen. But the casualty list as issued by the Netherlands East India Government says that the Japs did lose one carrier and probably a battleship, five cruisers and more than a dozen large troop transports. They also lost an indeterminate number of smaller transports and destroyers.

And so to the wars. . . .

Donald Duck announced at 12:45 that the captain was about to make an important announcement. At one o'clock everybody aboard who could get to a speaker was there. The captain spoke simply and slowly and for a wonder his voice was easily understood over the antiquated address system.

"I told you," he said, "that I should keep you advised of our future activities as plans for them matured. I am able now to tell you that on the morning of the day after tomorrow—Saturday— we shall bombard important Japanese positions. We shall act in conjunction with other ships of this force before, during and after a severe air attack." He spoke of the necessity for drill and of the security that comes of perfection in defense. "We are likely," he said, "to receive some opposition. And we prefer it that way. Nobody wants to bet on a sure thing. But we shall be able to hold our end up because we are equipped and trained to do just that. . . . I wish you luck."

In connection with his examples of what good comes from drill, he mentioned yesterday's fiasco with the tanker. An accident to the steering apparatus had been corrected by a man who once before had been in a similar mess in the steering engine room and on that occasion hadn't known what to do. This time he did know.

"And," said the captain, "his knowledge, his ability to act in an emergency, undoubtedly saved the ship from very severe damage. . . . He has been recommended to the Navy Department for recognition. His name is Lorisco, seaman first class. . . ."

That ended the matter so far as the crew will know about it until Saturday morning. We came away from the loud-speaker aware that we had listened to a very good speech. There had been no oratory. No *forte* passage, no quavers, no trick emotional appeals, no flag waving. But so far as a job of morale building was concerned, Rockne between halves never did better.

Half an hour later Donald Duck, the seagoing muezzin, called

WRECKAGE OF THE U.S.S. "ARIZONA"

Photo by Underwood-Stratton

FIRST ARMY PHOTO OF THE BOMBING OF HAWAII, DECEMBER 7, 1941
Rear view of Hangar 11, Hickam Field, Hawaii.

Photo by Press Association, Inc.

NOT DAMAGE BUT CONSTRUCTION
New buildings rise rapidly at Pearl Harbor, center of the Japanese surprise attack on December 7. Much of this new construction is announced
as at least partially bombproof.

the faithful to drill. "This," he said, "will be a dress rehearsal for the action in which we shall take part day after tomorrow."

Later an announcement of the general situation gave us our first idea of what sort of bases the Japs are maintaining on the Marshalls. "We are to destroy an enemy base known to be defended by aircraft, submarines, possible surface craft and six-inch guns. . . . This," he said deliberately, "is a drill. The term emergency will not be used again unless an emergency exists."

I went up to the signal bridge to look at this dress rehearsal and saw the crews of the five-inch batteries breaking out their shiny new gas masks. These things have a filter tank that hangs across the back of the neck and an exhaust valve under the nose. They make the wearer look more like a large-eyed wolfhound than any other contrivance of the sort yet devised.

There was some very smart loading drill around the one-one pompoms. Clips of shell were passing out of the magazine and into the feeder racks and out again just about as fast as you'd expect the guns to shoot. The eight-inch guns were waving about like trees in a wind.

I went to the bridge where I passed a pleasant hour watching the whole fleet moving about on the same problem we were working out—tossing theoretical shell into forts as yet unseen, strewing dynamite on grounded planes in duplication of the Pearl Harbor technique (grounded planes still grounded somewhere far beyond the horizon), sinking cruisers that in this dream world had come out of nothing to oppose us.

Dress rehearsals, as everyone knows, are sometimes no criterion of what the show is going to be like. But I must say that ours was most gratifying in its very dullness. Some nine hundred men went through motions as limited as the routine of a ballet dancer, as unstudied as the beating of a pendulum. And there was no noise whatever, no untoward incident nor anything else to keep one from hurrying back to his nap.

Commander Chappell took me into the chartroom where he explained sundry mysteries such as the depth finder and the robot that checks on variations from a set course, and an amazing thing like a power-driven pantograph that actually marked our course accurately on a chart as we went along.

After the battle we played bingo in the wardroom. There was

no further excitement except for the roar of airplanes that came across almost scraping our superstructure as they dropped messages about one thing or another in connection with Saturday morning's assignments.

It becomes apparent that we are not going to attack Jaluit—at least not at first. Maybe that job is left to the force on our left. That unit will strike to the south of the Marshalls while we go to the north.

Commander Chappell agreed with me that the element of surprise had quite likely been wrung out of this enterprise some time ago. But he said that the strafing would be important anyway. These targets of ours are submarine and air bases. They have to be maintained. And even though the planes and ships have been moved away from them they are still important objectives. They will have flying fields and docks and oil supplies and repair facilities. If we smash up those assets the Japs will have to move their subs to Truk—a thousand miles farther on—which means that they will be a thousand miles farther away from their enemy, to wit ourselves. They will have to travel a thousand miles farther to get at us. If we then go on and destroy Truk we may be able to drive them back all the way to Japan. Anyway it's a nice thought to take into battle.

It was surprising today to see the captain's smiling calm. Yesterday's episode with the tanker would have put many a good skipper into a state of nerves. But not the captain.

"Yesterday," as Sandburg says, "is a bucket of ashes—a sun gone down. . . ."

He told me cheerfully enough what had happened. It seems that in the steering apparatus on the bridge is a motor which works in conjunction with another motor in the steering engine room. Sometime since we left Pearl Harbor the motor in the steering column got hot and melted some rubber insulation which flowed down onto the contact points. Yesterday of a sudden there wasn't enough juice going down from the bridge to work the steering motor below. The ship had been thrown hard a-starboard and stayed that way.

The steersman, however, saw by an indicator at his side that the wheel was having no effect. So he threw a lever which blew a siren in the engine room indicating that the ship was out of control. Captain Zacharias in the meantime rushed to the starboard end of the bridge and megaphoned to the captain of the ship alongside what had happened and advised him to take a course ninety degrees to starboard. He did, while down in the steering engine room our Mr. Lorisco was hooking up some new controls and hauling the rudder back amidships.

So the ships swung around to the right together with us, snuggling in a dangerous fashion. Miraculously no damage was done save that we lost about three feet off the end of a boom—an hour's repair job.

One funny thing deserves a note in mention of this near catastrophe. From the time the tanker came alongside a gob on the signal bridge tried at two-minute intervals to cast a line onto our deck. He reminded me of a movie I once saw about the history of the bicycle which showed in the first scene a man trying ludicrously to balance himself on a single wheel and in the last scene showed the very same thing. . . . Everytime you looked up at this lad he was trying to toss a line. He was still doing it when the ship came towering over us and anybody could have touched her side by holding out his hand. Some of us were falling back pretty rapidly toward the port rail—but not one oily lad who sat with a spanner in his hand astride the fuel hose.

"Throw it now, Bud," he advised. "You'll never get any nearer."

The carrier sent over some puzzled inquiry today. The admiral or somebody wanted to know why we had more oil than we should have had considering what we'd got from the tanker. The captain sent back as an answer the report he had received from Commander Kobey, the engineer officer: "Five hundred barrels extra discovered in inventory." The admiral is probably still worrying about how you manage to mislay five hundred barrels of oil.

January 30, Friday. At sea. On the night of Thursday, January 29, we crossed the 180th meridian westbound and so Friday the thirtieth is lost. What kind of a day it was I shall never know.

23

EVE OF BATTLE

JANUARY 31, *Saturday*. At sea. Cool. Clear. Some overcast near horizon. Sea a little choppy but not much.

Just before the battle, Mother. . . .

I got up this morning before dawn and went to general quarters just for the practice of the thing—to find out a quick route through the blackout from the cabin to the searchlight bridge with a minimum of barked shins and falls through open hatches. The sunrise was no show because of a cloud bank to the east. But the Southern Cross was more visible than it used to be and Polaris could also be seen if you looked hard enough. I can't see, come to think about it, that I have learned anything likely to do me any good when the bombs begin to drop.

The only incident of the morning was the departure of the planes on the morning patrol from the carrier. They swept into the air traveling directly toward us, their twin exhausts wreathed in flame so that they looked like huge dragon flies with burning eyes.

Our schedule at the moment—it has changed before and may change again—is to attack an atoll, the name of which escapes me, at the north end of the Marshall group. This ship and another heavy cruiser will go into action after a preliminary fifteen-minute strafe by fighter planes from the carrier. We dash in and shell all the harbor works and anything we may see afloat.

There is a catch in this. Our atoll is a submarine base, so I have been told. And it is hardly likely that fighter planes will eliminate many subs by machine-gunning them as part of a general scene for fifteen minutes. In that time they ought to be able to submerge and cook up a reception for us.

The rest of the force will be split up to cover other atolls of the group. The other task force operating with us will take the south end of the line including Jaluit. Another cruiser gets one base where a 16,000-ton transport maru is said to be lying. That, of course, is the prize target.

Some orders were issued today about preparations for battle. The men are to take baths tonight and are to wear clean clothes inside and out to general quarters tomorrow. There is something reminiscent of vesting for Solemn High Mass about it but the idea probably springs from the doctors who know the danger of dirty rags in wounds—so it's hardly ceremonial.

I don't know whether or not I've made a note of it before but this is a good time to recall it: Reports of the sinking of an Army transport by Japs north of Oahu turns out to be true but not very important. The ship was a tug in inter-island service out of Honolulu and was listed by the Army as a transport. The submarine that put it down was also sunk.

Along about 10:30 this morning the weather turned perfectly beautiful—brilliant sun, deep-blue sea with scattering feathers and, on deck, a delightful breeze. Donald Duck announced that the captain would discuss the forthcoming operation with the officers at a meeting in the wardroom. I attended by invitation.

I wonder how many scenes like this I have run into—the same huddle of officers, the same calm, scientific dissection of a job that involves something like a major catastrophe for a lot of people including possibly ourselves.

Captain Zacharias outlined the plan in the main as noted. Reveille 3:45. Breakfast 4:15. General Quarters 5:15. Dawn 6:15 and attack immediately afterward. The planes will be on the target before daylight. We close in to suitable range for bombardment when they quit.

There was an endless array of detail—the disposition of the ships, the nature of targets, the rate of fire, the spotting process, the frequency to be used by spotting planes in reports, food, water, access to latrines, powder lot, ventilation, bombs, depth charges, airplane fuel. It is some twenty-five years later, maybe, and the wardroom of this ship isn't exactly like a wet shack on the slope of Vauquois Hill, but otherwise this is just the same affair as our business meeting with Major Rearden on the night of our attack in the first phase of the Argonne. . . . Only a little less did it resemble the briefing of the pilots of the bomber command of the R.A.F. the night they set out to destroy Turin.

The captain was cheerful and businesslike, the officers grave and interested but no more excited than they might have been over a prospective target competition. I recall that the officers of the *Valiant* after a tough year of shells and bombs were much less eager, much more likely to discuss the effect of enemy dive bombers than our own noble and undefeatable purpose. One lives, and if one continues to live, one learns.

Our objective, to put a name to it finally, is the atoll of Wotje. It must be important since two heavy cruisers have been assigned to give it a going over. Apparently it isn't expected that we shall have much thrown back at us. The idea is that most of the Jap strength will be drawn to the combat in the south. If that guess is wrong we may be in for a bad time.

Among other things of battle import the captain read a new order just decoded with great pain and travail: "Hereafter all officers will wear uniforms at all times except in the home when no more than three guests are present."

The notion was roundly cheered.

Cairo tonight confirmed the report that Rommel had retaken Benghazi and that a force of Indian troops had probably been trapped.

The Jap radio broadcast in English pooh-poohed the casualty lists from the Straits of Malacca. "We have lost four transports," said the commentator. "But if America, the Dutch East Indies and Australia and Great Britain want to falsify their communiqués, it's all right with us." He said also that Germany had sunk forty-two ships off the U. S. coast in the last month.

It became pretty evident that Singapore is in for a bit of hell. The Japs are only about eighteen miles from the Johore causeway—the only route the defending troops can take across the strait—and it appears that the Japs have air superiority in that area.

Somebody turned on the submarine-detector tonight. It's a fascinating gadget. The only trouble with it was that some traffic manager at the Salt Lake City airport kept breaking in to tell Flight Fifteen how to get over the Wasatch Mountains.

Dinner tonight was much as usual despite the momentous thing ahead of us. There seemed to be no ruffled, nervous or overexcited people in the neighborhood. There wouldn't be. It's the code that a naval officer knows no fear publicly. The postprandial movement as usual was toward bridge, chess and acey deucey. I suppose that every one of us ought to be feeling like a bride on the eve of her wedding, and I felt like a frequent widow getting set for a familiar role. But the calm is contagious, however phony it may be. I guess though that each one of us wishes he could find some species of juju like the international date line whereby we could steam a few miles and be safe in the middle of tomorrow night.

24

BOMBARDMENT

February 1, *Sunday*. At sea. Mostly clear with occasional overcast. A beautiful day to die in.

At this writing we don't know where one of our cruisers is. She took a walloping from high-level bombers at Kwajalein atoll and got a direct hit on her well deck. The carrier is slightly damaged. She just threw one of her planes overboard after a strafing that made the afternoon one of anxiety and prayer. We have only one plane left in commission out of four. (We lost one in a landing accident this morning. The other two were shot up on deck by our own ack-ack in action.) We are now theoretically on our way back to Pearl Harbor but I alas have no faith in these offhand pronouncements by our guides and guardians. More than once today we looked at the bottom. We'll get to Pearl Harbor when we get there . . . when and if.

Here is the chronology of a day of battle—as weird a day as I have ever experienced in war.

Commander Chappell woke me at about half-past four. I had slept through the noise of the alarm clock and he said that he didn't want me to sleep through a battle. I went down to the wardroom and ate a hearty breakfast of ham and eggs (simulated). After that in a leisurely fashion I gathered up my life belt, gas mask, field glasses, ear plugs, paper and fountain pen. And I clambered up through the dark to the searchlight platform just above sky control on the foremast. There with Bob Landry I watched the moon fight it out with a pale sun and eventually lose.

6 a.m. Moon full—yellow. For a moment a band of cloud slips over it like the belt of Saturn. But it remains brilliant, too brilliant. Aft, the planes begin to gurgle and roar.

6:15 A.M. Guns of after turrets are swung skyward. The planes get off one after another in quick and noisy sequence. They are gray blots against a gray sky with a ghastly blue halo of burning gases accompanying them.

6:40. The sun is struggling up through low-lying clouds. Eight seaplanes go off toward the west in ragged formation. Land is taking shape hazily like a narrow streamer of smoke on the starboard horizon.

6:45. Lookout sings out smoke coming from island dead ahead. This blackish cloud, round and rolling, is clearly visible in spite of hue of the dawn's early light.

6:59. We swing farther in toward land and turn loose forward guns in bombardment. We hear no commands. We see no unusual preparations but this is an historic moment. This is the first time in this war (save for some ack-ack at Pearl Harbor) that the Pacific fleet has fired on an enemy. The island is a typical atoll hardly visible save for the breakers along its coral reefs. Planes are on our starboard, low. Some anxiety until they are identified as our own. The carrier planes have gone home and for better or worse this show from now on is ours.

7:05. Lookout: "Ship dead ahead, sir!" And there it is! About halfway between us and the horizon. . . . A little thing like an ocean-going tug, which has come blithely out of the dawn to run squarely across the bows of a destroyer. A bit of irony. We increase speed to eighteen knots and turn slightly to starboard. The destroyer keeps on after the unfortunate tub—and starts firing. The sea around the Jap is tufted with white splashes. There are yellow-white glares from the Jap's deck—several of them—which from where I sit indicate that he has four guns and is using them.

7:10. The Jap turns parallel to our course. So does the destroyer. They exchange shots without result—several salvos knock down, drag out, toe to toe.

7:11. A destroyer is spotted on the horizon. The guns swivel and we lie back to blast. But it's one of our own coming back from a sub-hunt. There is some more to-do about a wandering plane that turns out to be an SBD returning to the carrier somewhere over the horizon.

7:12. A.A. flashes from the island. The ———, our associate cruiser, is throwing out salvos that burst with a green color. The coral beach is festooned with smoke plumes. The destroyer continues to fire. So does the Jap. This is an inspiring duel but it's beginning to look like a bad piece of gunnery.

7:16. Our eight-inch batteries go off and wreathe the ship and surrounding sea with a yellow acrid haze. We keep firing at halfminute intervals—following the lead of the ————. I was thrown flat on my face at the first blast and so far have been unable to get up any farther than my knees.

The light is getting better and we have a chance to view the fantasy of eight-inch guns painstakingly blowing a mangy, palmdandruffed atoll to pieces. The great battle between the destroyer and the seagoing barge proceeds with much noise and smoke and no end of dangerous-looking waterspouts. But the issue remains in doubt. I'm beginning to bet on the little guy.

7:26. The Jap is still up. . . . Seems likely to stay up indefinitely. We shift our fire. . . .

This atoll like so many of its kind in the Pacific is really a string of small islands about a lagoon, remnants possibly of coral erections on the rim of a volcanic crater. The entrance to the lagoon of Wotje is to the left of us as we look at the island but straight ahead of us the land dips abruptly into the sea, presenting an opening about a quarter of a mile wide through which we can see a large part of the lagoon.

And now, like something in a worn and hazy movie, an 8,000-ton freighter has steamed out from behind the island on the north of the opening and into plain view. There will be no better protection for her in back of the south island than she had when she started but in theory a moving target is harder to hit than a stationary one. . . . Our shells are smashing into the lagoon alongside her—two over, two short—a vicious bracket. Ack-ack begins to smash all around us. This is odd inasmuch as no planes are near us but there's no reason to suppose that a five-inch ack-ack shell won't bother us if it crashes into the bridge or sky control or, for that matter, almost anywhere else above the decks.

7:27. Somebody sights a submarine moving out of the lagoon toward the south passage. While we are assimilating that one the warning is passed to be on the alert for bombers inasmuch as near-by bases must now be aware of our attack. Everything seems to be happening at once—or on the verge of it.

7:28. Comes a terrific mixture of splashes about the Jap ship. You might take the bursts for bomb explosions but there are no planes above. Probably the destroyer crews are putting out something special in the way of quick fire. . . . We have completed our first run across the face of the island. We turn about with the other cruiser. The ship in the lagoon is still moving through a mist of spray and smoke. She appears to have been hit. The destroyer goes on with its interesting and interminable work.

7:32. The guns turn loose all at once with a brain-jolting slap and your diaphragm caves in. The yellow smoke blots out the target for a moment. Then clears. The hiss of compressed air cleaning the gun tubes comes as an obbligato. This is an ideal day for a battle. But it has a stiff wind which we are now heading into. It's enough to blow your eyeballs out.

7:33. The struggle between the destroyer and the Jap spitkit comes to a quick end. The destroyer makes a hit on the starboard and disables two guns. Apparently the Jap commander has one gun left on the port side. He is listing badly but he swings slowly around as more clunks rain on him and churn up the sea. He fires one last erratic shot with his remaining gun. He sinks.

"Well," says the navigator, "if the Japs want to put up a monument to that little guy I'll contribute."

7:40. Firing is fairly regular on the atoll now but doesn't show many results. We can see now—as the day advances—two more ships just over the reef in the lagoon. The one we were shooting at first is behind the south island, up or down I can't say. One of the pair now visible seems to be turning around. The other begins to move southward across the open space. Apparently the crews of both ships were taken by surprise and they've been until now getting the engines started. There is something of Pearl Harbor in this in more ways than one.

7:41. Destroyer milling about scene of kill is far away on our horizon now. It has large bone in its teeth and seems to be on the way to rejoin us.

7:45. The sun hits Wotje's low profile and shows color of its straggly palms and moth-eaten verdure. It is like all other south-sea atolls—a top of delicate green, an outcrop of grayish coral and yellowish beach. Over the front of it spin shreds of black smoke.

7:55. Sky control announces two submarines coming out of the harbor. The ship which first began to move from the trap beyond the open reef now swings south to get protection of the south island. One salvo seems to bracket it—to "straddle" it as they say in the Navy. It leans over to starboard and seems about to capsize. But it recovers and steams on with green and blue plumes of bursting shell in its wake.

8:15. We are beginning to notice artillery resistance other than the five-inch ack-ack that has kept sprinkling us liberally. Perhaps they've been working unobserved in the dim light of the morning but at the moment we are in no doubt about their being here. A couple of them are tossing six-inch shells out here with no hint of economy. The sea between us and the island is tufted with them. And now and then, in the fashion of another and better war, they throw a bit of time-fuse shell at us for adjustment. Some of this probably was mixed up with the ack-ack. If so it wouldn't have been discoverable.

Our five-inch batteries have turned loose to strafe the beach. They are probably the noisiest contrivance ever invented by man. Their effort mixed with the sickening roar of the main battery produces a din that nears the limit of human endurance. Lots of odd things come out of the five-inch tubes along with the shell, including odd bits of ashes, and red fire balls.

8:16. The barrage on the ship remaining in sight in the lagoon has been steady—and terrible. Now comes a bracket so close that most of the superstructure is hidden by an upheaval of water like Old Faithful. The ship starts down by the head, shivers, leans over to starboard. . . . In a matter of seconds she is gone.

8:20. Firing ceases. Brass shell cases of the five-inch batteries are dumped overboard. In the lull you have time to note numerous fires along Wotje beach. We seem to be withdrawing. Our destroyer is far on the western horizon.

8:25. I guessed wrong. The clamor is on again worse than before. Almost immediately we see results. There is a burst of red flame and a tremendous black cloud rolls skyward. Oil, would be my guess, and a big tank of it. Lieutenant Jim Brewer in fire control announces that twelve torpedo planes and seven bombers have taken off from a Jap island—apparently one where our preliminary attack wasn't strong enough to hold them. The fire burns mostly black with darting spears of red in it. Another ship comes across the open space in the lagoon streaking for protection back of the north island.

8:30. Our fire has shifted to the north end of the atoll. It's not so spectacular now as the bursts go over the crest but we've been told that three or four naval auxiliaries are in there. Shells from the shore batteries are falling nearer—the last batch about 200 yards off the port side and square in deflection.

8:35. A group of four shells tosses white water to starboard. We're bracketed.

Our turrets are working faster but not on the land battery. Maybe we don't recognize it socially. Continuous concussion caves in your stomach. Five-inch guns firing into the sunlight throw off large golden rings of burning vapor that chokes you when it comes back. Cotton in your ears is small comfort now.

8:41. Another string of geysers ahead of us. The Jap battery is in no hurry but, boy! it's working well. The range is now perfect. Deflection which has to change as we move is not badly calculated. Over on the island four white plumes are rising—wooden buildings maybe.

8:45. Three shells just smashed in front of us. Another came closer to scraping our stern. From our platform we can see a widening circle of green—like an excrescence in a swamp—spreading out over the deep blue water. Our fantail cuts off the view of one side of the patch—which shows how close the shell came. . . . Apparently the bridge is going to do something about this. We can hear the telephone men relaying an order already sent over the engine-room telegraph—left rudder. We swing about as on a pivot. The top rolls over until we are looking down into blue water. You'd think the whole thing would keep going right on over into the drink. But we come up with a jerk at right angles to our original course and right side up. Four shells, all in a pattern, fall astern and to port. So we've come out of the bracket.

8:50. Our guns fire from the stern. There is a crash from the flight deck. A muzzle burst in Gun No. 8 of the five-inch battery.

The tube miraculously held together although it is bulged to a bottle shape, and nobody was hurt.

Shells begin to pile up on the end of the island where the land battery is flashing at us. We are doing a sort of cumbersome adagio dance, the sort of movement you might expect of an elephant in bayonet drill. . . . Our wake, a broad path of light blue with fringes of white on a stretch of calm cobalt, is a glittering corkscrew. . . . "The rolling English drunkard made the rolling English road. . . ."

8:52. Geysers around the cruiser ahead of us. . . . Apparently a second battery has been working on her. She shifts. A second salvo falls short of her. The Jap firing is accurate enough but the guns seem to be working at the limit of their range—there are few overs.

8:53. We let loose a fine salvo at a ship in the lagoon which seems already headed for the beach. I shall make a note of it, to paste in my hat for study if I ever have to go to a gunnery school again, or to consult when anybody says anything about the law of averages. . . . Five guns fired—the two forward turrets; two shells went over, two were short and very near and the fifth made an error of fifty mills to the right, smashed into the coral right at water level, hit a subterranean oil storage and started the biggest fire ever seen in the south Pacific. I pause for a reply. . . . The ship goes on toward the beach.

8:53. Another black fire starts from the previous column of smoke and north of it. Almost immediately two smaller blazes spring up to the north of that.

The air is filled with beautiful little white birds that come out from the land to look at us and go away again. In the sunlight they look like butterflies or flying fish.

It is a pleasure to report that we are now maneuvering well out of range of the shore batteries whose efforts continue to pockmark the ocean between here and the shore.

8:54. A third fire of first magnitude but with more red in its black plumes has burst out well toward the north end of the north island—far to the right of the other principal blazes. The smoke column is now hundreds of feet high and spreading out in a cloud toward the south over the atoll.

8:55. We plaster the land batteries with everything we've got— a smash that makes the ship lean back and slide sideways in the water—and turn about. The northernmost fire and the one we touched off in error in the middle of the island seem to have combined in one fine blaze. It is now erupting gray and black smoke with high bursts of red in it where hot gases belatedly ignite.

8:57. A lookout announces: "Plane approaching—bearing two-five-oh." Lieutenant Brewer, on the platform below this one, repeats it into the telephone. . . .

"Our plane!" bawls the lookout and Brewer repeats that. Then he puts down the telephone and signals for an orderly to inform the Marine battery—the pompom ack-ack outfit. "Our plane!" he calls. "Tell it to the Marines."

The island fire has all the characteristics of oil except for the gray mixture which may indicate explosives, I hope.

9:00. We draw away. We are now about ten miles off Wotje. Bursts are leaping up on the south end of the island. The destroyer is still in there firing incessantly. It probably went in close to finish off the ships inside the lagoon. We are headed mostly south. . . . A string of signals breaks out on our halyard, another string on the ————. It's my guess the first phase of the show is over.

9:05. Here's a startling mystery. There was an odd noise—like a burst alongside amidships. A detail went to look into the matter but there's no answer to it unless the five-inch battery has had another muzzle burst.

9:10. The far-away atoll now seems to have no height. It is a long white-green streak on the horizon with flame running over it and smoke plumes like a couple of black waterspouts balanced on it. There are occasionally three distinct columns of smoke, two black, one gray—all about three hundred feet high.

9:30. "Periscope dead astern!" Thus the lookout. Speed and twist! Speed and twist! The destroyers leap like flying fish. Thud go the depth charges.

9:35. "Periscope off port beam." Speed and twist! Speed and twist! The periscope couldn't be a half-filled five-inch shell casing, could it? Who can say? Speed and twist!

9:40. All planes returning. You can see the rendezvous far astern. Our destroyer seems to have finished its job and is coming up like a fox terrier with its tail in the air.

10:00. Planes overhead but only seven. Eight took off. We

slow down to pick up planes. Four go to the other cruiser. So it's one of ours that's gone. Which?

10:10. The missing plane comes streaking in from the west. Cheers.

10:16. Last of the trio that came back first is taken aboard. So we learn that the late-comer is Davis who apparently is still flirting with a jinx. He circles about, heads down into the slick on the starboard side.

10:20. He's down . . . heads in. The signalman isn't very deft and Davis gets the signal to cut off too late. He slides too far and his engine conks. Before he can start again a wave throws him against the side of the ship. A wing crumples.

10:23. The plane is astern with Davis and his radioman sitting on the wings of it. The floats are submerged.

10:24. So begins a ponderous maneuver to launch a powerboat. The key to the winch is missing. Find it. There's no plug for the bottom of the boat. Whittle one. Why doesn't someone start the winch? Why not?

10:25. The ship is moving about the plane in a narrowing circle. The cockpits are under water now. The aviators have inflated their rubber boat and are preparing to get into it.

10:29. A destroyer goes by. The boat crew is still hopelessly fiddling with the gear. The destroyer seems to be awaiting a signal before going in to pick the lads up. In the meantime their situation is getting critical. There goes . . .

10:30. General Quarters with bells and bugle! Eight planes reported about fifteen minutes away and heading toward us. The can is left to do what can be done about picking up Davis.

10:42. Plane off port bow flying erratically.

10:43. Plane identified as a bird. . . . The captain says that the report of the approaching Japanese planes came from the carrier— which we ought to be picking up presently—and that fighter planes are being sent off to deal with the situation. All seems well and yet this would be the time to feel uncomfortable if we intended to.

10:44. Lookout sings out: "Plane approaching bearing two-two-oh." We zigzag. The plane, if any, takes off somewhere. We see nothing of it.

10:45. The captain has received a report that the cruiser which left to attack another atoll was severely bombed for nearly an hour. She got one hit on the well deck which killed about eight men. She is now steaming back to the rendezvous at a speed which would indicate that she's not seriously damaged. She apparently stepped into something. The island she attacked was supposed to be without air defense. It had plenty.

10:55. "Two planes off port beam!" Invisible to me. After a while I could make one of them out. It seemed to be heading in the direction of Wotje whose smoke plumes are still visible above the horizon.

10:56. Lieutenant Brewer calls into telephone: "Find out how many or how few are going in or coming out."

10:58. He gets his answer—three fighters over the island. Very likely ours. The air of uneasiness is getting noticeable. Obviously we know that the Japs are on the prowl but with our planes up it's difficult to tell where they're prowling.

11:04. Ship on horizon. She's identified as our carrier. All this identification business is done by the lookouts. I can't see anything on the horizon at all except a wisp or two of smoke from Wotje.

11:15. Near-by planes identified as friendly. The carrier now looms up over the rim of the sea as we zigzag toward her. She looks as big as the *Queen Mary.*

11:20. The atoll is now completely out of sight but the smoke of the oil fires is still thickly visible sixty miles above the horizon. Two more warships are coming into sight near the carrier—also quantities of planes.

Report to the bridge from the carrier: Eight Jap planes managed to get off during the attack on Kwajalein—heavy bombers. They followed our bombers back to the carrier. Carrier fighters got four of them.

11:25. The carrier swings northeast. So do we. We are still at general quarters.

11:58. Secure from general quarters. A tired, dirty mob troops down the iron ladders. Details start out to clean up the ship, to put electric-light globes back in their sockets and to take mirrors and other flat glassware off the floor, and to turn on the water. The first lieutenant's detail goes around inspecting damage which is considerable as a result of detonation.

12:20. Buffet luncheon: Beans, cold meat, pickles, stewed peaches. . . . Very acceptable.

1:15. I go to bed feeling as if I could sleep for a week.

1:45. Bugle and bawl of Donald Duck to general quarters. "Planes approaching!"

1:50. This time there's no fooling about it. Five planes—big bombers—come slanting out of the overcast which is thick above 2,000 feet and start in a long glide straight for the carrier. This is the first time I have ever seen dive bombing attempted by two-engine planes the size of a Douglas transport. All the ack-ack in the group lets loose.

At less than 2,000 feet they straighten out and drop their clunks. It's a fine job of bombing. Water rises to a height of 200 feet and covers the carrier for her entire length. It seems impossible that any of her should be left.

But the water comes down and the mist disperses and we see that the carrier has spun about. The bombs fell precisely where she was when the planes came out of the cloud. But by the time they hit she was somewhere else. The planes come back for another glide. Where our fighters are I'll never tell. Maybe I'll never know.

2:00. Four more bombs—half-ton clunks—drop astern and to the starboard of the carrier as we come about parallel. Another plane streaks out of the clouds on a long glide. Our ack-ack blasts. The plane seems almost to stop in midair as it bursts into flames. Then it continues on toward the deck of the carrier.

We'll never know whether the pilot was alive or dead when the plane came to its finish. In either case he probably had no time to know that his attempt failed. The big bomber hit the end of the flight deck, all right, its momentum virtually spent. It crashed one plane and slid over into the sea.

The marine gunner who accomplished most of this miracle looks startled: "He was there and now he's gone," he said. Which is true. There's no trace of him or his crew—not even a spot of oil.

2:10. This is the fastest I've ever traveled except in a speedboat somewhere on a calm lake. We are sticking our nose into it and flinging spray up over the bridge. Our wake looks like a waving green stair carpet with white fringe and no particular pattern on a blue floor.

2:30. The radio continues to report planes—obviously Japanese—in various quarters at no great distance. Obviously this will keep going on all day. The price you pay for raiding bases is that you get strafed by landplanes which are difficult competition.

3:00. The other cruiser lets off a blast—about four salvos of ack-ack for no reason that we can see.

3:10. Now and then the cans on the horizon do some shooting.

3:20. Black bursts low on horizon—a torpedo attack. The trouble is that we don't know what happened or how it came out. Apparently you don't mention battles in this war so long as they don't affect anybody but yourself. Your own worries are particularly your own.

3:30. Radio announces two or three planes fifty miles away and inbound. The sun is getting low, making observation to the west more and more difficult. The sky is covered with spotty clouds.

3:45. The atmosphere aboardship reminds me of the *Valiant* in a similar situation. There is no sound save the throb of the blowers and the vibration of the hard-driven engines. There is little motion as the gun crews man their guns and the fire-control details stand with heads bent and their hands clapped over their headphones. Somewhere out there are the Japs. They have made one attack and have missed and have lost face. They will have to make another attempt.

3:59. And here they come. The lookout sings: "Two planes approaching bearing two-four-oh. They seem to be heavy bombers." There is a clamorous conference among the observers: a moment's excitement and then calm again. . . . After all the air has been pretty well filled with Grummans.

4:00. The first lookout calls: "They're just coming out of a patch of cloud. There they are. Both of them. They certainly are heavy bombers. Most certainly!" Then another lookout and another: "Enemy aircraft approaching bearing two-five-oh." "Enemy aircraft approaching at 6,000 feet."

Then sky control: "Commence firing."

Once more bedlam. I was on my knees under the ship's bell on the searchlight platform when the riot started. I had trouble getting to my feet with the shock and plunge of the ship. I smashed my head against the bell and battered my bones on the rails and skinned my knees.

Two bombers came over at 5,000 feet, sailing as usual toward the carrier. Their shooting was pretty good.

4:02. Four bombs drop near the carrier. One bursts almost dead ahead and no great distance off. The water piles up on the carrier deck but apparently there's no damage.

4:04. It is plain from the position of the bursts that our five-inch ack-ack isn't bothering the raiders much. Their altitude is beyond the range of machine guns and minor ack-acks. But as in other combats of the sort I've seen, they continue to fire anyway.

4:05. Two of our fighters come from somewhere and begin to climb. We cease firing save for a few odd shots from the other cruiser and a destroyer. The fighters get altitude with amazing speed and take off after the bombers to the southwest.

It is difficult to get yourself adjusted to the silence that comes now. It has been a weird afternoon—everything you could ask for except a cavalry charge.

4:10. We sit down again to wait. So long as the Japs have bombers to fly we shan't be safe for the rest of the afternoon— and even sundown won't bring complete respite. We'll have a full moon in a reasonably clear sky. It's obvious, however, that if the Japs are going to attack they'll most likely do it before six o'clock. They were taught the rule that your bombing is better by day.

5:00. The carrier's planes begin to come back and land.

5:10. The bridge has received a message that the carrier planes shot down one of the two bombers.

5:20. I start down the ladders from my perch and run into one of the gunnery officers. He says a message has just been received that a torpedo plane has been intercepted about five miles dead astern and is now in a dogfight with our planes. . . . What a day!

5:45. Down to the wardroom to get a cup of coffee. "Secure from general quarters." We relax once more. Somebody comes in to report that the dogfight has ended satisfactorily for our side and that our planes are coming back to the carrier.

Crowley, apparently suffering from no trace of fatigue, is bragging about the effects of "The Zacharias Zombie" as he calls a diabolical gadget consisting of one bomb and one large bottle of gasoline. It made an impressive fire, he says.

With what the aviators know and what reports come down from the bridge we are able to reconstruct something of the scene on the atoll. It was like an army camp, Crowley says, with big wooden buildings close together. The defense forces were driven under cover by the strafing attack and one oil fire had already been started when we came in to bombard. The cruiser aviators set fire to a hangar, a storehouse and a set of buildings that appeared to be repair sheds. One ship was sunk outside the harbor, four definitely sunk inside the harbor and three driven onto coral reefs where the water was too shallow for them to be completely submerged. The magazines and oil dumps were set afire. In other words this base was rendered useless for many days, not to say months.

7:30. Buffet supper. I was too tired to swallow a bite of it. I am going to bed.

7:45. Call to general quarters by Donald Duck. There was no bugle but he informed us that he wasn't fooling. I got a few clothes on and went up to the bridge. The radio had picked up a couple of planes—judging by their speed, torpedo planes—about thirty miles astern and coming our way. We changed course and there was some more waiting under a brilliant yellow moon. I feel awfully naked.

8:30. The planes apparently have missed us. I went down to the wardroom for a cup of coffee but I went to sleep in my chair while drinking it. So I shall go back to bed. I shall sleep with my clothes on because all the lights in my end of the ship are out—including the battle circuit—and both my flashlights have gone *phut.* If there's a real attack somebody may have to wake me.

25

THE OPERATION WAS SUCCESSFUL

FEBRUARY 2, *Monday*. At sea. Coolish. Fairly calm. Cloudy. I awoke this morning to find everything back in normal routine. I hadn't batted an eye throughout the nervous night. The mess attendant who came into the room before I was dressed said that we had finally shaken off our pursuers about two this morning.

We appear to be still on our way north. I don't know whether or not the cruiser that was hit has joined up with us. Can't see much through the surrounding mist. I went down for breakfast and found the boys setting up a rig to transfer supplies to a destroyer. Under the circumstances the fog is very acceptable.

The captain sent in a copy of the news report on our performance. It went something like this: The Navy Department has released a communiqué in Washington to the effect that the Pacific fleet went into action against Japanese bases in the Marshall and Gilbert Islands in a large-scale battle raid. Large units of the fleet attacked a number of important positions with air and surface craft, destroyed large quantities of stores and materiel and completed the raid with slight losses. Damage to the enemy included many naval auxiliaries sunk.

I remember that even in the last war I always wondered who was the talented workman of the communiqués who could make even a battle sound dull and violent death a commonplace.

There was considerable, if minor, damage to the ship during the bombardment. Concussion loosened quantities of cork insulation from bulkheads in the wardroom and captain's quarters. . . . That's probably a blessing inasmuch as it takes away that much fire hazard. Some mirrors were smashed and Jim Brewer now hasn't any washbowl. He comes in here to shave. The smashing of

158

plumbing is an indication of why they shut off the water during action.

We got another message a little belated this morning. It was from the destroyer announcing that they had recovered Davis and his radioman unharmed. They had sunk the ruined SOC with machine-gun fire.

At luncheon the officers assembled to G.A.R. about yesterday's performance. Who did what and where, how and why?

We learned that the carrier had caught some splinters on her flight deck when the downbound bomber crashed her. She had to dump the remains of one ruined plane shortly afterward. There was some criticism of an outfit of pompom gunners who kept firing on a plane that they couldn't reach and some recrimination about a telephone line that had been taken away from them for some other purpose. There were regrets that we hadn't been allowed to shoot rapid fire, which the gunnery officer contends is the only kind that will sink a ship in a hurry. There were other plaints that we had not gone back to unstick anything that we had left on the atoll. But these yelps generally were recognizable hindsight. The sort of scuttle butt that you hear after all engagements on the water just the same as on the land.

We came just about 400 miles last night. Tonight should see us about a thousand miles northeast of Wotje and 500 miles from the spot where the Japs lost track of us.

Just as an example of how news gets around, I must make note of a bulletin brought into the wardroom by somebody who had heard it from somebody else: "The Russians have opened an attack on the Japanese in Manchuria." There weren't any details but the source was convincing. The news was said to have come from that center of Russian information, Shreveport, Louisiana. Today there has been no whisper of the matter in the official news. The navigator says it probably came from the CPO's headquarters where so many glad tidings originate.

I heard a funny one at luncheon about the one-one A.A. battery near the bridge, the one that shot down the bomber. There had been some worry about the supply of ammunition from a converted cubbyhole on the deck below. But yesterday just as the firing was due to stop a little fire started in the magazine and burned out the telephone line. Despite the gunnery sergeant's bleat the ammunition continued to come up the conveyor. It piled all over the position, threatening to invade the charthouse and bridge, and recalled the story of the German pilot whose life raft inflated accidentally and pushed him out of the cockpit. The ammunition problem was solved by some genius who thought to feed the clips back into the magazine via the disposal chute for empty cases.

Afternoon: The world is covered with a thick, wet mist. The forecastle and decks are foggy with spray. So far as vision tells us we are alone except for one tin-can riding bravely along on our starboard beam.

At 5 o'clock the sea has become flat and oily and gray. We have run into a perceptible ground swell and we have some pitch. News tonight was vague except for one announcement over the Jap radio that we had attacked the Marshall Islands and had been driven off. The Japs sank one of our carriers, four cruisers and two destroyers. And so go the communiqués. You listen to them and if you get any truth out of them, that's so much lagniappe.

5:20. With no warning at all the five-inch guns began to go— not in battery but slowly and deliberately and we swung over on our beam-ends. I tumbled out onto deck to find nobody particularly perturbed. A sailor in the stern gun crew was picking up the muzzle cover of his piece. Somebody had sighted a submarine, he said, and they had taken a crack at the white ruffle that marked the trail of the periscope. . . . A destroyer was dropping back to look after it and it was no longer any concern of ours. We were going too fast to have to worry about it or any other sub that didn't happen to be perfectly set and waiting for us as we came by. Speed and the law of averages (which militates against such accidents) are our protectors.

The incident gave us a bit of a scare, however, so the fuelling of the destroyer was postponed until 9 P.M. We're hitting such a pace that we may be out of this lovely protective murk by that time but at the moment (7 P.M.) it looks as if we were going to escape the attention of the large unblacked-out moon that gave us so much concern last night.

Donald Duck just contributed something to our condition of

well-being. He announced that the general alarm is out of order. It sounded as if he said that the general alarm is now in order, and you could interpret a remark like that only by grabbing your life jacket and starting for the upper areas.

At 9 o'clock promptly the destroyer came alongside. The moon was reasonably bright, even in a cloudy sky, so bright that I was able to write the notes from which this is being typed.

The visit as always was a weird and interesting sight, the more so, of course, now that an element of danger was mixed in with it. We sent over a net filled with flour and ice cream. They asked for bread but we couldn't give them any. We haven't any for ourselves. (Destroyers always want bread. They haven't any ovens of their own.)

The chief engineer told the engineer of the destroyer that his oil was mixed with Diesel oil and had to be used at 160 degrees. I thought to myself that you never get any such service at filling stations ashore. You had to find out for yourself about the Diesel oil.

The most recent Jap propaganda is that we attacked the mandated islands with the Atlantic fleet, which of course they defeated quite easily. Their bag, in this report, consisted of a carrier and five cruisers.

On top of this discouraging news from Tokio we received a dispatch from Admiral Halsey, our commander (Haul with Halsey).

"Commander Task Force Eight to Task Force Eight: Well done! You have made history in the Marshalls. I am proud to have the honor to command you. God bless you! (Signed) Halsey."

Our latest information is that we lost eleven planes in the operation. No detail of what happened to them is given and inasmuch as we heard no reports of Jap fighters it seems very unlikely that they could have been shot down—not that many of them. I'm wondering if navigation—the search for a single ship in an area where there are no railroads or landmarks or roof-signs—couldn't be classed right now as Japan's secret weapon against air attack.

26

POST MORTEM

February 2, *Monday (continued)*. At sea. Sunny. Pleasant. Fairly cool. Rough. And now we cross the 180th meridian eastbound so it continues to be February 2.

There is a prodigious groundswell that kept me awake most of the night—not through seasickness but through the necessity for either hanging onto the bunk or dashing my brains out on the floor.

I got up just too late for breakfast and went down to get some coffee. Fell in with Lieutenant Coggins who was conducting a post mortem in an effort to prepare an official report of our raid.

His questioning of the officers produced some interesting items about the bombing of the carrier. There was some divergence of opinion, for instance, as to whether the attacking planes had had four engines or two. I held out for two. There was enough argument over this to remind me of accident cases in Chicago courts, and yet everybody who saw the bombing at all seemed to have observed it closely and to have carried away a tremendous amount of detail. The navigator, for instance, was able to tell the exact position of every ship in the group from the time the planes first appeared until they went away.... The carrier had swung quickly— quickly enough to escape a mess of bombs that just about scraped her sides as they fell. We had maneuvered also and so had the other cruiser so that when one of the bombers was shot down it was between us and the carrier. That makes it appear that our battery of pompoms didn't get the bomber—but it also makes it appear that nobody will ever know who did. The operation at the moment is beginning to look like a dance of the whirling dervishes.

There was a little discussion about the number of planes. The lookouts who first reported the attack said six. The navigator and a brace of aviators said they had counted six in the dive. The aviators said that the diving planes weren't four-engined bombers but large ones with two engines. Everybody agreed that they were large planes, painted a battleship gray and without markings, with long, wide, tapered wings. All agreed that they seemed to be brand new and of extremely modern design.

"They looked to me," said Lieutenant Brewer, the gunnery observer, "like just about the latest thing in the air—super-bloopers with extra streamy extreme streamlining."

It was finally decided that six had come over and four had taken the dive and dropped their bombs. It was then figured out that the pair which remained aloof were the ones that had come back later. Observers of the second attack said that this pair had looked like Douglas DC-3's—as indeed they did.

In the middle of this interesting discussion an alarm came: "Submarine to starboard." We picked up speed at once and swung over so sharply that chairs and other oddments started to roll all over the wardroom.

I got onto the deck in time to see our pet destroyer spraying the air with flags and veering off full speed at an angle to our starboard; she could have passed us easily. As we looked she dropped three depth charges, then swung about to look over her particular section of the ocean. The signal flags read definitely "Submarine in Square Three." There were no qualifications, no "possible sub" or "probable sub," and the skipper of the destroyer is conservative. He wasn't the sort who would go tearing after the spume of a blackfish flipper. There had been a plain sight of a periscope somewhere. How the sub got out here I'll not attempt to say. At any rate it was surely an accident that put him in our path after such an erratic course as the one we've been following since we left Wotje.

This morning we were twelve hundred miles from Pearl Harbor. We expect to get there on the evening of Feb. 5 or the morning of Feb. 6. There was no drill today. Instead everybody turned loose to clean up the ship.

The chief engineer is still experimenting with a heatproof suit to wear when turning off valves in a room filled with live steam. He can find plenty of guinea pigs to try it on but no room to use for a laboratory.

During the afternoon the sky clouded a bit and the weather turned definitely cold. The ground swell continued. Brewer, looking over at the carrier, said her deck looked like a street in San Francisco.

There's a nice paragraph in the "Plan of the Day" for tomorrow. If the captain gets any more chewing gum on his shoes the sale of it is going to be stopped.

February 3, Tuesday. At sea. Still rolling. Fair. Cool. Nothing much went on today save a vigorous return to routine activities such as painting the ship and shooting insect powder around the hold.

The captain held a meeting of officers in the wardroom this afternoon for a sort of critique of Sunday's operation. . . . Have I told you about my operation? . . . All of the officers indulged in the conversation and you got the idea that a great deed which yesterday had seemed like one of the most brilliant, audacious and effective naval performances of modern times was really something we ought to be ashamed of. It seems we had confusion in communications, that the spotting was useless on targets we fired at and that the spotter couldn't get us to fire on the targets he spotted, that splash colors couldn't be identified from on top, that the first wave of carrier planes went home without leaving us any information, that lookouts were hysterical and reported submarines coming out of the lagoon at a point where there was no outlet—and more to the same effect.

The captain made note of these complaints but he said he was satisfied. I think his point was well taken. Our only sins as far as I could see were due to our complete lack of knowledge of what lay on the island and our overenthusiastic use of ack-ack, the common failing of all who fire it.

I sat up late reading the report of the lad who operates the director for the main battery. Our shooting seems to have been pretty good. Remainder of evening I spent getting copy prepared for the censor and conversing with Crowley, Commander Tyree, the gunnery officer, and others coming off watch.

I heard one puzzling and important thing: One of the ships we knocked over at Wotje had a Norwegian flag painted on her side.

February 4, Wednesday. At sea. Rolling sea that looks like blue jelly. Sunny. Cool.

We get in sometime tomorrow morning, God willing. The kids have started an agitation to put the brooms out on the yardarm. But the captain only smiles. There seems to be an idea aboard this ship that maybe the Navy did enough bragging before Dec. 7 to last it for the rest of the year.

The news today seems to be about the same as usual. We are getting the pants kicked off of us in sundry places. There is a new retreat in Libya, from Derna this time. . . . "We are concentrating our forces in positions better suited to the furtherance of the battle plan." Singapore is getting ready for a last stand. The Dutch are taking a terrible punishment from bombers.

(If I've mentioned this before I shall someday be finding out: Pearl Harbor in Navy argot was Torpedo Junction. Now the term seems to apply to any battle contact. A fight between little boats, such as the recent patrol boat and our destroyer, is called a spitkit spat.)

Dr. Coggins, who has custody of the Jap officer captured when a one-man sub ran aground at Kaneohe, says that his prisoner won't sleep in bed. He rolls up clothes in a bundle to look like a human form, puts that in bed for the bombs to hit, and sleeps underneath. Novel idea, eh what?

February 5, Thursday. Honolulu. Hot. Rainy. Muggy. Hawaii was visible through a thick haze when I woke up this morning. We roamed around a bit, then made a run for the slot through lanes of destroyers. We entered the channel about 10. Landry and I hurried ashore with our copy in the mailboat and so were the first to hear that the censors had decided to hold it up for a week or ten days.

This seems to me to be on a par with the best thought of censors everywhere. The Japs knew we were there. They know we got away intact no matter what sort of bull they may be issuing in their communiqués. And furthermore the Navy Department told all about it in a press release. . . . So what!

I skipped a press conference this afternoon. I've had enough of fine interviews that you can't reveal to anybody. I reopened my diggings at the seaside bungalows and began to wonder how even a salamander could contrive to live in such a climate as this.

There was some mail from home—also a box of jam, a Christmas present from Nan. There was little else to make me feel I ought to abstain from cutting my throat.

The town is just as haywire as usual. The Royal Hawaiian has been taken over by the Navy and the Moana shuts up its dining room at 5:15 P.M. You can't get a taxi after 4 P.M. Some new agency is dashing about trying to get another set of my finger-prints. Probably J. Edgar Hoover who has about twenty-five auto-graphed sets already.

Even in this Indian reservation that thinks it ought to be admitted to statehood you see as fine a cultivation of good old 100-per-cent American wool-wittedness as you'd find in Washington, D. C. We never heard about foresight, we never heard about fore-handedness, we never heard about moderation, or tolerance or even good manners. . . . We never heard.

God! I wonder what ever made this place seem beautiful to me. I sit here now and see in it only the epitomization of the things that might very well make us lose this war.

When I dropped in to see Drake this afternoon and air my ideas about the latest suppression order, he wasn't there. But a communications officer was—one I'd met in the wrangle over the censorship. With no cue from me he began to talk about stupidity. He sounded to me like a he-Cassandra.

So I came out here to the beach and unwrapped the phono-graph and a few books. . . . To hell with it!

I learned today that Knick and Joe Harsche didn't get back to our expedition. They are presumably still in Pago Pago, waiting for the rain, no doubt. (And what became of Sadie Thompson?)

27

POLISH UP THE HANDLE

February 6, *Friday*. Honolulu. Sunny. Humid. But surprisingly cool in spots. I got up this morning, loaded a suitcase and moved to the Young. Got a good, big, blacked-out room in the front of the building and may be comfortable—as comfortable as one could expect under the circumstances.

Drake was running another press conference this afternoon—more interviews with the brass hats who had directed the ships in our endeavor—a chance to get more information about a story that we're not going to have a chance to send out for ten days or two weeks. I asked him if he could arrange for some other interviews about other mellow subjects such as the battle of Manila. And I stayed home.

I spent most of the afternoon getting located. Had dinner with Keith Wheeler who, as it turned out, is the only other eyewitness reporter affected by the delay ruling. After dinner we got a call from Roy Vitousek. Journeyed up to room 443 where we found the chief of police, a brace of police commissioners, and half a dozen newspapermen.

We learned from the chief that the town is under an alert—has been for the past four days. General Emmons walked out of a dinner party tonight. Not an Army man is in town. Machine guns are scattered all over the premises.

I don't attach much significance to all of this. I suppose everybody knows that the Japs will exact some sort of reprisal for the Marshall Island affair and this may as well be the target as any other. Maybe that's another reason for the general befuddlement of the lads at the Navy yard.

February 7, Saturday. Honolulu. Misty. Cool. I was awakened by Commander Chappell who arrived with a suit of clothes I had left on the ship. He says the alert is on generally all over the Pacific—Midway, Samoa, Juneau, Seattle, etc. No matter which way the cat flops the Cincus can say, "I told you so."

I borrowed ten gallons of gasoline from the landlords of my rented car and went out to the Beach for more stuff.

At 3:30 went over to the police station with Foster Hailey at the invitation of Chief Gabrielson and he drove us out to his place on the other side of the island—a perfectly beautiful cottage on a high bluff with broken green mountains sticking into feathery mists behind and above it and a shimmering coral bay below.

Mrs. Gabrielson had us stay for dinner and we had a restful pleasant evening that took my mind away somewhat from the madhouse of Honolulu and Pearl.

However, we heard many strange stories of the bombardment and of the advance of the engineers on Punahou School. Heard also some statistics on profiteering, which by the way we are not allowed to mention in the dispatches: Two carrots for fifteen cents. Eighty cents for a head of lettuce. A quarter for a grade-two pine-apple. Seventy cents for a pound of pork. . . . Eat more pork!

About nine the chief drove us back to town over the Pali—a bloodcurdling drive in the blackout. I went out with Hailey to get a cup of coffee at the Black Cat and discovered that the all-night restaurants are now closing at 9 P.M.

I have just remembered a conversation that I had today with Captain Z. whom I met in the lobby of the Young. He says that apparently the Navy for once is taking its own warning seriously. His ship was to have gone into dry dock. Instead it is being re-fitted and refueled and made ready to go back to sea on an hour's notice.

February 8, Sunday. Honolulu. Cool. Pleasant. Had breakfast with Hailey who commented on slick anti-Hitler cartoon in the morning *Advertiser.* The cartoonist is an Irishman who for a long time drew anti-British pictures for one of the local Jap papers. After the troubled times he was taken over by the Army to do propaganda stuff, and he has certainly obliged.

February 9, Monday. Honolulu. Cool. (A little warmer than yesterday.) I went around to the Iliani Palace this morning to get some new gas tickets. To get my ration I had to write a letter to the military governor explaining my needs. I'll probably be allowed five gallons a month after the war is over. I understand on good authority that the guy who runs the gas rationing is a director of the tram lines.

Last night I started negotiations for a trip on a bomber doing patrol work around the islands. It will probably be monotonous as hell but no matter, it ought to produce a story and the Army promises to get it turned loose immediately.

Learned today that the FBI has finally folded up—not that anybody ever knew it was in business. Somebody was wise enough to figure out with a little aid from the Army and Navy that this is no time to go about playing cops and robbers.

Most of the smaller craft shot up in Pearl Harbor are in service again and the Navy engineers say all can be salvaged. Both the *Downes* and the *Cassin* have been cleaned up in their burned docks, and the *Shaw* has been fitted with a new bow. . . . Nobody who saw the *Cassin* and *Downes*, burned black and warped with terrific heat, would have believed that anything could ever be done about them. And Honolulu is beginning to feel the war as France did late in 1939. . . . The Pearl Harbor business was somebody else's hard luck. All the lads killed there were strangers. But it seems that the Army tub torpedoed during our absence was bringing a lot of local draftees from one island to another and thirty-two of them got killed.

Wrote a piece about preparations for battle and turned it in for eventual transmission to the *Daily News*. I learned that my stuff is passing the censor with no word changed. That's the irony of it. The censors for the moment at least are acting reasonably and intelligently. It's the Navy Department that's being stupid. . . . And with no great effort.

Signed up tonight for a trip in a bomber somewhere tomorrow. I feel willing to go anywhere with anybody who hasn't anything to do with the Navy.

I made a will tonight. These bomber trips are dangerous.

BOOK THREE

MARCUS

"All Hands to Repel Enemy Aircraft"

28

WITH THE AIR PATROL

FEBRUARY 10, *Tuesday*. Honolulu. Warmish and Misty. Got up at 6 A.M. (Five now that War Time is with us.) Waited indefinitely for an Army escort and eventually got to Hickam Field. More delay. 'Twas decided two fortresses would take off together. One ship—taking Dick Haller and me—would be photographed by newsreel men in the other. After that we were to separate and go our various ways in the air. Colonel Lamey was piloting the other plane. As we roared down the runway—about 150 miles an hour—one of his engines conked. He swung over into our path, missing us by inches. Our pilot automatically sheered off into the rough. We bounced squarely toward a string of automobiles in front of a pile of loose pipe and we took off just in time.

Almost immediately we knew that something else was wrong. The smell of burning rubber was all over the ship. We circled over Honolulu harbor and came down.

On the runway another fortress was taking off and as we came down it swerved just as the first had done and we escaped by another quick breath. The perils of flights in fortresses seem to be on the ground.

Our pilot, a young major, found another crate and we took off again for an expedition over the islands.

9:30. We were in the air. I sat in the forward gunner's coop in the nose.

9:45. We began to run along with a 360-degree rainbow.

9:55. Rain begins to weave delicate threads on turret glass. I feel something like a guinea hen *sous-cloche*. It's terribly noisy up here. The vibration is enough to take your teeth out in handsful.

10:00. We go up. My ears ache. We seem to be getting above the fleecy clouds. Only occasionally do we glimpse the blue water below and in perspective it looks like a continuation of the sky. The wool gets thicker and we try to burrow out of it. Not so happy. Nobody knows who may be up ahead in this veiling. And we have trouble enough keeping out of people's pockets on solid ground.

10:05. We fall into a clean spot in this vastness of cream puff. Cold. . . . Cold and lumpy.

10:15. Land off starboard bow—streak of deep green shading to green-white on edge of blue sea. Slate gray where it mingles with mists against the background of sky-fluff.

10:16. Sailboat below. In the sunlight it seems to be made of orange-colored tile.

10:19. Headlands on the right like Rapa Nui. The sun reaches us as we edge downward. Warmer.

10:25. We are nearing the flat reaches of a valley where it opens out to the sea—green with an occasional square pattern of black. There are strange black roads twisting through it to mark the edges of unearthly gardens. All of these islands look like something dredged up from the bottom of an aquarium. The beach is curving, yellow and broken by black basalt outcrops and shelves colored with red, yellow and green algae. The water, save for the white curve of the breakers, is clear amethyst.

So up along the rosary of the islands to the northwest and back again. Eventually we turn in over John Rodgers Airport and Pearl Harbor, come into the wind above Hickam and land. I feel as Lindbergh must have felt when he got out of his plane at Le Bourget—surprised to be able to get out and walk.

I went to town to look in on my prospects for a gasoline ticket and found that the boys hadn't heard of me. So I went to luncheon with Dick Haller and Chauncey Wightman, who used to be with the A.P. and is now vice-president or something of the HSPA, the Hawaiian Sugar Planters Association.

Wightman says that at Punahou school the engineers certainly carried out the scorched-earth policy.

The food in this town is getting pretty terrible. There was a shortage of butter so the Navy released 65,000 pounds all of which was rancid. That's complaint No. 1. Wendell Webb sat for some time at dinner with Keith Wheeler and me. His bleat was not so much over the quality of the grub as the stupidity of the yahoos who serve it. As he arose he put a quarter under a dish. "Hide it till I'm gone," he said. "I don't want to have him see me tipping him."

29

BACK TO SEA

FEBRUARY 11, *Wednesday*. Honolulu. Sunny. Warm. Sticky.

Waldo says we may go on a new jaunt soon—maybe to Ponape or Truk, I suppose, although that's just guessing.

It doesn't make much difference at the moment. Singapore is about to fold up and no other news will amount to very much. Re the fall of Singapore, Z. was in the hotel last night and he said he wasn't perturbed about it.

The Japs are extending themselves too far, he said. Once we can get enough airplanes over there to take care of them they'll be a setup.

I hope he's right and take consolation in the fact that he knows his subject.

Somebody said today that there are four wars in Hawaii: (1) The war with Japan, which doesn't concern anybody locally very much. (2) The big war between the Army and the Navy. (3) The lesser war between the Marines and both the Army and the Navy. (4) The major war between the district and the fleet.

Our story of the Marshalls seems ready to collapse as a news feature. Singapore, whether it's important or not, is just on the verge. The latest flashes tonight put the Japs in the outskirts of the city and the guns of the forts seem to be pointing the wrong way. We'll be lucky if we land on Page 28.

There are reports here—and they come from pretty good sources—that the elder Nisei Japanese (U. S. born, over twenty-five and under forty) are quite favorable to the son of heaven. The kids about sixteen years old on the other hand want the U. S. to win, and there are some swell family fights. The authorities are beginning to feel that in the event of an attack the inevitable rise of a fifth column would be checked by this element within itself.

February 12, Thursday. Honolulu. Clear. Warmish but not too hot.

Got a highly encouraging cable from the office about the Marshall Island stuff. Went out to the Bungalows last night and removed the last of my belongings. Stopped on the way back to buy a trunk in which I can store all my lares and penates if I go to sea again.

I was sitting in my room with Keith Wheeler during the afternoon when Waldo Drake phoned. He was sorry to inform me that the Navy Department intended to release our story to the A.M. papers owing to the fact that Knox owns an afternoon paper. It might be well to set out the facts of the case.

In the first place an embargo was put on this story as soon as we got back. The object of this was theoretically to keep the Japs from knowing that the fleet had returned and that the prowl of the Pacific was temporarily off. The stories could have been given some phony date line, our presence in Honolulu disguised and the whereabouts of the fleet kept secret. But no matter. After much harangue we received assurances from Admiral Nimitz that the copy would go out on Wednesday for release at 6:30 A.M. Honolulu time on Friday, Feb. 13—twelve days after our return. (6:30 A.M. Honolulu time is noon New York time.)

This we took to be a promise as well as a regulation of conduct. We made no further representations to our newspapers and we let the thing ride as it went. We thought that the word of a ranking naval officer ought to be good.

It is obvious that the A.M.'s have been putting the heat on Colonel Knox and that he has leaned over backwards to avoid a lot of talk. So by the time the *Daily News* heard of the business the Chicago *Tribune* had been out on the street a couple of hours. In this connection it might be well to note that the A. M.'s got the break on the original communiqué also.

This, it seemed to me, made the noon E.S.T. release void. So I asked about it. Waldo asked Admiral Nimitz. Admiral Nimitz— Waldo said—called Admiral Hepburn. Admiral Hepburn, we are informed, said no. And if you can make any sense out of that you are pretty good.

Take the case of Foster Hailey who is here for the New York *Times*. The *Times* can print the Navy's handout Friday morning, scooping itself on Hailey's commentary which it won't be able to print until Saturday morning. Now, I ask you!

Foster Hailey and Keith Wheeler joined me on the mourners' bench in my room. We played *Ruddigore* on the phonograph. Would have cut my throat but haven't anything but a safety razor.

February 13, Friday. Honolulu. Fair. Warm but bearable. The morning paper was filled with the story of the Marshalls. No way of telling whether or not the release was observed because it was built to fit Honolulu time. Morning paper here observed it definitely.

Took Keith Wheeler out to Waikiki to consult Minah-bird catcher. He wasn't at home so we returned via Kanaohe and the Pali road. I have never seen Honolulu or its environs so beautiful. You wonder at the mentality of the men who sold out the interests of the country to bring cheap labor here—eventually perfecting a system where a fleet operates out of a base surrounded by 40,000 Japanese.

At the hotel were conciliatory messages from Paul and Carroll overlooking my suggestion that I come home. Apparently God was good to the Navy Department. The collapse of Singapore was oddly delayed. The *Gneisenau* and *Scharnhorst* and *Prinz Eugen* got free of Brest but slipped through the Straits of Dover without provoking anything more newsy than a row in Parliament over the responsibility. So the affair of the Marshalls, which should have been as timely as a dispatch about the burning of Rome, lit on the front pages and, apparently, splashed.

Wheeler and Hailey came to my room after dinner and we played *The Gondoliers* and the *Pirates*. I read a bit in a book about Japanese psychology and came to the conclusion that the "oriental twist" is a feature that we detect in intellects other than our own. For devious thought processes I don't think you need go any farther than our own leaders in this terrifically tragic war. In which happy frame of mind to bed.

February 14, Saturday. Honolulu. Clear. Warm. Just a little sticky. I was awakened at 7:45 to get cable. So, being up, I went down to breakfast. Hailey was there just biting into a waffle when Drake called. Could we get out to the sub base prepared to travel by 11:30? We said yes.

I had to send some cables, check out of my room at the Seaside Bungalows, turn in the key to my rented car, cancel a dinner engagement with Dick Haller, pack some paper and shirts, buy some books and get a cab.

We reached the sub base on time but with nothing to spare. Hailey and I found ourselves assigned to the old *Swayback Maru*, which pleased both of us. Keith and Joe Custer of U.P. went to the carrier. A lad from the *Bulletin* was assigned to the other cruiser. But when we got out into the harbor we discovered that the carrier was just hauling in her gangway. Our men got aboard and we started for the cruiser berths. The cruiser flagship was on her way out. Which meant that the *Bulletin* lad would have to wait two days for other transportation. We cut over to our cruiser which was getting under way. As we came alongside they dropped a cargo net for us and we clambered aboard amid cheers. Welcome home! The mob seemed to figure that I am a sort of harbinger of luck. Well, maybe.

For a time after we left the harbor we loitered about in sight of Diamond Head. A four-piper showed up on the horizon dragging a ship target. The heavy cruisers worked on it for a while. I learned later that it is impossible to judge naval shooting with a pair of binoculars from a fire-control top. I thought the other ship's shooting was lousy and ours swell. The aviators said afterward that we hadn't been near the target whereas our rivals had been just about perfect.

Crawled down from the fighting top and met the captain and Commander Carter, the new executive officer. We got a cheery welcome and also some information. We are on our way to Midway and then to one of the Jap strongholds in the Carolines. We shall approach these objectives from the north which gives us a chance for decent weather.

Four of our planes had been sent off for the target practice. Davis is not with us this trip. He was left in Honolulu for a rest that nobody will deny he needed. He had two pretty narrow squeaks. . . .

The planes that were damaged by the concussion of the five-inch guns have been replaced. Two new ones were cracked up yesterday before the ship had received any march orders. There must be a special factory somewhere making planes for the *Sway-back Maru*.

Life aboard this ship has settled back into its customary placid way. No matter what's been done to you ashore or what may be done by the Japs tomorrow, it's hard to run up a high blood pressure.

Lingered during the late afternoon in the wardroom talking with Crowley about airplanes. And like others of my more intelligent acquaintances he is loudly critical of the bull that has been fed the great American public on this subject. Nobody now thinks Russia will come into this mess unless forced by Japan which seems unlikely at this writing. So it becomes necessary for us to find some way to lambaste Tokio without the use of Russian bases. Crowley says some of the new Consolidated ships may have the answer. And he thinks that designers when they get down to it can put out workable bombers (workable as in distinction to conversational) that will easily do four thousand miles with a full load of bombs.

The PBY flying boats will carry about the same load of bombs as a B-17E for the same distance. Their lack is speed and altitude but somewhere between their efficiency and the flash performance of the flying fortress may be found the bomber to demolish Japan.

John Lambert (first assistant chief engineer) dropped into the cabin after dinner to exchange a bit of gossip about the ship and our prospects and similar things. He said the personnel, including the officers, had been deceived by the issue of forty rounds of target ammunition. They thought they were going for a routine cruise. And then we came aboard.

"It was all over the ship in two minutes," he said. "Everybody knew you wouldn't be coming out for a boat ride."

Commander Chappell came in and asked Lambert to find him some steel wool so that he could de-rust the strings of his steel guitar.

"Your what?" inquired Mr. Lambert.

"You heard me—my steel guitar," said Commander Chappell definitely.

"I thought that was what you said," mentioned Mr. Lambert. "But it surprises me. Can you play it?"

"Like Heifetz and Kreisler and Houdini rolled into one," said the commander. "I shall demonstrate."

So he took out the guitar and played "Old Black Joe."

"This is my masterpiece," he said, breaking into the commercial in the middle of it. "I can play one or two other pieces but this is the one I do best with. You might call it my repertoire if you wanted to. . . ." So he played. And then Lambert contracted to find him some steel wool. When the commander gets the steel wool and works on the strings it is likely that he'll be able to play "Old Black Joe" even better.

30

ODD ROUTINE OF WAR'S BUSINESS

FEBRUARY 15, *Sunday*. At sea. Bright. Cool. Choppy. I got up earlier than usual because the lights came on in the cabin. But I didn't miss much sleep because I am still sleeping on Honolulu time. I looked out and discovered a tanker with us. We are plodding along at about seventeen knots and the chief engineer has been notified to "keep a light brown haze" over the stacks—an indication of the most economical oil consumption. It looks as if we might be out a long time.

The captain made an announcement of our purposes at 9:30. He gave few details but said that our mission is quite similar to the one we recently completed and that he hoped for the best. . . .

The morning news was reasonably dull. Jap parachute troops attacking Sumatra had been pushed back by the Dutch—it is alleged. Twenty flying fortresses took part in the assault on Jap shipping in the straits of Macassar. Evidence is offered that the weather over Dover was too thick to cut when the *Scharnhorst* and *Gneisenau* made their dash.

Reference to the news reminds me that I neglected to put down a bit of information I got just as we were leaving Honolulu. On the night of Feb. 12, Lincoln's birthday, unidentified snipers attacked sentries and killed some on the island of Maui.

Hailey came in to announce that we were going to be dive-bombed by an outfit from the carrier. So I crawled up onto the mast to take a look at the operation. It didn't amount to much except that it got me out into the open air. I got my face sunburned and walloped my head on the big bell when I tried to straighten out and so far as I could determine I was the only casualty.

The bombers dropped darts on a float towed behind us. It wasn't a bad performance although I didn't see anybody hit the target. I'm beginning to hope that after all we may be able to escape the divers by pulling our necks into our collars and standing still.

An order came down from the bridge forbidding any of our gun crews to train on the visiting planes. Apparently the skipper wasn't taking any chances on the loose trigger fingers of young gentlemen who see airplanes on the cross hairs of their sights.

The ocean today looked as if it had been made by a designer of German postal cards. The air is soft and languorous. And life is very lovely, or at least as lovely as it could be on a mess of floating scrap iron like this.

However, it's apparent that we are getting ready for war. From our coop up on the mast we could see the boys wrestling with Mr. Crowley's airplanes. Apparently two are to be kept in the cradles on the catapult ready for flight. The two others are to be hauled inboard, their wings folded back and their tails tucked in, to protect them from the backwash of the five-inch guns. That means of course that we shall probably have to content ourselves with two planes instead of four. But Crowley says he doesn't think it will make any difference. Two SOC's apparently are enough for anybody.

None of our planes went off today. Apparently the carrier is looking out for us. We are pursuing a leisurely course to accommodate the tanker and at the moment are about 450 miles out. We seem to be bearing slightly north.

Evening. The radio just announced the surrender of Singapore. It was not, of course, unexpected, but it seems to put the war squarely in our laps . . . and maybe we know what we are going to do with it.

The navigator says that in about a week we'll be in position to start on our job. How long we'll be out neither he nor anybody else seems to know. Since the war began, he says, this ship has traveled more than the total distance of a peacetime year's schedule. Twenty thousand miles a year was supposed to be just about what was necessary to keep the ships in good order and ready for anything. We went 8,000-odd miles to Wotje and we seem to be making a nice thing out of our voyage to Midway. Lieutenant Brewer who was listening to this conversation said that we are getting too conventionalized in our role. From now on when anybody in Washington wants an atoll sunk—says Brewer—he'll call in his secretary and say: "Who was that admiral we had down there in the South Pacific—Appley . . . that's not it. . . . Admiral Paisley . . . Admiral, Admiral. . . . The one that knocked off the Marshalls . . . Halsey! That's it, Admiral Halsey!"

And, Brewer says, when we get a reputation and Halsey is known to the press as Knock-'em-Down Halsey, we'll be lucky if they don't send us into Yokohama accompanied by the *Baltimore* (one of Dewey's old tubs) and a couple of four-pipers.

His mention of the *Baltimore* prompted Chappell to remark that we'd better be in a hurry if we're going to run it to Yokohama. It's been sold to a Honolulu scrap-iron concern.

Recently, after years of lying at anchor in Pearl Harbor, the old crate had an adventure. One night a couple of somewhat inflamed young gentlemen were returning from leave when they noticed that the *Baltimore* was completely without camouflage. Particularly she was without a painted bow wave which at the time was a well-thought-of bit of decorative hokum. So they got some paint and returned. With the paint they brought a couple of smoke bombs and some flags.

It was their interesting purpose to drop the bombs into the stacks just at dawn, run up the signal flags which would inquire: "Have I your permission to proceed?"

In the middle of their work a patrol boat came along and the commander of the patrol said that he intended to toss them both into the can. However, he seems to have been a reasonable creature. When they explained their idea he became enthusiastic in its favor. He ordered his crew to assist in the painting.

There, unfortunately, the great plan died. The bombs weren't set off, the flags weren't hoisted, and everybody thought that the bow waves were just some official—if humorous—experiment in camouflage.

February 16, Monday. At sea. Choppy. Rainy. Cool.

Last night I could have used a blanket. I'd almost forgotten what one looked like.

When I went out on the deck at 9 o'clock the sea looked like a somewhat bluer North Atlantic. Late for breakfast I went down to Ship's Service for some coca-cola and found plenty of conversation with the gobs. They are eager for more fighting—which is an unaccountable phenomenon in youth. Most of them hope for a continuation of our luck—which they believe to have been considerable.

One of the lads invited me to come down to the engine room for the next battle. . . . That's where you really see a naval action, he said. And I'm about willing to believe him though not yet willing to parboil in that hole while listening to the roar of a battle that I can't see. It's like being a broiled blind man.

Judging from my morning below decks, the morale on this ship is high, the attitude toward further conflict—as you might expect after an initiation such as ours—is that of veterans. You notice a contrast for instance between the attitude of the old officers and five new ensigns who reached Honolulu from Annapolis just in time for this trip. They've been sleeping in spots where sundry portions of the night watch walk over them and they don't get much rest or peace of mind. To them each rush of feet is an air-raid alarm, each clatter of iron a bomb.

My day so far, however, has not been entirely wasted. I have learned the derivation of the phrase "scuttle butt." I knew that in the Navy it means the same as bull, grapevine, gossip, but what I didn't know is that it takes its name from the actual scuttle butt— a water tap where everybody congregated and, presumably, exchanged gossip—the old Town Pump idea.

All hands were ordered to quarters immediately after luncheon. Everybody except Hailey and me stood at attention while division commanders harangued them about something we couldn't determine. We suspected it was another pep talk. I went back to the cabin to read in bed. I didn't have much success at it although the book *Midway to Murder* by Margaret Tayler Yates, a Navy wife, is very good—and timely. My eyes are burning and I'm so dopey I can hardly hold my head up.

One of the yeomen came in and asked for my transportation order. I gave it to him. Wonder what would happen if it turned out to be not all right. They could hardly put me ashore at this spot, and they've got enough mugs scrubbing floors and peeling potatoes without me.

The news today is run of the mill.

Blanche Bates died. Jehovah's Witnesses are suing somebody because they weren't allowed to bury Judge Rutherford in his own back yard. Most of the British and Australian troops seem to have got out of Singapore and moved to Sumatra. The Russians are closing in on Smolensk. Cairo reports a slight victory in Libya! Hooray.

The navigator says that the weather is unlikely to get any better as we roll along. Well, nobody hears me kicking. The ship is still hot to the touch from the month we spent on the equator.

Evening. Dive-bombing practice this afternoon was fairly good. As on yesterday we trailed a mat about a quarter of a mile astern and planes from the carrier came over and worked on it with small bombs and machine guns. The target was small, well submerged and tossed up very little white water, so it wouldn't have been surprising if the pilots aloft had failed to see it at all. But they saw, all right. The first came down from 10,000 feet on what was practically a plumb line. His bomb fixed up the mat so it was even less of a target thereafter. None of the divers missed by a margin that would have been comfortable for anybody on a ship in the place where the mat was.

It was interesting to see how the crew of this ship banked all over the stern on life rafts, ladders, masts and the tops of turrets. They were a sober and critical group. Yesterday wild bombing, indicating just how far a diver could miss his target, gave them considerable encouragement. Today's not so much.

Meantime we've been getting a battle drill in preparation for a possible meeting with the Jap fleet. . . . Possible! We should, with reason, hope for better intelligence this time than we had before, but you never can tell.

It was just about a year ago that I was besieging the British in Alexandria in an attempt to get a ride with the Mediterranean fleet. I wonder what would have happened if at that time I could have looked ahead a year to see this. I wonder if I had a chance to look forward a year right now, would I dare to do it. The answer is No.

Just over the horizon somewhere is the *President Hayes* on which I came home from Bombay to New York. That, of course, means a convoy to somewhere. She is being escorted by a task force working somewhere to the south of us.

Knowing these simple facts you could get up a good case for the possible re-occupation of Wake and maybe Guam. You could set up a good case and convince nobody—including yourself. But the fact that the idea at the moment is thoroughly fantastic makes me wonder more and more what we are going to do with a shipload of marines.

The clock went back another hour tonight. It's still very cold.

I had a long discussion with the navigator today about why you lose a day at the 180th meridian and he finally gave me an explanation that will let me go to sleep tonight. The baffling part of the trick lies in the fact that ships change time at midnight. If that were not the case, say that I came to the hour of midnight on Saturday when I was still ten minutes' sailing time away from the 180th meridian. I should then be out of Saturday and into Sunday. But in ten minutes I should arrive at the date line and be out of Sunday and into Monday. It's simpler to lump the whole thing and jump right from Saturday to Monday—or is it?

The navigator told me about a woman to whom all this was painstakingly explained on a transport.

"I get it," she said. "When we get to the international date line I shall turn my watch back twenty-four hours."

February 17, Tuesday. At sea. Cool. Bright. Choppy. Rolling a little. A beautiful day.

The turning on of the lights (because somebody had forgotten to turn the switch in this cabin after blackout last night) and the routine call to general quarters got me up at 5:30 and I couldn't go back to sleep. Went down to breakfast. Learned that we are progressing without any revision of orders. However the mysterious transport seems to be out of our calculations. She's aground somewhere—or was this morning. The other task force, of course, will stick around to guard her.

After breakfast I went to Ship's Service to buy a new fountain pen and there ran into Sergeant Tim O'Donoghue of the Marines. With him I took a trip back to CPO quarters for a cup of coffee and spent a couple of pleasant if not hilarious hours. Sergeant Hughes came in—he is a typical Marine sergeant, looks as if he might have come right out of *What Price Glory*, and we talked about the broad world as it existed in the days when there were only minor wars in it. But mostly we talked of China. He was there during Chang Tsu Lin's operations and his reminiscences were boisterous.

Hughes's best story had to do with an Army truck driver who ran over a Chinese soldier. After much palaver the Chinese army presented a bill for $500 which was duly paid.

"I never knew this to be done before," said Hughes. "But I guess it's true what they say about Chinese being honest. They sent back $150. They said the lad who was killed hadn't been a very good soldier to start off with."

31

ENCOURAGING ACK-ACK

FEBRUARY 17 (*Continued*). At 10 o'clock we got word that we would have ack-ack practice at 10:15. According to this plan the carrier would toss up a time-fuse shell and we would fire at the burst. So I climbed to the searchlight platform and managed to keep from cracking my skull on the big bell. It was a beautiful day, cool, almost windless.

On schedule the carrier tossed up its shell. Our five-inch guns pushed up four shots to starboard—not too far away from the target, not too close—a fair-to-middling ack-ack performance but definitely unspectacular.

The next target shell burst off port and the first shot of our battery exploded squarely in the middle of the smoke puff it had left. I may record here and now that in all my years of attention to ack-ack artillery this was the first target shot I had ever seen.

For the third act the other ships fired wide and we sent up a couple of duds.

During all of this we were in a fine, stately column—cruisers, carrier, tanker, with destroyers roaming about on the sides, close in to avoid splinters. Our stern, I noticed, was unprotected.

The fourth target burst was to port. The carrier fired a couple of her own guns for a close, neat pattern. But our No. 2 gun tore squarely into it—a second target. Believe it or not, a second target. Dark brown gooney birds—a small edition of the northern albatross—were romping about us. They were airily unconcerned about our shooting.

There was another try off to starboard. One shot was quite bad, about fifty mils off in deflection and completely out of range. Somebody, remembering the patrol-boat battle at Wotje, said that our favorite destroyer must be shooting. . . . Red tracers, like Roman-candle balls, travel with our five-inch shells. They are very pretty but they have a cockeyed trajectory which, I hope, bears no resemblance at all to that of the projectile.

In a spot like this on a calm day with no reprisals, you get a chance to study ack-ack dispassionately. What you notice first is the complete silence in all the early stages of the procedure—the yellow flash from the carrier's gun; the report isn't loud enough to be heard over the dull pulsation of the engines. Then a burst spreading out mysteriously black over the light blue satin of the sky. And only seconds later do we hear the *plop-plop* of the bursts. Then, of course, we hear our own guns. No difficulty about that— and we feel the concussion of them in our diaphragms. We cheer for the target shots and we find excuses for the other kind. Ack-ack the world over is about the same—the waste shots are always too low or behind, never too high or ahead.

The carrier next threw a high dud to starboard. From the flash of the gun we knew it had gone almost straight up. We waited interminably and in silence for the burst that didn't come. Then we spent other seconds in a useless study of the horizon to see it splash. There wasn't any splash. Apparently it stayed up there.

The next target was high and to starboard. The carrier's following shots were bad. Two others, from the other cruiser or one of the destroyers, were close. Our shot was almost a third target— closer than any of the others. The range was so long that the *bump-bump* of the bursts came back to us like the barely audible slam of a barn door in the next block. So far this has been an amazing lot of shooting.

The final test burst from the carrier was high and off port. The other cruiser fired first and came close but to the right. We fired next and covered the fading black of the original puff with a thicker, richer cloud—our third target of the day. I'd never have believed it possible.

That finished the practice. Our column of ships did a sort of squads right and we began to spread out over the tumbling blue Pacific again. Lieutenant Brewer seemed quite cheered as he ordered the gun crews to unload and return ammunition to cases. I must confess that I feel a little more optimistic about the future. The safety factor appears to have been greatly improved.

The noon news told of the evacuation and burning of the oil port of Palambang, a submarine attack on the S.O. station at Aruba in the Caribbean 700 miles from the canal, another retreat in Burma fifty miles from the railway that serves the Burma Road, and a new attack in preparation against MacArthur's troops on the Bataan Peninsula. . . . Bad news forever.

At 1:15 I got inveigled into the engine room to see a test of Commander Kobey's fire and steam-fighting suit. It is a grotesque affair of asbestos contrived on the lines of a diving suit and labeled the "Man From Mars." It turned out to be an interesting contraption and effective in such conditions as are likely to obtain should the enemy sock a tin-fish into a steam line. But somehow you can't get up much enthusiasm for a show like this when you stand in 150 degrees of heat and feel your eyeballs hardening like over-boiled eggs. We cheered loudly when—minus the oxygen-breathing apparatus which wouldn't work—a man in the heatproof armor went to work against a jet of live steam. Then we beat it out of there, just as enthusiastically, for the chilly upper world where, no doubt, we contracted pneumonia.

Completely exhausted by this or something else, I slept a couple of hours and, much refreshed, dashed down to a dinner which seems worth mentioning: Welsh rabbit, toast, roast pork, apple-sauce, potatoes, corn on cob, dressing, gravy, banana-cream cake, coffee.

We must be getting somewhere near the equator or else our cooks are losing their sense of direction. One equator, one roast of pork—that's the way it always goes.

Talk at dinner was desultory and totally unserious. . . . About the loveliness of Rio and the scintillant sunsets off the delta of the Amazon. There is a thin moon tonight. The captain looked at it with considerable pleasure. Six days from now, he says significantly, it will be at the quarter. And it won't be lingering in the sky to bother us at sunrise.

Hailey contributed the brightest jape at dinner. To a place at the foot of our table came Crowley whose planes haven't been off the catapult since the day after we left. "Fine," said Hailey. "All the passengers down here together."

Subs were reported in our neighborhood about 9 P.M.—picked up by the detector on one of the cans I suppose. There was some suspense for an hour but by that time the submarines, if any, had been left behind. We are still traveling at the most economical speed, and at that speed we must be, let us say, cautious. We aren't exactly a setup for the subs but we aren't outdistancing them much if they come at us from the stern when we aren't looking.

The evening is cool and comfortable. I could sleep under a blanket if I had one. With another hour in that boiler room I'd be looking for one of those eiderdown sleeping bags that were so popular up in the Yukon territory two months, or was it 200 years ago. . . .

At sea 1500 miles west of Honolulu somewhere near the 180th meridian. (The navigator says we'll stumble over it sometime tonight.)

This is another bright and beautiful day. I was grateful for the pounding of feet in the flat overhead (which is a gun position) and the slamming of a distant punch press (which is an automatic loading device) because they woke me. With blacked-out ports it's no trouble sleeping forever. You get used to routine noises and it's always night.

I got down in time for some toast and heard that the pompoms were going to have some target practice shooting at a sock towed by one of the planes. Hailey and I went up on top and saw beautiful maneuvering by a lot of Voughts flying about like a trey of clubs. On deck we found the doctor also keeping a vigil. He had heard somewhere that a lot of big planes were coming to look at us from Honolulu. They were due at 9 o'clock but they didn't come. I sat for a long time watching the lazy angling of the carrier as she headed into the wind and the wallowing of the tanker unable to keep up with her.

The Voughts landed and we went into the wardroom. There we heard that the Honolulu planes had come out after us yesterday, and, having failed to find us, had gone home again. Crowley was the source of this information. He thought some others would be out—probably from Midway—toward which, by the way, we seem to be making only indifferent progress.

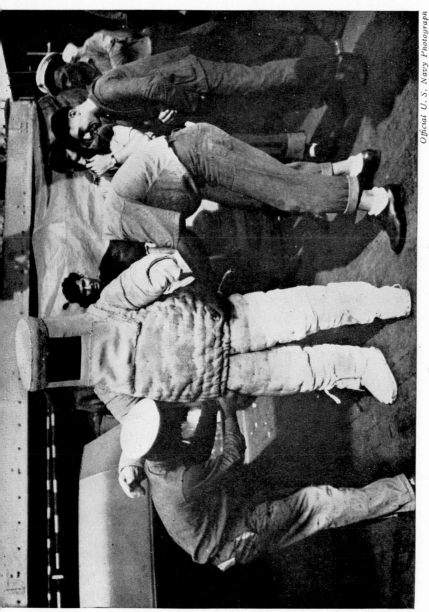

"THE MAN FROM MARS"

Commander Kobey's fire and steam-fighting suit. "It's got everything but air conditioning," says the lucky gob who gets a chance to try it out on a sweltering day.

ANTIAIRCRAFT MACHINE-GUN BATTERY AT BATTLE STATIONS

Members of an antiaircraft machine-gun battery at battle stations after repelling a Japanese bomber in an attempted suicide plunge on a U.S.N.

Official U. S. Navy Photograph

We drank a couple of quarts of coffee while Crowley discussed progress in aviation. He told us pointedly of an aged monk in Santa Barbara whom he had once visited on the trail of an aviation improvement.

"He was a very nice old guy and a learned scientist," he said. "But he was totally detached from the world. The gadgets he had devised were practical all right. He had developed them all without a bit of help from anybody and they represented about as fine a job of constructive thinking as I've ever seen. But some of his devices had been used by Germany in lighter-than-air ships shortly after the last war—a balancing system with movable weights in it. All of his ideas were sound. They were only theoretical with him but, although he didn't know it, every one of them had had practical demonstration. The only trouble with him was that he developed them twenty years after somebody else developed them. . . . And he did it all by himself—without any help whatever!"

How like so many of us who spend our days inventing new kinds of horseweights and buggy whips.

About 11:00 the PBY's came over, interrupting the pompom practice. The captain came up to our coop while we were investigating all this. He had a story from somewhere that the Japs are running out of gasoline. . . . One hopes. One certainly does hope.

At 2 o'clock we had a little practice for the pompoms. A five-inch gun threw out a shell and the pompoms fired at the burst. The less said about this undertaking the better.

At 2:45 there was another attempt. The pompoms finally got a shot into the burst. Some 1921 machine guns were, unfortunately, doing better.

There was quite a spectacle ahead—gray weather closing in, gray ships darkening against it, all in line as far as the misty horizon, the carrier wreathed in smoke of its own firing. Puffs dotted the sky off to the starboard with wisps of cloud drifting over them. Noise of firing came back dimly like echoes of Fourth of July at Cubs Park.

At 2:55 we fired again, a high burst in the clouds. The pompoms went after it hopefully. But we who live in the prospect of attacks by planes draw little consolation. The weather mercifully put an end to this exhibition.

I am not certain yet where we are headed for, now. Midway is behind us. Possibly we go to Eniwetok which seems to be on the northeastern curl of the Caroline group. We were headed for there once before.

When I went out onto the deck just before the blackout I discovered that the hue and cry was on for one of the carrier's aviators. He had gone away into a very bad lot of weather and while he was supposed to be close at hand he was making no progress finding us. We, in the meantime, had come too close to enemy territory to turn the radio loose. So every ship in the formation began to make smoke. The black clouds strung out through the gray clouds like a ribbon woven through lace, and eventually they came into the lost pilot's vision. We got a wigwag report from the carrier. I dare say it's unofficial: "He says he's glad to get back."

There was some comment at dinner on a report from the West Coast that the *Shaw*—whose bow was blasted off in Pearl Harbor— had arrived for repairs. She had come in under her own steam with a temporary bridge and a false front.

"The *Shaw*," announced the executive officer in a fair imitation of a commentator's lead, "came into Mare Island navy yard today to take a bow."

32

PALAVER IN THE FACE OF DEATH

FEBRUARY 19, *Thursday*. We have just crossed the date line so there isn't any February 19, Thursday. Some day I shall take time off to think what I might have done with it.

Meantime:

February 20, Friday. At sea. Clear. Bright. Beautiful. There is a noticeable swell.

I open this day's notes with an observation on the uncertain quality of news even when it originates in so close a corporation as this and is distributed through so confined an area as a ship. For example our lost aviators: They haven't been recovered—at least they were still at large at midnight last night. So it was impossible that the pilot could have made the observations brightly wigwagged from the carrier—or reported to have been wigwagged. There is a revised version of the incident which may turn out to be more reliable. It seems we did put out the smoke and that it didn't do any good. At 9 P.M. there was an end to all news of the lost plane. The fleet had altered course toward the spot where they'd been last heard from. This maneuver was not so grandiose as one might suppose inasmuch as we have a lot of time to kill in this neighborhood anyway.

The pilot of the plane flashed the carrier that he was in trouble along about 6:15. A radio was uncorked long enough to answer him with information that he seemed to be about 75 miles away. Thereafter he didn't signal the carrier any more but he carried on a conversation with one of his back-seat associates who apparently was an officer with no particular knowledge of aviation or how you worked the switch on the radio.

The officer, in talking with the pilot over the interphone, had pushed the wrong button so that the conversation went out onto the air and we picked it up:

"How much gas have you left?"

"Fifteen gallons."

"How far will that take us?"

(Answer unintelligible.)

"What kind of a thing is this radio beam?"

(Answer unintelligible.)

The pilot: "Do you want to go down now while we still have some light and power or see how close we can get before we fall in?"

The officer: "I think we'd better try to get a little closer, anyway."

After that there was no further conversation. The ships turned toward the position indicated by the radio and steamed a hundred miles. At 11 o'clock they turned back on their course. The hunt, temporarily at least, was over. We went to bed repeating the last message from the bridge: Maybe we can pick them up tomorrow. Maybe tomorrow. . . . Maybe.

Well, to return to other matters, I got up early today to look at the ack-ack fire drill scheduled for 7:30 A.M. But there wasn't any. Somebody had called off the whole business to put the planes to better use looking for the lost aviators.

About 8:00 the navigator came down to breakfast with encouraging news. He reported that an SBD plane had come back from early-morning patrol and had dropped a message on the deck of the carrier. Immediately thereafter a can steamed off over the horizon. He believed that the lads had been located.

Lieutenant Commander Kobey was philosophical over the whole business.

"We've got to be practical about this matter of lost aviators," he said. "Even if we are too calloused to get upset about a couple of men dying out there in a rubber boat, we ought to get a defense worker's urge to save a valuable product for the country. It costs about $40,000 to train an aviator at Pensacola. And by the time one of them qualifies to fly planes off a carrier the government has an investment of about $100,000 in him—what with crackups, spare parts, and all. . . ."

We left the discussion there while the destroyer went out looking for the $100,000 investment, not counting such dubious assets as might have been contained in the person of the accompanying officer. If you add in the expense of a trip through Annapolis I guess the total would justify a rescue expedition as big as the one they had for Amelia Earhart.

The weather continues beautiful and cool beyond description. Commander Chappell came out of the wardroom, looked at it, and recalled the ancient chestnut that used to be emblazoned over the dock of the Catalina Island boats at Wilmington: "In all the world no trip like this."

From all I can gather this expedition is going to be about four times as murderous as the one from which we recently returned. There isn't so much as a rowboat left in Pearl Harbor. Four carriers are on the prowl. Two or three sets of cruisers are slipping about in waters south of us. We are apparently about to move in on the Carolines in a sort of pincers movement. We have been more like professionals on this trip than on the last. We have less precautionary restriction for the sake of caution alone. It is obvious for instance that if we were to meet a sub out here it would be only by the merest accident. And if we were to meet him under circumstances that would permit his damaging us it would show that the law of averages had quit work. So, for instance, we showed some lights last night while looking for the lost plane. On the other hand our carefree chatter over the radio—such as that which made our stay off Samoa so notable and uncertain—has been completely cut out. We move in silence like the night.

Commander Howeth, the communications officer, is the ship's most pathetic victim of the international date line. Today if there had been any today would have been his birthday. He howled picturesquely as so many owners of lost birthdays have done before him.

There's some news that the Japs attacked Port Darwin with seventy-two twin-engined bombers. Apparently there's a great to-do about it, although what anybody could do to Darwin to make it worse than it was to begin with I can't at the moment say.

The Japs still seem to be active about Sumatra but their progress is slow. MacArthur apparently is taking another beating on the Bataan Peninsula.

The machine guns and pompoms began to sound off at 11

o'clock. This, I gathered, was the 7:30 A.M. performance that I had lost my sleep to observe. So I wasn't enthusiastic about it. I saw only about four runs and the white sock flying in the wake of the SBD plane seemed to be at no time in any danger.

It was a fairly interesting spectacle, however. Off to the starboard the plane would maneuver for altitude and then the sock would seem to be totally independent of it, streaking across the blue at right angles to the plane's course, diving sometimes when the plane sloped upward, fluttering weirdly when a cross wind found it with the tow-rope slack.

Our rosary of tracer bullets never came near the target while I was looking at it, though the navigator said that the pompoms had done well on a couple of runs. For my money the ancient Lewis gun still looks pretty good.

At lunch some of the official scuttle butt indicated that the firing on the whole had been definitely ungood. However Brewer and Tyree took some consolation from the tendency of the gunners to see their own errors. "You learn to shoot right by shooting wrong," said the gunnery officer, "or maybe not."

Well, there was some good news to brighten the day. A can signaled that she had picked up the floating fliers and was coming back to formation with them. They will be returned to the carrier on the occasion of some fueling program maybe. Or, possibly, they may have the dubious pleasure of rolling around on a can for the remainder of this expedition.

Of course this note—as is the case with so many others in this record—is based on such information as happens to be at hand. It is totally within the possibilities that the lads are still out there in their little rubber boat—no less a possibility that they never were in an airplane and never reported themselves lost and never fell into the broad blue drink at all. One gets skeptical.

All hands were summoned to flight quarters at 1 P. M. to catapult three planes and then were chased back. We aren't straining our planes much this trip. Crowley, who will probably survive everything that the Japs can throw at him, didn't seem to care much. Brewer says he has plenty of water in his plane and a few arrangements for sailing it backwards to San Francisco if he should be forced down. And Brewer says he'll get there, too.

I suggested that all one of the SOC's needed was an anchor. And I found out that the Navy had been ahead of me. These lively crates that stand still in a twenty-five-mile wind came completely equipped with a fifty-pound anchor. Nobody seems to know what for.

Since first I came onto this ship back in the dim reaches of time when the Japs were still sitting serenely on their atolls in the Southwest Pacific I have found out that sleep is difficult. The program makers try to provide something every minute—from lunar rainbows to funerals at sea. So I was not surprised at all when the navigator came in during the afternoon and announced that we'd be having some more ack-ack practice at 2:45. . . .

Well, I got out of my carpet slippers and into my shoes. It's hardly worth mentioning the rest of it save for the fact that I've wasted a couple of paragraphs on preliminaries. I got into my shoes. I climbed to the top of the foremast. I put cotton in my ears. I looked at my watch. I went below and bought two coca-colas. For this, it seems, was a drill in "dry firing"—noiseless gunnery which I first attended with simulated cotton in my ears and then with the simulated presence of the ears. Actually I had taken them back to the wardroom where there is a fine chair with deep cushions.

I brought back with me from the soda fountain one thought: The lads in the Jap ships aren't trooping down from drill to buy chocolate ice cream. They are probably on a strict diet of dried fish and rice which they cook for themselves on deck.

The ice cream on this ship compares very favorably with any that I've had on the mainland. Captain Cobb of the Marines (he has charge of Ship's Service) told me that he had captured a load of "mix" intended for the Royal Hawaiian before it was taken over. It's far and away better than any I've ever had outside of such places as Kranz's, Fred Harvey's or the Drake. It costs a dime for two scoops (a helping called a "gee-dunk") and no matter how far from payday there is no lack of business at the fountain.

The ship's store, adjoining the fountain, is open less frequently but does an important business. Its stock is limited—cigarettes mostly—soap, shaving materials, writing paper, toilet articles and sometimes canned goods and candy.

5 P.M. The plan of the day has just been brought in. It con-

firms the rescue news, incidentally establishing the fact that there had been an accident and that somebody had to be rescued. It also revealed that three men instead of two had remained out on the broad bosom of the Pacific all night. Here is the intelligence: "(2) The task-force commander was pleased to inform the task force that the three men lost yesterday in one of the carrier's planes were safely recovered by one of the destroyers and returned safely aboard the carrier."

There is a significant item cautioning everybody against wearing hat bands bearing the names of ships. History repeats itself only this time it is the chief of the bureau of navigation who sends this note and he can hardly be talking about H.M.S. *Malaya*.

Dinner conversation was placid—had to do mostly with the leadership and tactics of the Civil War. In the middle of it Crowley pricked up his ears. He thought he'd heard the sound of shooting. We went outside but were unable to trace any shots—although one of the cans might have let off a few as they frequently do. Thus you arrive at an interesting situation. Here you are aboard a super-blooper man-of-war and you can't tell whether or not a battle is going on because the radio is making too much racket.

It was pretty hot in the wardroom. . . . Maybe we've begun to turn south. From now on possibly we'll be able to give a little attention to the battle concerning which we've heard so much since we left Pearl Harbor.

33

ENEMY AIRCRAFT APPROACHING

FEBRUARY 21, *Saturday.* At sea somewhere near Wake Island.
The sea is rolling a bit, as you can tell when you try to spoon
your soup, but to the eye it is as calm as a sea could be. In all my
life I have never seen more glorious days than these. It is difficult to
think that the war lies just around the corner. So most of us probably don't think of it.

I got up rather earlier than usual after a fretful sleep and went
aft to the top of a gun turret to watch the dive-bombing exercises.
It was a dreamy, beautiful scene across the gray bulk of our stern
and beyond that across an empty sea to an empty horizon, depthless
planes of varying blue with a vague smear across the middle where
the "light brown haze" from our funnels lay in the still air.

The dive bombers are getting to be pretty good. They no
longer glide in as if they were trying to make a landing. Nowadays
they come down vertically and are almost on top of the target when
they level off. The gunnery officers are complaining that they are
cutting up too many of our mats.

I don't know what the practice is with the Japs, Germans,
Italians, French, Dutch, or what have you, but it is something of a
novelty for me to ride out to the wars (accompanied by a shipload
of veterans) to have shell fire every day in addition to the regular
drill, a sort of unending dress rehearsal. Battle is going to be only
another bit of extra work when we finally get around to it.

From scraps of conversation about the ship I gather that we are
doing something on a reasonably large scale—at any rate our performance is a portion of a big operation. One of the big English
liners is due in San Francisco tomorrow and there is some talk
about transporting 72,000 troops. It is, of course, too much to hope

that they'd be sending a sizable relief to MacArthur. Probably I shall learn more of this later. The thicker the hush-hush the sooner you work through it and the more questions you ask the more you learn.

We had a little excitement just before noon. One of the destroyers came tearing across our course so fast she looked as if she might be ready to take off. But what had looked to be a periscope was really a glass ball—about as big as a two-quart fish globe—of the sort used by the Jap fishermen to float their nets. The Pacific is filled with them.

This, by the way, is an anniversary. It was a year ago today that I boarded H.M.S. *Valiant* at Ras-el-Tin on a job like this one. I mention it without comment.

Among the bits of intelligence received at noon was a message so important that it was delivered to the executive officer in tape form as he sat at lunch. Three aviators lost by the carrier on our first trip (Jan. 16) have been picked up on Pukapuka. And that of course arouses surges of memory: Would it be possible that Frisbie, who wrote *The Book of Puka-Puka*, is still there, and if so is he as screwy as he was in the old days? And are the natives as fantastic now as they were when he saw them—or were they ever as fantastic as when he saw them? It's too much of a strain for a dreamy afternoon. But I wish I could contrive an interview with those fliers when we get back to Pearl Harbor.

Some more fair news came in the official dispatches this afternoon. It seems that the *Lexington*—we think it was the *Lexington*—operating with a task force south of ours sent out planes to meet a Jap bomber force near our old playground at Wotje. Eighteen of thirty enemy planes were shot down.

You don't have to have much additional information about that to know what happened. Somebody came down from the radio room of the *Lexington* and mentioned with excusable excitement that he had just spotted a mass of planes, about seventy-five or eighty miles away headed in a southeasterly direction. And you don't need any moving pictures to show you how the fighters took off immediately, formed their wedges in the sky and rode off on their quest.

You could do with a little detail from the Japanese, maybe. It would be nice to know how the commander of that force felt when suddenly out of the sun forty U.S. planes began to streak down on top of him. . . . Surprise! Surprise!

Lieutenant Hawkins drew a highly consoling picture from such materials as he had at hand regarding the Jap war effort against us. Their fliers go to Rangoon and get knocked out of the air by American Volunteers who have set the ratio of one P-40 for seventeen Japs. They bomb one of our cruisers in the Marshalls and as a result of the operation lose thirty-one planes when they re-arm. They try to bomb the carrier and three, possibly five out of six heavy bombers are destroyed. They go out on some mission with thirty bombers probably to restock one of the atolls we smashed up, and more than half of them are shot down before they know they're in a fight. Lieutenant Hawkins thinks that by this time even a Jap ought to know that he's not getting the right kind of service out of his material.

At the moment we are about 170 degrees east latitude and almost on the Tropic of Cancer. That puts us northeast of Wake.

The navigator says we have been following a fairly straight course with none of the coy maneuvering that marked our last effort. But he says we lost nearly a day looking for the floating aviators from the carrier. Also, for the record, we lost a day by crossing the international date line.

The evening's news, while not anything to make the people light bonfires and dance in the streets, was at least not discouraging. Darwin got it again yesterday. Flame throwers are being hauled up for use against MacArthur. There are signs of a major offensive shaping up in Java. American troops are landing in Java. There are signs that we are getting an army on its way somewhere off the Pacific coast. Meantime you get shreds of rumor from the communicators who get it the same way that a major battle is being fought off the end of Sumatra and on the tip of Java—air, land and sea. . . . At any rate we haven't lost that one yet.

The Japs announced over Tokio radio tonight that they had sunk the USS *Houston* with Admiral Hart aboard. There are circumstances which indicate that this may be true.

February 22, Sunday. At sea. Morning cool. Bright. Calm. A gray rain was falling by noon.

I woke to the noise of a can coming alongside and the clamor of men on our decks setting up a rig to transfer mail or something.

Went below and stumbled upon one of the oddest accidents in a somewhat full experience.

It seems that one of the eager young men on the can had been assigned to shoot a line over to us with a handgun, a contraption like a short rifle powered with a forty-five caliber, seventy-grain shell. The rifle throws a slug about eight inches long to which a heavy cord is attached.

I've been watching the working of these gadgets since first we left Pearl Harbor in January. And at the risk of looking like a hind-sighted prophet—or a diarist—I must say that I've been expecting something to happen. A slug of steel eight inches long and half an inch thick is going to make a hole in something if it hits. . . . And today was the day. . . .

The lad on the can aimed this contrivance at the passageway across our deck behind the washroom amidships and let go. The slug cleared everything except a sailor who had just turned the corner on the port side. It hit him in the face just below the left eye, went through him and out at the back of his neck, threading a cord behind it.

The sailor of course was extremely lucky not to have been killed on the spot. But he is still on the edge of the grave. The doctor is much worried. As well he might be.

The morning news says that the Japs have landed at Bali and that the battle for Java is definitely on. The British seem to be holding Burma, thanks to a definite air superiority. MacArthur is taking a bombardment of incendiary shells but there's no change in his situation from that of a week ago.

Foster Hailey and I were invited to luncheon with the captain at 12:30.

So at the appointed hour we strolled into Captain Zacharias' quarters and got on with our meal amid merry quip and jest. The weather was turning a bit sour. It had rained off and on for a couple of hours and there was a noticeable swell. But there was no more indication of trouble than usual. You more or less expect hell to break loose at mealtimes. . . .

At 12:40 Donald Duck squawked an order for flight quarters. . . . "Man all stations to launch aircraft."

The captain was just a little puzzled. He got up, went to the interphone and asked the bridge what had come up. The bridge said that the order was from the admiral. You could see that he was a little anxious about the situation. He explained to us that the weather was bad and that launching would be difficult because two of the planes had been launched inboard, out of the blast of the five-inch guns. We suggested that we postpone luncheon until the job was finished and for a moment he seemed to think it was a good idea. . . . However he figured out that it would take some time to get the engines warmed up. We could go on eating until that time—possibly as far as dessert.

There was an excellent lamb curry which we had disposed of down to the final bit of chutney before any of the plane motors showed signs of life. The captain congratulated himself.

"Good thing we waited," he said. "We can have our dessert probably before they get the catapult swung out. It's baked apple and very well contrived. . . ."

The waiter brought the baked apple with some thick cream and a large helping of coffee and we forgot the lowering skies that muffled the portholes. I was just about to put a spoon into the apple before me when Donald Duck took over once more. He seemed hysterical:

"Enemy aircraft approaching at 220 degrees. . . ."

So we stood up just as the bugle sounded and the gun crews began their heavy-footed stampede up the iron ladders to battle stations. The captain disappeared. I went to my room, picked up my tin hat and life jacket and climbed up to the searchlight platform. Below me all visible decks were filled with eager, laughing kids. They waved at me as if seeing me for the first time since I came aboard at Pearl Harbor, shouting "Good luck" and "Here we go again!" You got the idea all right that these kids were spoiling for a fight. . . . It's a fine game blasting the enemy to bits, particularly if you can live long enough to see it done. . . . And furthermore! Who was that goddam gunnery officer who was so snotty about the shooting of the pompoms and the fifty calibers yesterday? . . . Well, there was going to be some more artillery practice right away. And maybe he'd like to see some of that! Maybe he'd like to stand around and be shown!

From our perch on the foremast where Hailey presently joined me it looked as if the fleet were strewn all over the Pacific. The other cruiser had been nursing when we went to luncheon. Now she was nowhere to be seen. Nor was the tanker. You figured they might be somewhere out there under a black smudge on the gray horizon. But there was no telling.

All the observation apparatus at the gun positions was turned toward a 220-degree bearing whence the enemy plane was supposed to be coming. A couple of our planes snapped off the catapults. I don't know what for. Lieutenant Brewer at the observation post for the secondary battery told the telephone that three SOC's were now aloft. After that came silence and another of those fantastic waits.

The plane reported by the carrier is probably a patrol craft from Wake, unarmed and slow, an enemy of no particular significance to us save for what reports it may be able to relay to its base before somebody knocks it down. If it gets close enough to take inventory of us before we sink it, that cuts it! They'll know we're in the vicinity. They'll be sitting up waiting for us with everything they've got.

1:15. The wind up here is about 50 knots and cold. I sit in the so-called lee of the mast and try to keep from rolling off the platform the while I think of the baked apple with my spoon in it.

We swing and angle until it looks as if we intend to run each other down. The other cruiser and the tanker are coming up out of the muck—gray ghosts on the foggy horizon ahead.

1:20. The rain has stopped and the sun is plentiful but there are still heavy cloud banks covering the sky and wooly patches of black dead ahead. No planes as yet have gone up from the carrier which we now can see vaguely over to starboard and astern. Maybe the entire defense action is to be fought by our SOC's crawling like beetles over what we can see of the sky.

1:25. A new cry goes up. Some object seems to be a plane at 330 degrees. The main director swings around and somebody takes a look through the range finder. April fool! It's a meteorological balloon—a hell of a long way from home.

1:28. All personnel engaged in launching or landing of planes ordered back to stations immediately. We get ready to toss off another one.

1:30. Plane reported 220 degrees, very high. Almost immediately it turns out to be another balloon and the gun crews settle back moodily on their heels. The marines at the pompoms are outspoken in their belief that the balloons are Jap balloons and that their presence indicates something pretty sinister.

The ships of the fleet dodge and switch and cavort. The wakes of half a dozen of them cross and blend like waving peacocks' tails over the dirty blue. And here is a startling picture. We are headed one way and the carrier is headed in the same direction on our starboard. Streaking in the opposite direction and bearing squarely down on top of us come the tanker and a couple of cans with all the speed the tanker can put out. They pass between us and the carrier with much agitation such as wigwagging and the hoisting of signal flags. The soiled brown gooney birds ride gaily in the slicks that they've left over the choppy sea. In a moment we are all moving away from one another on courses like the spokes of a wheel.

1:40. And while you're contemplating this phenomenon some more signals go up on the carrier's yard. Mr. Brewer and Captain Cobb do a bit of telephoning and on the steel balconies beneath you can see the reluctant gunners putting the hoods back on the guns. Secure! This excellent performance has been the result of a false alarm.

We went below. The captain remained on the bridge to send off the fourth of our planes. The sea was getting rougher and grayer.

About 2:10. Captain Zacharias came down from the bridge and we took up the baked apple where we had left it. There was no explanation for our battle scare save that the carrier probably had picked up the trail of an SOC launched from a cruiser earlier.

The captain said that we'd not be dropping in on Eniwetok this trip. Tomorrow we'll be able to take a running jump at our objective which in this instance turns out to be Wake. The other units of the fleet apparently have been put to some job other than raiding atolls. I suspect a lot of them are working with transport convoys to Australia and the East.

By the time the captain had arrived the ship was sizzling with a report received in CPO quarters that the Japanese had been given a considerable licking in their attempt to land on Bali.

A check on several bulletins produced a variety of items in the casualty list but it is apparent that sixteen Japanese ships were affected by the attack, one cruiser was blown up, two destroyers were sunk, damage was done to several transports. That much appears to be certain.

From Batavia comes a report that one cruiser was blown up, two others sunk less spectacularly, two damaged and left in a sinking condition, four destroyers sunk, eight transports and tenders sunk.

Some Jap transports aren't much bigger than sampans and observers have a way of mistaking ships of no great importance for cruisers. But making all allowances it appears to have been a bad day for the Son of Heaven. The Japs can't take a beating of this sort forever. I'm not sure what their cruiser strength was before the war but as of this date there is good reason for the belief that fifteen of their cruisers have been sunk.

We talked most of the afternoon—or what was left of it—with the captain who as usual was greatly cheered by the prospects for our side. He thinks the Japs may yet be forced to try some sculduggery against Hawaii or the Pacific coast. He hopes they do. In that event he believes we can cut them off and demolish them.

The weather went from bad to worse as we talked. By 4 P. M. the ship was rolling so we could hardly stand up. Lookouts called down that visibility was about a thousand yards and getting less. Our planes came in and kept in sight. You'd hardly blame them.

If this keeps up we'll have an ideal setup for a bombardment. But the carrier planes will get to the target and back only by instinct.

34

IF YOU'RE BORN TO BE HANGED

The night was filled with music when we went down to dinner. The Japs had sent out a radio broadcast to the effect that they had just wiped out the entire Asiatic fleet—U.S., British, Dutch. Previously they had reported the sinking of the *Houston* with Admiral Hart aboard. We're not inclined to believe this latest communiqué.

The navigator told an interesting story apropos of nothing. An Army inspector recently stopped off at Palmyra to look over some machine-gun emplacements. As he stepped ashore he was surprised to see the personnel of the principal anti-landing battery scattered all over the top of a sand dune. Angrily he asked for an explanation of why they had left their position. And they gave it to him by leading him back to the gun pit.

There had been a storm. High waves had broken over the beach and filled the emplacement with water. But that wasn't all. A shark had been blown in there with the water and he was still alive and peevish at the unusual restrictions of his new quarters.

We continue to hear yarns about December 7. Maybe it takes this long to mellow them in the memory. Maybe it takes this long to make them up. A recent one has to do with the flying fortresses that came to Honolulu on the morning of December 7 while the Japs were still attacking. Out on one end of the island is a machine-gun school whose instructors, thanks to daily practice, are pretty good. When the attack started they trained on anything that passed within range and knocked down several planes. One of the incoming fortress pilots noticed the space so carefully avoided by the visiting Japanese. He therefore went out to meet any loose Jap planes that might be in the neighborhood and lured them over the school machine guns. . . .

And I'll admit that the story doesn't sound so hot to me, either.

Crowley told of a friend of his from the carrier who started in to the naval air base that Sunday afternoon. The ack-ack went to work on him and pinked him in the leg. He went out to sea and the ack-ack of a shore station went to work on him. A wing came off and he went down. He got out his rubber boat and started to paddle in. Soldiers on the beach shot at him with machine guns. He finally saved his life by standing up on his remaining leg and waving his hat. The gunners figured that if a Jap waved his hat it wouldn't be that kind of hat.

Hailey contributed a bit he got from Colonel Flood at Wheeler Field. When the ruckus came, all the lads dashed out to planes— five lads, four planes. One pilot went after his parachute. The spare lad swiped the plane. He was shot down over Hickam Field half an hour later.

About 6:30 the roll had quit. The ship was easing along with no perceptible motion. But it was beginning to get cold. Boy! It was getting cold. I daresay we've just missed a fine storm somewhere.

Somebody in the wardroom was talking of a plot to move across the international date line eastbound on a Sunday. That would give the padre two days' work in succession.

The padre came in, heard the discussion and seemed much cheered. Then he told of his experience today with his cabin mate, one of Mr. Crowley's rebounding aviators. The padre had noticed that things always happen on Sunday, and that church services have been held when-and-if since Dec. 7, which was also a Sunday.

"It will happen again," he said to his roommate. "Church is set for one o'clock tomorrow. It is now one o'clock Saturday, courtesy of the international date line. I'll bet you that we have a general alarm within the next twenty-four hours."

The aviator accused him of being jittery and an old woman but he made the bet—a double gee-dunk—to be paid immediately after Sunday service if there should have been no alarm by one o'clock.

At five minutes to one today the lad came into the cabin where the padre was looking over the notes for his sermon.

"I'll take the gee-dunk now," he said. "It will be quicker that way and the ice cream may be all melted by the time you get through with the sermon."

"I have five minutes," said the padre. "I'll pay on time."

The aviator went out and was back in two minutes with the same argument. He kept it up for a full minute before the padre got a chance to answer. The padre looked at his watch. "I still have two minutes," he said. "But I don't think I'll need that much time. . . ." And he didn't. At one minute to one the bugles were blowing and the rush to the guns was on.

Well, tomorrow ought to bring us to the zero hour. And yet as I sit here—partly freezing, so help me—I can't get up too much enthusiasm about it. If our intelligence is correct we'll have another job of shooting fish in a barrel. And while that may be healthy practice the time is fast approaching when it will cease to be news.

Midnight. The weather is clearing a little, which helps. Good weather to work in, bad weather to run away in, I always say.

February 23, Monday. At sea. Nearing Wake Island from the northeast. Weather clear and very cold for this latitude. Sea choppy.

We're definitely on the last lap.

The captain addressed an officers' conference in the wardroom this morning and explained the program. It's the same picture as Wotje except for the geography. The planes soften up the island at fifteen minutes before dawn. We go in and bombard. If we're lucky we clean up and go home.

I don't know what happened to the task forces that were supposed to operate with us. It appears that the *Lexington's* encounter with the Jap planes tipped them off to our whereabouts in that neighborhood and changed the whole strategy. It is quite likely that the *Yorktown* which was a part of our group went south to keep the Japs from cutting over in behind the *Lexington* force. Both carriers may be out working with convoys. We probably shan't know till we get out of here.

The lad who got hit by the slug from the line gun was running a fever this morning but the doctor still thinks he will pull through. The doctor rates it all as a sort of miracle, which of course it was. The slug, instead of traveling around under the skin as previously reported, went straight through his head from below the left cheekbone to the back of his neck. It passed through veins, arteries and nerve ganglia and apparently didn't rupture any of them.

A warrant officer cut the line loose and pulled the slug out. After that the boy walked to the sick bay and retained consciousness while Dr. Hays worked on him.

There is an apocryphal bit circulating about the ship in connection with this odd accident. It originates with Chief Quartermaster Peck (who somehow doesn't stack up too well as an authentic source) but it might well be true and before this voyage is out will probably rate with the better legends of the fleet. It seems that this boy was in the camera room Saturday afternoon discussing the imminence of the new battle. Peck quotes him as having said:

"I'm not afraid of it. The only bullet that will get you is the one that's got your name on it and my name's hard to spell."

Whether or not he said it he is certainly the world's outstanding proof by example of the theory.

35

THE GIRDING OF THE LOINS

DESPITE my freezing during the night it turned out to be another lovely day—turquoise matrix sky, white-tufted, a rumbling purple sea with feathers strewn over it. Down through the hatch to starboard you could see beyond the lattice structure of the main deck to the white water scudding past. We are making fine speed but there is no sense of motion.

I talked for a time with the gobs who still seem interested in other people's troubles and wanted to know particularly what you did when dive bombers came. I told them I didn't know but that I had hopes for the pompoms. So had they, despite the battle of the sock a couple of days ago.

I went below and discovered that the captain had addressed the troops and had conveyed the intelligence that we were probably going along as an escort to the carrier. The planes would go in and destroy Wake while we lay off somewhere and got the news (presumably) over the Jap radio.

By luncheon time, however, we got word that this idea had been given up. Halsey had received some pictures—probably they were delivered by the PBY that came over us a day or so ago—and had figured out the opposition. He was now prepared to have us go in and blow the place up.

One of the gunnery lads expressed himself:

"We go in. We destroy three shore batteries and sixteen tanks like railroad tank cars on the ground and such buildings as stick up over the six-foot hill. A destroyer that we know to be there comes out shooting. After that a squadron of planes takes off from subterranean hangars and chases us, bombs dropping en route. It continues to chase us for several days during which we fire back when

213

we can get the chance. We clean up and repair the damage for two days. Then we can go down and shave."

The captain came into the wardroom at 12:45. Everybody stood up until he took his place at the head of the main table.

"Since I last spoke to you," he said, "there have been further changes in our plans. As it now stands we carry out the same operation that we carried on against Wotje. The aircraft portion of the attack will be different inasmuch as we have many more planes than we had then. I anticipate that we shall launch planes an hour before sunrise as we did before. So tonight we shall rig the planes out for launching. . . ."

Mr. Crowley asked a question about bombs. Spotting planes, it appears, were not supposed to carry them. The captain said the rigging orders would probably be received later in the day. "But we'll anticipate them. We can change details as we have to. . . .

"We are going south now and we can expect better weather all the time. I feel that this rate is enough to bring us to our objective in time to do what we propose to do. I don't anticipate much opposition but we had better be prepared."

He looked about the table and smiled as a new thought struck him: "I hope that we shall be as successful as we have been at Bali," he said. "According to news which I received at noon, between seventeen and thirty-five Japanese ships have been sunk or damaged there. It was a very fine achievement. . . .

"To get on with our work—the gunnery officer is now preparing the details. One matter that should be taken up is condition watches. . . ."

The executive contributed one on that subject:

"Everybody will be buttoned up and ready to go at 6 o'clock," he said.

Commander Tyree explained his arrangement for gun watches. The captain seemed satisfied.

"That takes care of just about everything," he said. "I shall make an announcement to the crew at 1:20. I may not give them the name of the objective. . . ." (We waited for an explanation of that bit of reticence but none came.) "I shall tell them that the operation will be the same as the one at Wotje and that we expect the same results."

The chief engineer wanted to know about lighting off eight boilers. The captain said to have them cut in at 4 o'clock. He didn't foresee likelihood of any immediate change in speed. The navigator mentioned that at noon we had been 400 miles from Wake.

"Then present speed should get us there on time," the captain calculated. "Are there any questions or suggestions?"

The doctor stood up.

"I'd like to make an announcement," he said. "If all officers without identification tags will lay to the carpenter shop this afternoon they will be supplied. And I'd like all officers to wear their identification tags on a string around their necks." There was a grim laugh at that.

"Well," said the captain. "After all this is a routine matter. Let us go about it with no undue excitement. And that will be all, gentlemen, until tomorrow."

There wasn't so much advance discussion of this fight as there had been of the last. But the gunnery officer—a smart artilleryman and a keen psychologist—contributed one that may do as a motif:

"I don't get much of a thrill out of bombarding Wake. You just naturally hate like hell to smash up your own stuff."

The second in command of the Jap air force is said to be visiting this neighborhood on a tour of inspection—our intelligence seems to be getting more diversified if not better. If he came escorted we may find a lot of planes that we didn't know were in the picture. On the other hand he may have come on a cruiser or a tender. As one lad remarked: "It is the function of the air force to gouge service out of the Army or Navy when and if possible."

I slept most of the afternoon on the theory that I may not get much sleep on the morrow. At about 5 o'clock, Lane, the mess boy, came in to roll up the rug and commit other nuisances about the cabin—nuisances looked upon with favor by the distant authorities as preparations for battle. He was personally all done up with a hard-oil polish, wrapped in fine linen, and stinking of lilac perfume—some relic of voodoo, no doubt, that bids the warrior pretty himself against the nasty dawn.

I got up somewhat dopily, took a shower and sat down to meditation upon how little you get to know about a war even when you're riding around in a cruiser in a striking force. And I recalled with great sadness the business of communiqués. We listen to these things each night and ask ourselves what proportion may be true. They have been mostly of a pattern—the Russian, German, Japanese, British-Libyan, British-Malayan, our own precisely true but thoroughly misleading box score of Pearl Harbor, our own thundering bull about what we were doing in the tank and airplane businesses. And it comes to me that of all the world—in competition with experts who have had a couple of years free-handed practice—we have qualified as the most complete and expert liars.

There will be a normal breakfast for the men tomorrow. It seems that last time they didn't think much of "steak, dinner size" as a diet before battle. They were like kids at Christmas with appetites suited to their mood.

There are said to be one large "maru" and four smaller "marus" in the lagoon at Wake or anchored off. There is no proof that a couple of eight-inch cruisers have not also moved in. However there has been no evidence today that they see necessity for maintaining a decent air patrol. We shall probably get into shooting distance with no great trouble.

Here is the plan of the day:

03:00. Call cooks, messmen.

03:15. Reveille.

03:45. Mess gear.

04:15. Relieve the watch.

05:45. Pass word "General Quarters. All Hands Man Your Battle Stations."

06:30. Engine room be prepared for full power on all boilers.

07:00. Be prepared to launch two aircraft.

Forenoon. Task force will attack enemy objectives.

Noon. Meal will be served when and where directed.

Recover aircraft when directed.

Set condition watch when directed.

16:00. (About) Mess gear.

16:20. Relieve the watch.

Fifteen Minutes Before Sunset. Close all battle ports.

Sunset. Darken Ship. Set Condition 2.

I went up on the signal bridge with Hailey along about 8:45. The moon was pretty bright for a first quarter but clumps of cloud were scudding across the sky. It looked as if the weather would be on our side.

Orders Before Battle

Issued on the evening of February 23.

(1) All hands are directed to answer calls of nature prior to going to their general quarters stations in the morning.

(2) The small red and yellow pieces of bunting that have been placed at the first-aid boxes throughout the ship are to be used when a man has been given an injection of morphine by a morphine syrette. Tie one piece of bunting to the man's clothing, wrist, etc. By this indication the doctor will know that the man has had an injection of morphine.

(3) The cause of most of the upper respiratory diseases is due to infectious droplets being coughed and sneezed out into the air. In the ship at present we are having a great number of these cases— especially of acute catarrhal fever (colds). It is well known that people in the early stages of this disease can easily transmit the disease by coughing and sneezing infectious droplets out into the air. As the ship at present is crowded, great care should be taken to cover the mouth with the handkerchief when coughing or sneezing in order not to spray small particles of oral and nasal secretions laden with these organisms out in the air. A shipmate will breathe these small infectious droplets and if his resistance is lowered, if he gets an overwhelming dose he will catch the disease. The disease is not to be taken lightly as some cases are forerunners of pneumonia, a very serious disease. When you feel sick report to the sick bay to see the medical officer. The mission of the medical corps is to keep as many men in top condition as many days as possible.

And beat him if he sneezes for tomorrow he dies.

36

FIELD DAY AT WAKE ISLAND

FEBRUARY 24, *Tuesday*. Day of Battle.

I got up at 4:00 as the ship was coming within striking distance of Wake Island.

I went down to a breakfast that reminded me of an assemblage of sleepy lads in a bus station getting ready for a morning run. The waiters were the only anxious ones in the room. They had to convert the premises into a hospital right away—or as soon as we gave them a chance.

Before getting into my war paint I took a look outside. There was a dark sky with scattered lumps of cloud. But it wasn't going to be any gray day. You could see that. I went to the cabin and gathered up my impedimenta and returned to the platform above sky control.

5:45. No moon. Black water everywhere. A star that looked like Mars and probably wasn't blazed red near the horizon to the east. We were steering straight for the Southern Cross. The other ships of this unit weren't visible. Nobody was moving about in our shadows. If you walked the decks you stumbled over kids stealing a little sleep about the gun positions.

The attack was scheduled to begin at daylight with the cruisers and the destroyers taking part. But to one sitting in this murk it seemed unlikely that daybreak would ever come. Out in the gloom Lieutenant Brewer was mumbling about lights that turned out to be meteors masked in clouds. The navigator complained that he was going to have to learn to navigate in Braille.

6:30. The sky begins to lighten and we turn east. There is an absolutely terrific wind and the sea promises to be the roughest we've been in since we left home. It's virtually impossible to stand on the searchlight platform without hanging onto something. My tin hat is rising from my head and flopping down again, uncomfortably and, for the men on the platform below, dangerously.

7:00. A salmon-pink glow is spreading out slowly ahead. But it's no magnificent sunrise. The whole sky up there, clear or cloudy, is faded and washed-out looking. The wind is working up to hurricane velocity. It literally blows the ink out of this fountain pen and spatters it over everything. I can't think of a suitable harness to hold down my tin hat. Wish I had a shawl.

Below and aft our planes are warming up. Oddly enough you can hear them in spite of the gale. Whether or not they get off it's going to be interesting to see them try. The wind will probably dump them over backwards or hold them steady in the middle of the track when the catapult lets go. My eyeballs are sore and cold. This promises to be a hell of a day. Even without a battle it would be that.

The carrier, it appears in the dawn's early light, is not with us. None of her planes is in sight at the moment. The signs and portents are accumulating and without a crystal ball you can see it's going to be a clear beautiful blue day with a constant gale and a violent sea.

7:02. You can hear the roar of the motor crescendo as the planes warm up. The sound is a sort of obbligato now to the screaming bedlam in the rigging. You don't know how you can hear or how you can possibly distinguish one sound from another. You just pile one din on a worse din and your growing deafness sorts them out as individual plagues.

7:05. Horizon still empty but getting brighter.

7:06. String of signals slides up onto the yardarm. I keep smelling something like burned powder and marvel at it. You can call it prescience or bad judgment, or suspect we have run into a gas cloud left by one of the other ships in the force. They could easily have let off a couple of salvos without our hearing them. This promises to be the sort of battle you used to see on the screen in the days of silent film—hours of terrific activity and no sound at all save the whirr of the theater ventilator or the click of the projector.

7:10. Broad day now although the sun is still behind a cloud bank. You can make out a motley crew on the iron terraces below—

blue flash suits, denims, khaki overalls, life jackets, headphones, blue tin hats. They're all alive and moving now, trying to balance their regalia and themselves against the wind.

7:12. The first of the U.S.S. *Ark's** planes comes off. Foster Hailey discovers that he can light a cigarette by sticking his head up inside the ship's bell. The wind has widened a rip in my left pants' leg and threatens to remove the leg.

7:13. Crash! Flame! The ship shivers. A plane comes off the the port catapult, probably the disappointed Crowley. He's not allowed to carry any Zacharias Zombies this trip. Admiral says no extra weight may be added to bombs or planes without special order. And Crowley, so goes the ship's conviction, had planned to improve the Zombie this time, dolling it up with a couple of flags and a whistle.

7:14. A starboard plane takes off—the second of our scheduled contribution of two. The catapult jangles back into place.

7:15. Second *Ark* plane comes off.

7:17. Four planes, so close together that they seem to be tied up in a bundle, circle about overhead, gray crosshatches on the gray morning. So far everything seems proceeding according to schedule except that there's no sign of the carrier planes. Maybe we're too far out to see them anyway.

7:18. *Ark* lets go her third plane. Crews are moving our remaining pair to be ready for launching or maybe only to be out of the way of the backwash of the five-inch guns. Five SOC planes are now bobbing about prettily on the wings of the morning to no good end.

7:19. We are rolling along into the sun, a thin, gray column. The sea is purple to port, corpse-colored to starboard.

7:20. Starboard pompoms fire string of red tracers like gaudy necklace across the mulatto sky. The planes, answering the signal, turn north but don't seem to be getting far away from us.

7:21. The sun is beginning to edge the top of the cloud bank with a white-hot light. The *Ark* puts off her fourth plane.

7:25. The *Ark* swings right. So do we. We're lining up in a sort of company front and parading northeast. Roll and pitch and

---

* A nom de guerre.

shock and shiver. Water over our bows and spray over our control platforms. . . . And always the howl of the ghastly wind.

7:28. Flash of ack-ack from the *Ark*.

You look unbelievingly. And there it is. High up in the whitening sky you can see the cross of a plane—a plane that looks something like one of our SOC's—a single-seater flying boat—streaking across our course to the north. We join in the hunt in split seconds. Our snarling five-inch guns shake us and push in our diaphragms and constrict our throats and jar our teeth. But nothing else much happens. The fight, apparently, is on. But we're not in it yet.

The sky is covered with hearse plumes, rolling on their way at hurricane speed. We've straightened into column again—a wavering column. The sun has come up over the cloud bank and is looking us squarely in the face downwind.

7:31. The Jap bomber or another one like it is high in the sky off the starboard of the *Ark* and squarely above our group of SOC's. The ack-ack goes wild over him and the sky is mazed with the cockeyed patterns of tracers that don't—thank God—trace anything.

7:34. The Jap dives straight down across the *Ark* toward the cluster of SOC's. The fall is so nearly vertical that we look for the smoke burst that would indicate that he had been hit. It's an odd dive. Halfway down the Jap turns toward the *Ark*. A can alongside sends a string of flack and the Jap changes course again, dives at it and releases the bomb. The can slides sideways as the bomb bursts. For a moment it is concealed in the upended ocean. Then it goes its way. Nobody knows why.

7:35. Several more flashes from the can and the cruiser. There is a mass of muck overhead—cloud scraps and the debris of artillery. A geyser rises just ahead of the *Ark*. A close one. Very close. We head into the wind and readjust the cotton in our ears. For a moment the shriek of the gale is soothing. Our five-inch guns are quiet.

7:38. Sickly yellow flashes from the *Ark*. A plane between us off to starboard. Our ack-ack turns loose in quantity. The plane starts a high, shallow dive.

7:42. Bomb to port of *Ark*. Wonder why all this concentration. Japs must be taking her for a carrier. Our ack-ack goes to work in a slow, dignified, deliberate tempo. The Jap plane is visible only for a second as it turns into the sun at the end of its run. The *Ark* swings, piling up white water in front of her and flattening a punkah of green behind her.

7:45. The *Ark* fires again. I can't see the plane. In looking for it as everybody zigzags I catch a glimpse of Wake—a glistening white streak over to the starboard—to the south of us. We cut loose a tattoo of Chicago pianos to port. . . . So does the *Ark*.

7:46. Another smash of ack-ack blackens the sky about a target I can't see. It must be very high. The *Ark* edges for a position parallel to the beach of Peale Island, one of the trio that makes up Wake. Apparently we're not going to worry about the loose bombers. The *Ark* cuts loose with her main battery. We can tell that from the wreath of fumes that wraps her up. We also open up with the eight-inch guns, a blessed respite after the bark of the fives. And we watch the beginning of a line of fires.

7:47. Two land batteries are firing at us. The shells seem about six-inch—maybe five. The guns have pretty good range. . . . We remember that our Marines sank a cruiser and a couple of destroyers here with just such guns no great time ago. Two fountains leap up short of the *Ark*. . . . One between that and us. One is long in range.

7:50. Smoke puffs roll and coalesce on Wake. We are blasting with the two forward turrets and seem to have landed a shell approximately in the lap of one of the batteries. However there are others. You can see the yellow glare of their flashes against the black of the spreading fires. Most of the bursts are still short of us but not enough. A series of shots lands between the tumbling destroyer and the *Ark*. The destroyer, traveling at top speed, seems submerged most of the time.

7:55. The entire column of our ships is covered with a green-yellow smoke. Something appears to have smashed in the *Ark's* rigging. A mess of gear is hanging down from the top of the foremast. Shells are screaming over us—three shells. Burst to starboard, 2,000 feet wide. Another flash from the land battery. This time over and short. Bracket! Odd that even this dangerous situation doesn't look serious. The shots all seem too far away no matter what a straddle is supposed to do.

7:58. There are about five batteries working on us. . . . My tin hat just blew off. Hailey rescued it before it could fly down and decapitate a marine in the pompom crew. It is impossible now to wear glasses in the wind—barely possible to stand up when the forward turrets rock the ship.

The scene with all the geysers leaping up about us reminds me of the ancient cyclorama I saw as a kid in Chicago: "The Battle of Manila."

There's a new roar. The five-inchers—about whose song I have already said enough—are going *ad lib*. So are my ears in spite of cotton packs. All the ships in the line are now trailing yellow smoke and wreaths of shining spray.

8:05. Continuous noise. Four bursts over. Three splashes short. I count fifteen fires on the island—basing inventory on thick columns in spreading cumulus of smoke. . . . There may be more. We're overlooking Wake and Peale Islands. . . . Can't see what's going on across the lagoon where the carrier planes presumably are at work on the alleged marus. Our shooting is much better than at Wotje—more selective. A salvo here—an eruption of burning oil. A couple of shells there—a burst of debris from a seaplane dock installation. . . . There are no waste shots in the barrage that clunks down on the material sheds. You can see those results plainly and without need for field glasses.

The garbage tossed out by our five-inch ammunition dots the sea in front of us like hail and tosses bits of soot and ashes back into our faces.

8:10. Maybe some land batteries are out. I can't tell. At least three are still working. You have no difficulty seeing the flashes and counting the shells coming out at you. But it is silent only for a minute. Two fountains rise short of us. A white gush stirs the blue beyond.

8:12. Two more jets short. Captain Cobb yells something about splashes over. I've been missing something.

8:13. Direct hit on Wake oil tank—orange ball melts into black. Another battery flashes in the middle of the island. Two spouts rise about the *Ark.* . . . Straddle. One strikes near us. Short.

8:14. Smoke drifts enough for us to see the white tower of the power station in mid-island. Flames right and left of it but not touching.

8:16. Another rich orange blaze. The land guns hit close— much too close—to the can on the *Ark's* starboard. The dive bombers haven't come back. We hope they've been caught on the ground somewhere rearming.

8:17. Another shell near the can. One over about 200 yards from our port bow.

8:18. Another hot orange puff on the island.

Undisturbed gooney birds are still riding along with us. They seem to like the slicks the shells leave. Or maybe they're looking for dead fish.

Four guns on the island fire almost at the same time.

8:20. A fine red burst on Wake. We were told that the Japs had brought in about a dozen tanks such as are used on American railroads for oil storage. We seem to be picking them off one after another or else the fire is reaching them in leisurely rotation.

8:20. Battery at right end of island as we look at it fires one gun. Geyser far short and astern of us.

8:22. Lance of flame starts through shrouds of smoke on island near powerhouse. One battery seems to have gone west. The fire seems to be settling down to a routine of red and black gushes almost in a rhythm. The battery at the west end keeps diligently at it and should be given points for perseverance. But it's not getting anywhere. The last bursts seemed about as far away from us as from the island.

It would seem we're pulling out a bit. The five-inch guns have stopped completely. Our stern turrets rumble and shake the fantail.

8:23. Sweet Lady! It's good to give your ears a rest. Everything is silent except for the screaming gale which you hardly notice. The shore batteries are firing at the limit of their range obviously to keep us out here. A few odd ack-ack puffs slam up against the cloud where our spotters are hidden.

There is a seething cascade of red fire through the black at the west end of the island. You hope it's a battery, plus magazine or ammunition dump, and you know it isn't. Flames are weaving in and out of black in a sort of rag-rug pattern all across the objective.

One lone five-inch fires a shot at God knows what.

8:25. The island, as smoke drifts inshore, is fairly visible now. There are numerous white square buildings in addition to the power

plant. The whole thing looks something like a U. S. Army canton-
ment or construction camp, which, of course, it was. There is a big
white building where Jervis and Wake join. We haven't wasted a
shell on it, nor for that matter on many of the sheds that stick out
so brilliantly from the background of smoke. In a while probably
the fire will get to them. If it doesn't, no matter. At the ends of the
island are piles of construction material, silvery tanks with flames
reaching out for them. You wonder what became of the hydro-
ponics plant where they raised fresh vegetables in a bottle or
something. Separating the islands from the sea is a stretch of white
beach a little whiter than the rest of the landscape. There are no
trees. There is no color at all to the scene save for the red and
orange bursts of fire. Jervis and Wake are just gaunt skeletons of
coral incapable of supporting human life without help from outside
or of protecting human life against a bombardment.

8:27. There is a plane after one of our SOC's. The can behind
us opens fire, probably just out of habit.

A course signal goes up. Maybe we're going back for another
run.

8:28. Maybe not.

8:29. We appear to be zigzagging but we're getting no closer to
the smoke-fog that marks Wake.

8:30. Zigzag. . . . Zig. . . . Zag. . . . It's obvious now that we
took Wake by surprise. There were no big ships out where we
could see them. Maybe they were sunk in advance by our planes.
Maybe they were over on the other side of the island. Maybe they
weren't there. I'll ask somebody about it some day.

8:32. The SOC's were coming back in formation (including the
one driven off by the destroyer astern of us). The can for the
moment is witholding fire. If these crates are going to attempt a
landing they have a fine day for it. . . . I am writing this inside the
ship's bell which weighs probably half a ton and is windproof.

8:34. So far the show is ours. The smoke on the horizon is thick
and ominous despite the force of the wind. Wake is another Wotje.

8:37. Off to the starboard with startling suddenness there is a
burst of black high above the horizon. It's a plane. It arcs toward
the sea on a black rainbow. The lookout calls: "It's a Jap! A four-
motored bomber!" And as he speaks the plane crashes into the

water. Its grave is marked by a tall black cloud like a cypress tree. Another object, perhaps a wing, perhaps a smaller plane, flutters down after it like a falling leaf. It is gone before we can make out what it is. The smoke clouds linger as densely as those which hang over the still-burning Wake.

The black cerements of the island are still marking the horizon astern of us though we have come miles away. We are headed east and there is no sign that we are likely to turn back for another run.

Donald Duck or somebody tells us that the crashed bomber was taken by one of our fighters who came upon him unseen and unsuspected in a cloud bank. It was headed for us when it came flaming out of the murk. It lit on a bearing of 110 almost on our starboard bow. And the thought comes that we are undoubtedly dodging some more of the same kind.

Maybe—you toy cheerily with the thought—maybe this was the ship that brought the Jap air marshal to Wake on his inspection tour.

8:42. The other cruiser is swinging to the left, almost at right angles to the course, and we follow. The idea of another run on Wake, now only hazily visible astern, is getting more and more remote.

8:44. Smoke of the sunken bomber is rolling over to mingle with the fire-born cloud bank we are leaving. About it the sky seems to be empty, although everywhere you turn there's a lookout with his glass fixed in that direction. According to the ancient Irish maxim: "Where there's two there's wan."

8:45. Wake is definitely astern. The gooneys have left us or maybe we have left the gooneys.

One of the destroyers shoots across the track of the other cruiser and seems interested in something that we can't see off starboard. Two planes, ours or theirs, angle into the sun. We follow the general shift.

8:46. The puffball of the burned airplane is dissolving and you take time off to remember—or possibly you realize for the first time—that from six to ten men just died in that flaming coffin, were dead when you first saw it, their corpses riding to the sea in a spectacular glory.

8:48. I've so far unsolved the reason for this beat to the east.

It seems too early to be going home. Too much of the island seems to be untouched, still usable by the enemy.

8:49. Destroyer off to port shooting at something. It turns out to be a small boat—probably a copra schooner about seventy-five feet long—painted black and hard to see against the dark water. She has no height to give a silhouette at a distance of a few miles.

First salvo of destroyer rakes bridge. Range-finder operator, looking through twenty-four-power lenses, says that four men dived into the sea off her fantail.

8:50. Two salvos. The Pacific is goose-pimpled with the destroyer's frantic firing.

8:51. Two more wild salvos. Over and to the right.

8:52. It goes on.

8:53. Terrific display of fireworks and colored fountains. Some of it occasionally comes close enough to blot the tub from sight. But not often.

8:55. The tub isn't firing. Doesn't seem to have any guns. Destroyer however retaining all caution. Why doesn't the skipper throw bottles at it or turn around and sink it with a wave?

9:05. Ship sinks. Probably her bottom was eaten through by seagoing termites or she got tired of it all, or something.

It's an interesting thought that if all the shells fired at her by the can had been piled on her deck the weight would have put her under.

9:08 The can is still scooting about looking for survivors or seashells.

Note—as we look back at the thinning smoke that marks our progress on Wake: One atoll looks pretty much like another atoll.

9:10. Six SOC's fly in from our starboard side in formation. So help me there's another blast from one of the destroyers astern. I don't know where those boys get to look at airplanes. An SOC certainly doesn't resemble anything but an SOC.

9:14. Stand by to recover planes. The diligent can that sank the spitkit is still over on the horizon carrying on its mysterious works.

9:33. Hook is swung out for one of the SOC's which shows up in circle for landing. Then over the stern, about five lookouts at once pick up a plane—a big bomber that certainly isn't ours. The bugle blows. The rush begins. The fight is on again. I take a second to wonder what's going to happen to our plane. Probably the pilot who also has spotted the bomber has some concern in the matter too.

Our yards are all covered over with flags standing straight out in the gale. Apparently, despite this new and important threat, we are going to make some effort to get our SOC home. But we're going to be cautious about it. The bomber scooting across the sky behind us out of range of our ack-ack is a four-engined flying boat like the one we saw shot down a moment ago. Probably the pilot of this one saw that shooting. At any rate he doesn't seem anxious to close in. But no matter, he is definitely a menace, particularly as none of our fighter planes appears to be about.

Donald Duck cuts into this tense moment to announce that the airfield on Wake was completely destroyed. The returning Mr. Crowley apparently supplied that information. We get what comfort we can out of it while watching the flight of the black cross in the sky behind us.

9:42. Our plane lands and is hooked while plunging up and down like an express elevator.

The sea, despite its wildness, is as beautiful as I have ever seen it. The water is "wine dark" as Homer or somebody described it, densely purple with dead black beads in it.

10:00. Jap bomber shows up again near horizon off port. This time it creates no great excitement.

10:05. Down to wardroom for cup of coffee. Find the doctor and his gadgets occupying most of the premises. The doctor's prize exhibit, the lad who got hit in the neck by the slug from the line gun, is lying on a stretcher near the magazine rack. The doctor is taking no chances on losing this fine case until he can land it in good condition at Pearl Harbor. Miracles don't happen in the experience of naval surgeons oftener than once in a lifetime.

10:45. Over Donald Duck comes some mumble about the Main Battery including the incredible information: "Steamer has been sighted."

. . . So I left the doctor and the prize patient in the wardroom and went aloft again. This time I went only as far as the bridge. Through the glasses I picked out a tramp of about 1,500 tons steaming along on our port side just this side of the horizon.

A destroyer was angling over toward it at a fast clip—not the one that had worked on the spitkit, I judged. She wouldn't have enough ammunition left.

Donald Duck contributed the next bit of intelligence: "The steamer that was previously reported appears to be a small tramp. She is about six miles distant off the port bow. A destroyer has gone over to investigate."

At that point the destroyer let loose a blast with everything she had on the starboard side.

"The investigation is completed," said the captain. "The destroyer has opened fire."

10:56. The destroyer is closing in and firing wildly.

10:58. Destroyer's artillery is fast. The sea is littered with plops, like the surface of a lake in a hailstorm. Nothing, however, is falling near the tramp.

11:00. Somebody says the tramp is a patrol boat. I shouldn't wonder. The destroyer is throwing everything but the engine-room tools.

11:08. The destroyer apparently realizes that there is no return fire, turns toward the target and charges point-blank. You get the idea she's going to drop a torpedo or maybe to ram.

11:10. Another harvest of dynamite for half a mile in the vicinity of the destroyer. Can it be possible? The patrol boat seems to be listing and raising her prow at the same time.

11:12. She's gone. Foundered. Sunk stern first, and once more you suspect the baneful influence of barnacles and teredos or whatever they call them.

11:20. It's reported that a shell is stuck in one of the five-inch guns. They're going to remove it, oddly, by firing another shell behind it. I may have misunderstood the details of this process. I hope I have.

11:30. The five-inch gun goes off. Apparently no casualties, at any rate no rush to the doctor's quarters in the wardroom. You realize, however, that you've been expecting some. Never, as somebody mentioned before, a dull moment.

37

IF YOU DODGE THE BOMBS MAYBE YOU LIVE

Luncheon was served at noon—a buffet affair of ham and beans. I went to bed at 12:30 with all my clothes on. I learned that trick on our last expedition. When the bugle blows you'd better be ready to hit the deck.

And so the bugle blew and I hit the deck.

4:20. Bugle and bells! I woke in time to see Chappell, who had been shaving, go scuttling out leaving his electric razor hanging. I picked up my tin hat and life belt on the fly and scrambled back to the foremast.

4:25. The news filters up to the searchlight platform—a bomber has been sighted in the sun astern. Apparently it's content to stay there. Everybody is looking up at the sky like a Parsee votary.

Where did the report come from? Anywhere except the *Ark's* beam antenna which is hanging in shreds from the foremast. Shot off or shaken off we probably won't know till we get home. We're running wet at the moment, very wet, driving into high swells and throwing up a spray that drenches the pompoms above the navigation bridge.

4:40. Comes Sergeant O'Donoghue to report that our spotters picked up something bearing 220. Shortly after that Lieutenant Brewer and a lookout saw a spot on the sun at about that bearing. Later the forward director saw a bomber at 140. That is very likely the same one that has been shadowing us all day, trying, no doubt, to pass the glad news to near-by bases or to the subs that may lie between us and Hawaii.

While we were discussing these matters Crowley came up top. He says that the falling leaf we saw dive into the sea alongside the Jap bomber was one of our fighters. Two attacked. One caught it.

At 4:45 I went below but not back to bed. Though I was pretty sleepy, almost dopey, I began to put these notes together. I was thinking about a spot of food at 6 P.M. when I heard the banging of iron feet on the gun deck overhead. I grabbed my helmet and was halfway up the stairs when the bugle went and with it all hell.

The ship had spun and was still slewing over to port when I came to the top of the stairs and skidded across the signal bridge. Over the starboard rail I saw the answer—the churning green of four bomb geysers about 200 yards away from us—the tumbling remnants of the glittering waterspout that a full ton of dynamite had tossed skyward instead of us. Our decks aft were awash with the descending tide.

The guns were cracking high up and momentarily we got a glimpse of a couple of bombers like those that attacked the carrier on the last trip—twin-engined things resembling the Douglas transports. They were—as later officially announced by the range-finder operator—13,600 feet up. They went back into the haze out of which they had come and stayed there.

6:05. There were stories from good sources that the captain had saved the ship. He had seen the bombers before anyone else and had swung the rudder hard to the left.

It begins to appear that nobody saw the planes arrive. No one—and that includes the captain—saw them before they released their bombs. Brewer says he saw them as they came out of the cloud. And by that time four 500-pound crumps were on their way down.

6:07. The sky is still bright blue at the zenith with cloud patches in layers below. A white moon hangs near the horizon. The sun is squarely astern with everybody, as usual, staring at it.

6:10. Zigzagging abruptly.

6:20. Lookout calls to Brewer. Spot on sun. Brewer passes it on. Another tense wait. Nothing happens.

6:30. Sun getting low. It oughtn't to be long now!

6:40. The sun's down. Night is on its way. It will soon be dark enough for you to break your neck wandering around here. I'm going below.

There was quite a lot of palaver at dinner about the uses if any of our battle. I am pleased to note that the Navy isn't being kidded even by its own strategists. The gist of the conversation was that we had done little or nothing and that we had done it the hard way.

Said one: You steam about ten thousand miles, you fire twenty-five rounds a gun. You go away leaving land batteries and ground installations and power plants and God knows what. And if those bombs had hit us an hour ago, you could rate this as a very expensive expedition, which isn't to say that you can't rate it like that anyway.

Also, why haven't we got some kind of a detector? The first anybody saw of the bombers this afternoon was the bombs.

"We weren't surprised," says Brewer. "We'd been waiting for those planes all afternoon. You could hardly say that we were surprised when they arrived. But we couldn't see them when they got here. That's something different."

The navigator said that he was out on the balcony to the starboard side of the bridge when he saw the bombs coming down.

"I ran in and skidded across the bridge and grabbed the bugler," he said. "I told him to sound flight quarters. That was the only thing I could think of that had anything to do with airplanes. Fortunately the bugler knows only one call and he blew it and everybody got to his station."

Tate, the aviator, thinks the turning of the ship was unimportant because, as he determined from a look at the wake, the bombs would have missed us anyway. But the turnabout looked nice.

"Well, it was certainly as close a shave as I want to see," said another of the pilots. "Those boys had us cold. . . ." And the navigator cut in:

"Why do you guys keep referring to this in the past tense?"

Apparently if we go twenty-five knots in this sea, we leave a wake visible halfway back to Japan. If we go slow they catch up with us in decent bombing distance by daylight tomorrow. You pays your money and takes your choice. . . .

We were 228 miles from Wake at 8 o'clock tonight.

I wonder if we'll be having any free-for-all critique on this operation as we had the last time. I wonder. . . .

38

HUSH-HUSH

FEBRUARY 25, *Wednesday*. At sea. Honolulu-bound? Bright. Beautiful. Cool. Rough.

We were supposed to pick up the carrier somewhere in this neighborhood during the night. But she's not around here now. She didn't answer our squawk when we were being trailed by the big bomber yesterday. Maybe she's tired of our company—as I am.

The morning news confirms the smashing and dispersion of the Jap invasion fleet off Bali and indicates that MacArthur may be able to hold on until the enemy brings up some reinforcements. The British seem not to be doing so well in front of Rangoon. Churchill has reorganized his cabinet. Nothing in the reorganization stirs me much.

Moscow claims advances and seems to be rolling right on. Mention of the ring about Leningrad appears in the communiqué but from the news as offered you conclude that the status quo there continues not so much because of German resistance as because the Russians haven't concentrated their main attack on that corner. Anyway the ring appears to be just about broken.

Russia says that 6,000,000 Germans have been killed or wounded since the beginning of the counteroffensive. They say that a new army of Russian reserves trained behind the Urals is now ready to fight. To one who has seen these things before it seems highly likely that the Germans have been training a new reserve army also. They ought to have the manpower unless breeding has fallen off from the expected averages.

I am writing these things only that I may be able to link up more important events with those going on around me if and when I ever have the opportunity and inclination to look back. Nobody can tell the importance of any event until he sees it in retrospect.

I missed breakfast after the best sleep I've had on this trip. Went down for a cup of coffee and there was accosted by the communications officer. He was very sweet about the sad duty he had to perform. . . .

I shall digress. The night before the attack some maps of Wake were passed around the table in the wardroom together with recent aerial photographs showing our objectives. . . . I turned one of the maps about and in fifty seconds had made a sketch of it in my notebook. Not a bad sketch I shall admit. When finished it showed the outline of Jervis and Wake Islands, the central road, the power plant, flying boat ramp, new pier, hotel, airfield and known land-battery positions. It was still in the notebook this morning when the communications officer said:

"To protect ourselves I shall have to ask you to destroy that sketch you made of the Wake Island map. It's supposed to be confidential. . . ." He had the grace to look sheepish as he said it.

"Of course I shall destroy it," I said. "Or better yet, I shall give it to you and you may destroy it. And I shall bring you down my map of the Pacific Ocean which shows Wake Island and you may destroy that, too. . . ."

There was more interchange on the same high plane. It seems as futile to record it as it was to say it save for the implications it carries:

What in God's name is the type of intelligence that goes to the effort to be rude to a bearer of Navy credentials about so confidential a matter as a map of Wake Island? Is there anybody in the Navy who thinks that the Japs are under the impression that they have taken some other island? Are we to go on being hush-hush about the installations we just blew down or are we to suppose that the Japs won't be able to inventory their losses until somebody smuggles in a copy of the secret map and points them out.

Nuts, I say, with a capital N.

We were 585 miles from Wake at noon.

We realized today that we hadn't heard Roosevelt's talk on the progress of the war. From the CPO quarters came a typical yarn concerning this important event. A few of the chiefs were gathered around the radio at 6 P.M. just as the bombers of the Son of Heaven came over.

"We shall hit the enemy with all our power," said Mr. Roosevelt. "With all our energy we shall seek him out and when we find him we shall smash him."

"Boom! Crash! Zowie!" replied four half-ton bombs bursting alongside the ship for sound effect.

The navigator is trying to get some recognition of a claim that the bridge ought to have some new window glass. All the windows up there were smashed yesterday. How to get new ones is a problem that bothers the first lieutenant. He doesn't think there is that much shatterproof glass in Honolulu. (I wrote it chatterproof and wish I'd left it that way.)

The navigator came into the cabin during the afternoon and poured oil. I was still miffed by the episode of the Wake Island map. Chappell read me naval regulations which seemed to me to be just about as silly as the proposition about the possession of home-made charts of the Pacific. But he was so cheery about it I quit wrangling. Life, I daresay, is too short. And anyway he isn't being kidded. He knows without looking through any official glasses when something is silly.

The navigator says we may be out for some time. At present we are headed north to rendezvous with the carrier which it appears didn't desert us after all. Then, he says, it is quite possible that we may continue to wander around doing good deeds when and if we have the opportunity.

The weather in the meantime is getting pretty snappy. The wind is still about as stiff as it was yesterday and it's cold enough to turn you blue.

Something in the condition of the atmosphere was indicated by Lane, the mess boy, who came into the room half an hour late in answer to the navigator's ring. He came into the place as if he had just thought up the idea all by himself and deposited a white blanket on the bed. Then he looked through a couple of drawers and, with all the appearances of deep respect, addressed Commander Chappell:

"Have you got enough blankets up where you are, sir? Because you got two blankets. There is this here one and the one you got on the bed and the one you got where you are on the bridge if you got one there. . . ."

"What are you talking about?" was the fair question of the commander. "Did you know I rang for you?"

"Was that today or yesterday?" Lane wanted to know.

"It was today," said the commander. Mr. Lane considered that with an expression of detached thoughtfulness.

"Oh yes," he said. "It was your shoes you wanted shined."

"It wasn't," replied Commander Chappell patiently. "It was a towel. I wanted a towel so that I could dry my face after washing. And I suggested that maybe Mr. Casey might need a towel so that he could dry his face, too."

Mr. Lane nodded his head.

"We have many towels," he said. "We have one, two, three towels." He took one out and proceeded to hang it on the hook by the washstand. Commander Chappell looked at him pityingly.

"There are two of us. And why should we have to use one towel?" he wanted to know.

"It must be the war," explained Mr. Lane. "It muddles my brain and affects my memory." He got out another towel. But the end had not yet arrived.

"And how about my laundry?" the commander pursued. "When might I expect to get that back?"

"I guess day after tomorrow," guessed Mr. Lane. "Two days, yes, I think it will be all right then."

"Has the war addled the brains down in the laundry?"

"Mr. Chappell, this war has set the whole ship back three or four days. It sets everybody back three or four days. I don't see why they have to have a war in the first place."

Mr. Lane made what you might call a good exit.

Tonight's news wasn't so hot. The British are preparing to evacuate Rangoon. Churchill admits the losses in Singapore were 73,000 or more. We are reported to have lost a destroyer and a supply ship in a storm off Newfoundland.

The executive officer spent a vigorous period during dinner inquiring of all and sundry what the general strategy was going to be. Nobody was able to tell him.

During the evening I sat over cocoa with Lieutenant Hawkins and the chaplain. We discussed the lost beauties of Spain, the fine qualities of the Spaniards and the devastating effects of civil war. We arrived a little platitudinously at the fact that somehow a country is beautiful only when its people are happy. And as a sort of corollary we came to complete agreement with Mayor Ed Kelly of Chicago who says "Great national philosophies are the bunk. They haven't any existence aside from political speeches. The status of nations toward other nations is reducible to one proposition: 'Are they as well fed and as comfortable as we are, or aren't they?'"

The padre was recently promoted to a senior lieutenancy but tonight he is still wearing the stripe and a half of junior lieutenancy. Hawkins asked him why he didn't put up proper insignia, and kept ahead of him when he tried to answer: Mr. Hawkins knew that there were no stripes aboard, there was no money to buy stripes, there was nobody with needle and thread to sew them on. . . . The padre shook his head.

"No," he said. "It isn't that. Every Sunday something happens to interfere with church services. We have artillery practice or we fight battles or we cross the international date line. So finally the paymaster said to me: 'No preachee, no paychee.' And so if I wear a half-stripe less I don't get docked quite so much."

The navigator came in about half past seven. He said that this was the first fog he'd seen since 1939 and that he didn't think there would be much of it.

"But you've got to make up your mind to put up with northern conditions," he said. "We're thirty-two degrees north and I feel it in my bones that we're going to do some hayraking in this neighborhood for some time to come."

We were still sitting when a lad from the radio came in with word from the carrier.

We are to proceed to an island named Marcus and bombard it.

Well, we looked up Marcus in the pilot book. It was discovered in 1847, visited shortly thereafter by the U.S.S. *Tuscarora*, and last reported by a French ship that called there in 1880. That's all any-body knows about it, apparently. On the chart, if you have a chart big enough to show it at all, it appears to be somewhere north of the

Tropic of Cancer and a little west of the 155th parallel East Lat. The navigator says that according to his best information it's about 1300 miles east of us. We'll get there in about four or five days from now and if we don't run into the whole Jap fleet cruising about in that area, we ought to be back in Pearl in a couple of weeks.

39

THE MYSTERIOUS ISLE OF GANGES

FEBRUARY 26, *Thursday*. At sea. Fairly calm. Increasingly cold.

I was awakened about 6 A.M. by the tooting of our whistle. Somehow I had wrapped myself in a blanket and felt the cold only by implication. But I stuck a hand out and there it was—icy.

The whistle went on and on with no particular rhythm. The intervals between blasts were sometimes two, sometimes three or four minutes. So there was no sleep. I crawled out and went up to the signal bridge.

We were wrapped up tight in an Aleutian fog. The visibility was just about nil and apparently getting worse. We weren't very far north, but the stiff winds and rolling seas we've been having might have told us there were storms somewhere about with conditions that storms usually produce. This bit of fog had moved down a couple of hundred miles from the locale where you'd generally expect to find it. Off in the distance now and then you could hear the yammering of one of the cans—short dots and then a bit of unintelligible code.

It was a weird, wet scene, with nothing in it to warrant my staying above decks. So I went below again filled with memories of the last trip when I carried my overcoat, woolies and heavy clothes to the blistering tropics. This time I have a straw hat.

Most of the afternoon was spent waddling about while somebody got ready to fuel. We launched a couple of planes and took note of the repairs that must be made on the blasted tails of the others. Spectators about the catapults reminded the fliers that if they come down they'll have to head for the Aleutians instead of Pukapuka. . . . And how do you like blubber, Mr. Crowley? And

have you a baseball bat to use on the walruses when you are fighting
them for a share of the fish . . . ?

You think as you listen to this persiflage that we'll be a lot
nearer the pole if we are unsuccessful in this undertaking than we
are at the moment. We'll have to retreat on a route to the northeast—and that probably with a large part of the Jap navy on our
tails. We'll run up along the islands in the general direction of
Dutch Harbor with wind in our faces right off the ice pack and
the fogs cutting us off from all the other ships in the fleet unless
we happen to run over them!

A can came alongside during our maneuvers and showed evi-
dences of what we'd been through during our race away from Wake
to this strange rendezvous in the mists. She had been plowing the
swells, tossing the spray over her topmast and condensing it on her
hot stack. Today the stack is white and glistening with salt—rather
beautiful, even if it isn't so well camouflaged as it was yesterday.

The tanker looks large and important at its present work. But
as you watch it battling to get alongside a big ship without sinking
it—and herself—you wonder what the recompense is for serving
with it. Life aboard a tanker, you figure as you look at it off there in
the wet, must be very close to a hell of an existence. The lads
aboard see none of the excitement. They get shot at by every sub
and every plane that chances to spot them. And ashore they get
no glory. "On a tanker? Oh, I thought you were in the Navy. . . ."

I drew a secret map today for Commander Howeth's benefit—
a sheet of white paper with a lone dot in the middle of it labeled
Marcus. I'm going to give it to him "to be destroyed by burning or
eaten" the day after we finish there—God willing.

Marcus! The place nobody has ever heard about. Hawkins says
he thinks it was located by radio ranging—a sort of electronic re-
section—on its transmitter. So—as one may say from experience
with such things—the island may still be a myth like the U.S.S.
Tuscarora (with her seven decks and straw bottom) that was one of
its discoverers.

Sergeant O'Donoghue says it's his opinion that we are going to
bombard Tokio to interrupt the Emperor's speech and pay off for
the sub that bombed Los What's-its-name when Roosevelt was
talking. It might be a better idea at that than the one we're following.

The worst of it, as suggested by the navigator in one of his afternoon visits, is that we may never see this mysterious island at all.

I'm not so sure I favor that sort of operation. The only reason I can see for our being here is to throw the fear of God into the Jap high command—to let the observers see a mobilization of force. The cruisers you bring up don't mean a thing unless you give the enemy a chance to see them. . . . Well anyway . . .

The Japs keep referring continuously to our "hit-and-run" technique in the Pacific. . . . Our tactics, we gather from their criticism, differ strangely from the unyielding, non-retreating, toe-to-toe slugging match that the Japs put on at Pearl Harbor.

Our planes came back at 5:05 and landed expeditiously in spite of a bad sea. I'm always glad to report the return of these things particularly in this latitude. It's all right to kid Crowley but this is no part of the Pacific to sail a rubber raft in.

February 27, Friday. At sea.

Still, it is presumed, we are on our way to Marcus. The weather is bitter cold and I slept under two bankets until late.

It's a gray day of the sort you remember as typical of the North Atlantic in winter. At 11:15 the ship, despite the fact that she hadn't been pitching much, took a pile of green water over her bow. It sounded as if our whole stern had been knocked off. But the ship shivered a couple of times and settled down again with no fuss. Donald Duck was silent. There were no footfalls on the iron ladders. So I continued dressing without haste.

I was too doggoned cold to sit around the cabin. I thought maybe the engine room might be a nice place to sit in and I started for there. On the way I passed the executive's door and loitered awhile to talk to him. He is the sort of man I used to think all naval officers were—big, hearty, smart, cheerful, bluff and friendly. He comes of a breed that knew no bunk and the uses of bunk are a mystery to him even when the product comes wrapped up in official endorsement.

He's a hard worker—he certainly has made this ship shine from stem to gudgeon (if there be any gudgeons). He is a stickler for discipline and order. But he sits up nights wondering about things, as for instance why Wake was left with most of the buildings standing, the material dumps untouched, the contractor's camp intact, the land batteries still blazing. He is interested in any discussion of the progress of the war and indications of its possible finish. He doesn't think it will end very soon if we keep on using a fly-swatter policy. I subscribed heartily to these ideas.

We went down to luncheon where Lieutenant Commander Kobey, the engineer officer, enlivened the proceedings by announcing that he'd discovered a new island near Marcus. He was looking through an atlas that came as a premium with soap wrappers, and he lit upon this island as plainly marked as Yokohama. The name of it—which proved that it was no fly speck—was "Ganges." This undersized dot was located—by the cartographer at least—about 350 miles northwest of Marcus. And there might be nothing mysterious about the whole business except that "Ganges," which is so plainly marked in Kobey's soap-wrapper almanac, is not mentioned on the hydrographic chart.

Somebody went out and got a globe of the world as created by Rand-McNally and there Ganges was as Kobey had said. Kobey got his map. Ganges was on it. And so was Marcus. But Wake wasn't. The dot indicating Ganges was bigger than the dot that marked Yokohama, but Kobey admitted that the size of the dots probably didn't mean anything.

Well, anyway, there it was and we began to wonder why the hydrographic office should ignore an island so close to the great circle course between the United States and Yokohama. Maybe somebody made a mistake in compiling Kobey's map. Maybe he should have used a different kind of soap. Maybe the island isn't there. Maybe it's the Kelly Field of Japan.

It isn't surprising, somebody told Kobey, that a fly should have alighted on a ten-cent map. Flies are not fastidious. What is remarkable is the fact that Kobey's fly was able to make labels.

The navigator thinks that the island isn't there at all. He considers it one of those points of dubious location that ceased to exist altogether during the 1923 earthquake.

We were informed at luncheon that the captain would conduct a critique of the Wake operation this evening. God attend him!

There isn't much to cheer about on this leg of the trip. We seem to be piling up futility on futility. Besides that the sea is grayer and rougher and the weather is bitter. We roll and pitch and dance and we slap our keel on the bottom with much discomfort, the while radio intelligence keeps us informed that the Japs have coagulated a fair-sized air force to hunt us down. They are ranging between Wotje and Wake and far out to sea toward Midway. It's quite apparent the Jap doesn't think we've gone home but he has a queer idea about where we are loitering.

Tonight we turned back the clock an hour. Tomorrow we take on fuel after the other cruiser. The carrier follows us and then we start on our so-called drive. The captain says we'll be two nights on the way, maybe three counting tonight.

9:00 P.M. The captain held his critique tonight because he said tomorrow may be too full of routine work. Nothing much came of the discussion except his frank statement that the delay in the arrival of the air force hampered the assault. We were subjected to some inconvenience, he said, and we could very well have been put on the spot. There was a general consensus that the technical handling of the ship and guns was all you'd ask in a peacetime drill.

As for our objective on this end of the trip the captain said:

"I think it will have a far-reaching effect because it will strike close to what the Japanese consider Japan proper. They've been wondering when we should start raids on their industrial centers no great distance from this island.

"That the attack on Wake has caused them considerable concern we now know. They don't know what is to follow. That is what upsets them most. As I have told you repeatedly when you upset a Japanese you render him incapable of action. This raid, I am convinced, will have a definite effect in causing the enemy to withdraw more and more forces from the south to protect bases up here. . . ."

After that he said good night and we sat about blowing on our blue fingers.

Just about a year ago today I was coming home from a jaunt through the Mediterranean with the British fleet. A year ago tomorrow I got smashed up at the Cairo station.

Naturally you keep on wondering how much tomorrow is going to look like yesterday.

I joined a scuttle-butt conference in the wardroom about nine.

Howeth came in while Tate and I were discussing the feasibility of refueling fortresses with carrier planes on long runs. (Just for the record it looks impossible. It would take ten planes nobody knows how long to supply the fuel load.)

Howeth mentioned that the Jap planes were right on our tail twenty-four hours ago and all the day before that. They covered most of the Pacific between Wake and Midway looking for us. But they couldn't know that we were headed west instead of east.

That gives us reason to wonder what's going to happen next time. We can't go very much farther west without bumping into Formosa or China or something.

We had a discussion that continued far into the night on the advisability of giving the crew more information about what's going on. At present they know only that they're headed for an island called Marcus. And on their dime-store maps Marcus is separated from the rest of Japan by less than the thickness of a cigarette paper and they're not feeling comfortable about it. I can't see how it's going to help us any to keep ourselves blindfolded in a spot where nobody could communicate with the enemy even if he wanted to. In the British navy everybody aboard ship was kept informed at all times by Donald Duck where we were going, how long it would take us to get there, when we might expect to meet the enemy. It didn't hurt anybody. It may have been an important factor in the unbreakable British morale.

Brewer added some words of explanation to the story of the can's ack-ack barrage against our SOC's at Wake.

"They came right out of the sun," he said, "from a direction where we didn't expect any of our planes to be. We couldn't recognize them in the glare. So we trained on them. We'd have fired, too, if the forward range-finder operator hadn't noticed the markings on one of them."

Another secret. We were firing over U.S.S. *Ark* during the action and we had one short burst. Says the captain: "I don't know whether we blew off the antenna or not." The inference, however, seems plain.

40

IN SILENCE LIKE THE NIGHT

FEBRUARY 28, *Saturday*. At sea. It is still cold and rough but the weather is brilliant, not to say beautiful.

The morning news indicates that our airplanes are still active about Java. We hope the communiqués from that region are reasonably accurate. If so it would appear that the P-40 is really a plane, despite our misgivings.

Foster and I have begun to wonder about our chronicle of Wake—which wasn't such a hot story to begin with. However there doesn't seem to be much danger of our getting scooped by the Navy Department—not immediately. The admiral—our admiral—hasn't sent out a peep about our transaction. He learned his lesson presumably at Wotje where he published the glad tidings and found a flock of bombers on his tail.

I suggested to the executive officer that the hovering-around program could be carried out more economically if we carried an anchor as a substitute for a lot of fuel bunkers. He didn't say what he thought. Ho-hum and so it goes. The boys will be willing after another day of this to retire Admiral Halsey and take away his medal.

They paid off the officers today—I don't know what for, and neither do they. I watched the proceedings for a while and then went out to get bored by contemplating the great empty sea. I came back to make some cocoa—the soda fountain having been filled up with freshly paid gobs. And I was working a crossword puzzle—carefully because I had to do it in ink—when the general alarm sounded.

There was a hell of a to-do about this. The ship had gone to Condition Three and the alarm meant that there must be some

245

reason for manning the main battery in a hurry. The navigator, passing to the stairs on the fly, said he thought it must be at least a couple of cruisers.

I didn't know what it was, except that it seemed unlikely enemy airplanes would be around here, and if they were I couldn't explain the whistle and bell. . . . It's been found easier to pass the word for the manning of the guns piecemeal; it keeps the mob from assaulting the ladders in one rush.

I went into the room. Nobody had shut any ports or put out any lights. So I leisurely got into my going-away costume (life jacket, tin hat, ear-cotton, notebook, pencil, binoculars) and started for the top.

On this trip I met Lieutenant Commander Tyree, the gunnery officer, who said it was a submarine contact.

That beat me. The reason for all the panic was something I couldn't reach for at the moment. We had had numerous submarine (or blackfish) contacts during the past six weeks, and I couldn't remember any such riots as this. However! If a sub had run dead across us, worse luck. By now we'd been spotted in a new position and the Japs would be looking for us in force. We had only one bit of luck that I could see. We were steaming east at the time of the alarm.

In five minutes came recall and I went below to remove my regalia none too disturbed. . . . As usual none of my acquaintances had seen the target.

Jim Brewer stuck his head in and said that this was like being in a firehouse and that he was going to agitate for a brass pole in reverse so he could slide to his station. On the same theory I am all for a gadget to harness me automatically with all my important accouterments, lacking which I may some day go to my death.

I noted that the day had turned warmer as we proceeded east. It was really quite lovely although the water right now is probably too cold to die in with comfort.

The navigator came in. He said the alarm had stemmed from some echo-ranging detector or something. He didn't think it had been any submarine. He disapproved of the general alarm as a means of dealing with the situation anyway. He repeated what he had said about the two cruisers.

"I didn't expect we could be running into anything less," he said. "So I looked around my room and inventoried everything and I thought, Well, I probably won't be seeing those things again. I noticed you had left your pajamas lying on the bed and I thought you wouldn't be wanting them right away. . . ."

The captain had had to pry himself out of the movies and fight his way through a company of Marines in the dark to get up topside. He had a harrowing experience. He was looking at a movie that had something to do with war—ships dashing around and changing course and shooting ack-ack and dropping depth charges and dodging bombs. And when the alarm sounded the captain didn't know whether it was real or part of the show.

Ah well, we're back at our old routine for the moment. Somebody just came in to the navigator with a message from the carrier that we'll set the clock ahead an hour at midnight. That means that we're going to continue on east. And it also indicates that maybe we've abandoned our expedition.

The navigator says it's just as well. If we'd been able to quit Wake, do our fueling and get on at once so that we'd have been able to drop our clunks on Marcus today, it would have been all right. But the Japs know about our being in the neighborhood now and they're likely to do something about it.

They could bomb us from Saipan and land their planes at Marcus. They could bomb us from Wake on the way back. They could bomb us from a base at Bayonnaise, concerning which I never heard anything until today.

I mention these things merely because they have been brought to my attention—and most of them by the navigator. The personnel seems to be distinctly acid toward the bright undertaking.

5:05 P.M. This date is put in merely to show a suitable lapse of time—say five or ten minutes—from the note above. The navigator had gone away. Speedily he came back. He said we had just received another message. We are not going to change time. What else we aren't going to do, he doesn't know. Unless the admiral has made up his mind finally to turn around and go back west, we are now just about in the position where we ought to be moving the clock forward an hour. Ah me! I suppose I shall let somebody else do the guessing.

I went down to dinner at 6:15 P.M. just as the executive was getting a message from the carrier. We are to fuel at daybreak. Well, maybe. I suppose we shall rig for refueling as we've done so many times before on this trip. And if the C.O. changes his mind again in the morning that won't be any novelty either.

In the meantime we have turned north and the weather is getting icy once more.

Dinner conversation was very cheery. It had nothing much to do with the war. We all swapped reminiscences about where was the best place to eat in New Orleans—Memphis—New York. And how were the automobile roads doing in Mississippi. And such matters.

On the whole this war isn't so far different from the last one except that it's more comfortable to live on a ship than in a trench. You try to keep as close to your old life as possible. Nothing else, not even the prospect of sudden death, interests you much.

The paymaster has been ill today with a bad cold. He got up to attend to some routine work, something in connection with disbursals. Somebody kidded him about his absence and he mentioned that he had arranged long ago for a leave to begin tomorrow. So now, he says, he will start it with a fine threat of double pneumonia on the way to a dubious reception at Marcus.

All in all, he says, it isn't the danger of pneumonia that bothers him at present.

41

ADVANCE NOTICE

MARCH 1, *Sunday*. At sea. Cool. Calm. Sunny. A truly magnificent day!

I got up just in time to see the stowage of the last of our fueling gear. It was apparent that we'd be on our way somewhere later in the afternoon. So far as I could discover nobody was more enthusiastic about the job than he'd been a couple of days ago. But by now everybody is resigned. The proper spirit.

Resignation, it may be added, takes odd forms. One lad, who had been very glad to think that we were heading for home, considered the situation over a cup of coffee and doped out for himself that the division commander is waiting for fresh news of the battle off Java. If he gets the right kind of encouragement he may skip Marcus and tear up a bit of the Japanese coast. That of course is merely the idea of this thoroughly resigned officer. When you get resigned you might as well get resigned to something big.

War is like that. The more I see of it the more I am reminded of the story of the Irishman who was poking a dollar bill through a crack in the sidewalk to make it worth his while to take up the walk and rescue a nickel that he had dropped there previously.

This morning we were about 600 miles due west of Midway—about 1,000 miles from Marcus. If we get going with speed we ought to be in attacking position sometime tomorrow night. So probably we'll turn loose Tuesday morning.

Our planes were launched at 11:30 to snoop about a bit. We then took over a patrol that lasted for the rest of the afternoon. The planes were called in at 4:40 which, I take it, may be considered the starting time for the present maneuver.

Well, despite the admiral's seeming choice in such matters, we

249

had a nice day for the fueling. Most of the time we were quite close to the other ships of the force but even had we not been, the air was so clear that we could have seen details ordinarily invisible with or without field glasses. The tanker and the carrier moved sedately like the waltzing elephants in *Fantasia* . . . painted ships (gray) upon a painted ocean (blue).

The carrier was full about a quarter to five and the tanker was bobbing around just about empty. The carrier apparently is going to make a trip somewhere.

The Japs put out an interesting communiqué today: "A force of U. S. naval vessels, a carrier, two cruisers and six destroyers, attacked Otori Island, formerly Wake, and did no damage. They were shelled, bombed, and repulsed. Fire was seen to have started in the stern of one of the cruisers and one of the destroyers was down by the bow as she went away at reduced speed." (Maybe the communiqué said there were two cruisers damaged. But no matter because none of it's true anyway.)

Our planes came in in good order. At 5 P.M. a lad came looking for the navigator with a dispatch from the admiral: "Resume operation." So at 5:01 we are resuming operation.

At 5:32 Donald Duck made an announcement: "Now here it is. The captain will make a statement presently." And presently the captain did, deliberately, slowly, pausing between sentences so that his talk could be relayed to other circuits. He said that we had finished refueling but that our trip home would be delayed two days because we were about to act as escort to the carrier on a little job she had to do. He assured us that there would be no bombardment and that we should be no closer than 600 miles to any island except our objective. There were indications, he said, that the carrier would be able to complete the bombing job promptly, after which we'd be free to head for Pearl Harbor.

Well, there it is . . .

We are setting Condition Two watch, which means we are taking some precautions against surface craft. Without paying too much attention to the sub-basement navigators' club with its two-bit globe and its inch-to-the-half-billion-mile maps, I'd say that we are reasonably likely to find traces of the Jap navy in and around here. If it isn't here it isn't anywhere.

ATTACK ON WAKE ISLAND BY U. S. NAVAL FORCES

February 24, 1942. Main battery of U. S. cruiser bombarding Japanese forces at Wake Island while antiaircraft crews stand by.

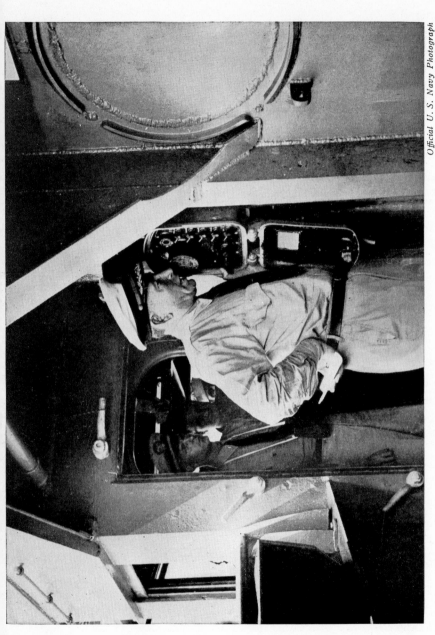

Official U. S. Navy Photograph

CAPTAIN ZACHARIAS ADDRESSES CREW BEFORE BATTLE

". . . We shall act in conjunction with other ships of this force before, during and after a severe air attack. We are likely to receive some opposition. And we prefer it that way. Nobody wants to bet on a sure thing. But we shall be able to hold our end up because we are equipped

I wonder just what was going on when the admiral sent us the message to set the clock forward and then decided to let it alone.

This then is March 1. A year ago I got broken up in Cairo and so entered upon what I thought was going to be an entirely new life. I'd get home, somehow, sometime, and sit down in a region free from war and lying communiqués and flea-witted censors. I'd read some good books and listen to some amusing phonograph records. Oh, yes, I would. . . .

So now I am here on the U.S.S. ———— engaged in what the navigator calls "pooping about." My legs appear to be all right.

I somehow don't mind the prospect of getting permanently dunked on such occasions as Wotje and Wake. I've more or less made up my mind to be resigned to the worst. But I hate the abruptness of general alarms that break in on you when you're doing something else. In the rush I never get adjusted properly—mentally I mean. I guess it boils down to the fact that you don't fear death unless it sneaks up from behind and snatches at you.

Over the radio tonight we got some details of the battle of Java. As I suspected, the bulletin of our great naval victory was a typical Libyan communiqué. The operation was successful but the patient died. The battle was won by our side but the Japs in the excitement managed to land at three places in Java. Fifty transports assisted them in this undertaking.

Reuters sent out a report from Batavia which is quite likely close to the truth: Five Jap cruisers sunk or damaged, several Jap destroyers blown up, fifteen transports sunk or damaged. But admitting all that, the situation seems nothing we can crow about. The Dutch admit the loss of two cruisers and damage to a third, and possible loss of three destroyers. No U. S. losses have come into the totals so far.

The night's news sheet contains the Jap communiqué regarding the attack on Wake. Everybody is wondering how they knew we had six destroyers with us when only two showed at the island and the Japs never did locate the carrier. A more interesting bit is from a U. S. sub commander who reported to Pearl Harbor that he had looked at Wake "and it seemed deserted." It's quite plain that some inkling of our expedition has got home, and for the moment at least, the Navy Department is wondering what it's all about. You live a long time for a day like this when you know all the news and the news sources don't know any.

The plan of the day (for Mon.) contains a word of praise from the admiral for the boys responsible for the visual signaling. Who was this man Marconi?

March 2, Monday. At sea. Midway between Midway and Marcus. Cold. Wet. Rough. Miserable. Another North Atlantic Day.

I got up early after a restless night. My hours, thanks to excursions and alarms, are getting all twisted. I went down to the deck, stuck my nose into the dismal day and began to wonder what good could possibly come of this.

The navigator had hoped that we'd be able to launch our planes tomorrow morning, start for home tomorrow afternoon, and be well out of the patrol zones by nightfall Wednesday.

But nobody's going to send planes out into this soup. If you launched them you'd never see them again. If they found the island, they'd never get back. Miracles just aren't repetitious.

Well, anyway, at the moment we're heading north. At this writing we've been shorn of our cans which probably stayed with the tanker to refuel and catch up with us later. Meanwhile we— two cruisers and the carrier—are pursuing our odd course toward the arctic alone.

Somebody got around to testing the whistle and siren this morning. The whistle was all right—that is it aroused no memories poignant or otherwise. But when the siren went *"whup whup whup"* it seemed incomplete. Nobody took over Donald Duck to bellow "Modern Design!"

In the wardroom the aviators were setting up a complete outfit of models of the Jap navy on racks recently installed for them. They are beautiful scale models and, I must say, look very impressive. I picked up the one I thought looked deadliest of the lot and was pleased to see that it was the *Haruna*, sunk by the late Captain Colin Kelly.

The smaller brands of Jap destroyer look very small indeed. Cheney (one of the aviators) says that they're in the guppy class.

And that caused somebody to recall a line in *Life* or *Liberty* describing a British corvette as "a bargain-basement destroyer."

Aside from that there was nothing much to enliven the morning except the navigator's story of a minah bird that used to scream outside his window and then say "Sh! Sh!" to itself.

Late-morning bulletins contained some news of the carrier's aviators who got to Pukapuka. It seems that they existed for thirty days on three fish and two birds. There were no details about how they got the birds. They stored drinking water by soaking their clothes in rain. The dispatch says that the survival of the three was due to the ingenuity of a machinist's mate who took charge when the cruise of the rubber boat began.*

Crowley, on reading these interesting tidings, checked over the things he wants for his rubber boat—not including keel, rudder, mast, sails and outboard motor. Kobey is making a still for him—a vacuum still to be worked by a smidgen of gasoline or alcohol. Crowley thinks he'll trade the rubber raft for a bigger contrivance—something like the *Queen Mary*.

Before noon sometime we turned almost due west which is encouraging. Whatever the job is, we'll get on with it.

The morning wasn't on the whole what you'd pick for warfare. It was bad at breakfast and it got worse with cross winds and breakers and spray all over everything. One of the carrier planes, a Grumman, returning from patrol out in the soup started to make a crooked landing, got flagged off, circled once, came in. Then his engine conked and he went into the sea. The other cruiser came alongside and picked up the pilot and his radioman.

After luncheon we listened to Radio Tokio where an unconvincing youth read bits about Japanese successes all over the world. You knew he lied when he mentioned definite losses inflicted upon definite units of the allied forces. But unfortunately you knew that in the main he was telling the truth when he indicated that the Japanese were swarming all over the place.

He said that the Japs had knocked out a total of six allied cruisers in the battle of Java. The Dutch admit the sinking of two and the damaging of a third. He said that this phase of the opera-

---

* The experiences of these three were the subject of *The Raft,* a best seller by Robert Trumbull.

tions could be considered finished and that Australia and New Zealand would be cut out next. He said that the Aussies were much disturbed about the smallness of the help they were getting from the United States and England and seemed to indicate that the great continent down under would be much happier under the genial and understanding Japs.

I guess I am recording this only because I know that some day I may wish to read a sample of the propaganda that is being dished out to us these days. One portion I should have found place for in any event:

"The decadence of the United States has been thoroughly demonstrated and the pitiful inadequacy of American arms made clear to the nations Roosevelt has been cajoling. We remember that Admiral Nimitz said boastingly that 'every sinew of American strength is now in use against the enemy.' Where is that strength? The Japanese forces have carried the war straight to the shores of California and have awakened some of the people so long kept in ignorance by the Roosevelt policies. We do not talk. We strike!"

There was something almost awesome in listening to this on a cruiser headed straight for Japan. Thank God for the Japanese. Were it possible that I should ever lose faith in the worth of our mission or the strength of our right arms, they would restore it for me.

The marines broke out their overcoats this afternoon and immediately took on the snug, smug, comfortable look of the men who never get caught out without their umbrellas. I don't belong to that class. This is the first jaunt I've ever taken since I left on the clipper for what in those days we called the war that I've left my coat somewhere else. If I don't freeze this time I'll not make the mistake again.

At dinner we talked of the Japanese situation. Nobody professes to know much about it or to gather much about it from the communiqués. However it seems to be the general feeling that the defense of Java won't be any better than the defense of Singapore. You'd wonder at that. If the Japs succeeded in landing every man out of the fifty transports they brought to this enterprise, they'd have a force not to exceed 75,000 men equipped with just what stuff they could manage to get ashore in a hurry. It seems to me that there ought to be enough troops in Java to stop a haphazard invasion by even 100,000 men—it seems to me.

We are bowling along straight westward and that caused some discussion of the admiral's possible plan. It looks now as if we'd be getting into dangerous waters by daylight. But maybe not. We'll be too late for a twilight smash at the island so very likely we shall proceed with our mysterious work on Wednesday morning.

Kobey was a little worried last night lest our positions and direction had been relayed by a submarine that stuck its head up in the neighborhood of our rendezvous the day after we left Wake. But he got some reassuring information. The sub wasn't theirs but ours. It came up and was immediately plastered with eggs from the carrier's planes homeward bound. The skipper sent out a message: "Am being bombed by strange carrier planes." And inasmuch as nobody at Pearl knows where we are and inasmuch as nobody there would tell him anyway, he still doesn't know we're in the vicinity. It would serve us right if he were to come along some night and put a tin fish into us. Turn and turn about.

42

SAD CASE OF THE REDUCTION GEAR

MARCH 3, *Tuesday*. At sea. En route to Marcus. Fine day. Cold but not painful.

On deck there is a noticeable and eye-pleasing change in costume. Officers are generally in blues. Last night in the dead cold of the midnight watch, they crawled into anything that happened to be at hand and the wardroom looked like a teamsters' convention in Winnipeg in winter.

The gyro compass was reported out of order about midnight. How do you fix a thing like that on a darkened ship? However, morning found it working again. Kobey changed a motor or something.

Late this afternoon the captain made a brief announcement over Donald Duck: "Tomorrow at about daylight the carrier will launch planes to attack our objective. After that we shall reverse course and head for home. After turning we must be on the alert to give the proper reception to anything that may be sent out after us. Tonight Condition Two will be set in the main battery and anti-aircraft battery. That is all."

The navigator was a little concerned about the wind. As it's running, the carrier would have to turn around to recover planes— a serious handicap in some circumstances. However, he doesn't look for much trouble and the wind may change. Kobey is still moaning about the noise the reduction gear makes. He hopes it will hold out but he's not sure. Maybe he ought to pray over it. I wonder why he reminds me of so many other chief engineers.

We have increased speed. We get to hop-off point at midnight . . . start back, it is alleged, at seven o'clock.

Everybody disappeared from the wardroom shortly after dinner as is the custom before battles. Everybody seems to want all the sleep he can get so he'll be bright and chipper in the morning, even though we're unlikely to know our part in the proceedings till we get home and read the Pearl Harbor press releases in the Honolulu papers. The boy who brought around the daily news sheet found me almost his only customer and he seemed a bit disturbed as a bearer of glad tidings at the dearth of interest in his wares.

"We certainly have a good press tonight," he said. I said I hoped so. He went out and I bored through the collection of pieces from baseball contracts, rubber priorities, and the blabbing of Sumner Welles to an unencouraging account of the battle of Java. Then I discovered that the good news was: The overseas paybill had been passed and under its provisions, officers at sea will receive an increase of 10 per cent in pay, enlisted men 20 per cent.

The news from Java wasn't too upsetting after what we've been getting recently from all parts of our battleground. The Japs had established no new beach heads. The allied fleet, although somewhat crippled, is still able to operate. The Japs lost at least one carrier and two destroyers besides numerous transport ships. U.S. losses were small. At least that's what they say.

I went out and took another look at the map gone so generally skew-gee. Japan ought to be upset if we hit Marcus effectively. If we could take and hold that island and put in an air base we could bomb Tokio *ad lib*. There might, of course, be a little trouble holding it—what with the Jap home fleet, etc.

John Lambert, assistant chief engineer, came in about 10 o'clock for a cup of coffee. I offered condolences about the reduction gear and he said nuts or words to that effect. "I've been listening to that gear for two years and a half," he said, "and it's sweeter sounding now than it was to begin with. If you don't like to listen to it you can get a pair of ear muffs."

Well, I thought, that's how it was. Tomorrow if I live that long I shall advise Kobey to pack his gear in grease and ground cork as used so extensively to cure noisy differentials back in the early twenties. You just pump it in and you don't tell the customer.

43

THE RAID ON MARCUS

MARCH 4, *Wednesday*. At sea. Off Marcus. Homeward bound. Rough.

I turned in at 4 A.M. and was awakened immediately by the sound of planes. I went up on deck and discovered the last of a string of bombers leaving the carrier. We'd sent out thirty-three and four fighters.

I looked at what the art critics used to call a "dramatic sky"— tumbling clouds with light finding its way around them to the sea—the full moon exploding through them every time a rift rode by on the gale. I went below.

We'll sit here and wait now. We shan't know what's going on until the planes get back and maybe not them. It's not the same as other vigils we've kept here. (1) We're not going to get the distraction of an active part in the mess. (2) This is a more dangerous situation.

The Japs aren't going to enjoy this unbirthday present for the Emperor. In two hours from now the whole western sky will be filled with planes. We may not see them—we hope—but they'll be there. The ether will be cluttered up with indignant and probably panicky Japanese. . . . Every sub between here and Pearl Harbor will have dropped all useful endeavor to look for us.

As I write this at 5:30 A.M., twenty minutes before general quarters from which we may not be released for a couple of hours, I feel that gift of clairvoyance which comes at least once to every diarist. So I make a prediction:

I don't think we are going to get into much trouble. Our planes have the advantage of surprise (the admiral has done very well this time) and fair weather. All of them ought to get back.

After they have been taken aboard and bedded down, the whole force will be streaking for healthier climes, and Jap planes—even if they knew where to hunt—would have a hard time catching us. If they did find us they'd have to contend not only with our ack-ack (which might be improved) but with a full force of planes better than theirs.

To get to our hop-off point the closest of them would have to fly 600 miles (a three-hour journey in which time we'll have gone another hundred miles). And because of the long haul they'll have to send bombers. Their fighters, which might protect the bombers against our Grummans, just aren't good enough to make the trip. In any sort of fight so far the Mitsubishi bombers have been a setup for the Grummans. . . . I shall go now and take another look at the setting moon and the living statuary around the five-inch guns.

6:45. The carrier sent out eight fighter planes. Shortly after that we got an order to secure from general quarters and went to breakfast.

7:15. "The attack has been successful. . . . Japanese planes were caught on the ground." Thus Donald Duck.

Some of the aviators came in with more information. There was some confusion about whether or not any of the Jap planes had got off. One squadron commander had reported that he thought they'd all been kept down. Another thought some had got up. And there it was.

Crowley had overheard a conversation between a squadron commander and a pilot. . . . Said the commander: "They're rolling planes onto the field. . . . Get them."

Answered the pilot: "Am getting them!"

And there was some smart horseplay. Over the air from one of the bombers came a message that may have caused worry and speculation in Tokio if any Japanese was unbusy enough at the moment to listen to it: "Ranger group! Department of Hawaii group! Attack in ten minutes. . . ." And this was repeated so that the Japs could get an idea of all our carriers massing along their shores.

8:00. Seventeen bombers came out of the western sky flying in close formation. Shortly after them a group of eight. It's apparent that they haven't taken any beating. Otherwise they'd not be doing any of this parade stuff. The stragglers would be coming over the horizon singly every five or ten minutes. . . .

As they circled overhead you could see that one had taken a charge of flack in his right wing. He was having a little trouble.

8:20. Carrier heads into wind. Leading plane lets down wheels.

8:35. Planes begin to land rapidly. . . . The wind is erratic but strong. The sea is rolling but not too rough. Thirty-one bombing planes landed without casualty. I'm going below now and read a good book. If we are going to get Japped I think the dust-up will come between 11:30 and 1 P.M.

10:00. And after. I didn't get to settle down in the chair. Lambert came in to tell me that the crash detail had been posted to pick up a bomber lost from the carrier. There was a chance, he said, that the plane would land in the water beside us. We went into the wardroom and waited for this glad event. But it didn't come off. The crippled plane got in all right, took a chance on the carrier and landed right side up. By 11 o'clock, when I finished this session, all hope had been abandoned for the other bomber. He had taken some slugs of ack-ack in the tank, apparently, and had reported that he was running short of gas. By now, of course, he was dead.

I slept through luncheon. There was no alarm during the noon hour. When I awoke at 4 P.M. I should have said that our position was excellent. The navigator came in and more or less verified this. We are about 600 miles from Wake, he said, but the planes that could come up out of that area would be just about pooped out by the time they got here. Our only worry is that we may be surprised—the word seems to be well chosen—by some of the regular patrols. And if that's all we can find to get nervous about our ingenuity must be getting pretty low.

The navigator says that the bombing expedition found a better bag than it had expected. There was a flying field on Marcus, complete with hangars and other installations. This was destroyed along with the radio station, docks, etc.

From source unrevealed word has come that two divisions of Jap battleships are operating in the waters through which we are at the moment retiring so hastily. I hardly need any blueprint to help me visualize the panic on those ships when they heard of our odd performance on Marcus. The sundry admirals will be sitting in conference for the next two weeks trying to find out what it all means—providing, of course, that we don't tangle with them before that. And when they do find out I hope they'll tell us.

At dinnertime San Francisco radio said that the Navy now admits or announces that on February 21 "a task force southwest of the Gilbert Islands had attacked a Japanese flying force and sunk eighteen planes with a loss to us of two planes and one pilot." This, of course, is the *Lexington's* performance about which there's been as much mystery as about our own operation at Wake. The Japs, one remembers, said that they had put this force out of action, damaging the carrier. The Navy communiqué says no warship was damaged. All of which sounds reasonable and encouraging.

There were some more bulletins. Steep increase in income tax and a strike by some builders of wooden boats at San Diego for double pay for overtime. 'Tis a mad world we live in, Horatio, and "Hut-Sut Rawlson on the rillerah . . ."

The radio tonight announced that Senator Bilbo of Mississippi was considering a plan to teach all soldiers and sailors of the United States how to swim. The hands are duly appreciative of his thoughtfulness.

44

MORE BOMBS ON HONOLULU

MARCH 5, *Thursday*. At sea. Bound northwest and presumably for Pearl Harbor. Another North Atlantic Day. Short gray rollers with fuzzy white collars. Gray sky. Wet decks. Most of the ships with us look as if they intended to submerge.

Last night at 11 o'clock we were out of danger of airplanes. At 6 P.M. we were 420 miles from Marcus and 580 from Wake. But we are still in danger of submarines if not battleships so it's likely that this runaway speed will be kept up for another several hours.

Inside the ship it's hot. Outside it's cold with a wind of fifty-eight knots across the deck. Everybody on watch is dressed in his best interpretation of an arctic costume.

With the first cold in the head I've had for a long time I couldn't sleep despite the late turn-in. So I got up before the call to general quarters this morning. Went down to the wardroom for coffee with Captain Cobb, a genial and intelligent soul if there ever was one. He doesn't advertise himself much so it's a surprise to learn that he speaks and reads Chinese—real Chinese, not the kind that passes for English in the communiqués.

So passed a pleasant morning with nothing much but the Marines, the artillery and China in it. Almost enough to make me homesick for life in a pup tent in a possible invasion of Norway—almost.

Commander Carter came in to breakfast with a thought about the plight of Admiral Kimmel before, during and after Pearl Harbor.

"He was damned if he did and damned if he didn't," the commander said. "He'd had orders to get on war footing. But it was very hush-hush. He couldn't let the word get down through the

262

fleet. He was on war footing but nobody had told him under what conditions he was to reveal that to the enemy.

"Suppose he'd taken his ships out here—as he undoubtedly would have done before December 9. Suppose he'd met the Japs out here on their way to Pearl Harbor. What was he to do? If he took their salute in friendship and let them get by, they could have gone in and destroyed Pearl Harbor just as they did anyway. If, as would have been more likely, he had met this force and attacked it, there would have been the overt act, the *casus belli*, originating with us. The people of the United States would have yelled that he'd got us into war. And they'd probably have got around to apologizing to Nomura and Saburo Kurusu.

"Whatever he did it was on the cards that he was going to get into trouble. And I think that a court-martial would so find."

Maybe. I think myself that Kimmel was let down terribly by some of his subordinates. He takes the rap as the final responsible officer—which is the way with armies and navies.

It's odd how your sleeping habits get twisted around so quickly when you've had no particular program for bed-going. Having stowed away at a proper hour last night I stayed awake until daylight which in these latitudes at this time of the year comes late. Immediately after breakfast I found I couldn't keep my eyes open and so went up and lay down on top of the covers of the bunk. I fell asleep over something by Jules Romains—an easy task even when you aren't sleepy. I slept through luncheon and most of the afternoon. The navigator came in after while and we swapped stories and comments on art and literature and the like.

Well, we don't get to Honolulu till after Tuesday. Somebody in the front office has received word that the Japs are going to do a bit of raiding of their own. So now instead of a group of homing pigeons we are an interception squad of tired hawks. According to the present intelligence we'll be at least a week on this job. However, everybody's fairly pleased with everything. We're better equipped to fight cruisers and planes and subs—even battleships—than we are to blow up outhouses on Wotje and Wake and Marcus. And there's consolation, too. If the Japs are sufficiently aroused to try a counter-raid, it means they have hauled something out of the southwest.

The news tonight was generally discouraging except for the fact that the Russians are still doing business on the southern part of their line. The R.A.F. succeeded in bombing the Renault works outside of Paris. There will be a fine hullaballoo about that in spite of the fact that nobody in his right mind thinks Renault now has any customers but Hitler. Java, if an old communiqué judger may judge from the current communiqués, is about to fold up. American planes and pilots are reported to be arriving in Australia. The British would appear to be falling back from the river Whosis in front of Burma, and Parliament is rushing a plan to grant dominion status to India. More U. S. troops have landed in Northern Ireland—which, I take it, presages a campaign through Norway to protect the Russian supply line.

The *pièce de résistance* in the night's grist comes from Tokio relayed via Los Angeles (KNX) where an announcer cautions us to remember its source and take it for what it is worth. "Forty U. S. planes bombed Whosisowara Island. [It seems that Marcus was traveling under an alias on the hydrographic charts.] Eight people were killed. Some buildings were hit. No great damage was done and eight of the attacking planes were shot down."

"That ain't the way I heered it, Jahnny!"

More mysterious than the attack on Marcus we find a flash that Honolulu was bombed yesterday. Three bombs are said to have fallen outside the city limits and to have done no damage. The Army says that the bombs came from an enemy plane. . . . And that has caused a fine lot of speculation. What kind of plane was it? Where did it come from? Where did it go? How did it operate entirely in the dark?

Ted Kobey guesses it was a plane carried by a submarine, which would explain some of the mystery but not all. It's hard to see how a plane capable of carrying three bombs could be launched from the deck of a submarine and if it had been launched, how it could have found its way back and been recovered. It is also difficult to see how it could have carried enough gas to sustain it until there was enough light for it to return. There are many other reasons why it couldn't have been a submarine plane. So most likely it will turn out to have been one. My own theory is that a dirigible came over carrying a four-engined bomber plane in whose bomb-bay was a plane-carrying submarine. Let's have it simple.

It's not impossible of course that the plane was actually a Jap plane. (We'll stipulate that, also the Army's declaration that some bombs were dropped and that they exploded.) If we are able to get within socking distance of Marcus, we can't deny the possibility of Jap warships slipping through our guard near Hawaii. It has been done. It is conceivable that only a destroyer came—a destroyer carrying a catapult and one plane. With such equipment the Son of Heaven could expand his nuisance technique—the technique he has been employing on the California coast. With no risk of any important part of his fleet he could do a little genuine bombing to support the artillery practice of his submarines.

Later: Possibly inspired by the Hawaiian mystery, the news sheet tonight mentioned that Japan has twenty plane-carrying submarines and may be building more. Those that may be built, of course, don't mean anything to Honolulu at the moment one way or the other. And as for the twenty already built: "Ho hum!"

I went farther into the oddities of the report that originated with a certain appropriateness in Oahu (pronounced Wahoo). One of the novel features of the situation was the manner in which it became public. There are quite a lot of important brass hats in Honolulu—Cincpac, the military governor, the provost marshal, the civil governor and the press relations officers of the fleet and G2. But the announcement of the outrage if any came from none of these but from the mayor—who has previously taken no part in the conversation.

So our shipboard committees of experts went into session to review the whole case and decided that the explosions might have been:

(1) Ack-ack from some Army artillery practice.

(2) Bombs jettisoned in the wrong place by some lad returning from patrol.

(3) Blasting.

Contrariwise it was decided that it was not:

(1) A visitation by long-distance land-based planes.

(2) Debut of some carrier-borne experimental bomber.
(3) Miracle.

In the late news there were some more details of the *Lexington's* exploit near the Gilberts. The Japs attacked the carrier in two waves of nine planes each. Of the first wave three got in close enough to drop bombs. Thirty minutes later five of the second wave got through. Of the eight that came to striking distance none made a hit because of the heavy flack and quick maneuvering of the ship. One Jap attempted a crash landing on the deck of the carrier—that seems to be the new technique of *Bushido*—but he was blown up at 100 yards by ack-ack. When the final score was totted up sixteen of the eighteen attacking planes had been shot down—six of them by Lieutenant (J.G.) O'Hare of St. Louis. We lost two planes and recovered one pilot.

The one bit of news that causes most speculation tonight is the detailed account of the bombing of the Renault works by the R.A.F. The French report 1,000 injured, 600 dead in one of the most thorough-going destructions of this war. Petain was almost lyrical in his outcry:

"The bloody attack of the night of March 3-4, striking only at the civilian population, will arouse indignation as it takes on the character of a national catastrophe."

French politicians never learn. Wistfully I remember the rolling mills of the Moselle blazing in the sky a couple of miles from blacked-out Nancy—the foundries of the last war that weren't bombarded by Petain's own artillery over there in the Verdun sector even while they were turning out shell for Germany. And I remember the amicable setups of the international steel cartel in Luxembourg. And I haven't forgotten the day when Fritz Thyssen, the inventor of Hitler, came in and sat next to me at luncheon in the Crillon. . . . That wasn't many days before the Nazis were cracking through at Sedan.

So there will be bitter resentment at the English for killing Frenchmen on French soil even though the Frenchmen are turning out tanks with which the Germans, unless the Russians get there first, can kill a few Englishmen.

Moscow reports that the Red army is "methodically destroying" the 90,000 men of the German 16th army, encircled at Starya. I hope so.

From the Philippines comes a dispatch saying that MacArthur's almost nonexistent air force had gone out to Subic Bay on a raid and sunk a 12,000-ton ship, an 8,000-ton ship and two motor ships of 100 tons apiece, and had damaged numerous smaller craft. Before returning the fliers set fire to the Jap fuel dumps at Olongapo, the former U. S. naval base.

Late tonight the commentator on the Columbia broadcast from San F. repeated the Japanese bulletin about our bombing of Marcus.

"We don't quite understand this," he said. "Nobody in the U. S. seems to know anything about such a raid. All that we know is through the Tokio report and it's not immediately evident why such news should come from this source unless the Japs wish to get to the U. S. with the news first and forestall worse reports or prepare the home folks for the possibility of a raid on Tokio."

Tokio had an air-raid alert for the first time yesterday afternoon. You don't know why but you rather guess it was an echo of the Marcus affair. After so close a call as that nobody will be able to burst a paper bag in Tokio without starting the sirens.

The voice from Java about midnight said all the news was bad. The Australians are looking for an attack on their east coast via Port Moresby.

The clock has advanced an hour.

45

TWO-MAN SUBS

MARCH 6, *Friday*. At sea. Cold. Damp. Gray.

"Bad Weather Halsey," they called him in them days.

We're not quarreling about it particularly. If any Jap aviator finds us in this he'll be an ignorant mug who never heard about the law of averages.

I went down after breakfast to the sick bay to have my head blown out but no go. My nose is so completely stopped up that the doctor suggested using the main battery or a depth charge.

I discovered that the doc's prize patient, the lad who got hit with the line shot, is up and about. The only mark on him is a little spot under his left eye. All he'll need will be replacement of a couple of his left upper teeth.

I'm going to take my cold to bed—not that it's serious but I've nothing else to do with it.

The weather turned decent during the afternoon—or so I hear.

We cross the date line tonight so tomorrow will still be today. I got out of bed at midnight just to make note of that interesting phenomenon.

The 180th Meridian.

March 6, Friday. At sea for the second March 6. Bright. Very rough.

Commander Chappell brought in news that we've abandoned the hunt for possible Jap raiders and are on our way to Pearl once more. He says not to bet on it, however, because too many people can change their minds too often in five days.

The captain dropped in for a minute during the afternoon. He says that from information reaching him from various sources, it's obvious that the Japs are upset about the Marcus business. They are reassigning fleet units and presumably hiking their battleships to a safer venue. Foster Hailey says that if we can make them burn as much fuel oil as we burned getting into position to drop a few crumps on Marcus we may call it a Mexican standoff.

There's some more news about MacArthur's recent air operation in Subic Bay. The lads put down not two large Jap ships but three—a total of 30,000 tons. They were loaded transports and the loss of life must have been considerable.

It seems odd that the only shred of news that can give any consolation to our side should be coming from the abandoned Philippines. Somebody came in with reports that the brass hats are meeting in Washington to consider a revision of their strategy in the Pacific. That comes as news to me. I never knew they had any.

Went down late to the wardroom and so heard an odd announcement from Radio Tokio. The *Bushido*-bushed Japanese thought it was time to admit that they had seven submarines lying on the bottom of Pearl Harbor on the morning of December 7. These subs remained in a recumbent position until late afternoon, long after the air attack was finished, at which time they popped up and knocked off the ships in sight including the *Arizona*. Medals are to be awarded posthumously in most cases to the heroic commanders of those seven submarines.

All of this of course is interesting chiefly as fantasy. We know how many subs there were in Pearl Harbor that morning—namely three. Two were sunk in a few minutes after the attack began. A third which had left before the planes arrived went aground near Kaneohe. No sub got a chance to fire a shot inside the harbor even at the *Arizona*. No U. S. warship has been sunk by a submarine torpedo in the Pacific up to this moment.

You'd think that of all the places in the world from which the worthy Japs might hope for correct intelligence, tops would be Hawaii. But you begin to wonder. It becomes more and more evident, as you sit listening to the Tokio commentators putting out flat statements to provoke flat answers, that maybe they don't know yet just what was in their bag at Pearl Harbor.

With the planes that made the attack, or some of them at least, back in Japan it would seem that the high command should know precisely what happened that morning. It was all according to schedule and the schedule undoubtedly had been contrived months before Saburo Kurusu brought his message of good will to Washington. You'd think a Jap brass hat would only have to look at his blueprints to estimate the damage. You'd think that. But stories like this cockeyed bit about the seven submarines make you wonder.

About the only offhand explanation one can give to the announcement is that the Jap air force is getting a bit too cocky and the admiralty wants to put it into its place. As against that, of course, we have the always interesting theory of our intelligence that none of the attacking planes got back to tell what happened. The O.N.I. officers explain the reports of the showing of moving pictures of the bombing in Japan, with the suggestion that a couple of unarmed, high-flying observation planes might have been able to make the trip to and from the carrier in safety. The bombers shot down or cracked up about Oahu, they say, were all virtually out of gas despite the belly tanks they carried to Honolulu and dropped before the attack. In keeping with this theory we now have some of the best thought in the Navy holding that the carrier was parked 190 miles or better from Honolulu at a point southwest of the island of Hawaii. The proponents of this theory discount the suggestion that the attack sneaked in by way of the Aleutians. For, they say, a carrier and escort coming that way would have been too easily spotted by ships on the great circle course, by the Army fortress flight actually in the air at the time, or perhaps by a clipper. Anyway it has its elements as a puzzle.

March 7, Saturday. At sea. Very rough even for the Pacific. Bright. Somewhat cool. At 8 o'clock last night we were 1,045 miles from Honolulu. We ought to be there late Monday afternoon.

The weather is terrific. Water is sluicing the decks sometimes to a depth of a foot and a half. The wind is howling like cats in a loud-speaker. We have most of the makings of a storm except an overcast sky. The sun is shining brightly. The constant spray weaves through the light and makes a rainbow off starboard.

The radio this morning announced an air-raid alarm in Honolulu. Everybody was warned to take shelter. Then the radio went dead. Knowing what we do about the whereabouts of the Jap fleet we're inclined to think it's just another of those things. However in a war where nothing happens but the impossible, you can't be sure.

6 P.M. Nothing new about Honolulu. The general feeling on the ship is that the authorities are testing their new sirens on some screwy evacuation scheme. (They have a plan to chase all civilians out of town into the hills.)

The news tonight is all bad. Java has all but collapsed. Burma isn't doing so well. The Australians are getting all set for invasion. There was a bit of H₂S taken on the rebound from the London *Dyely Mile* to the effect that hordes of Americans are now on their way to the relief of Australia—a magnificent convoy of planes, tanks, artillery and what have you. Convoys have been going down there regularly so I can't explain why this item sounds phony. Maybe the Navy is giving it publicity to cheer the customers at a time when they certainly need cheering.

Home news is much brighter. It seems that the manufacture of juke boxes and pin-ball machines has been stopped by federal order. The factories are going to make something nifty for use in national defense. Probably loaded dice.

To bed late. Choppy all night. One roll 26 degrees port to 27 degrees starboard. It sounds as if the ship were falling to pieces. As I sat in the wardroom noting all this down Jim Brewer came in. He had been tossed out of his bunk and he sought the safety of the wardroom davenport. It turned over on top of him.

March 8, Sunday. At sea. Still rough. Bright. Cool.

The navigator when he came in this morning said that he'd stick to his first guess that we'd get into Pearl Harbor Tuesday morning.

I find that my cold is better, which is a matter of great importance to me if not to posterity.

We've learned enough to pay attention when Donald Duck calls for Condition One in the A.A. battery. The bugle didn't blow but nobody could have heard it anyway in the clatter of feet on the iron ladders. I got into my costume and hit the gun deck just as the lights went out and the doors of the watertight compartments began to clang shut all over the ship. As often as I've been through this mill it sent a shiver up my back.

On the deck a telephone man announced the situation to a belated gunnery officer. A plane had been picked up off the port bow twenty miles away. If it hadn't been for the excursions and alarms from Honolulu we might have been more interested in this plane. We were near Midway and it seemed more likely to be one of ours than a Jap. On the other hand it might be an enemy carrier plane. So we stood at attention until a PBY showed on the horizon, came to look at us, dipped in salute and went away again.

Foster Hailey and I went to lunch in the CPO mess at noon and fought for our soup and chicken all over the galloping table. We finally conquered by wrapping one leg apiece around a stanchion, holding the dishes with one hand and eating with the other hand.

Here we listened to the Honolulu news report. Some Jap general was reported to have committed suicide—hara-kiri as we called it in them days—because he hadn't been able to get rid of MacArthur. MacArthur in the meantime had counterattacked and wiped out most of a relief regiment.

Honolulu apparently is sticking to the theory that the air-raid alarm was legitimate. The Japs gave some verisimilitude by paraphrasing the Army announcement of March 4 that "four small bombs" had been dropped on the outskirts of the city "by a lone airplane." The Jap version was a little different: "Naval planes rained tons of bombs on the city and Pearl Harbor," read this sprightly bit.

The Russians, one gathers, continue to do well. What would I have said in my bed of pain in Cairo a year ago if anyone had suggested that one day the only cheering news of this war would be coming out of Russia!

Went down to the wardroom after dinner and found no reason for staying. The evening's news was even more dismal than that we'd been listening to at noon. The only bright bit was a quote from the London newspapers wondering if the catastrophe in the southwest Pacific might not have been due to faulty American strategy. No doubt it was—particularly the faulty American strategy that failed to put a back on the Singapore base.

The night is one of the roughest in my experience. The ship heels about twenty-five degrees to starboard most of the time, and when she goes all the way over she snaps the foremast. She also has a trick of dropping flat for fifteen or twenty feet. A torpedo jolt would be no new experience.

We were 540 miles from Honolulu at 8 P.M. We're making little progress at fifteen knots on account of the head wind which must be doing seventy-five knots across the deck.

46

HEAVY WEATHER, ETC.

MARCH 9, *Monday*. At sea. We are 360 miles from Pearl this morning so we'll be in tomorrow unless we break something or the wind gets worse.

The gale is still roaring and the sea is lumpy. I'm beginning to ache in the joints. We certainly have been taking a beating during the past few days whether we realized it or not. The navigator says he doesn't know whether it's a storm somewhere or just \March. Anyway he doesn't like it.

I don't suppose there is anything quite so boresome as the trip home out of battle. Your work is done. The prospects for excitement as you know from experience are nil. You've read all the books—most of them for a second time inasmuch as the available library consists mainly of two-bit pocket books. And you can't sleep (a) because you're not sleepy all the time, (b) because nobody will let you.

The Navy life is of course the favored life in warfare. But it has its drawbacks. In the army you lived like a dog—or a duck—and you walked in the aura of discomfort from the time you went into the line until the day they signed the Armistice. But usually there was something going on—all the time. Battles were not a matter of a couple of hours' fighting. They went on and on with plenty of noise and no end of incident to distract one's attention from his condition in life. There never was any sense of security. On the other hand there never was much boredom—at least not in the war I fought, although it's highly probable that the boys who had experience with the immobilized wrangle of the trenches would disagree with me. . . .

Anyway the point I'm making is that we travel something like twenty thousand miles in two months for a total of about five hours of tense action.

Foster Hailey came in about 10:30 to announce a bit of good news. It doesn't have to be *very* good news these days to rate the label. He reported that one of our subs—or maybe a couple of them—attacked a Jap task force, sank a couple of destroyers, got two hits on a carrier and one on a cruiser.

The important part of that to me is that it indicates a new phase of our conduct of the war in the Pacific. Everybody knows we had plenty of submarines over in Asiatic waters at the beginning of the riot. And the folks at home have been wondering what became of them. This bit of news would indicate that the scouts that have been lying doggo out there with orders not to attack, now have been told to pour it in. I hope so.

March 10, Tuesday. Honolulu. We came in at 10:30 this morning. The weather was sunny but cool coming in, sunny turning to rain when we arrived.

About 8:30 Hawaiian time the land came up out of the mist to port. Presently we were part of the turmoil that has become characteristic of Honolulu. All about us were four-pipers and motorboats of the patrol—big boats, little boats, all dashing about like the ferries in New York harbor. Gobs in starched white were breaking out on the decks like a species of popcorn. Home again.

We swung in past the buoys with no delay, the last ship in the line. Crowley, who had been supervising the job of swinging his planes outboard for taxi-ing to the seaplane base, came up to the rail for a minute as we neared Ford Island. "All the boys of the repair shop go to general quarters automatically when they see us coming in," he said.

We came ashore about 11 o'clock to find the usual bedlam. We now have two censorships where one grew before. Fleet and general. The general is a new setup, a version of Byron Price's "National Censorship," and its field officer is a former circulation manager of one of the local news sheets. Its inevitable head, I am told, is a former insurance agent. The agency men tell me it operates only part time. The fleet "supervision," as they laughingly call it, embraces a going-over by all sorts of experts on operations, aviation, communications and possibly caligraphy and cartography. If any real story were to break under this setup the public would find out about it a year after the armistice, if any.

Foster Hailey, it turns out, is in the middle of a mystery. Three days ago word was sent out to all the fleet that his credentials had been revoked. He found out about it this A.M. when Captain Zacharias told him.

Ashore Waldo Drake told him that the orders had come from Washington because he had avoided censorship. He wired his office and it looks as if a fine row might be in the offing.

I seem to have raised a stink with the Marshall Island story because it circulated where the pundits could read it. James (M. E. of the *Times*) cabled Hailey wanting to know if I was the only reporter on the trip and why. I think I shall send in another resignation today. All of this tires me.

Liquor is back and you can drink all you want to between 7 A.M. and 5 P.M. or later if you have a supply. But if you get drunk they may give you as much as five months in jail and a fine of $500 or under.

There was one consolation. Stan Johnston is here for the *Tribune*. He came up to the hotel during the afternoon and we refought the blitz of France and London where censors were so silly we little thought sillier ones could be contrived.

The lads who sailed a thousand miles and thirty-four days in the rubber boat after falling into the drink on our first expedition were in town and all the locals were interviewing them as we arrived. They seemed perfectly well.

March 11, Wednesday. Honolulu. Wet. Alternately cool and muggy. Miserable weather. I wasn't able to sleep because of the cold at night. Felt rotten all morning. Had luncheon with Stan Johnston and Walter Farr, *Daily Mail* correspondent who kicked up an international row with his story of the convoy that wasn't going any place and hadn't started anyway. He said he had an alibi for his story—which I guess he may be going to need. He seems to be a pleasant boy, and bright.

The feature of the day was that we wasted a couple of hours at a press conference with Captain Browning of the carrier on the subject of the Wake-Marcus business. The purpose of the meeting was to give some of the non-seagoing correspondents a chance to find out what we had done on our journey. They didn't find out anything including the time of day from Captain Browning.

I probably never realized before the gap that exists between the naval mind and the facts of life as they exist in a democracy at the midpoint of the twentieth century. I had a chance to compare what I had seen for myself with what was dished out in the official report. And I had a hard time imagining them to be the same thing. The captain dismissed the operation with a gesture as not worth mentioning. He named the places, recited that we had destroyed the usual inventory of stuff, and apologized for having taken up our time. He did not tell us why his planes had been so late that he virtually had no reason to suggest his own connection with the engagement.

He was right on the whole about our little raid having had no significance as a naval operation. But what got me was his casual assumption that nobody in the United States needed to know anything about the U. S. fleet unless it happened to be fighting some new battles of Trafalgar. Henceforth, I suppose our motto must be: "Silence until the New Jutland!"

March 12, Thursday. Honolulu. The chief feature of this day was a luncheon at the Pacific Club in honor of Commander Robert Berry who was sent out from Washington during our absence to look over press relations.

I found out after he had finished his speech that my service message to the office had been held up. That means I am incommunicado. I then raised hell, most of which was listened to by Roy Howard who had just arrived in Honolulu for reasons known only to himself.

I am getting very disheartened over this business. If the Navy can't get such a small thing as a press office operating without a lot of internal politics knocking it to bits every time it is set up, then what on earth is the condition of departments that have really important work to do?

We have seen here the bitter quarrel between the district and the fleet, for instance, over who shall control the press, and between individual officers of each of those organizations as to which one should have the dubious honor.

This is the most important naval news center in our world. The local publicity office should be handled by somebody of decent rank and considerable tact and experience, but most of all by somebody who can look at a clock and tell what time it is.

I came home and tried to soothe the shattered blood pressure. I shall cultivate an abiding calm until such time as I can get out of this to some place where I am trusted enough to send a cablegram to my editor.

March 13, Friday. Honolulu. Hot. Went to the censors (the national censors so called) to complain of being kept in internment. I discovered that this civilian institution was run by Navy personnel which made it more difficult to understand. Eventually I found Commander Kelser who since our arrival here has been pointed out as the Big Bad Wolf of the censorship. He and Lieutenant Clissold, of his office, turned out to be fairly decent gents. I presented my case and they seemed inclined to listen to reason. So they let me send out a message to the office asking them to fix up my income tax. They said it would go through all right and I can only hope it does. However, if it fails and I get sent to Atlanta I can console myself with the thought that they have no censors there.

47

VARIATION ON AN OLD THEME . . .

MARCH 14, *Saturday*. Honolulu. Damp. Warm.

My birthday, so help me.

This began like all other days but took a turn to novelty about 9:40 with an air-raid alarm. Over my short-wave radio I could hear the Army transmitters in a strange gibberish: "Agnes Brown from Control, Agnes Brown, Agnes Brown, alert all flights immediately . . ." And more such stuff. I went over to the police station with Foster Hailey and Keith Wheeler and sat there until the end of the disturbance. I noticed on the way that this alert save for geography might be in Paris or in London—the same public reactions—the same lack of concern—the same disinclination to get to shelters—the same unimpressed attitude toward the same type of diffident or overbearing auxiliary wardens.

At 10:52 the business was over. Army and Navy announced that unidentified airplanes later had been identified as friendly.

At 5 P.M. Dick Haller picked me up at the hotel and we went to dinner with Chauncey Wightman and his charming wife somewhere up in the flowering hills. On the way we dropped in to pay a brief call on the Sam Stewarts where we presently turned out to be participants in an old-home week. Mrs. Stewart, who used to be a reporter on the Portland *Oregonian*, questioned me about the Paul Mowrers. It seems she went to school with Mrs. Mowrer in Paris.

The Wightmans are due for gifts of orchids or something from me. They not only gave me the best meal I've had in weeks but they saved me from cutting my throat on my own birthday.

March 15, Sunday. Honolulu. Bright. Fairly cool.

Went to 9-o'clock Mass at the cathedral. Struggled with a bit of decaying turkey and a pat of rancid butter for luncheon and then went to the movies out near Koko Head somewhere with Hailey. The town is deader than usual, if such a thing were possible.

Dr. Hays and Paymaster Bird came visiting from the ship. They want us to put in for another voyage with them. We're willing but Hailey at the moment is definitely in the doghouse.

March 16, Monday. Honolulu. Misty rain in the morning with sunshine sifting through it. Went out to Pearl Harbor to see medals given to Admiral Halsey and the crew of the rubber boat that went to Pukapuka. The ceremonies were aboard the carrier.

There was the usual comedy relief. The Signal Corps sent over a photographic truck and the naval authorities said it couldn't proceed to the medal-pinning because the sacred rites were being exemplified in such a frightfully restricted area Then there was an arrangement whereby the Army photographer could accompany the correspondents if he left his camera behind. Finally somebody broke down—presumably after the Army had identified itself as a non-spying institution maintained by the United States for good and honest purposes—and the truck was allowed to wallow over to the dry docks.

After a brief row with Jim Bassett over being held incommunicado I went to luncheon with Jim Wahl of the NBC. He wants the visiting firemen to join in a round-table program this week. The idea isn't so hot but the luncheon, served in a cool, high-roofed, nipa-thatched place out near Waikiki, was marvelous.

Heard today that 140 of our planes had attacked a large chunk of the Jap fleet in the Solomon Islands and had sunk three cruisers, four destroyers and five auxiliaries.

Commander Berry started for home with our stories today—it is alleged. There is talk that they may be released Thursday or Friday. Again I doubt it.

March 17, Tuesday. Honolulu. Fair and unaccountably cool.

I wrote a long letter to Paul Mowrer today outlining what I think of the censorship business. I took it out to Waldo who gulped a couple of times and said he would pass it. He was starting it on its rounds among the brass hats at headquarters when I left. Maybe something will come of it—maybe.

I went to dinner at the home of the Stewarts with Dick Haller and there met about half the headquarters staff of the Department of Hawaii. It was a pleasant evening. Wonderful. It's so interesting to discover that people still live in houses and cook up things that are fit to eat.

March 18, Wednesday. Honolulu. Fair. Cool. Waldo phoned to say that my letter had been sent and also to mention that a new trip is in prospect. I put in my bid for passage on Captain Zach's ship, the so-called *Swayback Maru.* Waldo thought maybe I'd prefer to sit here and wait for the office to act on my resignation. I said it wouldn't be the best idea.

March 19, Thursday. Honolulu. Rainy but cool. Went shopping with Stan Johnston and picked up my uniform.

Despite the ennui that comes to me in Honolulu I got up energy enough to go out to a vaudeville show and supper at Red Hill with Doc and Dorothy Benyas, Naomi Pollard, Dick Pollard, Foster Hailey *et al.* The show was old-fashioned and unbelievably good— and it gave me a chance to see something of the amazing work of catacomb building for the storage of Pearl Harbor's oil. I also got a glimpse of the green patch on the hill that represents about 3,000 graves.

Returned home to find out that the release dates on our stories are off and nobody knows or cares when they'll appear.

March 20, Friday. Honolulu. Still fairly cool. Dined at Fort Shafter Officers' Club with Frank and Betty Tremayne. Came home to find that the credentials of our old friend Farr had been suspended. The odd part of his trouble is that the Army wants his scalp, whereas the Navy is all for him. The reason for that appears to be that his story of the convoy was innocuous until the naval censor mutilated it. The lads at Fort Shafter have sent some protests on his behalf to the War Department. It seems odd that anybody should give him the works for a story submitted to the censor, mauled by the censor and passed by the censor. But I'm thinking I don't know much about official muddling—and official injustice.

48

BOREDOM IN PARADISE

MARCH 21, *Saturday*. Honolulu. Fair. Cool. Went to Pearl Harbor and Shafter with Dick Haller just for the ride and found everything merry and bright. Had lunch at the club with Dick, Forrest Allen, and Commander Gelly of the Coast Guard whom I knew a long time ago in Washington.

March 22, Sunday. Honolulu. Fair. Cool. Not to say cold. A day of thumb-twiddling.

March 23, Monday. Honolulu. Fair. Misty. Cool. I am all packed up and ready to go. But ungo.

I saw Captain Zacharias in the hotel lobby this afternoon. He says Commander John Ford who yesterday was Hollywood's most important producer is going with us.

I spent the evening reading *Huck Finn*. It's still good.

March 24, Tuesday. Honolulu. Cool. Still here. Farr is still rowing with the Army. The War Department says now that there wasn't any convoy, that he didn't go anywhere, that he invented the whole business. The Navy still says the Army is wrong. I wonder how it's going to come out. Go it, Husband. Go it, Bear.

I sympathize with Farr who has an amazingly pleasant personality and is really a very good kid. But my tears would flow more freely if I didn't realize that he's getting just what the British equivalent of our asses handed out to me for a couple of years.

Bought some Dwight Fiske records today unheard. After listening to them I judge that they will come in handy as the old records you have to have nowadays to get new records. I also got a copy of Gracie Fields' biggest aspidistra which I shall present as a prize to the Navy public-relations officer who qualifies as the biggest aspidistra in Honolulu. It will be a sort of judgment of Paris.

P. S. It looks as if we'll be some more time getting started. The cruiser fleet went out on a two-day errand—presumably to pose for pictures by Commander Ford.

March 25, Wednesday. Honolulu. Our stories were released today—so I hear. There were some telegrams from home mentioning it. I have been barred from the correspondents' broadcast probably because of office rules. All things considered and considering how sappy such things generally sound I guess it's just as well. Foster Hailey, still excommunicated from the Navy, is going on anyway. He has revised his script so that wherever it once read "Navy" it now reads "Army." I had luncheon with Jeff Garth, my old friend from McCann Erickson Co. in Chicago. He's a lieutenant in the Navy. Spent part of the afternoon with Captain Zach. Heard my pals on the radio this evening. Their broadcast was as I had expected uproariously funny. They now rate easily as the second biggest aspidistras in the world.

March 26, Thursday. Honolulu. Cool. Sunny. Lovely.

Coming up in the elevator at noon Jerry Garner, the trick censor, congratulated me on the tenor of the messages I had received from the office. I asked him how he knew about them. . . . Oh for the privacy that the goldfish had.

March 27, Friday. Honolulu. Cool.

March 28, Saturday. Honolulu. Beautiful day.

March 29, Sunday. Honolulu. Another fine day.

March 30, Monday. Honolulu. Fine weather. Looked around for some radio tubes because my set has quit. Everybody was out of the kind I needed. So I went home and replaced the old ones. They now work all right. Dined with the Wightmans after a successful cocktail party in which I met a practicing admiral and

Colonel Fielder, head of the local G2, who did fine card tricks. The colonel explained that nowadays you have to be a Chinese magician to have anything to do with G2.

March 31, Tuesday. Honolulu. Fine day. The navigator was in after luncheon. He's cheery about everything but he decries hysteria ashore. Even that doesn't bother much. He thinks the country will outlive it.

49

GUNS OR STUFF

April 1, *Wednesday*. Honolulu. Lovely day. Wandered about aimlessly and so found myself looking at a movie, *The Gracie Allen Murder*. It was quite soothing, particularly in the spot where she tells the detective she has a lot of clues in her clues closet. After dinner at the Wagon Wheel we went over to Bob Trumbull's house. (Bob is city editor of the *Advertiser* if I haven't mentioned it.) Soon after the blackout the windows rattled and the floors shook although there was no noise from without. The Scotty dog could hear, even if we couldn't. He whimpered and got under the divan.

"It's just guns or stuff," said Mrs. Trumbull with the practicality of a woman who has learned the sounds of target practice not to mention war.

April 2, Thursday. Honolulu. Cool. Nothing much doing during the day. Heard some civilian bleats about foolish use of cargo space—there was one ship that came over with two holds filled with water for ballast. They couldn't get the holds dry enough to take sugar so she went back empty—and much more of the same sort of stuff. I yawn listening to it even though it's the sort of muddling that may starve us tomorrow.

Dinner with Frank Coll, editor of the *Advertiser*. The night began to get muggy and was oppressive enough to foster all sorts of civilian fears. Around Coll's house out near Diamond Head the searchlights worked constantly and eerily against the low ceiling. Twenty or thirty patrol planes were rumbling about in the air above the clouds.

April 3, Good Friday. Honolulu. Bright. Sometimes cool. But muggy. I got a telephone call from Marie who seems to be all right. She had sense enough not to try to say much.

Pearl Harbor says that we haven't been forgotten. The fleet will get out some day.

I went out this evening with the other correspondents to the home of General Wells, Head of the HSPA, in Manoa Valley. A magnificent dinner with a roast of beef as big as the ones they used to have at Simpson's. . . . And this Good Friday!

One of the features of the dinner was ice cream made out of coconut milk. It was the best I've had since coming here.

April 4, Saturday. Honolulu. Hot. The *Aquitania* got in today. The gray old lady just about filled up the harbor. Three new correspondents arrived with her, including Claussen, a new A.P. chief. Mr. Claussen once served with G2 and he told us confidentially that he had come over chiefly to fix things up. He promised us that he will have everything straightened out in a day or two. I wish I could sit around and watch his education.

Farr is still at large. Hailey's status is all gummed up again. Yesterday they told him that his cable privileges would be restored but that he couldn't use his own name. Today they said that was the wrong interpretation of the message they got from Washington. So he's thinking of moving over to the other side of the island where for the moment there is peace.

D. L. Chambers (Bobbs-Merrill) wired me today that it would cost $146 to mail me ten copies of my book.

Spent the afternoon reading *Telefair* by Craig Rice. *Telefair* is a good enough book of the *Wuthering Heights* school—grim suspense and dire foreboding. And you wonder why the central characters in novels like this are unvaryingly such unconscionable saps.

April 5, Easter Sunday. Honolulu. Hot. Rain.

April 6, Monday. Honolulu. Cooler. News from Pearl Harbor indicates that the time may be getting closer. We went out this afternoon to the Royal Hawaiian and there met Lieutenant Commander Hutchinson, skipper of a returned submarine that had sunk a couple of tankers somewhere off the Carolines. With the Commander was Admiral Thomas Withers, commanding the submarine division. It was an interesting interview but not particularly news.

In the evening Chief Gabrielson and Roy Vitousek poured at a farewell dinner just preceding which we were notified to be out at the yard at 8:30 A.M.

A Mr. Richard Tregaskis, newest adjunct of the INS, was also present. He was informed during the evening that his presence would be required at Pearl Harbor in the morning. Whereupon he got up and went away for an hour. When he returned he had a soapbox filled with canned corned beef, canned salmon and, presumably, pemmican. He didn't want to go hungry while traveling with the Navy, he said.

April 7, Tuesday. Pearl Harbor. Cool. Got up at seven to get a telephone message that our going would be delayed. At 11 o'clock Keith Wheeler and I thoughtfully got a sandwich just to be prepared. And at 12:30 we were out in the yard. We scooted about the harbor dumping correspondents at various places: Field, of *Life*, his photographer Ralph Morse, and Tregaskis to the carrier; Jack Rice and Hawkins of Reuters to the other carrier; Wheeler and Joe Custer to destroyers. I came alone to the old ship where I was greeted with cheering warmth.

The torpedo nets were still about the cruisers and there didn't seem to be much indication that we were ever going anywhere. I learned that our departure had been delayed because a plane bringing Admiral Halsey from a mainland conference had been held up by bad weather. The admiral made up for it, however, by arriving this morning with three clippers.

Went ashore briefly during the afternoon where I met Mrs. Chappell, a lovely person and a brave spirit. I begin to think that maybe the Navy was right psychologically as well as practically in evacuating Navy wives. When they're in California and their husbands are here, they have only the one parting and none of the reminders of battle that foster worry. Here there's a new death in the family every time a ship goes out.

One of the surprises of the day came from a civilian engineer who has been working on the Pearl Harbor salvage. He says that the *Arizona* probably will be hauled up and put back into service. From where you see her as you scoot past in a launch she seems to be split in two, with her foremast tilted forward and her after structure leaning far astern. The divers report, however, that virtually all the damage was forward of the foremast, that the rest of the ship does not show many signs of damage, that her engine room is in better shape than those of the others, and that her motive power can be more easily put in order. They are talking now about fitting her with a false bow as they did the *Shaw* and sending her over to Mare Island. . . . I'm beginning to think that maybe we missed a bet on the *Maine*.

We were all called back to the ship on the five-o'clock boat. All of the crew had come back from liberty by that time. So the launches were hoisted aboard and we were buttoned up for the night.

Had a pleasant dinner with a lot of old friends and discovered that we have a new and better cook. Interviewed Ted Kobey on the reduction gear. I was assured that it has been fixed or hypnotized or something and that it is probably in no danger of pushing out through the side of the ship this trip. This is a great relief. We can now sit down and worry about something else.

50

FAR FROM THE MADDING WAR

APRIL 8, *Wednesday*. At sea. Cool. We sailed shortly before noon and, though I say it as shouldn't, we look like the same old Punch and Judy show.

We'd had dreams this time, I am realizing, of a mighty sweep across the Pacific with numerous carriers and battleships and cruisers and destroyers. The dreams are back in lavender. We rate, reading from left to right, "Halsey's collection of aquatic marvels"—carrier, our ship and another cruiser, tanker, four destroyers. Maybe things are going to be different. But on the surface this looks like another assault on the outhouses of Wake.

I had little or no sleep during the take-off. Most of the night I was kept awake by train whistles, a strange curse for a man on a warship.

As we slipped out to sea very close to the green reefs we passed a battered submarine coming in. She was making good time and seemed okay but she showed several signs of a beating outside of the sea growths around her hatch. Her bow was dented and a section of her forward rail was missing. A few thin sailors stood on the deck and listlessly waved to us. They were pale as ghosts as probably they had every reason to be.... These ships go out for months at a stretch and during that time seventy-five per cent of the men aboard never go through a hatch! What a life.

Right outside the reef we hit the cold. The weather was sunny and we were only a step from the sweaty streets of Honolulu but I began to be glad I'd brought my overcoat along.

About midafternoon we were away from the track of the four-pipe destroyer patrols and on our own headed west. I then began to inquire—judiciously—where we were going. And I made an interesting discovery. The captain doesn't know any more about it than I do. Two days ago he had ideas. But now he hasn't got any.

It seems likely that Admiral Halsey brought back some high-powered plan straight from King. But if he has he hasn't told anybody about it. Well, I'm beginning to think it really doesn't matter. I want to be surprised. And the name of the next atoll that we shoot up won't make any difference to me or the people who pay three cents for my newspaper.

April 9, Thursday. At sea. Gray. Cold. We've been heading northwest. This course, if unchanged will take us right into Yokohama Harbor.

The voyage is starting off like other crusades I've been on. I stayed in bed as long as I could—what with the cold and the choppy sea, etc.—but I finally came around about lunchtime. I sat down to spoon my soup amid talk about our new depth bombs and how good the beans were at Annapolis.

I sat around the wardroom for a while gathering information that Bataan peninsula was about to pass into the hands of the Japs and that the German thrust into Libya had not yet amounted to much. Then I went to the cabin to get under a blanket and read.

Commander John Ford came in about 4:30 looking for mystery stories. Then he sat down and talked of shoes and ships and sealing wax. Somehow I'd always pictured him as different from the rest of Hollywood but I'd never realized how completely different. He's just the same sort of humorous harp that I was always meeting at the wakes of Clem Lane's friends and relatives.

I was pleased to discover in him a kindred spirit insofar as the publicity situation is concerned. He thinks that the people of the United States ought to know a little of what's going on. He says pointedly that bad news is the finest cure in the world for smugness and apathy.

He also thinks that the present voyage is not too hot. He hopes we may be on our way to a rendezvous with other forces in the north. But there's no evidence.

"All we know is that it's some sort of suicide," he remarked cheerily. "It won't matter to us so much because we've seen the show. But I feel sorry for the kids. . . ."

I had dinner with him and the captain. There wasn't too much of war and naval strategy in the conversation. Ford wanted to know principally about his "old fellow countryman and co-religionist—that big harp who was in the hooch racket . . ." To wit Spike O'Donnell. And I told him. It was a hilarious evening.

April 10, Friday. At sea. Cold. Sunnier. Smoother. Farther north. The navigator says that the chief engineers and communications officers are the victims of occupational noises. An engineer goes along with all his senses intent on one racket. And then all of a sudden something distracts him and he hears another one. . . . It isn't a new noise. It's been going on for twenty years. But he hasn't noticed it before. So he begins to worry. And he begins to share his worries with everybody else. And people try to avoid him and that makes him introspective and eventually he becomes what you see.

And communicators are the same, he thinks. Before they get into that job they are normal gents speaking English even as you and I. But stick them in the radio room and in two weeks they've sprouted false whiskers and are talking in numbers—"We'll PBX that to MYK very QSL" and all that sort of stuff. . . .

Ford came in during the afternoon to gas about sundry mutual friends—Hal O'Flaherty, Ben Hecht, Wallace Smith, Hazel Macdonald, Bill Donovan, Phil Chancellor, Bishop Charley Buddy. It seems strange that we should know so many of the same people, that we should also know so many people who came from St. Mary's, Kansas, a school he had never heard of before today. He went away at 2 to take a picture of the launching of some planes.

I did a bit of rewrite for the ship's paper this afternoon and got bawled out by the new gunnery officer for making a noise with my typewriter. He doesn't like the typewriter by day. The first lieutenant doesn't like it by night. Writing in this Navy I discover—and with no surprise—is still being done with quill pens.

The British announced the sinking of the cruisers *Dorsetshire* and *Cornwall* and the ancient plane carrier *Hermes*. The manufacturer of the communiqué is still the same old chump that we knew in the ministry of information. He softens the blow by mentioning that the two cruisers are not the same ones claimed by the Japs in the battle for Ceylon but two other ones.

There was a special dinner tonight in the wardroom for the captain and Commander Ford. It was a howling success, thanks to Ford. He told how he got into the movies as a stooge for his brother with the old Universal.

"My brother got up on top of a boxcar on the trestle and started scowling and shooting. I didn't notice what he was shooting at. All I saw was that the boxcar was sixty feet above the water because the tide was out. So after while he got through shooting and went away. I stayed there and put on his frock coat and sideburns and slouch hat. And pretty soon they yelled at me, 'Get on the boxcar.' So I got on. And there was an express train coming straight for the trestle and me at ninety miles an hour—it looked like that. There was no chance to get out of the way. So when they yelled, 'Jump!' I got the idea. I made the sign of the cross and jumped. Halfway down I hit my fanny on a lot of telegraph wires and I spun and when I hit the water the wreck of the boxcar came down on top of me. But I got to land somehow and my brother took a swipe at me. He said I'd spoiled the whole picture by blessing myself before I took the dive. . . . I didn't think I had." And more of that. I didn't start for bed till long after midnight.

BOOK FOUR

MYSTERY CRUISE

"Darken Ship!"

51

SHIPS GOING SOMEWHERE

APRIL 11, *Saturday*. At sea. Still headed northwest. Cold. We're about clear of the islands now and presently will be outside the zone of the Midway patrol and strictly on our own.

There was dive-bombing practice this morning with us towing the target. But I didn't hear anything about it until everything was over. We're getting pretty blasé nowadays.

When I got wind of the proceedings I went out to investigate. I ran into Tate. Tate is senior aviator now, vice Crowley who went to the flagship to be squadron commander. He looked at me with a very serious mien. He says that he is glad to be alive and more than ever aware that man's time upon this earth is fleeting. Yesterday he came back from patrol and was within thirty-five miles of the outfit when he discovered that he was lost. At the time he had passed us and was heading away—although naturally he didn't know that. His gas was getting low as it always does at the end of a patrol.

He thought he saw a dot on the horizon and called to his radioman to look. The radioman said it was a patch of cloud or a stationary gooney bird or something.

He switched on his radio and asked for a homing beam. But his receiver wasn't working and there wasn't any homing beam. He decided then to look into the matter of the dark spot on the horizon. He headed toward it against a forty-knot wind and for half an hour it got no larger. He was willing to believe that it was nothing but a spot on his own vision when it suddenly took shape as the stack of the carrier.

Nice interesting work, aviation.

The gunnery officer is howling about the cold on the midnight watch. And with reason. He put the bite on the supply officer for a suit of winter underwear. He thought he really ought to have two suits so that he could keep one in the wash. Lieutenant Boland says he really ought to have three because we're heading into a "three-coat winter." He can wear two at a time and unsew only the outer covering when he wants to change over.

We're still headed northwest, just about on a straight line for Kamchatka. The clock went back an hour tonight. We're about 350 miles from the international date line at 8 P.M. The day has been cold and crisp but rather beautiful, the sea calm. The tub proceeds on its mysterious way.

Reveille has been at 6 A.M. hitherto. On the plan of the day it has been boosted to 4 A.M. All hands will turn out for general quarters at 4:20 with life jackets. The vacation seems to be just about finished although nobody yet knows where we're going or what we're supposed to be doing.

Talked late with sundry officers in the wardroom. The exec says we are still pursuing evasive tactics. That's a new name for the Haul-with-Halsey idea. The navigator ventured an opinion that we probably would be dodging a lot of bombs before we got back. And nobody gave him credit for very original thought or second sight on that one.

Ted Kobey was grousing about having to light off extra boilers as part of the GQ program in the morning. It will take 250 gallons of oil and he says cheerfully that 250 gallons of oil may be just the reserve we'll need sometime for a spurt to take us away from a whistle bomb or a tin fish.

In view of the extent and cultivation of his worrying processes I wasn't so upset as I might have been over his estimate of Japan's steel resources. He pointed to the record to show that the Japs, thanks to the gifts from the Allied Nations at the beginning of the blitz, now have more ship tonnage than they had in the beginning. So he says that the reserve of scrap iron we sold them, plus the loot of Singapore, Penang, Batavia, Hongkong and Shanghai, will last them a couple of years.

The navigator pointed out that the Japs had used up great quantities of their steel reserves supplying an army of a couple of million men, enlarging factories and making equipment other than ships.

As he talked I felt that the navigator must be nearly right but I got once more the old sinking feeling when I remembered how little we actually knew, how at the beginning of the war we hadn't been certain just how many battleships Japan had.

My current reading is appropriately *Wuthering Heights*. Everybody in it is nuts. So you don't have to worry much about what anybody is going to do in a pinch.

April 12, Sunday. At sea. Clear. Colder. Got up to discover that word had been received—presumably in a revelation from on high—that we are to meet a couple of companions today or tomorrow. Out here in the boundless boundlessness it's a consolation to know that we aren't scheduled for another one-man Punch and Judy show like Marcus. We are still headed almost due north. Wonder what Petropavlovsk looks like.

I learned about the Jap prisoners the destroyer picked up after the ruckus at Wake. They finally talked, all four of them, and said that they were the sole survivors of forty. When the shells began to come over (the first took a section off the little bridge) the captain started to put on a wholesale hara-kiri. He turned a machine gun on the crew, four of whom were killed instantly. Eight were wounded but able to dive overboard. The ones we picked up had managed to dive off the fantail before the captain saw them. As they departed he was shooting himself.

Officers of the destroyer that picked them up say that they weren't hoping for any favors. A couple of them were taken forward to the head just as a routine machine-gun test started. The two who remained behind went into hysterics. They thought the executions had begun. The patrol was a regular naval detachment that had been in Kamchatkan waters and was recently transferred to Wake.

Just before noon there was considerable machine-gunning as dive bombers from our carrier came to work on the target we'd thrown out astern. I didn't even go out to look at the performance but got my information from Lane the mess boy who reported

"Some of 'em come down straight and hit! Some of 'em come down smooth and easy and miss. I guess maybe they're scairt."

Had luncheon with the CPO's—a banquet as usual. Afterward I went aloft with Sergeant O'Donoghue to see a bit of anti-aircraft practice which had got itself postponed when the carrier lost the target sock. However, the trip to my old coop was justified. I found out that the big bell is gone. You can now walk around the platform without braining yourself. The view is un-obstructed and the wind, as usual, is about ninety miles an hour.

The ships ahead of us in line on a glowing blue sea were misty gray like a procession of Gothic cathedrals. I stood for a time freezing and drinking in the terrific beauty of it all. Then I went below and fell asleep as soon as I had hit a chair in the ward-room.

Dinner was odd. . . . Maybe my attention was detached but the conversation sounded like a transcript of the Mad Hatter's tea party. Talk of ack-ack, fuse settings, what sort of shirt to wear with blues (Kobey had broken out with blues, by the way), the antipathy of an old carrier skipper to the overseas caps of aviators, the dubious beauty of overseas caps anyway, the need for some battle headgear to replace the impractical cap, the types and condi-tions of aircraft carriers, the high rents in Honolulu . . .

Commander Shaw, the new gunnery officer, says that the *Lex-ington* could take seven torpedoes without sinking. "Of course," he said. "She would then be drawing forty-six feet and unable to get into any port in the world for repair. She'd just have to stay at sea from then on. . . ."

We sipped our coffee in silent contemplation of this terrible catastrophe—to have to stay at sea from then on. . . .

The weather seemed a little warmer this evening but that was only because the wind had shifted. By midnight I was beginning to remember the log fire in the hotel at White Horse.

I sat in the wardroom where the warmth was a little greater and listened apathetically to the radio. Jack Benny doesn't sound very funny out here—although perhaps that's not a fair test of local conditions. And nobody seemed to get much amusement out of the pontifical SOB who followed him with "words of good cheer from Hollywood to our boys in the Navy out there. . . ."

There was a somewhat cheering report from Corregidor that the Japs had lost another cruiser off Manila. However, nobody can find any dope on the class of cruiser described. So it will probably turn out to be a sampan.

There was fog in the early evening, phosphorescence at night. Numerous lookouts were reporting flares and there was considerable tension until we began to run out of the patch at midnight.

April 13, Monday. At sea. Clear day. Rolling sea. White caps. Cold.

This morning we met some new cruisers and destroyers.

Commander Chappell came in to tell me this glad news after a bitter-cold night, and also to spread the tidings that we are on a patrol mission. Somebody thinks we may run into surface action in the northwest.

News of our mission was all over the ship when I got down to the deck at 9:30. It seems that the operation orders were transmitted from the carrier by semaphore which virtually everybody aboard the ship can read. I have learned that at sea in a man-of-war there is no such thing as hush-hush.

There were movies as usual this afternoon. It's the beauty of the Navy that everything is always as usual. In weather like this it may be comfortable down there in the iron catacombs of the mess hall where they display this undoubtedly interesting cinema. But I too shall act as usual. I shall skip it.

The steam heat is on in our cabin for the first time since the ship came out of the Atlantic a couple of years ago. The ports are battened down and it's still none too warm.

Kobey came around this afternoon to contribute an amusing bit. His wife and five-year-old daughter are still in Honolulu, and the little girl somewhere has picked up enough information to make her interested in the shooting of Japs. She was full of the subject last week when he came home from target practice.

She: Were you out shooting Japs?

He: No, we were just practicing shooting.

She: My goodness, do you mean you don't know how to shoot *yet?*

Ford was talking last night to a man on watch in sky control who spent much of the four hours telling him of the evils of drink.

"I'm off the stuff," he said. "And I can't tell you how much good it's done me. I feel snappier in the morning, much more alert. My appetite is better. I've got a new interest in life since I've been on the wagon."

"And how long have you been on?" Ford inquired.

"Since we sailed," answered the gob.

Here lies
April 14, a Tuesday,
sacrificed to the west-bound crossing of the
international date line.

April 15, Wednesday. At sea. About 1,500 miles east of Japan.

It is a little warmer, maybe, but this morning brought fog, a howling, frightening wind and a pitching sea.

The afternoon has been brisk but tolerably clear. You get a little consolation if not thrill in looking out at the clutter of ships between here and the horizon. Maybe we're assembling the artillery to blow the holes in the Swiss cheese. But anyway it's a lot of artillery.

After dinner a Marine orderly showed up in the wardroom with an odd message: "The captain requests the assistance of Mr. Casey in disposing of a box of fudge." So I went up and helped with the disposal. It was accompanied by much conversation with John Ford, as usual, contributing the major share.

Here is one sample for the book: Ford went below today to get a haircut and encountered the best barber he'd ever met. He was profuse in compliment which he rounded off by asking: "Where have you been all my life?" And the barber answered: "Oh, not in the Navy. Mostly around Hollywood."

Mystery is abroad if you may judge from grapevine comment on recent dispatches: Somewhere out on this broad drink is "a friendly merchant ship." And what the hell might that be and what the hell might it be doing out here? We've come to strange place in the road when the friendliness of a ship is enough of an oddity to get it into the dispatches.

April 16, Thursday. Cold. Gray. But unfoggy. (The sun

came out for a while but not long enough to make this scene look like anything but the North Atlantic.)

The other day John Ford had the mess boys lined up trying to discover enough graduates of the Hampton choir to make a double quartet. Bland, a bright-eyed little guy who looks eternally surprised (but isn't), acted as spokesman for the boys. He was much interested although he didn't think any of his outfit "could sing very good." And none of them had been to Hampton. No chorus came out of Ford's negotiations, but if energy and a quick brain could produce "good singin'" you got the idea that somehow Mr. Bland would provide.

So today we weren't surprised when we heard that Bland had organized a gun crew. His mess boys are now the reserve unit—the second team, you might call it—of the stern starboard five-inch battery. "Gunnery is a good life," said Bland as he put his blue-lipped Nubians through their stuff in a stinging spray and a polar wind. "It gits you out in the open."

You might think that an afternoon in a cabin on a cruiser would be something like a ditto in a cell in a monastery. But today came Church Chappell who owns this place, and the chief engineer to see what was the matter with the radiator, and an electrician to fix up a bunk light, the paymaster to borrow a book and John Ford to discuss some matters that had just come to his attention. This motley convention talked of authorship, Captain Yardley (the *Black Chamber* expositor), military intelligence, naval codes, the Japs and the Irish. As I remember it the Irish won.

(Yardley came in for quite a lot of comment by Church. He said that the publication of *The American Black Chamber*, which revealed all our cipher tricks and caused our Jap friends to revise their obsolete code system, was a backhanded blessing to the Navy. It gave the impression that with the closing of Mr. Yardley's cipher bureau the U. S. was left with no eyes or ears at international keyholes. So the O.N.I. was able to continue its work—which Church says was farther advanced than Yardley's—free from interference from the old folks at home and unsuspected by interested persons abroad.)

52

TROUBLE COMES FOR HIROHITO

APRIL 17, *Friday*. At sea. Clear. Choppy.

I was awakened by two messengers arriving simultaneously. One brought a message from Keith Wheeler, saying that his destroyer has been detached, howling at his luck and asking me to cover for him or get him taken aboard with me. . . . And another from John Lambert asking for the loan of the *G-String Murders* by Gypsy Rose Lee.

I straightened out this congestion and went abroad to see what could be done for Keith. The captain was duly appreciative of his plight and willing enough to take him aboard. But he pointed out that Keith would have to be taken off the destroyer in a breeches buoy and in such a sea as this the removal would be precarious. He was willing to try it even at that but didn't think Halsey could be sold on the idea. So we dropped it with a message to Keith: "I am doing all I can"—signed "Charles E. Erbstein, Elgin, Ill."

The mess boys' gun crew made its first impression on the ship consciousness this morning. When the call came to general quarters the boys reported not to their stations in the powder magazine but to their stations as substitute gunners. Somebody is now going to iron out this dual-personality business.

At 6 P.M. we were in a roaring tempest and odd noises filled the ship—not including the contribution of somebody practicing on the trombone—the usual creak of strained rivets, the bang of iron doors plus the breathless whispering of the tumult outside, the offstage conversation of the wind, the clatter of sliding gear. . . . Roll and pitch and toss and smash! I've known few evenings like this.

We are pretty well up toward the Aleutians now. Our patrol

ought to be getting where it's going soon. The mystery deepens. Nobody seems to know what we're doing or why.

Dinner—I suppose that under the circumstances I should make note of it—was fried chicken, ice cream and cake. There was no overpressure in the wardroom atmosphere. Uncertainty was there, of course, and puzzlement. You'd not expect anything else where nobody knows anything and thinks he may be dying tomorrow in some unforeseen and novel fashion. The executive thinks we ought to start a hammering operation against the few and badly protected units of the Jap fleet still left in this neighborhood. And that's the way I feel about it.

Late this night I went down to the wardroom and gabbled with the lads on the changing watch. Somebody commented on the fact that the plan of the day never has a battle order in it any more. It's routine from reveille to lights out—drill and clean and scrub and drill.

April 18, Saturday. At sea. North of Marcus. Cold. Seventy-five-mile gale. Rough.

I got up at general-quarter call. Went on deck to face the howling wind. Sky gray. Sea pitching. I stood it for a while and went down half-frozen to the wardroom for coffee. The place was filled with officers but nobody was much concerned with the weird inconsequence of our lives. Water is rolling down the decks, sometimes a couple of feet deep. It's hard keeping upright.

The carrier has been sending up a lot of planes in spite of the weather. I don't know what that proves except that an airplane will actually fly in this soup. I wouldn't have believed it.

7:00. Breakfast. Ack-ack alerted. Mysterious surface craft reported to the north. May be a destroyer. After a moment's hesitation the assistant gunnery officer is allowed to eat his cakes in peace.

7:45. Report something sighted off our port bow. Carrier queries our report. Object unseen by plane patrol. We verify. It's a junk or sampan or trawler. Considerable activity aloft. I go up into the wind.

8:00. One of our new cruisers swings out of line to port. Starts firing almost immediately. Terrific barrage with fifteen six-inch guns. Shells are tossed like machine-gun bullets—eight salvos in the air at once. Flashes run around ship like lights on an electric sign.

8:10. Dive bombers attack. Trawler visible momentarily against whiteness of shell geysers. She seems to be about 600 tons. Cruiser chases Jap tub to horizon slapping shell at it generously.

Got call from bridge about 1:30. We'd picked up another spit-kit. As I got to the signal bridge the cruiser, standing off from formation, let loose a blast at her. The sampan hoisted a white flag. The cruiser was ordered to go in, take the crew prisoner and sink the ship.

The day had turned out gloriously except for the turbulence of the sea and the earsplitting wind, which on the other hand may not have been exceptional at all. The carrier moved out a lot of SBD's. Several of these took the air along with a couple of squadrons already aloft. They hopped around in a sort of circus that didn't seem to have much purpose. Then about 3 P.M. they began to land. One nosed over on the deck. The crack washed out the plane but apparently did little damage to the pilot and his aids. Another plane fell into the sea astern of the carrier. A destroyer picked up the crew. It was difficult to see how many planes got back to the carriers which were rolling like yachts.

2:30. Tokio radio announced an air raid.

We clustered about for details of news that the world—our part of it—had been waiting for since the morning of December 7. Unidentified planes had come over the town about noon. Bombs had been dropped on numerous nonmilitary objectives. Children had been killed. Temples had been blasted. . . . And all the customary indignation.

Excuse us, please, for wondering if by chance our journey up here might have been synchronized to this raid for some purpose.

5:00. The reports have been continuing all afternoon. The Japs claim to have shot down nine of the bombers immediately. Whose planes they turned out to be we are still waiting to hear.

9:00. We are turning eastward. . . . But definitely we are high-tailing east. And what do you make of that?

53

THE PLAINTIVE VOICE OF TOKIO

It was a weird experience, this, listening to what you might call Japan's Pearl Harbor.* That afternoon we weren't given much information about whose they were or what had happened to them. But we were kept in no doubt at all about what they had done. We were close enough to hear the crescendo of Tokio's hysteria, to read in the tone rather than in the substance of the popular outcry the fear that had seized upon the capital. And there at sea, fluttering about on a patrol that seemed too timely for pure coincidence, we got perspectives on the raid that never did come out in the official reports.

Whatever might have been the effect of bombs on factories and railroad centers and the like, the upheaval in the morale of a people whose stoicism had seemed their chief national characteristic was complete. We weren't to know for many a day what material damage had been done on Honshu Island. But had we based our estimates on what we heard that night as relays of hysterical announcers pushed a somewhat unintelligible commentary in English over the beam to America, we should have thought the whole of Japan in ashes.

On one of the domestic frequencies a shrieking woman broke in repeatedly, hour after hour, to call for donors to a hitherto neglected blood bank. The captain of our ship, who had been listening to the bulletins with close interest, interpreted her plea with some surprise.

"The woman's had a shock," he said, "*a bad shock*. Japanese

*Now, as these notes are being prepared for the printer, we have been told that the planes which interrupted Tokio's radio idyll about the security of life in Japan were Gen. Jimmy Doolittle's B-25's.

women don't get that way over nothing. Maybe this bombing amounts to something after all. . . ."

The woman was chattering disjointedly of the horrors of bombing—broken bodies and tenuously held lives. She spoke when she was coherent at all in the language of the hospitals, of first-degree burns and amputations, severed arteries and tourniquets, blood types and blood transfusions—an amazing program for a people supposed to care nothing about human life. But even if she'd been talking about nothing more unusual than new ways to cook rice you'd have known that the terror had arrived in Tokio. It was her voice rather than her subject matter that conveyed her message of panic. Her choking intensity gave you the notion that she was one citizen of Japan who wouldn't give much for her chances of being alive tomorrow.

The captain, long a student of the Japanese language and philosophies, read the principal message of her jeremiad in the things she left unsaid.

"It's fear, of course," he said. "She thinks this is going to be something like the 1923 earthquake only worse. But she's bewildered, too. The Japanese high command said that it couldn't happen. And it has happened. However it was done, it was done. And the generals, the protectors of the Emperor, have lost face—and death would be preferable to that. This woman sees catastrophe threatening the country's leadership. . . ."

The woman went on with her keening: "Give your blood as the men at the front are giving theirs. Your lives are in danger. Your country is in danger. Tomorrow—even tonight—your children may be blown to bits. Give your blood. Save them. Save yourselves. Save Japan." The captain nodded gravely.

"An interesting moment, gentlemen," he said.

For perhaps an hour afterward the air was filled with messages between ship and shore stations, and bases and ships and Tokio—plain-language messages, which was significant. If you could judge anything from the type of transmission hereabouts their fear of another bombing was so great that they no longer cared whether or not we found out about it. We got some evidence of futile movements to block the planes whose havoc had already been totted up in half a dozen cities to mark this, the blackest day Japan had ever known. We judged that carriers and cruisers were coming out to look—to look for what? An odd hegira with their radios wide open where any ship could get a bearing and plain-language conversation bandied about where anybody with a knowledge of Japanese might read it.

The voice of one of Tokio's graduates of the University of Missouri who had been teamed with "Tokio Rose" in English-language transmissions to the West Coast came then to advise the world of àn unspeakable outrage.

"Tokio has been bombed—is being bombed," he said in some surprise, and then he read somewhat haltingly from what seemed to be a badly written script: "There has been no damage at all to military objectives, but several schools, hospitals and shrines have been destroyed. Thirty primary school children on their way home from morning classes were machine-gunned in the street."

One of the officers in the close-packed group about the radio asked the senior aviator about that. He said No.

"Those planes had to be big ones to do the job at all," he said as the agitated commentator struggled on with his story of unimportant carnage. "You notice that nobody on the Jap radio yet knows whose planes they were. They give themselves away guessing. So put it all together and it means that those planes came over sailing high, that nobody saw them come and no ack-ack got at them. They wouldn't be likely to give up the advantage of altitude to machine-gun a lot of school kids, no matter how good an idea it might have been. On the face of the evidence it looks as if this bombing has been a great success."

The announcer rose to new heights of *Bushido*.

"This attack on the civilian population, this killing of little helpless children, was quickly dealt with," he said chokingly. "Our patrol planes were already in the air when this armada of Chinese, American and Russian planes came in from the sea. Our antiaircraft batteries went into action at once. Nine of the enemy bombers were shot down. The others were turned about and forced to fly southward. Others are being pursued by our fighters and they won't escape us. . . ." There was a lull, and then another voice mumbling offstage in Japanese. The commentator resumed as if reading from a new script.

"Nine unidentified planes have been shot down. Scores of unidentified planes have been driven from the skies over Tokio. The damage save for one small area on the outskirts of the city is slight."

The senior aviator laughed.

"More evidence the bombing was a success," he said, "and whoever did it got away clean. 'We have shot down nine planes but we don't know whose.' "

The commentator, a little less excited now, went on:

"Japan rejoices because our emperor escaped all harm in this cowardly attack. The prime minister, the chiefs of the victorious forces of Japan on land and sea and in the air immediately paid calls at the palace to reassure His Majesty and to explain what steps have been taken to drive off such attacks as this and fortify the security of Japan."

Only a few hours ago—only last night—this same announcer, less worried perhaps but no better informed, was announcing to the world that Japan could never be bombed, that the military chiefs had said so, that the United States, powerless to act at long distances, had been unable to deliver a single airplane to Russia.

"Japanese invention has produced a new air arm that will paralyze our enemies," he had boasted. "It is equal in all ways and superior in many ways to the English Hurricane and the American Flying Fortress." (We had wondered about that odd combination of resemblances.) "It has made invasion of our shores impossible. And in our invincible security we ask ourselves: 'What has become of the advertised American air power? What has become of the British and American fleets?' "

The gunnery officer, as did everybody else in the wardroom, recalled these things without reminder as the bulletins of the bombing went on.

"And now," he said, "they're hoping to be able to get out of town before Tokio burns down. And they're not interested in asking where the fleet is. They're afraid they'll find out."

The quavering voice of Tokio went on into the night.

"Tokio was raided today by unidentified land planes," came a repetitious bulletin about 9 P.M. It was apparent that the high command was scrapping its theory about a joint attack by Chinese, Russians and Americans.

"The raid was quickly dispersed. Nine enemy planes were shot down, many probably damaged by our fighters. There was no damage."

An hour later another commentator furnished the information that "a study of tail markings" had led the experts to believe that all the planes (including no doubt the unidentified nine that had been presumably shot down) had been American.

"They did no damage," he reiterated. "They did no damage."

"Fires started by the alleged bombing in Nagoya and Kobe are now under control." This announcement came at about 9:10 P.M. Tokio time—ten hours after a shocked radio propagandist had announced the fall of the first bomb on old Yeddo. Even if the bulletins had begun unaccountably to tell the truth, it was evident that the "alleged bombing" had done pretty well—probably not well enough to justify the dither in which the capital's English-speaking radio personalities found themselves, but well enough.

There came presently "a study of the situation by a home strategist." He turned out to be quite like any number of American radio experts:

"The bombers which struck Tokio were large planes capable of carrying a heavy load," he was quoted pompously by some rough-voiced member of the studio staff. And that was the last point at which he seemed to make any sense.

"They came to Japan over three possible routes," he said. "The first possibility is that they came from the South—from China or the Philippines. The second is that they operated from the Aleutian Islands. The third, of course, is that they were based on some secret airfield in Japan proper." The suggestion of the secret air base interested the executive officer who thought maybe that was the sort of job that had brought us wandering around the Pacific, the establishment of secret air bases in Japan.

"The guy didn't think that one up by himself," he said. "Somebody's talking that way in Japan and giving Tojo a lot of jitters."

For hours this went on. Even in our end of the ocean we got bearings on ships moving about restlessly in a wide zone along the Japanese coast. Toward morning we got a fantastic explanation of the activity. The Japanese planes and ships had gone out to look for a possible carrier—a super-carrier capable of launching big bombers. And before the commentary got completely unintelligible along toward midnight the announcers were talking about a ship with a flight deck a quarter of a mile long.

In the morning a commentator who indicated that somebody got around to develop some Signal Corps photographs of the raid said that the bombers had been North American B-25's. Knowing his previous accuracy we figured that they might have been Messerschmitts.

Noon dispatches mentioned that General Muto, former chief of home defense, had been ordered to a line regiment with a possible stopover at Hara-kiri. Muto was asked how the bombing happened and apparently he didn't know any more of the answers than anybody else. He realized that he had seen the accomplishment of an epoch-making turn in aerial war technique. But there was nothing in his experience to tell him how the trick was worked.

They order things better in Shangri-La.

54

PROGRESS TO NOWHERE

APRIL 19, *Sunday*. At sea. Clear. Rough.

We are still hauling with Halsey.

Everybody got out of circulation early tonight. Every so often on a voyage like this, the wardroom is overcome with a great lassitude. After all there isn't much to do. You can play only so much acey-deucey without tendencies to murder. The darts get busted up on the steel bulkheads and the only souls who try to read the ancient magazines that were aboard when Pearl Harbor froze the mails are those who are training for a trip to a dentist's office.

April 20, Monday. At sea. Rough. Fair visibility. Gray sky. Cool.

I was awakened by the roll of the ship at about 5 A.M.; I stayed in bed somewhat miraculously but everything loose on the premises piled up against the port bulkhead. I got up for no reason that occurs to me at present and went below to wait a couple of hours for breakfast. A lot of other early risers joined me. We slept in chairs in the wardroom—chairs conveniently lashed down—until the mess boys began to put out the ham and eggs.

It was obvious when we went on deck after pinning down our breakfast that the ship is heading mostly south. The navigator confirmed our observation. So the word spread that we were about to play a return engagement with Wake.

There was no reason for this, of course, except for the fact that Wake is about the nearest, and in a generally southerly direction. We are east of Wake at the moment, a novel position if such an attack were intended. However, the rumor got around the ship and

aroused plenty of enthusiasm—enough enthusiasm to show that nobody is quite satisfied with our current job—whatever it is.

I discovered about 2 o'clock how to make a six-strand square
braid with shoe strings and so passed a pleasant afternoon. The navigator suggested that it was a sort of occupational therapy. I believe
he's right.

Today we had abandon-ship drill and I found out for the first
time since I came aboard in January that my station in such a predicament is Life Raft No. 18. This is of course academic. In battle
when you abandon ship you don't have to follow out the technique of the drill. You get blown or tossed into the water (unless
you disintegrate) and I doubt very much if you ever land anywhere near Raft No. 18.

4 p.m. An order just came over shifting our course back due
east. You can forget about Wake.

April 21, Tuesday. At sea. Still rough. Sunny and beautiful.
Cold.

The carrier lost another plane today. A pilot, considerably off
his homing course, signaled that he had twelve minutes of gas. The
carrier gave him the beam and he started in. We could hear him
talking to his radioman: "Think we ought to go onto CW. Sure,
it's all right now. We'll make it all right. . . ." Seventeen minutes
later he was still on the air: "We're overdue now. . . . Gauge doesn't
show any gas. This goddam thing must be running on air."

He was in sight of the carrier when he crashed. We could see
the splash on the horizon. A destroyer leaped forward. But there
was no trace of him or his radioman. We went on east.

Laval made an announcement today regarding his new government. He was somewhat ominous: "Everybody knows what I
intend to do," he said. "Nobody has to guess about it. I have repeatedly said that the destiny of France lies with Germany." So now
we have the French fleet to worry about again.

At 4 p.m. we ran into some fog and warmer weather—not too
warm, but warm—and a heavier swell. We have picked up our
tankers and are now definitely on the course to Honolulu.

What price battles! In this great expedition our only danger
seems to have been in coming out of Pearl Harbor.

Date line crossed sometime today so it's once more April 21, Tuesday. At sea. Foggy. Windy. Rough. We've changed course and are now proceeding about twenty degrees south. We ought to get to Honolulu Saturday.

The *cafard* has fallen over everything. Our job whatever it was is done and what we have contributed is anybody's guess. The great adventure we had hoped for has all been about as exciting as a ride on the Staten Island Ferry. The captain is no more informed about our prospects than he was at the beginning but he seems greatly cheered at reports of the recent raid on Tokio and our planes appear to have landed safely, all of them. The Japs are still in a dither about what happened and what may happen.

Japanese bombers today raided Chinese airports, obviously looking for American visitors. They didn't claim to have hit anything, so it's very obvious that they didn't.

The other important piece of news was that O'Hare got promoted to Lieutenant Commander and was given the Congressional Medal by Roosevelt in person.

I sat up until late talking to Ford, mostly about the great cities which I feel that I am unlikely to see any more—London, Paris, Berlin. . . . An odd subject perhaps when the ship is on her beam-ends and the sea is rolling and the sputtering radio talks of war. But of course it is really the customary thing. You talk of the things you know best and you bring back some shred of a better life in nostalgic recollection. No amount of experience can make war anything but the greatest of all unrealities no matter how close you are to it.

Went to bed. Couldn't sleep. Sat up all night reading a novel in French about the Haut Jura. The weather has turned cold again. We're still headed southeast.

55

APPENDICITIS OPERATION

APRIL 22, *Wednesday*. At sea. Rough. Foggy. Warm.

I sat reading through reveille and the call to general quarters. Started to bed when the clattering feet on the ladders indicated "secure." I was awakened at noon by the navigator who himself had piled out of bed only about an hour before.

There was a fine commotion out on the big drink. The carrier launched some planes and had to swing about into the wind. A signal of intent was transmitted to the nearest ship by blinker and that ship passed it on to any other ship that might be in range of vision in the fog. So some ships saw it and some didn't and presently there were ships all over about twenty miles of ocean.

I managed to get something to eat at luncheon which I pretended was breakfast. I told myself I liked thick soup for breakfast—thick soup and meat loaf and spaghetti and fried potatoes and pie. I did a little work during the afternoon but not much.

Ford came in to say that the executive had asked him if he minded being placed next to me in an abandon-ship station. Ford had replied that he didn't mind very much, which was fine of him indeed. And then Church Chappell told a story of a destroyer commander in the Philippines who made abandon-ship drill the *pièce de résistance* of his operations. He was quite the best ship-abandoner in the U. S. Navy. He got out the charts and the muster roll and assigned all hands to stations and so arrived at the distressing discovery that he had one man too many. He looked about for additional flotation gear and hit upon the meat block. Seaman First Class Joe Glotz was assigned to an abandon-ship station on the meat block.

Glotz protested with no satisfaction. The skipper would not be thwarted. . . . Persistence in that attitude was what eventually landed Glotz in a booby hatch. But no matter. The commander was adamant and Seaman Glotz remained on the block.

There came a day finally when abandon-ship drill was put on with full regalia and ruffles. Joe Glotz and some friends rushed the meat block out onto the deck and swung it on the davits. The skipper was greatly pleased with the performance until he ordered "secure from drill." The friends of Mr. Glotz secured by letting go the rope. The meat block fell into the water and sank like a rock.

Along about midafternoon Sergeant Timothy O'Donoghue came and gathered me up for a light supper of hash, corn fritters and baked beans in the CPO mess. It was a fine idea. As I came back through the wardroom (I had come forward below decks because the following sea was washing everything untied off the decks) the ship heeled about thirty degrees. All the crockery on the tables for the officers' mess slid onto a pile on the floor. I sighed at the thought of the lads who hadn't been fortunate enough to get invited to dine with the CPO's. This is rough weather.

April 23, Thursday. At sea. Murky. Warmer. Terribly rough.

We roll, we pitch, we shiver. When I looked out of the bunk to which by some miracle I had held during the night, I saw a room strewn with furniture, paper and toothbrushes. I arose for breakfast which was unmemorable save for the comment of an ensign who came in with me off the wet deck: "Why," he inquired, "doesn't the sun ever come out in a war?"

Somehow the question sent me back to the Argonne where I spent quite a lot of my time puzzling over the same fascinating subject. . . . Why doesn't the sun come out in wars?

Went back to the cabin to discover a brace of electricians wiring it for fluorescent lighting. They explained that there's too big a load on the battle circuit. . . .

Ships, it seems, are always in a state of flux. The people who live in them apparently have full right to change anything they don't like so long as they don't have to go into a navy yard to do it. It is said that as soon as a ship comes off the ways somebody is always standing there with an acetylene torch ready to put the bow where the stern used to be and vice versa.

Torpedo-attack practice was scheduled for this morning. I went up to look at it. It turned out to be some trick diving at the carrier which didn't amount to much. I met Sergeant O'Donoghue who had turned sour on gunnery officers.

"This shooting's all getting too complicated," he complained. "There's just too goddam much high-school algebra and not enough lookin' through the sights."

General Wang, spokesman at Chungking, today declined to comment on the route of the U. S. planes in the recent raid on Tokio. However, he says, there is no doubt that Tokio was bombed.

The sea was terrific today. I'm going to tire of talking about it some day but until then I can go on reminding myself that we have about as good a weather man as Hitler. . . . When you haul with Halsey, you do it with fine natural camouflage and no visibility.

We've been rolling so it's unsafe to go up or down a ladder, almost suicide to stand up straight in your own room. From the decks you get a better idea of the roll by looking at the new cruiser ahead of us. She's always just about to tip over, particularly when on a zigzag and she gets a following sea. She steers erratically and she meets the swells with a sort of yielding motion. Then she heels over until the red plastic on her bottom is out of water two or three feet. With blue water rising behind her and our point of view swinging downward toward her as we roll ourselves, about half the time she seems to be lying on her beam-ends on the ocean.

These bobtailed cruisers are excellent ships, about the most modern thing afloat. They are said to have been constructed to meet a Japanese threat of a similar type. They are light. They have two or three knots more than we have. They can shoot like machine guns—and I hope more accurately than one might judge from their recent demonstration. They have thicker belt and deck armor than ours—or so it is alleged. I get most of this information out of a two-bit book that I bought at Pearl Harbor. The navigator thinks it's accurate because the publishers probably got all their information from the Japanese.

Rain! Rain!

I tried to kill the *cafard* by going to bed but you don't get much sleep in this place. I was awakened by a Marine sergeant talking

FIRST PHOTOGRAPH OF THE BATTLE OF MIDWAY—JUNE 1942

A Japanese heavy cruiser of the *Mogami* class after having been bombed
by U. S. carrier-based naval aircraft.

JAPANESE BOMBER SCORES HIT ON U.S.S. "YORKTOWN"

A Japanese bomber scores a direct hit on the U.S.S. *Yorktown*, aircraft
carrier, despite a tornado of antiaircraft fire.

snappily to the navigator. Ford wanted me down on deck. I muttered okay and Commander Chappell said: "Tell Mr. Ford that Mr. Casey's been asleep but that he's now bright-eyed and bushy-tailed and will be with him forthwith." The marine went below and gave the message precisely as sent. I checked on that afterward. Which shows that Marines are pretty smart and unsurprised by anything. Ford didn't want much. He and Commander Carter were holding a conference about down-trodden people, the Silver Shirts, and Father Coughlin.

At dinner a call came for Dr. Hays. Some lad had an acute case of appendicitis. There was talk about driving on to Pearl at twenty-five knots so that the lad could be taken care of in a hospital where the floor stayed quiet for a minute at a time. But when that was transmitted to the admiral he said No. The doc, so informed, called out cheerily to somebody to get the operating room ready. He finished a meal of considerable size, tossed in his napkin and went below.

Ford commented on it as a great spectacle—the little doctor growing about seven feet tall in the emergency as frightened kids stuck their heads around the corners of the sick bay to watch his strange and skillful ritual.

"Tell the bridge the operation is about to commence," he says and thereafter braces himself against the pitching sea to save a man's life. The operation was successful.

The captain thinks that the Japs will be back for another crack at Pearl Harbor. He didn't think so at first but he thinks so now. It's a question of face saving.

He has made one or two other forecasts that have come true. So I'm making a note of this one. It seems to make sense.

April 24, Friday. At sea. Bright and rolling at 6 A.M. Foggy at 9:00 and from then on.

I was up most of last night. Slept most of today.

Today's radio says that four U. S. ships have been sunk in the Atlantic. Moscow says that one of our airplanes from the Tokio raid had been interned along with its crew. Interesting if true. The Japs are closing in on the Burma defenses.

I got up during the afternoon to see the planes come in. It's always a good show and the more you look at it the less pleasant it becomes—the more you wonder how any SOC pilot lives to draw his first week's pay. (I'll still wonder despite the fact Crowley says their casualties are fewer than those of other brands of aviation.)

This is a bad, gray, rainy day. We cracked up one plane, but it didn't sink. So we got all four of them aboard. And just in time. The crane was shooting the last one out of the water when the ship drove into a rain squall black as ink. In a matter of seconds the rest of the fleet disappeared. At precisely that moment a plane came over us at a couple of hundred feet, an SOC and SOL. As nearly as we could discover later, the plane belonged to one of our new companions, but in the murk the pilot hadn't been able to distinguish his ship—if indeed he'd been able to locate it when by luck he found the fleet before the squall blotted it out.

Somehow after leaving us he got over another cruiser and wouldn't go away. That ship offered to pick him up but about that time his own outfit turned on a searchlight—the first I've seen at sea in this war. The beams roamed about for about ten minutes, breaking themselves off short on the black ceiling. When they died out we figured correctly that their gone goose had come home.

Our aviators are all unenthusiastic about the efficiency of airplane detectors in Honolulu. And all of them agree with Captain Zach that we shall have another attack. The next edition of the Emperor's Birthday is on April 28.

April 25, Saturday. At sea. And Honolulu.

The day turned out to be brilliantly beautiful as we approached Pearl Harbor. The carriers launched their planes early. Then they rode in line like a brace of battleships shunning the escort. We were sliding into Harbor about 11 o'clock. It's surprising how this place changes from week to week as the damage of the Jap visit disappears.

I went back to the Young and checked in—probably because all my lares and penates were there.

All of our press stuff has been stopped, of course. This doesn't mean anything to me. But what does mean something is that we have another new censorship setup. The work has been taken out of the hands of the press-relations section and given to fleet intelligence. I expect no good to come of that.

BOOK FIVE

CORAL SEA

"All Hands Man Your Battle Stations!"

56

THE REBOUNDING MAIN

APRIL 26, *Sunday*. Honolulu. Hot! Kona weather!

I was up most of the night on account of the oppressive heat.

At 11 P.M. Dick Haller called. Mauna Loa, the most recently active volcano in Hawaii, had blown up. The Army is trying to keep it quiet. . . . And just how do you go about trying to shush a volcano? I wrote a story to file with the censor for release when and if. After I had trotted over to Bishop Street with the copy I came back and called Fort Shafter to reserve transportation over there on a bomber.

April 27, Monday. Honolulu. Hot.

I went over this morning and registered for the draft with Major Cost. Returned to the hotel. Keith Wheeler reported that the Army looking coyly over its volcano had decided to send only four men—reporters for the three agencies and one photographer. I set up a yelp about that on the ground that the Army had plenty of planes and that our syndicate represented a bigger circulation than some of the wire services. I said that if the Army were going to be parsimonious it should bar the whole works.

At 3:30 Foster Hailey called up in an exceptionally high dudgeon to mention that everybody and his brother had been taken on the trip except the three of us. I still don't run much blood pressure on account of this for the reason that I didn't come over here to cover volcanos, censored or otherwise. But I must confess that I dislike finding out how much Army public relations resemble Navy public relations.

April 28, Tuesday. Honolulu. Cooler.

The Army assures us that a plane will take us to the volcano (and presumably dump us into it) tomorrow at 8:30 A.M. from Hickam Field. The volcano, according to some of my friends in Navy intelligence who are always glad to talk about anything that looks like Army foolishness and not theirs, is letting up.

Evening. Keith came in a short time ago with Hailey, both of them blistered by the work of the program committee. However Keith brought news that we go aboard tomorrow. So the Army may upshove its volcano and lasting luck to it.

April 29, Wednesday. Honolulu. Hot. Perhaps we might have gone out to look at the volcano after all, because the summons to Pearl Harbor didn't come until afternoon. I spent a weird morning buying books and jigsaw puzzles and knitting equipment. Once I proved my thesis that the kids of one generation will be interested in what was interesting to kids of another generation. And in the same fashion I have come to the conclusion that the things that passed the time on liners will do the same thing on warships. The knitting (done with a spool and four brads) is an added starter.

I rode out with Keith to face the customary jamboree at press headquarters. There Waldo Drake took me aside to inform me in a mysterious fashion that "everybody" had been complaining about my being aboard the same ship continuously—"because you get all the good stories." Who "everybody" is he didn't specify. No matter. The admiral is said to have listened to the complaints. So I have been transferred to another cruiser. Captain Zacharias showed up and looked a little peeved. Keith, who drew my old assignment, tried to make a trade. But I declined to enter any protest or take an active part in theirs.

Well, we tooled out to the ship and I clambered aboard with Ralph Morse, *Life* photographer, feeling much the same as I did when I arrived for my first day with the Army at Springfield twenty-five years ago. A new ship—the same sort of old collection of iron and rope as that I'd lived with for about four months, but for all that a different world.

However, it might be worse. Tom O'Connell, the supply officer, came over to Honolulu with me on the ship from San Francisco, and Staff Crowley, aboard as cruiser air-squadron commander of our task force, used to be our senior aviator.

I met Crowley a minute or two after we came aboard. He was going ashore for an hour or two at the officers' club and I went with him. Met Chappell and one or two other old friends who showed proper distress at my removal. I fixed it up with Chappell to rent our room to Keith.

Got back to the ship for 6 P.M. supper and sat up late listening to hopeful forecasts that maybe we're going to earn our keep.

April 30, Thursday. At sea. Southbound. Hot and getting hotter.

This morning about eight o'clock we sailed—the usual string of ships of Halsey's task force plus another carrier, one additional cruiser and about four extra cans. One other cruiser will join us after two more days in dry dock. She will clip along by herself at her best speed and will catch up with us in about five days' sailing time. That would seem to indicate that we'll have no action before May seventh or eighth.

I stood on the deck forward of the turrets to watch the familiar maneuver through Pearl's water lanes. Salvaging operations seem to have ceased for the time being on the *Oklahoma*. But the *Arizona*, wonder of wonders, shows signs of coming up.

Out we went through the green waters of the reef while eight fortresses came hammering overhead, their wheels almost touching our foremast. Beyond the harbor entrance the four-stackers are playing about. You wonder if they ever go in for a rest. But we don't linger long in their company. With our own cans clustering about us we ease into a choppy sea off Maui for target practice.

This too is a bit of routine. The ship was battened down and stripped of all breakables—light globes, mirrors, glassware and such. All hands stood at battle stations bearing the toil and heat of the day. And the eight-inch batteries popped off a couple of salvos. I don't know how good they were because I never did see the target.

There is one novelty about the proceedings, however—a bugle sounding over the loud-speaker to let the faithful know what's going on. The bugler is good and the calls are out of the Army book so it doesn't make any difference whether I can understand Donald Duck or not.

Donald Duck, by the way, has had his tonsils removed (or something) by the local sound engineers and at times he talks quite intelligibly. I wonder if that doesn't put him in a position to be prosecuted for conveying military information. They'd never bring that charge against the one on the *Swayback Maru*.

I talked for quite a time with Commander Crenshaw, the first lieutenant, out on deck, on this subject of military information. He agrees with me that some phases of the current hush-hush are difficult to understand. For instance a lot of fire-control apparatus that we got from the British in 1918 is still secret. . . .

Somehow we got onto the subject of antiaircraft fire for which he entertains the same high regard that I do.

"I knew Major Whosis of the Army who was set to develop the A.A. fire control for the Coast Guard," he said. "There was little or nothing for him to go on so the major announced that he would be pleased to entertain ideas should anybody care to submit them. He got hundreds of suggestions, most of them silly, but just as he was ready to despair, a letter came from some town in upper New York with what seemed to be a radical upheaval of the theory of this sort of gunnery.

"The writer said that he had been in an ack-ack battery during the last war and that he had never lost interest in the subject. It was apparent that he knew the limitations of all the current systems, and he offered what was virtually a new range table with all data pre-calculated, providing a four-dimensional barrage in anticipation of any move that a target airplane might make.

"The major was interested, not to say enthusiastic. He wrote to this correspondent asking him to come to Washington and work out the mathematical details of the scheme with his technicians. The government of course was ready to pay all the expenses and all that. But the answer was disheartening:

" 'I should love to come to Washington and be of all possible service without pay,' said the amateur ack-ack genius. 'But unfortunately I have been refused permission to travel by the chief psychiatrist and other officials of the institution in which I now live.' "

The commander says that gives you a pretty fair idea of antiaircraft fire.

Our course is southwest. Whether or not we shall meet up with the mysterious battleships and their fine escort of cruisers I don't know. I haven't the faintest inkling of our objective although from what I've heard of the massing of the Japanese fleet around Rabaul I might make a guess. What I do know for certain is that the heat is getting unbearable and that there's going to be no hope for a let-up.

May 1, Friday. At sea. Rolling. Bright. Hot.
I got up at 6:30 because somebody called Lieutenant Dancey at that time. That's one advantage of room-sharing. You keep all the watches with your mate.

My head was as thick as a pudding most of the morning but so far as I could see there were plenty of others just the same. Heat and the sea get in their licks at times despite experience and commissions. The atmosphere in the wardroom was moist and glum—approaching the peevish.

Tom O'Connell, who was stationed in Samoa for a couple of years, wiped his fevered brow and mentioned weakly that the weather would be nice in that vicinity now. The winter has set in, he thinks. Maybe he's right but at the moment I can't begin to think of such a thing as a cold day.

I learned today that the father of Sam Kelly, the navigator, was once owner and editor of the Tombstone *Epitaph*. Dancey's father was Baton Rouge correspondent for the New Orleans *Times-Democrat*. Ensign Grey's father was Zane Grey.

The day's news as we slither through this region where somebody shot the albatross is of no great interest. Tokio announces that a public exhibition has been made of two American planes shot down in the recent raid over Japanese cities. We have reason to doubt.

It is reported that the English have been using 2,000 planes a day in their eight-day bombing of French war factories. The only thing novel about 2,000 planes aloft in the present theater of their operation is that the planes are English.

May 2, Saturday. At sea. Fairly rough. Sunny. Hot.
Stewed in my own juice throughout the morning while the

officers went to quarters for inspection. Inspection! They looked very pretty in their starched white uniforms. They said it was cooler lined up on the sunny deck than it had been in the wardroom and I don't doubt that.

Sat up late discussing submarines with Crowley and O'Connell. They think the Jap losses off Hawaii and our west coast have been considerable. They declare that a lot of exhibits in the bag of blackfish shot up in that wild week after Pearl Harbor were really subs.

May 3, Sunday. At sea. Hot.

I was headachy when I got up today and I still am. In spite of that I spent the day finishing Woodward's *New American History* and Ellsberg's *Captain Paul*. You wouldn't know it was Sunday aboard—not even to the extent that it was unnoticeable on the other cruiser. We haven't any chaplain. Commander Schetky (who by the way is one of those large magnetic guys you take to instantly) says that when these ships were put together in a division two of them were provided with chaplains. The other two had dentists.

From unofficial sources I heard today that one of our subs, fresh from the East Coast, had knocked off a seaplane tender in the Coral Sea. All this bears out rumors of Jap concentrations thereabouts. Commander Crenshaw told me that he'd seen the operations order and that he thinks we'll get our money's worth this trip.

May 4, Monday. At sea. Hot.

We were about four degrees north of the equator at noon and about 170 degrees west. . . . Not far from Johnston Island. We'll cross probably tomorrow morning. Not that it means much to anybody.

Our course is veering a little more to the west and it is still stinking hot.

In the shade of the deck it is not so bad and we have come to the region of magnificent sunsets—flaming skies with cloud embers strewn about them—bands of weird luminous green at the horizon.

There was a general cleanup today—chipping rust, painting the raw spots, polishing metal. Always you have to have the old tub shining when you go into battle.

A dispatch has been received from somewhere in the southwest Pacific reporting a mixed bag of planes, warships, transports credited to bombers from one of our carriers. There seems to be some blur in the total in two versions of the story but conservatively it would appear that the score was four torpedo boats and one light cruiser and one seaplane tender sunk; one light cruiser beached and destroyed; one transport damaged; four seaplanes destroyed. Our losses were two planes, which, one infers, were lost on their way back to the carrier after the battle.

This action occurred at Tulagi off Florida Island in the Solomons, which leads one to suspect that we may have an assignment down there somewhere in the same general neighborhood. The score was excellent but, as so frequently happens in this war, the Japs hold the town. The showdown in that region, one judges, will have to come pretty soon. If we are to maintain a supply line to Australia, we can't afford to have the little brown buzzards moving in on us. We are led to believe from the wording of the communiqué that our carrier has not withdrawn any great distance from the Solomons and that the fight is still on. Which is as it should be.

It is—maybe I've mentioned that before—silly to make forecasts in a diary. If you're not on record you may be able to kid yourself when everything that you prophesied turns out wrong. But the temptation to play Cassandra for the purposes of the record is always strong. Adding up all the evidence to date, the steady movement of this double-face task force toward the southwest, the reports of other carrier forces in that region, the indication that a battle fleet is actually at sea somewhere near us, I believe that the action in the Solomons will presently shape up to proportions unheard of in recent sea warfare. There is no doubt whatever that we are heading into a fine fight and that it may be crucial.

I was shown an odd letter today—a printed form from Admiral Nimitz to the Pacific fleet under date of April 12. It has to deal with the care and feeding of war correspondents, their privileges if any and their restrictions, and mostly it is a repetition of ancient wisdom save for one rule which gives us a new censor. The commander of any ship on which a correspondent finds himself will receive all copy, etc., from the correspondent and decide whether or not it should be passed on to the fleet censor. The fleet censor in turn will decide whether or not to pass it on to our old friend the National Censor who will decide whether or not.

Maybe the admiral will want to look in on the mess. And then there'll be four. One lives in hope.

57

WHY DON'T THEY PICK COOL WEATHER?

MAY 5, *Tuesday*. At sea, south of the Equator. Hot. Calm.

We crossed the line early last night and are now somewhere in the south end of the doldrums—if there is any south end to the doldrums. I have spent the morning stewing not to say basting in my own juice—but somehow the ship feels cooler than it did yesterday, much as melted lead may be cooler than melted brass.

The days pass in target practice and drill and drill and target practice—and simulated battery-firing on a spotting board in the wardroom. There is no doubt in anybody's mind that we are getting whetted up for battle. Morale has been honed to a keen edge by the captain or the admiral or some other stroke-oar on this trireme who was doing his work before I got on. And we move about so equipped that we could get going with a minimum of effort no matter how short the notice. That, I am informed, is the reason why the wardroom ports, not to mention other ports on the ship, are kept closed day and night.

I dropped in one of those 'tween-watch conferences this morning in the wardroom and learned that one of our subs had popped off another Jap sub somewhere. There are no details and the mention of one Jap ship fails to excite anybody. It might have been another of those spitkits.

Scuttle butt has it that we are making a call at Samoa to deliver some airplanes to the Marines and, so we hear, to gather up two more carriers. I don't know how anybody found that out and I doubt it a little. If you have to deliver the planes off a carrier, then you have an empty carrier. And there seems to be something wrong about the proposition. It may be the carriers are carrying some knocked-down crates or a deck load. . . . It may be.

Crowley came in with an odd story about yesterday's maneuvers of the SOC squadron. Mickey Reeves, senior aviator of the ———, was leading the show. Tate, senior on my old cruiser, came abreast of him, waved his arm a couple of times and went away. His quartet then cavorted around a portion of the sky they had chosen for themselves while the bomb-target trailed behind their ship unnoticed and Halsey raised hell with the signal flags. After about an hour Mr. Tate's outfit blithely came back and the show went on. Crowley sent a "how-come" wigwag over to Tate and got no answer. I hope I survive this cruel war long enough to find out what it was all about.

After luncheon I went to see the planes get off. The equipment is newer and swankier than that of the other cruiser. There are a brace of life-sized hangars into which the SOC's fit easily when the wings are folded back.

The job got itself done expeditiously as I had expected it would. Meantime I had a chance to get an occasional breath of air. In appearance this is a day to get lyrical over—blue sea, calm as jelly, all one shade of cobalt clear out to the knife edge of the horizon, then the slow curving Delft pottery of the sky to a purpling zenith . . . a few cloud tufts but not much—not enough cloud to make a Dutchman's breeches. It is, however, still bleeding hot. The fans puncture little holes in the invisible blanket—the pipe blowers don't even penetrate. So I went back indoors after a brief look at the aerial circus. If you sit still the head doesn't bother you quite so much.

May 6, Wednesday. At sea. Hot. Calm.

Arose late and discovered that the chief difficulty of fighting a naval war is finding a place to sit down. Your roommate is always just off watch and sleeping and the wardroom is being used for spotting drill, buzzer instruction or the like. This ship reminds me of a hotel lobby—"Where do the guests go when they want to sit down?"

"They go to bed."

I discovered shortly after arising that "boots and saddles" played on a trumpet by Donald Duck doesn't mean that the horse-marines are going into action. It's just a call to flight quarters.

I met the captain this afternoon. I had gone up to one of the odd levels of the foremast and stopped to exchange quip and jest with Lieutenant Commander Walter Mayer, the gunnery officer. The captain emerged from somewhere with a news sheet, one line of which said that Colonel Knox refused to comment on the fall of Corregidor. I introduced myself and admitted that I hadn't heard about the fall of Corregidor either. And he went away. The captain seems to be genial in a New England sort of way. In appearance he reminds me somewhat of Captain Morgan of H.M.S. *Valiant*.

Throughout the day the weather continued lovely but unbearably hot. At dinner the officers at our table decided to roll the dice for ice cream. The cream had been too thin to serve at noon. We sent down for a sample at 6 P.M. and found it reasonably hard. But alas for samples. Maybe the mess boy went after it with a stack of. hot dishes or maybe he loitered by the engine room on the way back, but what we got was soup with a few bits of nuts floating about in it. There were useless lamentations but not from me. Free ice cream may not always be good but it certainly is never bad.

We passed land about a hundred miles off port today.

It will probably be another week before we get anywhere even if we don't repeat our performance of running up and down the coast of Samoa. The clock went back another hour tonight.

One of the cans made a sound contact last night but failed to shoot the fish or whatever it was.

My efforts at tatting are getting along marvelously. I now have about a yard of knitted rope for which I can see no possible use.

May 7, Thursday. At sea. Hot. Calmer than you'd expect with a tail wind.

Arose to the crash of a scratchy march on a phonograph and the conversation of two gobs in the outer companionway telling each other how well the town band played it at home. Missed breakfast unconcernedly. Who wants to eat on a day like this?

In search of air I crawled up to the searchlight platform which I found occupied by chippers and scrapers and painters, all discussing the heat in the accents of Jaw-jah. I'm beginning to wonder if anybody north of the Mason and Dixon line ever gets into the Navy. I was about to make some comment about painted ships upon painted oceans but thought better of it and went below.

Two kids turned up with TB on sick call last night. They're laid out on the well deck under an overhang of the gun deck and protected against rain by squares of canvas and cooled with air picked up by a canvas tube. One of them is so frail and bony you'd wonder how he managed to pass an entrance test—a nice-looking kid, too. I think I could work up quite a bit of emotion over such things as this if I let myself. What a pity that a nice boy like this should have to die before his time of a wasting disease instead of lasting long enough to be blown to atoms by a shell or bomb.

Across the deck a lot of southerners are scraping and sand-papering the gangplank. Their leader loves his work: "We keep it always bright and shining but we never do anything with it," he said.

Drooping and peevish we pushed aside the spotting boards and plane tables and buzzers and got to our luncheon. Everybody at our end of the table was too hot to talk. Everybody at the other end of the table was distantly interested in Tom O'Connell's weary discussion of something about the ten-per-cent raise in base pay. It seemed an academic discussion to everybody. What price base pay?

The *pièce de résistance* was shrimp salad with slim cuts of avocado. Crenshaw didn't want any. He's from Philadelphia and had to smell shrimp for twelve years, he says. Now he's not having any of them. So he gets a slice of cold meat. Somebody says shrimps have a lot of vitamins. He says he doesn't care what a shrimp has.

The vitamin discussion smolders languidly. What is a vitamin? Dr. Maloney answers. Kelly wants to know how the sunshine vitamin can be delivered by the sun. And there's some more heating palaver about that phenomenon. More silence. Somebody brings in a pipe catalogue for Crenshaw. It catches Mayer's eye. I don't think he cares a hoot about pipes but if you read you don't have to talk and you can forget the sweat running down your back. We spoon our shrimp. Somebody at a near-by table leans back and upsets an ash stand.

"Mah-jongg," says the commander in a dull voice.

The communications officer arrives late.

"The message," he says cryptically to Crowley. "It seems she took it in her boiler rooms and the buoyancy of her forward compartments is keeping her afloat. She can be towed...."

"What with?" murmurs the commander who seems to know what it's all about.

Nobody else seems to share the confidence of the communications officer. But what of it? Everybody is too hot to ask questions.

A ship probably got torpedoed.... It's too hot to talk.... She got it some place where towing is unlikely ... It's too hot to think.... What ship? Whose? No matter ... It's too hot ...

Mayer aroused himself long enough to call a waiter and ask about the ice-cream supply. It seems there is some and it's alleged to be edible. But we haven't any dice. Mayer remembers that he has a dice box and four dice. The commander—somebody remarks—has the other die.

"How did you know that?" the commander inquires. But he mops his beaded brow and doesn't listen to the answer, if there is any. The dice are brought. We roll them languidly ... languidly. Exertion boosts the blood pressure.

We had three submarine alarms today, the first at 2:30 A.M., second at 10:20 A.M., third about 3 P.M. On the last occasion a can went out and laid some depth charges with no results.

We're not disdainful of the subs in this area. Part of our daily grist of messages from headquarters consists of bearings on flashes from Jap submarines working near a task force such as this. So far we've not had such attentions—at least no sub has uncorked a radio anywhere near us. But we are getting closer every day to the places where plenty of Jap U boats ought to be if the Japs have them.

I finished *Captain Paul* today and was greatly reassured. The nation that let fuzz-witted incompetence, pettiness, pride, jealousy, nepotism, vanity, political expediency and two-bit dishonesty do their best to wreck the first American Navy has somehow survived. With a few alterations it is still working in the same old way although there are reports that this is a different war.

The afternoon was filled with novelty. . . . A lookout on the range-finder forward reported sighting a raft with five men on it. A destroyer dashed over to discover a floating log. A few minutes later a smoke cloud on the horizon, which the officer of the deck took to be a plane crash, turned out to be a waterspout.

And the day ended in untold magnificence. The sky had been rolling with thunderheads all day and great banks of them were on the western horizon at sundown. The sun slanted behind them. And presently the light was reflected upward, topping the cloud wall with white, mottling the sky with an iridescence like that of an abalone shell and streaking this pearly mosaic with wide brush strokes of deep purple light. Light faded with flashes of green and magenta. Nobody aboard had ever seen anything like it despite long travel in these strange waters.

58

DUST-UP IN THE CORAL SEA

WE CROSS the 180th meridian tonight.

Tomorrow will be May 9, Saturday. May 8 is another of those lost days.

May 9, Saturday. At sea. Cooler (a little). Choppy. Another of those deadly days.

Over the radio and in plain English at about 11 o'clock came a startled announcement: "Air raid in progress." And an hour later a similarly anonymous bleat: "All clear!" We probably will never know what that's all about.

The battle of the Coral Sea appears to be getting good. (Or else we're getting details of a second guess about the May fourth encounter at Tulagi.) The Australian radio lists one Japanese carrier sunk, another badly damaged, one heavy cruiser sunk and another damaged, then an inventory that sounds like the gunboats reported sunk in an attack on Rabaul.

A Washington broadcast said that the Navy Department is claiming nine ships sunk and three badly damaged. Late Australian sources raised the ante to eighteen and I began to remember those days of victory when the Allied Nations were knocking off sixty-five ships in the Straits of Macassar but failing to stop the Japs.

The scent of the fragrant fish, however, is not confined to our communiqués. The Japs are announcing that they have sunk the *California, Yorktown* and *Lexington* and severely damaged the *Warspite*. The British deny that they are having anything to do with the Coral Sea fracas and as for the *California*, if the Japs sank that they had to pull the cork on the dry dock in Pearl Harbor.

Madagascar—particularly the base at Diégo-Suarez—is in British hands after severe casualties. Vichy is howling about it and so presumably are the Japs.

I heard the evening BBC broadcast in Lieutenant Mayer's room. The British are greatly elated over our fight. They say it is the greatest naval engagement since Jutland. However big Jutland was. After the broadcast the New Zealand radio played "Franklin D. Roosevelt Jones."

May 10, Sunday. At sea. Cooler. A southeast trade wind is blowing and there are parts of the ship where you can really be comfortable.

This, it seems, is the second anniversary of the bombing of Nancy and the beginning of the big blitz. . . . How far away that seems. Or does it?

The reports were pretty certain today that the *Lex* got hit—and possibly also the *Yorktown* in the battle of the Coral Sea. The *Yorktown's* damage can't be much because she is still putting off planes and doing thirty knots. The *Lex,* however, continues silent which is ominous. And last reports from her indicated that she would have to have "extensive repairs." She's probably sunk.

Some of the wardroom strategists were afraid that the loss of a carrier, even temporarily, would cause us to retire from the action. I protested that if the loss of a single ship could change our whole operating policy then we ought to quit right now. But every hour makes the prophets of doom less credible. We are continuing on a straight course past Fiji to the southwest. In two days we'll have a bigger strength of planes and ships in the Coral Sea than we had on May 4. We are evidently not retiring and it is quite obvious that for the first time in months, the Japs have been set back on their heels.

In a matter of a few hours, if we continue on this course, we'll be right on the edge of trouble. But the prospect seems to make no more difference here than it made on the other cruiser. Came the doctor to luncheon today to howl that we are getting 25,000 calories a day instead of 1,500.

Somebody reminded him that this is the only ship in all the world that ever failed to serve roast pork when crossing the equator.

The "Just-Before-The-Battle" game here is cribbage. The mob on the other cruiser played bridge. Captain Horatio Hornblower played whist.

There was brief excitement last night. A voice came over the warning net from the skipper of one of the cans. "I've made a submarine contact," he said in a hollow voice that made the blacked-out bridge seem like the wing of a haunted house. "It's too metallic to be a fish. I'll take another look." He looked and apparently there was no sub—which leaves us nothing but the interesting note that the fish in these waters have metallic sounds.

Spent the afternoon reading *Captain Horatio Hornblower* and working a species of crossword puzzle known as the Double Crostics —a very tough form of amusement. I go down to bed at midnight with the serene faith that if the Japs ever get hold of all I know about the present operation, they wouldn't be surprised.

A year ago today I was getting ready to leave Cairo for home.

May 11, Monday. At sea. Calm enough. And a little cooler. Despite the fact that we fueled two days ago, we took on another load today. That would seem to mean that we have arrived at the jump-off. From this point we go in swinging. The tankers will go back to Pearl and maybe somebody will come out to oil us up again in a couple of weeks.

The other ships went through a similar routine during the day. The planes went off for Efate about noon.

We are headed into the Coral Sea.

It was a beautiful day out on deck and I strolled out there to loaf for a couple of hours. The doctor saw me with *Captain Hornblower* in my hand and asked me if I had heard of the bombing of H.M.S. *Liverpool*. I said I didn't know the details.

"Well," he said, "the executive officer was standing forward when the first bomb fell. It knocked him flat on his back. When he got up he saw twelve Heinkles diving at the ship from all quarters. About that time he became aware that his pants had been blown off and also the deck was tilting so that it was impossible to fire the ack-ack.

" 'I wonder,' he said, 'what Captain Hornblower would do now!' "

Came an odd bit of news tonight from our forgotten friends the Italians. A bulletin from Rome stated that Musso's April losses had been 97 in Russia, 105 in Libya and more than a thousand in the Balkans. Why didn't somebody tell them that gun was loaded?

May 12, Tuesday. At sea. Cool. But not definitely arctic.

It would appear that during the night and for as much of the day as has now gone by, we've been chasing a disabled Jap carrier and its cruiser escort.

A plane got lost from the new carrier's brood. . . . The old one hasn't been losing any lately. The whole fleet took off in the general direction of the point where the pilot should have been at the time when he let off his plaintive cry for help. He certainly had luck in picking a spot to get lost in.

The pilot, obviously inexperienced, transmitted the important intelligence that he didn't know where he was. Then, apparently, he failed to switch over from the air to his local communication system. (It's a common oversight.) So when he began to talk with his backseat driver he was also talking to as much of the listening world as happened to be paying attention at the moment:

"Get that receiver working. What's this little switch for? Boy, this is serious. Can't you hear anything? I can't hear anything either. What the hell do you suppose is wrong with that thing? It worked all right yesterday. What the hell good is a radio beam when you can't pick it up?"

Apparently the radioman, whose commentary on the pilot's navigational gifts is unrecorded, got the receiver working and the plane came along to meet the searching fleet. This is a hell of a place to be making free with radio bearings.

We had a brief band concert during the afternoon. Nine guys were playing "Hilo Hattie" while a tenth was plunking a gee-tar and looking at the score of "Moonlight and Roses."

After the concert there was a talk on first aid under the guns of Number Three turret on the fantail. It was sunny, hot.

The doctor was good at this sort of thing. He spoke simply and effectively of how you stop bleeding, how you treat burns, what you do in cases of coma and shock. He was matter-of-fact about it all though he stressed the imminence of our half-forgotten battle. "We can't waste too much time on first aid," he said. "We've got to keep the guns firing. That's our first job." He demonstrated the use of the rubber tourniquet, showed where to put it, spoke briefly of neck wounds, penetrating wounds, the use of pressure bandages. . . . "Handle these people, these patients, gently. Push them over to one side where you won't have to walk on them and leave them for the stretcher bearers."

As he talked you seemed to see a deck covered with gently handled patients pushed aside where no one would walk on them waiting for the transport that would take them to the dressing station. It was graphic and not too cheering.

Of course, whether we spend our time ruminating on the doctor's talk or playing acey-deucy in the wardroom, we can't avoid consciousness that the battle is only a short distance away from us. If the Jap fleet hadn't stepped back we'd probably be in the middle of it right now.

With full recognition of the situation, the department heads held long palaver just before dinner listing the weights of things they might be able to jettison in the event that we have to strip the old ship to save her.

It's the old question of: "How do you dump off a catapult?"

A lot of people have wanted to know that since Dec. 7 when a smart first lieutenant on the *Raleigh* saved the ship by tossing the silos and cranes into the water.

I was discussing the matter with Senior Aviator Mickey Reeves on the deck at sunset (a very mediocre performance for these parts) when I discovered that the ship had suddenly turned directly west and wasn't sparing the horses. The officers on the deck began to suggest that maybe we were moving into action. One of them said he hoped they'd sound general quarters for it. Otherwise, he complained, we might not ever hear a goddam thing about it.

An hour later. The purpose of the increased speed is still unexplained, the more so in that a dispatch was received soon after sunset to the effect that we'd be meeting friendly cruisers and destroyers during the night. . . . During the night! I'm feeling that friendly cruisers and destroyers would look more friendly at another time— say high noon.

Donald Duck announced at 7 o'clock that from now on all hands will carry gas masks at all times—a bloody nuisance if anybody ever heard of any.

There is no particular use in noting why a gas attack at sea looks to be an absurdity. It's evident that the naval intelligence has picked up something to indicate that the Little Brown Bothers might try a bit of mustard just to find out the effect. So from now on we'll carry these gadgets about with us when we're awake and tied to us when we're asleep. Nobody seems to be particular about life belts although the possibility of sinking would seem to me to be a better bet than the possibility of smothering.

There may be a battle north of here in the vicinity of Ocean Island in a day or two. It appears that a Jap cruiser division is moving in that direction. And how do we know that?

Apparently they think they have knocked out our air force in this region—and just as apparently we've knocked out theirs— so the cruisers are starting on their prowl without overhead protection. It has all the promise of a good fight. I merely mention it.

May 13, Wednesday. At sea. Cloudy. Cool outdoors; humid and smothering indoors.

We are still churning up the edge of the Coral Sea. Of course so far as the scenery is concerned we might be on one of those two-week cruises to nowhere that used to run out of New York. No matter where you are on this biggest ocean in the world you're never able to see anything of it except a puddle fifteen miles in diameter.

Today's nuisance has been—as previously advertised—the gas mask. You lug it around all over the ship. You eat with it and sleep with it. And presumably you drown with it. And I find that it's just as much in the way today, no matter what you're doing, as it was twenty-five years ago in France.

Of course, after Pearl Harbor, anybody will admit that the Japs are capable of trying anything and very likely to make the impossible happen. So it may be the part of a canny commander to make you keep your mask close at hand. But even after a day of discipline with it I am no more convinced than I was yesterday that I shall ever have to put it on.

At 6 P.M. the force was proceeding north. We are still to pick up two cruisers, and a couple of destroyers. Our two tankers and a brace of cans have started out in the general direction of home.

There was another magnificent sunset tonight with wheel-spoke rays in red, Nile green and magenta like the Aurora Borealis. I gave it my attention and then came in to finish *The Voyage of the Forgotten Men*, a story of the Russian Baltic Fleet's journey from Libau to the Korean Straits.

This is an astounding story and would have been even if the odyssey had had no important historical significance. It is provocative of much thought when you read it in the wardroom of a man-of-war in such a situation as this. For if Admiral Makaroff had lived and, as he might very well have done, had saved the Port Arthur fleet, and if Rojestvensky had won the wrangle with Togo, Japan would not now be terrorizing the Southwest Pacific—nor any other part of the globe. There can be, of course, no *if* in a military report but as you slide along here to another meeting with Togo's successors you can't help but wonder.

From some undetermined source a rumor spread around today that the *Lexington* had been much more severely damaged than previously admitted—so much so, in fact, that as some of us had suspected, she is now on the bottom. There is also a report that we are chasing a Jap carrier damaged by *Lexington* planes.

There are many reasons why I might decline to believe the yarn of ultimate catastrophe to the *Lex*. But whether I believe it or not it is a tale of great significance in its effect on the ship's company. I should say that at least half the officers believe it. They have seen bombs fall and they have heard of the *Ark Royal* and they are not deceived about the vulnerability of ships. The encouraging point of it all is that they don't seem worried.

Many years ago I made a note of the basic phenomenon of wars which apparently remains basic in this one: "It's the psychology of battles that somebody else's widow is going to collect the insurance."

May 14, Thursday. At sea. Warmer. Steamy.

This day has been a trip through hell's boiler room in a fur overcoat. It produced little of interest. Such days seldom do. Men who don't have to work sit around and look miserably at one another in steamy silence. This is no time for merry quip or even for intelligent comment on the destiny that may be cooking up for us in the thicker steam up ahead. Those who have work to do do it without zest or inspiration.

I came on deck and made a note that those two cruisers we've been expecting had not yet joined the party.

"The latest information is that they'll join up in the morning," said Dancey. "I'll be glad to see them but I'll confess I'd be even gladder to see the *Saratoga* and the *Illustrious*."

One of the associate officers of the ack-ack who was doing something with a slide rule in the wardroom looked up from his coffee.

"No hurry," he said. "I just read something by a lad named Pierre Huss. He says the war is going to last ten years. . . ." Commander Crenshaw and I looked at each other.

"I'll be walking in my sleep ten years from now," he said. And as for me I began to wonder whether or not my bones, ten years older, could be induced to hoist me through scuttle holes in battened hatches.

We have plenty of information now that we are right on the edge of some Class A Priority trouble. All of this region is crawling with Jap warcraft though not now to the same extent as it was before it met the *Lexington* and *Yorktown*. The daily drill of the gun crews goes on much in the fashion of signal practice on the eve of a big football game. . . . The simile might be more novel but it's descriptive. There isn't so much difference between passing a ball and passing a shell. . . .

The navigator reported today that he had heard a male quartet— part of the crew of the five-inch battery—singing as he came off watch last night.

"They were singing 'Onward Christian Soldiers,'" he said, "and the funny part of it was that they all knew the words."

We had dinner at 4:15 again tonight—just a few minutes after we'd got up from lunch. Inasmuch as dinner is always set at an hour before sunset on this ship, the 4:15 gong means that we have traveled mostly north during the past few days.

At seven o'clock there was a report of a submarine contact. Just before that I was sitting in Commander Crenshaw's room and he was telling me that he suspected some such thing because of a quick turnoff from our course and some otherwise unexplainable activity on the part of our destroyers. He was still telling me about it when the depth charges blew up. . . .

This was the first time I had ever heard any of these things, and I was impressed by their power. The ship shivered perceptibly and the hold boomed like an immense drum. There were four shots. I went out onto the deck, stumbling over half a dozen sailors sleeping just outside the wardroom door. Somehow I got to the rail and stopped there—fortunately. It was blacker than the inside of a bow-legged man's hat. Stars were edging out of the rain clouds but there was no moon. The Southern Cross was off our starboard bow which indicated that for the moment we were headed east. I could make nothing of that or of anything else. So, when my eyes had become sufficiently used to the darkness for me to venture away from my handhold, I stumbled back through the dark again. The depth charges were still beating their ghastly drum over a mile or so of remote control.

A little later a report came from the bridge that one of the destroyers had been ordered to remain behind and continue the search. After all it's not a fantastic idea that there should be a sub out there. If there weren't Jap submarines in these waters our naval intelligence would be staying awake nights trying to find out why not.

Our base course remains northwest—more north than west—across the end of the Coral Sea. At the moment we still appear to be chasing the disrupted Japs and we shan't be able to go very far in that direction without tripping over a big portion of Yamamoto's fleet. So far Halsey hasn't announced his intentions to anybody.

59

DEPTH BOMBS!

MAY 15, *Friday*. At sea. A light blue ocean. Hot and glassy.

We seem to be moving now along the east side of New Cale-
donia, apparently on a romp that will take us along the east side of
the Solomons. Our course, when the customary kinks and zigzags
are ironed out, is still generally northwest. I had a little trouble
realizing that when I went out on deck to take my bearings from the
sun. At noon the sun was dead ahead of us, which in Honolulu or
Chicago would have meant that we were going almost due south.
But I recalled after while that in these latitudes the sun is to the
north.

We had two more contacts last night. Who'll say positively that
they represented the noisier moments in the life of the blackfish?

While the depth charges were shaking the ship an emergency
operation for appendicitis was going on in our sick bay. Even if the
victim, a sailmaker, hadn't been as close to death as he's ever going
to get this side of the grave, there would have been twice the drama
about this performance that you'd find in a hospital ashore. Operations at sea seem always to have that quality although generally
they're about as well done and as successful as those turned out by
an ace surgeon in the cloistered quiet of Rochester.

Last night the sea was flat as a hospital floor which was one of the
unusual things about the operation. Until now the surgeons have
had to be acrobats. I guess we're lucky to have a couple of good
doctors and a real operating room. There have been several cases of
acute appendicitis since this task force began to wander about the
Pacific. In all of them the patients lived to go back to the dive-bomb
zone. We're a long way from situations like the one in *Mr. Glen-
cannon* where the chief engineer removed the first mate's appendix

with a jackknife assisted by an anatomical diagram, a slide rule and a pair of calipers.

Today, thanks to our position which we can no longer very well ignore, we talk of battle—but in a nice way and calmly and in a subdued voice. We are very detached not to say unconcerned.

This morning we passed through historic waters, the course that this ship and my old cruiser took a year ago on their trip to Brisbane. This journey, if one may judge from the continuous reference to it, must have been the greatest naval journey since Jason's trip after the golden fleece.

When we got into the artillery back in 1917 the old-timers in the National Guard dated everything from the Austin Hike. The voyage to Brisbane seems to have been the seagoing version of the Austin Hike.

Officers of the one-one ack-ack batteries are going around today cutting the ends off broom handles to make dummy shells. The gunnery officer says that from now on we'll have to get some short sweepers.

Picked up April 27 number of *Life* in the wardroom. (Come to think about it the mails must have been doing pretty well to get that over here by April 28 when we sailed.) In it I found a picture of Ray's photographic school in Chicago and another of George Rodger who was on the *Seaforth* with me from Glasgow to Lagos. I couldn't pick out Ray or Pat O'Brien from the assembled students of the photo school. At the moment the scene seemed to be dominated by Stuyvesant Peabody and a blonde girl with a brace of legs. From the Rodger picture I discovered the interesting truth that he had survived French Equatorial Africa and is now in Burma. I hope he likes it.

Shortly before noon came a message that nobody tried to keep secret: "Enemy planes trailing this unit." Conversation amplifying the news revealed that three planes had been picked up dead astern.

There was no alarm. There was a little futile discussion about "Have they sighted us or not?" in which it was pointed out that they'd hardly be following us if they hadn't. There was some more pointed argument about the distance a pilot could see the fleet on such a day as this, and the distance at which he could make out that we were escorting a couple of carriers. It all depended, one gathered, on the altitude.

At noon fourteen fighters went off from the carrier.

At 1 o'clock the vigil became interesting although most of the ship's company was more concerned with a supervised fist fight on the fantail. Our planes hadn't reported.

Most of the officers not on duty had left the wardroom hurriedly to get ringside seats for the air show. But all their forehandedness, not to mention their piety and wit, did them no good. The impending fight, if any, between the airplanes must remain just another of those hearsay fights between airplanes. Our future might depend on something that was going on over the horizon but it was nevertheless over the horizon. The sea was a gleaming spread of blue jelly from one snap-brimmed horizon to the other and the sky overhead was an empty porcelain tureen—hot and cloudless.

Crowley came along to say that he thought we were playing in unusually hard luck.

"They spotted us at sixty miles," he said. "They must have been awfully high up, and so far the fighters don't seem able to find them. . . ."

I went out onto the fantail then. Everybody knew the stage business of this particular melodrama. Spotter planes were following us. . . . Well, well. Everybody remembered a similar situation after Wake. Nobody had to be told that in an hour or two the bombs would probably be crashing down on us. But nobody was agitated. As veterans we can no longer let our blood pressure rise over things that we can't see.

I met a marine named Musa out on the quarterdeck. He wanted to talk about Chicago where he had first seen the light of day and to which some day, he assured me, he was going to return. He knew a few of the NBC crowd but I had difficulty following him then because he interrupted the discourse now and then to dunk a swab over the stern on the end of a rope. He wished the plane would hurry up and come or else go away for keeps. You can't give all your attention to ack-ack guns and a broom at the same time.

The pugilistic card on the fantail was a brawl under official direction to settle a quarrel that had begun without official direction between two gobs apparently unsatisfied with the regular ration of war. I didn't stay to see it or inquire the causes. But there were lots of spectators without me.

Throughout the afternoon the Jap planes were all about us though we don't seem to have done much about it. It turns out that we were first spotted this morning about 9:30 by a lone-wolf seaplane. Later visitations probably came from lads sent out to check on the first one.

Now, at 5:30, we have a call to general quarters. The guns are bared, manned, loaded and ready to fire. The lookouts are alert for what may come out of the sunset as it has in the past. We are speeding south on a zigzag course.

It would be thrilling if we didn't feel that nothing is likely to come of it. We're not likely to have two freak experiences like the one that overtook us coming from Wake.

There is a fishy smell in the breeze. It may be land. It may be a patch of floating kelp. On the fantail it's varied with a hot breath from the stacks as more boilers are lighted off.

May 16, Saturday. At sea. Hot. Calm. I got up this morning in time to see a terrific sunrise. One of those displays that envelop the whole horizon with fluffs of old rose and light gold. The black fleet looked impossible on the black water—like wooden models on a mirror. And the morning breeze was cool for a while and the clouds of flying fishes sped out from the froth of our bow wave. Oh what the what! War, they say this is!

We picked up two new additions to our force, the expected cruisers, soon after sunrise to fill up what space was left on our starboard horizon. They look exactly like each other. They brought three cans with them, all of which was announced by Donald Duck as "Bearing 270, two friendly cruisers and three destroyers, a total of four ships." Don't ask me how he arrived at that.

I heard an odd story today—one that will probably be a classic of this war and just as probably will be ticketed as fiction.

During the last stages of the battle of the Coral Sea a U. S. carrier, probably the *Lexington,* started in just before sunset to gather in its planes. The last one came down after dark and the deck crew was preparing to go below when another plane came circling about and then three more. The first plane switched on its riding lights and came slowly into the groove to land. About that time it became obvious that they were Jap planes and the ack-ack went to work on them with unpublished results. The Jap carrier was only thirty-five miles away.

Dinner was at 4:00 tonight. Somebody said if we kept on this way it would be served just before breakfast. Pretty soon 6 P.M. will be just about 6 A.M. and noon will be a week from last Tuesday.

Went up on the bridge with Commander Crenshaw but we were in heavy rain by the time I got out from cover and we couldn't see anything except two cruisers that can't be told apart even in good weather.

An emergency turn was ordered at twenty minutes to six. Donald Duck blew the alert. It was all a shadow show to us, what with the rain and the early sunset. But off in the dark the cans were at work. The ship throbbed with the depth charges—four of them.

The verdict as usual is withheld. Maybe it *was* an elephant!

May 17, Sunday. At sea. Wet morning. Hot.

As this is written about 10 A.M. we are still headed south through squalls and a sort of natural steam.

There was a muster this morning. After yesterday's inspection it looked a little like the polishing of the backs of the buttons and I kidded the executive about it.

"Well," he said, "I do it every week just to make 'em get into a clean suit." Not a bad idea.

Was talking to Commander Crenshaw this afternoon when an ensign came in with a message board to which were clipped the latest items from the decoding room. The commander read one of these and seemed surprised. But he couldn't tell me what he had read, of course, because the information is secret, confidential and all of that.

I wasn't disturbed. The messages couldn't have had to do with anything but future plans, and experience has taught me that today's future plans are always superseded by tomorrow's future plans.

What I know in advance will do me no good and battles can't be kept secret from you if you're there when they happen.

The afternoon was cooler. Kelly the navigator says that's because we're only 6,000 miles from Little America.

My old cruiser got orders today to proceed to Australia for some reason unstated. Keith Wheeler and a couple of photographers were transferred by boat during the afternoon to another cruiser.

We refuel tomorrow or next day and then maybe go someplace or continue to boil in these familiar waters. Wonder what happened to the Jap carrier we were chasing.

May 18, Monday. At sea. Cooler. Rougher. Sunny.

The cruiser left us this morning. Just in time, too. The Germans reported in their latest communiqué which reached us this A.M. that they had sunk a cruiser of the *Swayback Maru* class, and if it wasn't its sister ship it had to be the *Swayback Maru.* Poor old ghost! Sunk twice and burned once by the Japs and now at least 50 per cent sunk by Hitler.

There's a feeling all over the ship that we're going back to Pearl Harbor. Don't ask me why. Nobody has said anything. There have been no notices on the bulletin board, no unusual twist in the day's operating orders, but, whereas yesterday nobody would have tried to guess where we were going, today everybody knows we're headed home. We've 4,000 miles between us and Honolulu. The betting is that we'll be there in ten days.

Along about noon Domei reported that the good old task force had been sighted—the two carriers and some cruisers. If the people of the U. S. can't find out from us what the Navy is doing they can learn from Japan. . . . There's something fishy about this. I wonder why we got sighted in the first place, why we ran away— possibly for Honolulu—in the second place.

I was sitting at dinner, languidly shaking dice for a package of cigarettes or a tootsie roll, when Commander Maloney, the doctor, came running in all out of breath and reported a man overboard. We rushed out to find most of the crew milling about on the well deck.

It's a rule, of course, that if you fall overboard these days you stay overboard. The admiral isn't going to risk the fleet in a hot spot by halting it for a search. But in practice, nobody's quite that cold-blooded. Our first lieutenant as he got out onto the deck called to the bridge to sound flight quarters and got ready to launch an SOC. The plane couldn't pick him up of course but it could keep track of him.

Meantime the destroyers were beginning to coagulate on the horizon. Three of them came steaming along behind us as soon as they spotted our wake.

How the sailor came to go overboard I don't know. One witness says that he fell and rolled under the life-line at a point just aft of the propeller guard. Another gob says he leaned outward, caught hold of the lower life-line and dragged himself over. When he hit the water he disentangled himself from his gas mask and began to swim. In a few minutes the destroyers were almost out of sight in the wet haze behind us and it looked bad for our lost hand. But you never know. A quarter of an hour later Donald Duck announced that he had been picked up by the ———. I suppose he realizes how lucky he was.

60

THE QUICKEST ROAD HOME

MAY 19, *Tuesday*. At sea. Warmer. We continue to head northeastward.

One of our newest cruisers showed up this morning on our horizon. She came down from Pearl with the mail and probably will go back with us.

She didn't deliver the mail in person. She sublet the contract to a destroyer which came alongside at 5 P.M. It was a pleasure to see the efficiency with which the crew of the destroyer set up a cable and pulley rig between the two ships. About twenty sacks of mail were hauled over in a cargo net in fifteen minutes. Everybody on the ship turned out to see the performance. Some of the officers missed dinner. There wasn't much exciting about it but we are rapidly being brought to the state of yokels who make a daily trip to the depot to see the train come in.

I sat up late working puzzles and sweating. There seems to be no doubt now that we are heading home. I heard indirectly that some of our ranking officers wouldn't be surprised at an attack on Hawaii or Alaska. The Japs are likely to go in for anything that might take the heat off the Southwest Pacific.

May 20, Wednesday. At sea. Fair. Hot. Lat. this morning 12 south 178 east.

I slept hardly at all last night nor was I any better able to when chance offered this morning. I had just about conquered the heat and was dozing off when I discovered that most of my companions on the ship weren't able to sleep either. I'll never find out why people who can't sleep have such rotten taste in phonograph records.

Got up. Did little else.

Tonight at 5:30 P.M. we passed the 180th meridian eastbound. There was no noticeable jar.

So it's May 20, Wed., all over again. And still hot.

I slept hardly at all last night. I had just about conquered the heat, etc. . . . (That's all repeated too including the taste in phonograph records. Good old 180th meridian!)

The water supply is low, oddly enough because the temperature of the sea is increasing. I made some inquiry about that and discovered that the answer is really simple. The seawater is used as a condensing medium and when it gets to 85 degrees the condensation is much less rapid than it is at say 40 degrees.

Men off watch were permitted to go without their gas masks today. That's a break. I shall take advantage of it and also leave off my tin hat and my dunking-suit.

I learned a little today about the man who fell overboard. Dr. Maloney reports him as being well read, well educated, and generally a pretty good sailor. He recently seemed to be suffering from some abstruse nervous ailment and had had one fainting spell.

We are now (at noon) 2,000 miles off Honolulu. Very likely we'll be there by Sunday morning. We certainly aren't wasting any time. We've been going just as fast as the tankers (which we picked up somewhere) will let us. Nimitz apparently is anxious to get us back into Hawaiian waters. I might possibly figure out the strategy. But it's too hot.

At this writing the Reds are poking on into Kharkov but not doing so well on the Kerch peninsula.

May 21, Thursday. At sea. Hot. Calm. Still bound N. E. at 18 knots. No sleep. Everybody on our deck was awake before sunrise this morning and the ship was noisy as a charivari. We had air-attack and torpedo-attack drills today. You have to do something to break the monotony of these battles.

May 22, Friday. At sea. Hot. Calm. Heavy ground swell. We've slowed up a bit and the latest information is that we get into Honolulu Tuesday morning.

Yesterday we had a moment of concern when one of the engines went foul—something wrong with a condenser. The chief and his associates fixed it up in about half an hour and we were on our way again but I got a chance to meditate on the troubles of Rojestvensky with uncertain engines as his stumbling fleet passed not far from here on its way to Togo and the hereafter.

Engines certainly have improved in the past thirty-seven years. So have ships of war, and not merely in the development of super-dreadnaughts and great artillery carriers. In comparatively short time since the keels were laid on our pre-conference battleships we've worked out new steel alloys, lighter and tougher. This steel, plus advanced technique in welding, makes it possible to go to battle in ships with lighter armor and heavier guns, and take the punishment of heavier shelling. I wish they'd carry this out farther. Maybe we could be winning naval battles with no ships at all.

The first lieutenant is complaining of chain-locker disease on this ship. The anchor chain folds down into a compartment in the bow which in the nature of things can have no cross bracing in it as the other compartments do—no decks for instance below the main deck. In a heavy sea the shell plates of this compartment weave under pressure—"pant" as they call it. Eventually in the present series of maneuvers, they cracked and little jets of water came in from the sea. Plates were welded over the cracks and the whole business was shored up with wood braces and it promises to hold out until we get to dry dock which may be tomorrow and may be never.

Part of the symptoms as described to me by the first lieutenant is a phenomenon known as "weeping rivets." Weeping rivets seem to be the worst kind.

8:50. Donald Duck announced in a loud, clear and enthusiastic voice: "We are now crossing the equator." And that about ended my observations for the day. Once more in north latitude I loafed and worked a couple of puzzles.

The evening was overcast. That prevented the official personnel from going out on deck to look for the green flash. I've been looking at every sunset for a month and I haven't seen it yet. I'm still wondering if there is such a thing.

May 23, Saturday. At sea. Cooler maybe. Anyway there's a bit of a wind. There should be decent weather any day now—we're only a couple of days south of Honolulu. We're out of the doldrums although you'd never guess it looking at the attitudes of most of us. Lieutenant Commander Mayer, the gunnery officer, is protesting about "ice cream served at room temperature."

There is much discussion at the moment about where we shall go next. That, not to be too technical about it, depends on the Japs. It's obvious that they're going to attack somewhere, and at the moment we're popping up to a point where we can take care of their program to better advantage than might be possible if we were at say Little America. The bets at the moment favor Alaska for the next performance, and all without much information. As a matter of fact the attack may fall on Alaska or on Midway or Hawaii or to stretch things a bit farther, the Pacific Coast and the Panama Canal. Anyway no matter where it comes it won't be down here, and the weather up there will be cooler. The Japs, if the reports are to be trusted, are beginning to show some sense.

The navigator has been very coy about admitting that we are Honolulu-bound. When I asked him how long it would take to get to Pearl Harbor he inquired a bit sarcastically: "Is that where we're going?" But all the mysterious Mr. Kellys in the world couldn't alter the fact that the men got paid today—a fair indication that somebody, if only the paymaster, thinks we're going in. The censors begin to plow through tons of letters in the wardroom. One censor gave the pitch to the job by remarking that "the Navy's ready-letter-writer seems to be 'Dere Mabel.'" They sweat and fume and curse and would cut their throats if they thought they were making all these preparations for no purpose. Commander Crenshaw thinks we'll go in all right "but only for ten gallons of gas and a windshield wipe."

There was no green flash tonight—heavy clouds on the horizon. But the sunset turned out to be something worth looking at, a band of old rose completely encircling us. Crenshaw said: "I see the Army has released Mauna Loa tonight."

After catching myself on the edge of my bunk a couple of times I got up and sat in the wardroom until 2 A.M., mostly listening to a discussion about where you can get a good steak in Kansas City.

May 24, Sunday. At sea. Hot. Rolling.

On deck at 9:30. Heard Behan's radio delivering program from West Point on the Army Hour. Jimmy Doolittle made a noncommittal speech. Then Announcer Bill Sterns unleashed a terrible excitement over a trip in a bomber. He would probably go into hysterics over a ride in a freight train.

There is some conflicting news about Russia's progress at Kharkov. Apparently the world's greatest tank scrap is going on there.

It's a dull day.

The evening was a little brighter, thanks to discussion by competent authority about the difficulty of escorting corpses. It seems that you have to keep a closer watch over the dead than over the living because in the bad old days, thirsty people used to drink the alcohol in which the corpses were pickled.

Once this was disposed of we had an argument over the Christian requirement that we be kind to Japanese who are, after all, God's creatures. Oddly enough it was a Marine captain who got wrought up over the suggestion that a mass murder would solve the whole problem. There was also some talk about the opportunities of a war correspondent, if any, aboard the Flying Dutchman.

May 25, Monday. At sea. Overcast at dawn. Later sunny. Stiff wind. Hot.

We have still received no orders to go into Honolulu. Commander Crenshaw says that the war's getting too mysterious.

"I can see that there are reasons why we mightn't know what the Japs are going to do," he said. "But I don't see why we can't find out what we're going to do ourselves. . . ."

I went to the captain's office with my copy at 9:30 A.M. He was quite cheery. He said that, as some Englishman had put it, war is a long boredom broken now and then by periods of great excitement.

He said he didn't know whether or not we were going in. It seems silly to write such speculations when tomorrow will show whether we are in Pearl Harbor or not. But on the other hand it may be a matter of reminiscent interest that we are now one day away from Honolulu and still don't know whether to go in or stay out.

I finished reading *Mrs. Appleyard's Year*. I liked it.

I listened to the radio news flashes tonight in Crenshaw's cabin. The Japs now claim that they sank one cruiser, one carrier and one battleship of the *North Carolina* class in the Coral Sea engagement. The Navy denies the loss of any carrier or any battleship. (I wonder about that.) Australia reports the arrival of survivors from an allied ship which was severely bombed by the Japanese. The ship was set afire after a fight in which eight Japanese planes were destroyed. A ninth alighted in flames on the deck of the allied ship and set it afire. "When the blaze got out of control, the personnel was taken off and the ship was sunk by torpedos from another allied vessel."

I should like to feel that I am not being kidded by the oriental minds in the Navy Department. But there, save for the grace of God, goes the *Lexington*.

May 26, Tuesday. Honolulu. Hot. We crawled into Pearl Harbor about noon. I got ashore at 2:00 to look upon the well-remembered madhouse in Drake's office. Ralph Morse and I, after learning that we were due back on the ship in the morning, started to walk to a taxi stand, leaving our baggage in the administration building lobby. We got to the gate without any help. There an Army colonel came along in a jeep and transported us as far as the end of the King Street bus line. There we alighted in a rainstorm.

I had little time to do anything except buy a few books.

I talked in the evening with Walter Farr who has just been whitened by a board of officers of the Army and Navy in joint convention assembled. He is still without status because of finagling in Washington. I told him truthfully that I never realized the brotherhood that exists between the English and ourselves until I saw the muddle-minds put on their imitation of the ministry of information for his benefit.

I turned in at the Young and tried to get a little sleep in a scorching room.

BOOK SIX

MIDWAY!

"Secure from Flight Quarters . . ."

61

REVIVAL OF THE JITTERS

MAY 27, *Wednesday*. Pearl Harbor. Hot. Up early and out to Pearl. On the way, thanks to a meeting with a couple of Army men, I learned that the town had been in a state of alert for ten days, that Army pilots were standing watches in the cockpits of their planes, that Jap carriers had been sighted a thousand miles off Honolulu, that the *Lexington* had been sunk by a time bomb, that the big attack would hit Honolulu by way of Midway.

I put all of this away in a tired mind already filled with such stuff. But I did pause to recall a lot of similar chatter given us by the colonel who rescued us at the gate of Pearl Harbor. The colonel wasn't giving us any futures. He was talking history. And what history!

He had it on good authority that an advance detachment of the Japanese navy, complete with carriers, battleships and transports, had been sighted off Midway. It was a tremendous force, the colonel said. It had four battleships in it and at least five carriers and any number of destroyers and such stuff. This invasion fleet had been intercepted up north of Midway by a U. S. task force and there had been a knock-down and drag-out fight. He was afraid the U. S. losses had been heavy including a carrier, but Yamamoto's side had taken a worse beating. (They had lost two carriers and a battleship.) The Japs hadn't been destroyed but they had been drubbed so thoroughly that they broke off their plan to descend upon Honolulu and had retired to Wake for repairs. They were reorganizing in those waters for a renewal of the attack.

I told the colonel that the report was cockeyed—and I could be quite sure of that inasmuch as I knew where most of the avail-

361

able U. S. forces were at the moment and where they had been for the past ten days. I didn't tell him that we'd probably be on our way toward Midway in a few hours to see for ourselves whether such dreams as those of his informants in G2 ever come true.

On the way out to Pearl there was a reminder of the local alert and the general jitters. A little restaurant out near John Rodgers Airport had been burned during our absence. The charred pieces of the wooden walls stuck up like hop poles in the lush greenery of a garden.

"The Japs did it," said the Hawaiian driver. I looked at him questioningly.

"Why," I asked, "would the Japs want to burn down a joint like that? They didn't have to eat there, did they?"

"There was an alert on," said the driver. "We were told the planes would be here in an hour. And the blackout was black. And then they caught this guy setting fire to this joint. . . . It made a fine blaze, too, I can tell you. But the Japs didn't come in and this guy will go to jail for ten years for nothing."

I was stopped by one of the inner guards at Pearl and told despite my armed escort I should have to walk to the sub base. What with baggage and general resentment at being taken for a Jap spy, I declined. It probably takes an act of Congress or a regiment of Marines to get in here now.

Dick Haller came along and picked me up and brought me to people whose ears I wearied with my lamenting. It will do no good of course—none whatever.

We went aboard the ship at 10:00 and found out that she isn't sailing until tomorrow morning. I could have gone ashore but found the thought bothersome. My face is severely sunburned for one thing. For another my legs are stiff—too stiff for another jaunt halfway to Honolulu in search of a cab.

Ralph Morse went ashore and came back with some gossip. Stan Johnston was on the *Lexington*—very likely the only reporter on it, too. Foster Hailey's credentials arrived the day after our departure and the willing press department hoisted him aboard a tanker which in due course was supposed to overtake us. The tanker

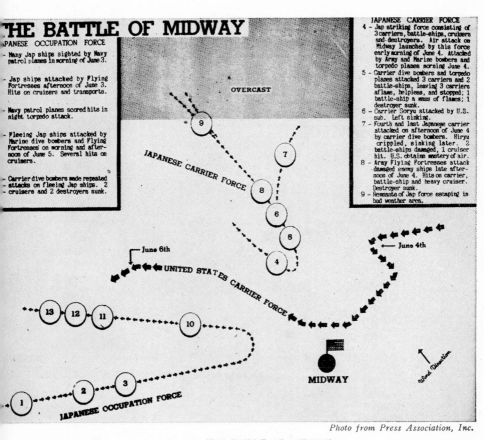

NAVY MAP OF THE BATTLE OF MIDWAY

In detailing the historic battle of Midway, which took place early in June, the Navy Department issued this map of the four-day action.

CREW OF THE "YORKTOWN" EXAMINES DAMAGE

Walking cautiously over the sloping deck of the crippled *Yorktown*, these hard-fighting crew members and fliers examine the damage done

didn't overtake us, and nobody knows where it is—or where Foster is either.

I am reading Oliver Onions' *The Beckoning Fair One*. The last time I read it was in the Athenaeum Court, London, the night they dropped a couple of clunks down the airshaft.

May 28, Thursday. At sea. Hot. We started to get out of Pearl Harbor at 10:30 A.M. We were in the middle of a mess of ships. The harbor is full. The battered *Yorktown* came in yesterday afternoon with two cruisers. The *Lexington* didn't. The *Yorktown* apparently wasn't damaged much. She didn't show any wreckage in a closeup view as we passed her.

At 11:00 we were heading out through the slot. The day had turned out well—cool enough. And the calm, sleepy atmosphere was broken only by black bursts from Fort Weaver ack-ack ominously thumping off our port bow.

It's apparent now that we're going northwest and the best thought on the subject suggests that we're heading for a slugging match. Admiral Spruance of the cruiser division is in charge of the expedition. Admiral Halsey has been sick and most of the lads are affectionately concerned about him. He's been a good leader.

According to the latest information the *Lexington* was hit by five torpedoes and stayed afloat just as Commander Shaw said she would. She righted herself, shook off her list, responded to rudder and retired at twenty-five knots. A fire which at first had appeared to be a minor affair then got out of control and reached a magazine. Her escort sank her.

Apparently the carrier crews started out badly and learned in a hurry. The first attack on Tulagi wasn't very successful. So the planes came back. They rearmed, readjusted their bomb sights and returned to Tulagi. They repeated three times. They were pleased to note improvement as one after another of the Jap ships, including four spitkits and a cruiser, piled up on the beach. By the time they ran into the Jap carrier the next day they were good. One torpedo division alone knocked the *Sziokaku* apart and turned it back toward Tokio at thirteen knots. Then they rearmed, met another carrier and sank it outright.

The skipper of the third carrier involved in these operations—apparently the one that sank the *Lexington*, although information about that is confused—reported in retiring that only twenty of his complement of planes were left. It would seem that the Japs lost about 160 planes or better in the two-day wrangle.

There are stories that we'll get into action quickly this time, maybe in a couple of days. That would seem to indicate that we'll start off from Midway. This information fits in with some of the Honolulu gossip. Army men said that a couple of B-17's had come in from patrol up in this neighborhood badly shot up. They reported a carrier and four cruisers north of the island.

Cincpac sent out a message to the task force: "Please publish at quarters: Although denied an opportunity in the cruise just ended to meet the enemy and to repeat the splendid achievement of past operations, I am confident that you used this time to prepare yourself for usefulness in future actions. In this cruise just starting you will have the opportunity to deal the enemy many heavy blows. You have done this before and I have confidence in your skill and ability to strike even harder blows. Good hunting and good luck."

The Navy has announced that a *Maryland*-class battleship sunk by the Italians off Brazil by means of a high-explosive communiqué two days ago was a Brazilian cargo ship of 5,000 tons.

62

FLIGHT QUARTERS

MAY 29, *Friday*. At sea. Nearing Midway. Calm. Cooler.

During the night we spoke a ship and inasmuch as we don't recognize ships socially any more we swung our guns about and got ready to shoot. Then we got a signal. The ship was one of our four-pipers towing a submarine back toward Honolulu.

This morning an announcement was made to officers on watch that we are shortly to contact the enemy who seems to be traveling in force. According to the best information available at present the Japs have mustered carriers, battleships and a large number of cruisers. We are not going to force a conclusive issue, the advice to the officers goes. (I should hope not.) But we are going to fight a war of attrition. We are going in. We are coming out. We are going to play the game of hit and run that we do so well.

As usual we seem to be holding the short end of the stick—this time shorter than usual. We muster carriers, cruisers, and about half a dozen destroyers to face one of the biggest fleets ever turned loose on the Pacific. An armada that rates as a good half of the Jap fleet and we're meeting it as usual with a fly swatter and a prayer.

An interesting point comes up here: We have just learned that the *Akagi*, one of the carriers in the setup facing us, was sent to dry dock for four months at the beginning of the war by the U. S. Submarine *Sailfish*. And the *Sailfish*, as we now know, is our old friend the *Squalus*, up and working.

Today we are heading almost due west. Tomorrow we will be in the waters about Midway. We're already in the patrol zone. A flying fortress went over us today.

Well, we might sit here and fret considerably about our present predicament. And if naval wars were still being doped as they were a few months ago, we'd have reason. But while our assets may be a little slim, they are good. We have our carriers and inasmuch as the Japs are going to run into this we may look upon Midway as another carrier—and unsinkable at that. And all the time we shall be within flying range of Honolulu reinforcements. So let us think in the grandiose fashion. . . . This is our great opportunity. If we could contrive to dunk the four battleships or the four carriers, this war would be very nearly over.

May 30, Saturday. At sea. Off Midway Islands. Cold and a little gray.

We finagled about all day to no apparent purpose and it got colder and grayer.

We're carrying gas masks again. The commander says we may run into trouble at any time now. In the meantime we improve the shining hour on the morrow by fueling. . . . We pick the oddest places for it.

May 31, Sunday. At sea. Off Midway. Cool. Calm. We took a lot of fuel this morning including about 150,000 gallons of aviation gasoline, all of which is right under my bed.

A useless day. Spent part of it falling asleep in a wardroom Morris chair, part in doing double crostics.

GQ—may its tribe increase—sent out a request today for somebody to take a lot of pictures of Jap battleships, etc., so that the profiles in the spotting books could be corrected. Except for this odd communication, which wasn't in the form of an order, we have heard nothing to suggest that there is any war going on in the neighborhood.

June 1, Monday. At sea off Midway. Cool and a bit foggy. (The fog is hearsay. I feel no urge to go out and look at it.) Last night I froze and was glad of the chance.

The morning's news says that the R.A.F. raided Cologne last night with more than a thousand bombers. This is definitely a different sort of news from what they were issuing when I left London. Only Heinie had a thousand bombers in those days and we could count them whenever we wanted to. The British claim also to have stopped Rommel's drive in Libya, and, as an old interpreter of Cairo communiqués, I should say that the news sounds authentic.

We are now really in Jap territory. We can tell that by the condition watches and the cockeyed course of the daylight zigzag. Odd that it should seem so much like any other part of the Pacific. We continue to contact sharks and small whales just as if there weren't plenty of Hirohito's subs in the vicinity.

Somebody spotted some smoke on the horizon today at 16,000 yards. It looked like a steamer hull-down on the horizon, but the forward director, which has a horizon of 26,000 yards, reported a column of smoke with flame at sea level—probably a fallen plane. The cans and the carrier's airplanes went over to look at it. So probably we shall hear no more about it. We never do.

Heard a story today about the strange behavior of our inter-ship Donald Duck, an ultra H.F. voice outfit through which the admirals spread their orders to the fleet. Last night this gadget began to cough in Morse code instead of lingual adenoids. A startled signal man took down the communication and found that he had a lot of gibberish in plain English, if there is any such thing. The messages went: "When are you going to Alaska?" "Why don't you drop your bomb?" "Are you going to take an admiral with you when you go to Dutch Harbor?" "How do you like it out there in Tokio?"

There was a hurried canvass of the ship but no electrical signal apparatus of any sort was found to be operating at the time—not even the practice buzzer in the wardroom. Mickey Reeves finally solved the mystery. Some of his pilots were practicing with a blinker tube which contains a small buzzer, weak enough to be fed by a single flashlight dry cell. This buzzer, apparently, was operating at Donald Duck frequency, although we'd have had some trouble believing that it could be heard. Wonder what the Japs thought if they picked it up.

At noon it was raining, a thick gray rain.

Boots and saddles for launching planes. Then un-boots and saddles for un-launching planes. Too wet. . . . Too thick.

About 4 P.M. there was an alarm, muck or no muck. Planes had been sighted off the starboard—just sighted. They made no approach and in the fog we had to take them on faith. Our SOC horses went out to look at them and presently came gallumphing home—PBY's.

We breathed more easily, well knowing that today's PBY's may be tomorrow's Mitsubishis.

"I was always a delicate kid," said Tom O'Connell apropos of nothing. "They used to wonder if I'd ever grow up. And sometimes even now I wonder if I'll ever see my thirty-second birthday."

"When is it?" somebody wanted to know.

"Next Thursday," replied Mr. O'Connell.

The aviators came in, red-faced from the wind, and wet, their yellow rubber jackets dripping and shiny. They had had a tough afternoon. However there was no unusual conversation at dinner save for Commander McCann's inquiry about what happened to Idaho baked potatoes during wars.

Overheard a little private conversation about some admiral:

"His private life was very unhappy . . ." etc. I had never realized before that admirals had private lives.

Sat up all night reading, and forgetting to listen to the sound of barking ash cans in the distance. No runs. No hits. No errors.

June 2, Tuesday. At sea. North of Midway. Foggy. Cool.

This morning about 3:00 I was tossed out of bed by a resonant thwack that set the ship back on her tail and shivered the plates until I expected them to fold back on top of me. I should like to treat this entry with the dramatic suspense that accompanied it in fact. For it's a long way to your socks when you're battened down in a lot of ironware and the noise is going on outside. But the denouement turned out to be unworthy of the stew I was in or the time I am wasting setting it down. Not to be too coy about it, we had hit a whale and apparently a large one. I'd feel sorry for him if I didn't know that the depth charges would be sure to get him in a couple of days anyway.

Here is a copy of the order of the day that explains our odd rendezvous out here. I got it belatedly out of the "Plan of the Day." To wit: "The following dispatch from Comtaskfor is quoted for your information—

" 'An attack for the purpose of capturing Midway is expected. The attacking force may be composed of all combatant types including four or five carriers plus transports and train vessels. If the presence of task forces remains unknown to the enemy, we should be able to make surprise flank attacks on the enemy carriers from a position northeast of Midway. Further operations will be based on the result of these attacks, damage inflicted by Midway forces, and information of enemy movements. The successful conclusion of the operation now commencing will be of great value to the country.' "

The dispatch doesn't mention it but four battleships are supposed to be with the attacking fleet. Our strength at the moment consists of carriers, cruisers and nine destroyers, and, I hope, a lot of luck. I knew our limitations a couple of days ago but it didn't look then as if we should be called upon to monkey with more than three carriers. Our present position is what you might call interesting but unpromising.

At 1 P.M. we had torpedo practice. During the rush to stations, a cruiser made a surface contact. Apparently nobody else got it and we figured that they'd picked up a cloud. The business remained a mystery when I went indoors again. The next time I went out onto the deck a couple of hours later, the *Yorktown* was on the horizon and with her two cruisers and an assortment of destroyers.

The new force stays aloofly over toward the horizon on our starboard side but they make a very inspiriting sight. The gunnery officer who until this moment has been unenthusiastic about our mission in life is now talking about a possible annihilation of the Jap fleet. Everybody now scoffs at the suggestion that the highly unpredictable enemy has slid around us and gone on to smash Honolulu or the coast or blow up the Canal. In naval war, apparently, you contrive to know not only where the other fellow is at all times but what he's going to do. The process is ten per cent navigation and ninety per cent ouija board.

June 3, Wednesday. Northeast of Midway. Choppy. Gray. Rough.

The striking event of the morning was a dispatch from Cincpac which said tersely: "Enemy planes attack Dutch Harbor."

Well, here it is. We didn't need any amplification. We'd been expecting that attack just as we are now expecting another one. Our advance information has been proved at least half correct.

So we spent the morning waiting alertly for developments. It looked as if we'd be seeing plenty of them at any time now.

The call to muster came at 9 A.M. and the men fell in at 9:05. At 9:06 Donald Duck joined the proceedings with a single startled cry: "Aircraft!" Then came the bugle, and for the first time since we've been aboard, the *beep-beep* of the general alarm. The trim ranks broke up like falling dominoes and the ladders began to fill with clambering gun crews. I picked up my tin hat and gas mask, puzzlebook and pencil and went aloft to the searchlight platform . on the foremast—a cold place and as windy as a similar observation coop on the lamented *Swayback Maru*.

Here as usual I could pick up a bit of gossip from sky control whose tin tubs (gun-position splinter shields) are just below this platform and behind the forward director. The *Yorktown* had made a contact "with a number of unidentified planes at thirty miles." Nobody seemed to think much of the alarm. We knew we must be reasonably close to the hour when the Jap planes might be giving us this sort of trouble, but it seemed hardly likely that, with air patrols out as they'd been since daybreak, we should have to depend on a radio contact to find out about an approaching enemy squadron at twenty-five or thirty miles.

However, we stood there in the biting wind, looking at a pretty fair bit of antiaircraft maneuvering through atmosphere hazy-blue with oil fumes. All ships were moving at full speed with white ruffs at their water lines, and white tails, looking for all the world like ships in a Greek lithograph. We did an amazing assortment of plunges and turns until nobody could have told what direction we were intending to follow or what was our position in the general line-up. Zigzag! Run ahead! Turn hard right! Turn hard left! Zigzag! . . .

Watching a naval battle, it occurs to me, is like watching a three-ring circus with clowns—you haven't enough eyes.

For half an hour we did a sort of cotillion, sometimes ahead of the carriers, sometimes between them, sometimes abeam or astern. As I write these notes of this performance we are all tangled up with the *Yorktown's* outfit, which until now has remained upstage and unneighborly on the horizon.

During all this, there has been no sign of the suspected planes and while waiting for them one gets a good chance to study the atmospherics. It's a fine day for an air raid. The ceiling is about 2,000 feet but it's a real ceiling. Planes could come a hundred miles through it with no chance of detection.

9:30. Word was relayed to the task forces that the *Yorktown* had picked up some of her own planes on the detector. So the bugle blew recall and we all came down out of the wind and the weather except the lads who had to stay on watch.

Met Commander Crenshaw as I hung up my mask and hat in his cabin.

"It had all the flavor of the real McCoy," he said. "And I feel in my bones that it's a sort of sign or portent or something. We'll probably be spending most of our time up there from now on. . . ."

At noon we heard another piece of news:

"A large body of the Japanese fleet moving on Midway has been located by Navy patrol planes 700 miles west. . . ."

Two days' travel for ships.

The planes should be going to work early tomorrow.

Another bit of news: Another carrier and accompanying cruisers are on their way to join up with us. They're said to be only "two bells and a bosun's pipe" behind.

Afternoon. There was much agitation and an oversupply of scuttle butt during the morning as more people went out—from Midway bases presumably—to look at the visiting Japs and contribute to the reports. The first news was modified after an hour or two. It was discovered by some observer who'd been working with the Honolulu patrol and knew the shapes of warships that this force was really an occupation division consisting of eleven ships, most of which were transport or supply vessels. The main body thus remained unlocated.

All in all the atmosphere should have been surcharged with the menace of war and sudden death—but somehow it wasn't. The principal topic of discussion at dinner was Ripley's cartoon of the passing Chinamen. The Commander said Ripley's premise was false. The caption of the cartoon had stated that if all the Chinamen in the world were to march past a given point they'd never get by; new ones would be born faster than those marching could die off. The first lieutenant put up a brief defense but the Commander wasn't having any.

"He's talking in the first place about Chinamen now living," he said, "and in the second place he's talking about Chinamen not yet born. And I doubt very much that all the Chinamen in the world would march past a given point just to accommodate Ripley anyway."

The ship was tightly buttoned up when I went to bed. I lay reading as the watches changed. All through the night. . . .

63

DAY OF BATTLE

June 4, *Thursday*. North of Midway Islands.

1:00. Just learned that the Army planes from Midway located another part of the Jap invasion force late Wednesday afternoon. They reported four heavy ships, at least two of which were battleships. They damaged one and left it "burning furiously."

Another report came in tonight. One of our subs sank three Jap subs and three merchant ships with eleven torpedoes at Wake. The submarine skipper was complaining in his report that his periscope was getting so cloudy he couldn't see through it. What might he have done if only he could have seen what he was doing!

6:00 A.M. I got up for reveille and looked out at a clotted sky, a black sea and odd gray moonlight.

If there is such a thing as a special atmosphere for battle, here it is!

Daybreak was late because, in deference to the land-based forces co-operating with us, we had gone back to "war time."

The day is warm and a little calmer—a fine day for whatever it is. If the Japs were 700 miles away as reported yesterday they must be about 350 miles nearer this morning and we, having traveled about 350 miles in their direction, must be almost on top of them. Of course both fleets may have changed direction since yesterday noon—quite possibly have.

Mickey Reeves turned down my offer to act as tail-end Charlie in one of his fine SOC's. He told in extenuation of how they took an overweight pilot to Samoa on the Marshall Islands expedition. When it came time to return to the ship the wind had died and the

SOC wouldn't take off. A message was sent to the admiral: "SOC unable take off account wind conditions. Extra weight one hundred gallons gasoline and pilot's overweight equivalent twenty gallons gasoline."

Two days later the plane got back. A report was sent to Halsey who replied promptly: "Hope you've recovered also your twenty-gallon pilot."

8:20. Donald Duck issued a call to quarters with the *beep-beep* that made it official. As we started for battle stations we were informed that the Japs had just attacked Midway, 170 miles to the southwest of us. We didn't have to be told as we swung about into launching position that we were going to take a flying leap at their carriers.

As I went into the wardroom to get my gas mask and tin hat I met Commander Crenshaw. "Okay," he said, "this is it. And don't go out without your rubbers." I crawled up to the searchlight platform and saw us start the ride into battle at the fastest speed this force has worked up to date.

We were going so fast that our protective can, half submerged and slapping green water over her bridge, had trouble keeping up with us. The sea was flat but still the can buried her nose in the green and tossed up a plume in her wake that looked like Old Faithful.

Behind us the sea was strange to look upon, crisscrossed by frothy white lines—miles of them in fanciful design, as wide and white as concrete roads—the boiling water left to mark the passage of heavy ships. From here the sea appears to be crowded with ships. Our little force has grown miraculously—and fortunately—through the addition of cruisers and such that have overtaken us in the night, and also through the companionship of the *Yorktown's* force, the stacks of whose destroyers look like black stumps on the horizon.

The officers of the secondary battery in sky control a few feet beneath this platform just got the story of the Army's battleship attack as I heard it during the night. They passed it on with cheers.

8:45. I'm beginning to have a great deal of respect for Admiral Spruance who is conducting this expedition. It is getting more and more apparent as we steam toward the west that we haven't been detected. . . . It's a miracle but that seems to be the way of it.

We have an inferior force. It's probably one of the largest the United States ever sent anywhere in a gesture of anger but what of it. About half the Jap navy—and not the worst end of it—is out there ahead.

Every one of the gun crews that I can see below me hanging to the guns to keep from being blown away now realizes that luck or superior information or something has given us a chance to get this war well on its way to a finish in the next couple of hours. If we can sink a couple of battleships and four carriers the sea road to Tokio is open, and to dominate the Pacific we won't need much more equipment than what we happen to have on hand.

Of course the dice may not roll that way. But somehow optimism has replaced the casual gloom of yesterday's outlook. We believe in Santa Claus again. . . . And besides Hirohito's carriers won't be expecting us.

The wind is stiffer up here than anywhere else on the ship and you can count on thirty knots of it no matter where you go. Even so the funnel fumes hang around here like a hearse plume. The heat is creating its own eddy currents, and breathing in this locality is getting very difficult.

The air beyond the light-brown haze of the stacks is strikingly clear although there is a thick cover of cloud overhead and the sun peeks through infrequently. The whole scene is blue and black, and the details of our carriers and cruisers draped on the starboard flank stand out like images in field glasses.

9:10. We make a right-angle turn. The wind stiffens, if that were possible, and the SBD's and STB's go off.

It's much too windy for me to hear what's being said in sky control so I don't know whether or not any contact has been made with the Japs. Anyway the haul isn't too far for these planes if they have to go all the way to Midway. It's comforting to see them up and something of a relief, too. It won't be long now one way or the other and if anything's coming to us we'll soon know it. If we don't get the Jap he'll certainly get us.

The white road in our wake goes straight back to the horizon, a four-lane highway on which ride two cruisers, fantastically unreal behind a curtain of exhaust fumes.

From here I can look down on the SOC's sitting in their cradles and definitely detached from the flight. . . . This is no work for children or fat men. Beyond the catapults the five-inch guns are bunched together on the flight deck, all of them with their muzzles in the air expectant of attack. Experience shows that there's nothing wrong with that premise or the technique.

These guns are manned by Marine crews who from a height present a change in color from that of the region where the gobs operate. Here instead of blue dungarees is a vista of shiny O.D., a mass of it and as motionless as Lorado Taft's statue of the "March of Time." Nothing on earth is so immobile as a cannoneer awaiting a chance to work.

Shells stand nose-down in the fuse cutters, colorful shell and dull varnished brass bases. The guns, somehow, look bright and new— freshly painted barrels with a red ring around the muzzles, brass elevation gears burnished with grease.

Somebody might make a fine picture here of the strain before battle—the strain that is somehow never manifested save in a deathlike impassivity such as this. But I have no time to enlarge on the theme. The sky is filling with planes. They circle the carriers, group themselves in two's and three's and quartets, and finally wing along under the high clouds in squadrons of fifteen. They are joined by a few gooneys—little ones, the first we've seen in weeks.

Why we've delayed so long in uncorking these planes nobody has told me but it's fairly obvious. It may be hard on Midway to let the Japs proceed with their attack in force, but it's going to be a lot easier to smash the carriers if the planes are busy somewhere else. It would seem that the carriers are sending up all they've got. The sky over toward the starboard horizon is filling up with little black crosses, so presumably the *Yorktown* is doing the same thing. Over the top and God bless!

From the signal yards the flags come down and the flags go up—red, yellow, blue, white, crossed, striped, checkered. Lads are running up and down the ladders of the foremast with dispatch blanks in their hands. It's all spectacular and beginning to be thrilling.

9:30. We're out of the fog banks and into a region of brilliant sky and glowing blue sea. Everybody aboard ship stands motionless, each man prayerful after his fashion as the planes go quickly out of sight off our starboard quarter. Few men, after all, have had a chance to look upon a spectacle like this. In the nature of things few will look on anything like it again.

The ship's bell tinkles the hour. As if it made any difference to anybody.

10:50. Everything is on its way now except for about ten fighters which loiter around us.

I went below to get my glasses and found everything shut up tight. Nobody's taking any chances with this ship no matter how far away or how preoccupied the Japs may be. I found a gob with a chisel or a permit or something to pry a scuttle cover off one of the hatches and so got below. Everything was darker than a coal mine and as stuffy as the inside of a rubber boot. Turret men and powder monkeys lay sprawled in the long passageways. A hell of a life. In the long vigils before battle they lie in the dark. During battles they go through a monotony of powder and shell-handing. The most vital moments they will ever experience are also the most drab.

Below decks you got an idea of the ship's speed from the sound of the water tearing at her shell plates as it went by. It's a sound deeper throated than a rumble and not far short of terrifying.

On the way back I stopped on the well deck for a look over the side. Here, close to the skittering foam, you got a greater sense of motion that you'd ever experience in a fast airplane. We are doing everything the engines will let us do. We dive into it and we roll. And every time the ship changes course the port rail goes under the water and the well deck takes a frothy ocean.

The day has turned out to be beautiful.

A report has come in that the Jap attack is divided into two sections—the striking force against which our planes have just moved and a reserve force between fifty and a hundred miles behind the striking force. The general course of these ships is on a line to the west of us.

10:30. We go into a terrific lateral-pass maneuver and the ships start running across each other's bows. Donald Duck raises his voice: "Antiaircraft stations stand by to repel attack."

I go back to my place on the foremast. Then comes the usual

wait and study of the sky. You can't help but think that this fine day which you were finding so useful to our bombers is going to be just as helpful to Hirohito's bombers.

10:35. Usual reports of approaching aircraft. . . . "Unidentified plane, bearing three-three-eight—forty-eight thousand." "Unidentified plane bearing two-seven-oh—fifty-two thousand. . . ." Everybody is tense of course because sometimes these hysterical shouts turn out to make sense.

We are now leading the procession abreast of the cans. A cruiser—a floating arsenal of ack-ack—has come over alongside our old carrier.

10:45. Ten planes show up off the starboard bow. They may be the *Yorktown's* SBD's. As we glower at them we get the answer—the step pyramid of the *Yorktown's* bridge structure comes up over the horizon. More planes are reported but the *Yorktown* claims them for her own and we withdraw from the contest.

We are still plowing along at top speed. On the lower decks the roar of the engines is so great that you have to shout to be heard a few feet. The cans, if we keep on at this rate, will have to refuel tonight. One lone gooney is sailing along with us easily and hopefully.

At the moment the carrier nearest us has sent out fighters, dive bombers and torpedo planes. If the *Yorktown* has contributed as many as our old carrier, there ought to be about 180 planes on the way to the attack, 105 of them bombers or torpedo carriers.

11:15. A report has come in that one of our fortresses has attacked and damaged a carrier, presumably in the reserve group. The attack on Midway has been driven off—eight planes shot down over the island, the Marines claiming a bag of thirty off shore.

It's odd how the battle is shaping up to fit the specifications of the story the medical colonel told me when we went into Honolulu after the Coral Sea. The Colonel said that the fight had already occurred. I said it hadn't. Nature as usual is imitating art.

11:35. We head now into the wind and it's very chilly. Some fighter planes are coming in, presumably part of our protective patrol. Against the sky they tumble along like a cloud of May flies. We're making crochet patterns all over the sea again.

11:40. There is some contact off the starboard quarter. Maybe that's why the fighters came in. They shoot over the rim of the sea and we continue our cotillion.

I'm getting sleepy. A gray half-moon hanging belatedly in the thin blue sky reminds me so much of myself.

11:45. Fighters come back to land on our carrier. Apparently a false alarm.

12:00. Mickey Reeves signaled me to come down to the bridge for a sandwich. So I was right at headquarters when first reports began to come in from our planes. The first message was brief. The Jap carriers had been located, a little belatedly, and they were virtually without air cover. . . . Apparently all their planes had been sent out to make the conquest of Midway quick and easy. However, the squadron commander of the TBD unit reporting, said that his planes were virtually out of fuel.

"Request permission," he called, "to withdraw from action and refuel."

The admiral's answer was terse.

"Attack at once."

So as I sat down in the chartroom to bite into a ham sandwich, the planes had begun to move in on the carriers. Whatever might be the result, we'd never be able to criticize the quality of our opportunity. . . .

I sat there thinking. The Jap air admiral undoubtedly had figured us as permanent fixtures in the southwest Pacific where last he had had word of us. So just about now he'd be looking up at the sky suddenly clouded with SBD's and asking himself the Japanese equivalent of "Where the hell did those things come from?"

12:45. Enemy planes reported off port at twelve miles. New alert sounds. The kids drop their food and sidle off to their guns. The Grummans once more leap off our carrier.

1:00. Still no sign of the visitors. I guess the contact was another of those phonies that breed so rapidly in times like this.

1:15. Fifteen of the ———'s bombers come over. The squadron is intact and in tight formation, its work, whatever it was, finished.

1:20. The carriers swing around, apparently getting ready to take on returning planes which are now showing up in two's and three's. Everything is set to repel an attack, and with good reason.

If these planes have failed in their mission or fought a draw or left the Jap carriers usable we may expect a quick and vicious attack in return. If by some remote juju we have put all four carriers out of commission we have just about gained mastery of the Pacific including the Japanese side of the international date line, or so the more educated of my spies tell me.

I went back to the wardroom and contemplated this phenomenon. Presently the word filtered back to us that the attack had been a complete success. All the carriers·had been hit and severely damaged. At least three of them were burning. One, apparently, had been sunk in the first two or three minutes of the engagement.

One battleship of the north group of the force that we had attacked was afire. A second battleship had been hit. Reports from the Army told of hits on two more battleships and another carrier. Discounting these messages to the fullest extent and recognizing how easy it is for one observer to duplicate the report of another, it was still obvious that we had had something of a field day, still obvious that the bulk of Japan's attacking planes must presently be going into the drink for want of any other place to land.

64

BOMBS BURSTING IN AIR

I LEANED back in the Morris chair and stretched out my legs and presently was sound asleep in that deep exhaustion that follows such moments of tension. I was aroused by the sound of some other chair-holders grabbing up their tin hats. I got out onto deck about 2:30. The time is uncertain. My watch was smashed.

There was no time to climb up to the coop on the foremast. A spot of ack-ack had burst over to port near the horizon and the air in that direction seemed to be covered with planes. Word came from nowhere—by the telepathy of battles, I guess—that the *Yorktown* was being attacked. The battle was already on and it would necessarily be brief. The ack-ack was ragged but the thunderheads of it blackened the horizon.

We had no way of telling how many Jap planes came in on that raid but there couldn't have been many. The blasting was short-lived. The carrier came up toward us obviously in good order and such planes as we could pick up with ordinary field glasses appeared to be ours.

A couple of heavy cruisers peeled off from our formation and streaked over toward the *Yorktown*. It seemed a little late for rescue work and a little unnecessary. The *Yorktown* had come through the assault without much aid and apparently wasn't needing any help to celebrate her escape. This, it seemed to me, might be like shooting stars over the rim of the sea.

As in the first attack this drama lasts only a matter of seconds. The black puffs attenuate and lose color and mingle with the stratus clouds in the low distance. The fires of the burning planes are quickly out. The carrier has gone over the horizon again and the ocean is as it was before save for one strange and terrifying thing—a column of smoke, like the greasy black cockade that marked Wotje after the Marshall Islands raid, is rising straight into the air to reach at last the dim levels of the ack-ack bursts. Something is afire over there. Commander Crenshaw thinks that maybe a destroyer got hit. We cross our fingers and hope it wasn't the carrier. At any rate it's serious.

We keep on our course with every rivet straining and we cast no regretful or anxious glances at the horizon. We haven't time. We keep our necks pulled well down into our collars and mind our business. Whatever happened to the carrier may be happening to us in very short order. The Japs will never overlook the flagship as long as they have a plane left.

(Emphasis inserted at midnight: As long as they have a plane left!)

6:05. An announcement was made over the loud-speaker to coagulate the rumors on which we have been subsisting since the planes went off this morning. We begin to realize that we have actually taken part in a decisive and important battle. Until now we have been kidding ourselves that this might be so. But now we know. Whatever else we may have done, we are now informed that we have "attacked and severely damaged four enemy aircraft carriers. . . ." A haul in itself if the carriers have been smashed enough to put them into dry dock for a few months, a terrific victory if they have been smashed badly enough to keep them from getting back to Tokio. . . . But there's a catch to this announcement and possibly an explanation for the smoke over on the horizon. . . . "One of our aircraft carriers was attacked in two waves and badly damaged. We suffered severe losses in airplanes. . . ." Battles, you are learning, are merely encounters in which the victor's losses are a little less than those of the loser.

About 6:10 I came in off the deck to a dimly lighted wardroom for a cup of coffee. I needed it. A lot of officers were there, most of them munching sandwiches automatically and in silence. If they spoke at all it was with the voices of men dead for sleep. . . .

"We sent out fifty-three TBD's and we got back five." "They had to land in the water—no gas." "If they attacked the carrier why don't they attack us? What's keeping them?" "I guess most of their planes are in the drink too." "If four carriers are smashed their planes are going to have a hell of a time finding a place to land." "Is the carrier still afloat?" "She's listing badly to starboard and down by the bow."

For a victory feast this was certainly a depressing session.

Out on deck again at 6:30. Either we had altered our course a bit or the carrier had altered hers. The carrier was now well up over the horizon, an appalling mass of smoke rolling off her flight deck.

6:40. Air alarm. I scrambled up to the searchlight platform again. As I passed the 20-mm. battery, Mickey Reeves came out of the charthouse. "Watch it on that side," he ordered. "They think they've got something coming in on the sun."

We swung about immediately and careened toward me so that I was hanging to the ladder like a fly trying to get a hold on the ceiling. When I got to the platform we were leaving the burning carrier behind us. Another carrier, undamaged, and her cruisers in new perspective were jet black against the reddening sky.

Down at the five-inch guns the Marine crews were staring into the sun, shading their eyes with their hands, their faces screwed into odd knots like those of characters in a Bellows drawing—alert but as usual immobile, concerned, perhaps, but not showing it.

One interesting thing occurred while I was looking at the guns: A carrier got lost. A moment ago she was there in plain sight. Now she was gone. And I wasn't the only person aboard who wondered about that.

7:30. Lieutenant Dancey, my ex-cabin-mate, came up the ladder bound for the fighting top. I crawled up after him and looked out upon a larger if no more watery world.

We had forgotten about the enemy plane at that time. It never showed up—if it ever existed—but as we took a long sweep on our zigzag, the wounded carrier did. Presently she rose over the rim like something in a magic-lantern show. Somebody apparently had tossed a miracle. She had straightened up. The list had been reduced so that it wasn't apparent through the glasses. The fire had gone out. Big, clean, beautiful, she filled a large section of our vision like a symmetrical island. She was like an island not only in her silhouette but in her immobility. Four cruisers stood by.

7:35. Dancey asked for a report on operations in progress and that's how we learned that we still had twenty-four torpedo planes out working on what was left of the mess we produced this morning. They may have some trouble getting back before dark.

7:40. The sun is getting low. The horizon is a band of glowing orange. And against it the battered carrier stands in her glorious aloofness. As we watch, four heavy cruisers steam off along the edge of the panorama toward the north and the cans follow. You look at all of this with a catch in your throat. And you brace yourself for the sentimental shock that must come presently when one of the cans turns about to put a tin fish into her. For there's no doubt now that the ship has been abandoned.

She was dead in the water, you could see that. You could guess at the sievelike condition of a hull so battered that her engines were finished. . . . So we'd sink her as we'd sunk the *Lexington* only a couple of weeks ago. We stood by and waited for the drop of the trap.

But it didn't come. The ships held to their course away from the deserted hulk. The carrier, until our course for the recovery of planes took us over the horizon and dropped her from our vision, stood majestically on the rim of the sea, the blazing sun behind her like the burst of light at the climax of a grand opera, her head up.

7:45. Once the carrier was out of sight we took our loss philosophically. After all to trade one carrier for three wasn't bad business, and despite the confused reports of the operation it was quite likely that the proportions of the bargain were even greater. I mentioned to Commander Mayer that for the first time since December 7 we were now able to meet the Japs with the odds even—with the odds even despite the fact that they outnumbered us still in ships and outclassed us in main battery-fire power. For the first time since I began to ride with this task force we had arrived at a point where we could trade the Japs carrier for carrier and still have enough left to lick them.

Mayer nodded.

"All this has worked out like the war games," he said. "We've been over this problem right here in these same waters a dozen times. Somebody realized a long time ago that the best way to beat the Japs would be to let them pick the battleground—but make it

INJURED CREWMAN IS CARRIED TO SAFETY FROM THE "YORKTOWN"
This graphic picture shows an injured member of the gallant crew of
the *Yorktown* being carried to the deck of a destroyer by means of a
breeches buoy.

THE "YORKTOWN" AFTER JAPANESE AIRCRAFT ATTACK JUNE 4, 1942

Listing heavily to the port side with smoke billowing from her single funnel, the *Yorktown* is shown after withstanding a successful, bruising attack by Japanese aircraft. But forty-eight hours later, a Japanese submarine scored two direct torpedo hits on the crippled aircraft carrier and she went to the bottom later. The picture shows a list in the d...

our battleground that they picked. The Japs wanted another Tsushima but we got it instead."

8:30. The carrier still close to us launches some fighters. About that time the missing one pokes her nose over the horizon dead ahead of us. How she got there is something I'll really never know. Her reappearance is reported immediately to a lot of interested folks below.

The TBD's are coming in to land. They are well bunched but in no particular formation. The recently released fighters romp about here and there over them in the darkening sky like a flock of blackbirds.

I recall a comment of Ralph Morse about torpedo bomber pilots. "They don't stand any watches. They don't have to go out and do patrol jobs. They don't have any dogfights to worry about. They may sit around playing poker for a month before they have to go out. . . . Then they go out and they don't come back."

Note at midnight: These lads, however, came back in good order. And they brought a puzzle. One of our carriers had sent out twenty-four planes, including her remaining TBD's. Thirty-five came back. The explanation of course is that some of the homing pigeons were part of the outfit from the ship put out of action.

8:35. The lookouts began their customary twilight field day.

"Large group planes bearing three-one-oh unidentified." Seven fighters streak out to investigate that one.

"Aircraft two-five-three relative reported friendly."

"Unidentified aircraft, sir, just passed overhead."

8:45. "Only unidentified plane now in sky is at one-one-eight relative. . . . Sixty thousand yards."

The last of the bombers is in. I am going below.

The wardroom scuttle-butt session was brief considering that we had just taken part in a first-class battle and, not only that, had come out intact and with an amazing success where most of us had expected to be sunk.

Crowley contributed a bit of common sense for the consideration of tired officers. "We have a lot of subs out there," he said. "It's to be expected that they are closing in on such ships as the bombers have partly wrecked and slowed down."

The officers listened to him politely and without argument. Most of them had been awake for twenty-four hours. All of them had been under constant strain for a long nightmarish if glorious day. One by one they went to sleep in their chairs or staggered off somewhere to lie down.

The score at present, unverified and of problematical accuracy, is this:

The Navy claims two carriers badly damaged and two completely destroyed.

Reports from Midway say that Army bombers damaged two carriers—which isn't so confusing when you figure that they were probably working on the "reserve force" somewhere detached from the main striking force. The Army bag is also said to include one battleship afire and one with a brace of torpedoes in it. Three ships are on fire between here and Midway, one probably a heavy cruiser and others unidentified.

Fantastic as these figures would have seemed yesterday when we were counting heads of our force and rechecking the report of what the Japs were bringing to us, it's now obvious that Admiral Yamamoto's outfit has taken a severe trimming. The figures seem less outrageous when you figure what the results of the trimming have been on Jap maneuvers. The big fleet is in full retreat as it probably would never have to be if the Japs could muster any planes at all. That means that if they had five carriers as advertised, then at the moment five of the five aren't working. How many are actually sunk we don't know at present—possibly none. But they're out of action and it's obvious that the resulting disaster to the Jap fleet is little short of disastrous. Tomorrow or next day may show the best part of this armada out of business, our mastery of the Pacific assured, the threat to Australia definitely removed, and this war on its way to a fine finish.

Seldom in the history of naval warfare has an admiral walked out so far into a trap with his chin so far out and seldom in naval warfare has a surprise stroke by a working minority meant so much.

The warning net carried the chatter of amazed Japs all morning, along with the less amazed but colorful conversation of our pilots. One Jap apparently was trying to confuse the Americans because after each of his messages in Japanese he would count up to five in English and say "Acknowledge." It was apparent that so far as the battle was concerned, he was an outsider. He probably knew that the carriers were being attacked but he pursued his job of patrolling with no thought that our bombers could have come from anywhere except Midway. Then suddenly he came out of a cloud or around a corner or something and a great light seemed to break upon him. He gasped, and when he spoke it was in the language with which he was most familiar—as one always does in shock. In his case it turned out to be good San Francisco high-school English:

"My God! The whole U. S. fleet is out here!"

He was wrong of course, but as we are going now, nobody in the Jap navy is likely to stay around here long enough to discover his error.

This is quite likely to become one of the most amazing battles since men began to set themselves up as naval experts. For example, despite the fact that we were outclassed by the fleet the Japs sent against us—they had a margin of four battleships and possibly three carriers—our task forces in combination made up the biggest armed force that the U. S. ever turned loose upon the waters for an act of war. We carried out our mission in good order, we took part in a major engagement which we appear to have won handily. *And we haven't fired a shot.* This is the first big naval battle fought entirely (or at least brought to its crisis entirely) by airplanes.

Mickey Reeves mentioned that it would be a good subject for a critique.

"Sure," said Crowley. "If you could find anybody who was there."

There is plenty of basis for his cynicism. . . . "They live the life of Riley. . . . They go out. . . . They never come back. . . ."

About 11 P.M. we got a report from the TBD's that carried out the late-afternoon expedition.

When they caught up with the Japs again only one carrier was present and that was afire. They worked on that briefly. Then they saw a battleship and dropped the rest of their eggs on it. As they left, fire was pouring out of its stacks and it was in obvious difficulties.

The submarine ———— also reported that she had put a couple of fish into a carrier of the *Soryu* class, and the story gets better and better.

It will take a couple of days of course to sort out the casualty list. For instance the battleship reported by the late evening bombing party may be a heavy cruiser. The three missing carriers may have fallen out of formation or may have taken another course to keep far over the horizon and well away from the beacon of a burning ship. The *Soryu*-class carrier reported torpedoed by the sub may be one of those reported damaged in previous communiqués. But at the worst construction you can put on the results, the knock-over seems to have been complete and startling.

I am going to bed. I am so damned tired that my legs are buckling under me.

65

PURSUIT

June 5, *Friday*. North of Midway. In pursuit of the Jap fleet. Calm, wet, misty.

Despite exhaustion I got little sleep. The lack of ventilation below made me come up for air at 3 A.M. Went out on deck again to give moral support to GQ. Came in again. It was dark and rainy, and obviously there wasn't going to be much of a sunrise.

We got a report from Midway along with the morning news sheet. The attack had damaged only a power plant and some odds and ends of sheds. The runways, hangars and gas storage were untouched. Eight Jap planes were knocked down by ack-ack. The Army airmen, realizing the strength behind the Japanese push, had been prepared to operate with light bomb loads and count on returning to Honolulu to land. But there'd been no necessity for that. They came down on Midway immediately after the first, and only, wave of the blitz.

All day we moved west without contact.

We got a bit of encouragement about the *Yorktown*. She's still afloat and promises to remain afloat. A fleet of minesweepers, Navy tugs and such craft is being rushed out from Pearl Harbor to tow her in.

6:20. We start through the rain at top speed apparently headed for the kill. We may have trouble locating our quarry. The fog is so thick that we can't see the other ships running alongside us.

This battle has taken on an odd complexion. We have a very fine chance to annihilate what is left of the Jap force, but what Crowley calls the "logistics" are beginning to enter into the problem. The cans are just about out of fuel. They can't tear along indefinitely at top speed and for that matter neither can we. Such maneuvering as this pursuit of a defeated fleet after twenty minutes of contact could never have been foreseen even by the chief of staff of a madhouse. So fuel will have to be brought to us from Honolulu if the chase is to continue with any hope of success.

As matters stand we still have enough oil to last us a couple of days and a tanker is said to be on its way out.

Pursuit is further complicated by the fact that we are pretty vulnerable. We don't want to get too close to a battery of sixteen-inch guns by day and we'd just as soon keep out of the reach of sneaking destroyers by night.

6:30. After a dull, not to say comatose day, sixty SBD's were shot off to look over a new combination of Japs. A group apparently from the reserve is ahead of us. It is said to be composed of two *Isei*-class battleships, the Japs second-best heavies, and two carriers, one of which is afire. The speed of this outfit is thirteen knots which would indicate that something very serious is wrong with at least one of the ships.

In yesterday's bombing a lot of SBD's worked on a battleship in the northern group, dropped a few 500-pound bombs on the deck without damaging it in any vital spot. They climaxed their work with a couple of near misses that fixed up the big flatiron as the *Bismarck* had been fixed up for slaughter. They damaged the rudder and from that time on the big battleship steamed about in circles.

7:00. Planes report contact.

8:45. Eight SBD's come back with bombs.

9:05. Fifty-two planes are still out and the sun is just about gone. A mob of men is standing silent on the decks hoping for a chance to welcome home the wanderer—an unusual and touching performance.

9:15. In the wardroom. A voice: "Is it getting dark out there?" Crowley: "A little. They'll have to make a night landing." Voice: "Boy, I'm glad I'm not with them."

9:30. I went out onto the deck. It was pretty dark with a dirty streak of orange ahead of the carrier. One by one the SBD's began to straggle in. By 9:35 the returning ones had turned on their running lights. They'd come across the southern sky from the west.

After while when the black got blacker, the carrier turned on her searchlight and waved it about, picking up a heavy cruiser a couple of miles away and making it look like a white model of itself. Mast lights appeared on all ships at the edge of the formation. And it still looked like an impossible job to get the wanderers home.

The Marine major looked at the lights and went in after his life jacket. "We may complete this recovery right square in the middle of the Jap fleet," he said.

About fifteen minutes later, however, the last plane came in and a ripple of cheering ran around the decks. The searchlight of the second carrier made one brief sweep and another light came on. The two met vertically and came apart. A blazing white "V" stood five thousand feet high in the black sky. The lights went out.

Taking inventory of the activities at the end of the second day, it would appear that there have been two forces of Jap ships engaged. (This aside from the train vessels which went out of the picture after the first attack by the PBY's and flying fortresses. Apparently they dropped back out of bombing range and so were well on their way home when the retreat started.) The northern group was the striking force. It consisted of two battleships, four carriers and assorted heavy cruisers and destroyers. Behind it at no great distance—possibly fifty to seventy-five miles—was a reserve force of two more battleships, one or possibly two carriers. The Army claims to have hit one carrier and two battleships of this group and the strafe is still on.

Admiral Nimitz issued a communiqué tonight: "A battle is in progress off Midway Island. All armed services are engaged. One battleship and one carrier of the enemy fleet have been damaged." Well, that's safe enough. Apparently Nimitz is taking no chances and is discounting in advance the messages that reach him from imaginative birdmen.

There may be good reason for his conservatism. We aren't completely in command of the situation yet although we are looking upon a pretty good imitation of it. A carrier is reported to be coming down from Dutch Harbor to work on us. Nobody minds this because with the carrier strength we have now we'd be more likely to go looking for the Jap than run away from him.

There is always, of course, the possibility of bad breaks. One can conceive of conditions under which the battered Japs might get free to Wake and thence to Japan, conditions under which they might lure us into a torpedo trap or something of the sort, or maneuver us into a position where the land planes could take care of us. (I mention this latter contingency just by way of imaginative flight because we know where Wake is, just as well as they do.) But at the moment, however cockeyed the reports, however lousy our reconnaissance work, however uncertain our next step in the attack, there is no doubt that we have gained a decisive and important victory.

10:00 P.M. We are about to cross the 180th meridian headed due west but are just going to ignore the loss of Saturday.

Midnight: There have been no reports from the bombers that took after the Jap remnants last evening. However Cincpac has ordered us to close in and polish off the leavings with light surface action.

We listen gravely and wonder. We certainly won't be sticking our necks out if the battleships are still doing well. We might carry on indefinitely, of course, slapping bombs at the retreating ships between here and, say, Marcus, and wearing them down to a point where we might go in and sink them with shell. But fuel is becoming a real problem. Tomorrow the Japs will still be within fortress bombing range but it is quite likely that tomorrow will be the last day for all of us.

One interesting bit has come out of the reports from Midway. It becomes apparent that despite their heavy losses the Little Brown Bothers were pursuing their customary technique. With at least four carriers smashed and all their planes gone, they drove on to within fifty miles of Midway. At that point, apparently, Yamamoto found out that all his carriers were down and sent an urgent message to his alleged chiefs to pick up their marbles and get out while they were still in one piece. So they went.

Oddly nobody has paid much attention to the Jap cruiser force—that is nobody but the SBD pilots who occasionally mention cruisers in their inventory. It now begins to be certain that two of the *Mogami* class (8,500 tons and well equipped) have been sunk. Others are reported afire here and there. And as Tom O'Connell points out, a cruiser fire never lasts long. She burns energetically two or three hours and then she sinks.

So we retire to our infrequent hay, pondering the wonder of it all.

June 6 (Or is it?), Saturday. At sea west of Midway. Sunny. Calm. Warmer.

We've headed a little southwest and are about 800 miles from Wake.

Shortly after breakfast the task-force air patrol spotted a carrier and six destroyers pursuing a southwesterly course at ten knots, 150 miles from here. The scouts reported a complete absence of enemy air protection—another indication of what we suspected yesterday, that all the Jap planes were destroyed in the first few hours of the attack, that the flight which attacked the *Yorktown* probably never found a carrier to land on.

We sent up some SOC's and then began a day of indubitably successful operation accompanied by cockeyed reconnaissance.

At 11 o'clock the latest batch of scout planes reported that the carrier wasn't a carrier but a battleship. This bulletin was somewhat authenticated at noon when Donald Duck announced, "We have just intercepted a message from the commander-in-chief of the Japanese fleet saying that he is being bombed."

But after that the communications began to get mysteriouser and mysteriouser. Soon after noon came another report from a new bombing expedition: "Have made hits on two ships. Carrier afire and seems badly damaged." On the heels of that a cruiser plane reported sighting "carrier and two heavy cruisers." "The carrier was sunk," he said. "I saw it sink."

Two of our SOC's, piloted by Mickey Reeves and Crowley, took off at 1:30 to look at what there was to see of the shambles. They were within twenty-five minutes' flying time of the scene when they were called back.

And as if that didn't add up to enough to muddle pretty nearly everybody, returning bombers reported that they'd had a field day with a battleship which they left well on its way to the bottom. We had only three torpedo planes left to send on the afternoon's mission but apparently they did pretty well.

The best explanation anybody can give to all the odd reports is that the Japs split their force into two groups reasonably close together, a battleship and six destroyers in one section, a carrier without planes, accompanied by two heavy cruisers, in the other.

We sent out three bombing attacks today. The first one worked on the carrier and cruisers, the second, looking for the same target, came upon the battleship. The returning pilots report a highly successful operation. Eighteen hits were planted in the big flatiron. The planes then stood off and watched preparations being made to abandon ship. They then landed several hits on the cruisers and used their remaining bombs to plaster destroyers. They came home convinced that they had left nothing afloat except men in life jackets whom it was impossible to count, let alone pick up.

It is estimated on the basis of today's reports that between 18,000 and 20,000 men were killed in this brief battle. While we aren't wasting too much sympathy on our enemy at the moment, we are awed by the catastrophe that overtook him. There is chill in the thought that there, but for the Grace of God, go we. Had we been seen . . . Had the Japs attacked us before making the try for Midway . . .

66

OH! THAT WE MAY BELIEVE!

JUNE 6, *Saturday (later)*.

Little by little as a dense Aleutian fog (somewhat appropriately) rolls down over us we begin to see as in a revealing light what actually was done in this fantastic battle. In the last few hours we started out on what looked like another of those hit-and-run jobs that we've been doing so well. We had no illusions. . . . You wouldn't have when you could look out of any convenient porthole and count the ships that we were sending into action against the biggest fleet ever assembled in the Pacific—or maybe anywhere. The best we might have hoped for, as we clasped our St. Christopher medal in our left hand, our fly swatter in our right, and set Condition One in the main battery, was to snipe a carrier or two out of Hirohito's varied collection. The impression was general—and logically enough—that he'd probably never miss them.

That was a matter of hours ago—so recently that we can't yet realize that it's all over—and now it turns out that we have fought a major engagement—one of the biggest naval battles of all time. And miracle of miracles, we have won. It was too stupendous to contemplate as we lolled in a mist of nervous exhaustion, mumbling to one another in senseless monosyllables, falling to sleep over our coffee. This incredible Navy has come of age and, not too greatly to the surprise of one who has lived with it in recent months, it is as good as it thought it was.

I don't know how much detail of this we shall ever be allowed to tell, but in the meantime there is no percentage in hush-hushing ourselves: We started for this slaughter with a couple of carriers, half a dozen cruisers and about as many cans. We picked up the battered *Yorktown* and a couple more cruisers on the eve of the big smash. What we had a right to expect from an outfit like that against the competition that was massing on Midway only the experts can explain.

And now we have wrecked the best portion of the Japanese fleet. We have canceled the threat of any all-out naval assault on the Hawaiian Islands or the West Coast of the mainland perhaps forever. In other words, we who a couple of months ago were shuddering at the sight of Pearl Harbor, have taken control of the Pacific. It is no criticism of the skill, endurance, and foresight of the strategists of this action—nor does it imply any lack of the usual confidence in our brass hats—to mention that most of us look at the score with dizzy unbelief.

As the news filters back to us from a score or more sources it appears now that four—possibly five—Japanese carriers have been sunk. (There is no doubt about four of them.) Three battleships have been damaged or sunk, and perhaps a fourth was hit. (One was set afire, another disabled and steaming erratically.) Four cruisers and four transports were damaged or sunk.

Navy communiqués that reach us over the radio indicate that the old conservatism hasn't been jarred any more by victory than it was by defeat. But as matters stand there's nothing to prevent our writing our own ticket on Japanese losses. As a matter of fact nobody, not even the bomber pilots, can tell you how many Japanese ships were sent to the bottom in the murderous sweep of our carrier planes—nobody but the Japs and it will be a long time before they get around to telling the truth to anybody, even themselves. This was a cataclysm observed by tens of thousands of eyes and yet a spectacle that no man saw. Hundreds of men brought back their little bits of it—bits that sometimes fitted together and sometimes didn't—to make the mosaic in which we may one day see the picture of what happened at Midway. As for the amazing battle, its tactics and its mass movements, its development and its collapse, it will be a long time probably before anybody can get the straight of that either, for it lacked the pattern of other battles of similar importance in the world's history. It was, more nearly than any other naval engagement ever fought since man put to sea in war canoes, an attack by individuals. Its operational technique can be reduced to the formula of the SBD pilot much quoted after the Marcus Island affair: "Saw sub sank same."

Looking back over it with the keenness that seems to be so characteristic of hindsight I can't see that anybody was unduly upset when word was received from the PBY's that they had located the main body of the Jap fleet northwest of Midway. (As a matter of fact that report was excusably in error. What the patrols picked up was the occupation force with an escort of heavy warships. The striking force wasn't located until after the attack on Midway on the morning of June fourth. A point, just now, of no particular importance.)

One recalls that the cribbage game in the wardroom was no longer and no louder than usual and a couple of outbound lads on the midwatch found time to make customary allusions to the quality of the coffee. One or two of the night hawks went on reading stale magazines. Most of the ship as usual went to sleep in the old uncomfortable spots near the magazines, turrets, hatches and such. Tomorrow's worries would have to stand in line and take their turn.

Yet we knew even then what sort of trouble was coming to us. And I daresay that most of us, knowing something about the law of averages, figured that we stood an excellent chance of being dead in a few hours.

The fleet that was roaring down on us from the northwest was one of the most powerful ever gathered together in this or any other war. It was obvious that the Japs realized that as well as we did—and very likely knew all about our potential strength as well. . . . Though perhaps not *all* about it. Full of confidence, arrogance and spiritual saki Yamamoto's admirals apparently weren't considering any possibility of defeat—hardly any possibility of opposition. For as it turned out they were hammering down through the established lanes, making no attempt to conceal their movement or to camouflage their intent.

The inventory of the fleet had varied from time to time inasmuch as no observer could possibly see more than a part of it at once. But it was generally believed that four battleships were in the array, five carriers and possibly six, from twelve to sixteen cruisers, thirty destroyers, and a train of transports, tenders and supply vessels bringing the total to more than seventy all together.

In the new order of things, with aircraft carriers ranking definitely as capital ships, this was a bigger organization than Togo took into action against the Russians at Tsushima. Probably never since the invention of the dreadnaught had a battle line like this been given a test. Nobody on our ship—or on any of the other ships in our odd expedition—had to be told that this was going to be a slugging match. There wouldn't be any chance for hit-and-run tactics—not while they had ships as fast as ours and twice as many carriers. We'd have to finesse this one somehow. And no matter how we played it a lot of ships—somebody's ships—were going to be sunk.

What with recent upsets in the Coral Sea, things hadn't been going too well for Yamamoto's navy. It had been more or less obvious for some time that he would have to do something about the sundry menaces based on Hawaii.

We weren't deceived, either, by the aiming of the fleet at Midway Islands any more than we'd been drawn off by the noisy feint toward Dutch Harbor. Midway would have been of little use to Japan as an air base for operation against Pearl Harbor. To date we had no evidence of any Jap bombers able to work at that distance. Contrariwise a Jap field on, say, Sand Island would have been a simple target for routine operation of the flying fortresses from Hickam. So we gathered with no strain on the imagination that Hirohito was sending his battleships for an attack on Pearl Harbor or, should he have the luck he might expect with our naval aircraft cover, a possible visit to the Pacific Coast of the mainland.

I toy with the latter idea which might have seemed preposterous a week ago and looks like the architect's model for logic right now. If Yamamoto had done to us on June 4 what we did to him— and the chances for his doing it were very good indeed—then there is no reason at all to suppose that he would have stopped at smashing the empty harbors of Oahu. We might well have been moving our bases to a more suitable place—such as the bottom of the Grand Canyon.

Anybody who reads Jane's *Fighting Ships* can guess what we would have mustered at Midway if we had taken up every available aircraft carrier. And now that the loss of the *Lexington* is known, the guess can be much more accurate. So, again looking backward, I find excuse for the fact that some of us were vocally concerned when we first heard what we were up against—not on the eve of the fight but before that. We may have recalled with a certain nostalgia those other occasions when all we had to worry about was land batteries and high-altitude bombers. We thought that for once, maybe, we were giving away a little too much weight. There was no pre-funeral air about the ship, of course, but definitely there was a hint of realism and savvy. And, as everybody in the Navy continues to remark with unfailing originality, you can't make an omelet without breaking eggs.

Well, anyway, here we were looking somewhat cagily for trouble north of Midway when the news was brought that Dutch Harbor had been attacked. Somehow everybody seemed pleased at that. The navigator looked up from his waffle and nodded his head as if congratulating himself on his own good judgment.

"We ought to be getting into it any day now," he said. "It's going to be a fine opportunity." Somehow that sounded a little familiar. It reminded me of one night before the Germans came into Luxemburg—the beauty and the chivalry of the Duchy gathered for a cocktail party in the home of George Waller, the U. S. Minister, and the U. S. Minister playing Bert Williams on the phonograph: "Fine opportunity for somebody! Somebody else! Not me!"

Then we went out to attend to the air-raid alarm and never after that got much of a chance to sit down until just now. The Navy patrols spotted the occupation squadron; the fortresses plastered their battleship; our strategists plotted rates of speed and guessed at where the rest of the attacking fleet might be; our roving carrier patrols were up continuously without running into any of the hostile bombers that we expected momentarily. And that took up most of the day.

And, still with the omniscience of retrospection, we seem to have assimilated the affairs of the next day with no particular strain. We took in our customary stride the stresses of the morning's vigil when doom might have been just around the corner. And we were hardly conscious of personal danger—or, indeed, of a possible upset of all our plans—when some Jap planes appeared out of nowhere (and on their way to nowhere) to bomb the *Yorktown*. We were pretty certain that night that we had tossed a miracle. But we still didn't realize how much of a miracle it was.

As a matter of fact the battle was fought and won in the twenty-five minutes between 11:55 A.M. and 12:20 P.M., June 4.

At five minutes before noon the torpedo-plane squadron came up to the carrier group of the striking force, paused briefly to suggest refueling, and attacked. By twelve-twenty the carriers were afire and sinking—so hashed up that the planes aloft could no longer land on them and the planes below decks could not be launched.

For those of us sitting in the charthouse listening to conversations of pilots and their reports as they were relayed over the warning net it was almost frightening to think that this encounter, which immediately had taken on the proportions of a decisive action, had been taken on and finished in a matter of minutes. This much we knew even then—if we had wrecked their carriers, then we had won.

We were in no doubt about the damage done to the carriers. We heard the report of one calm, level-voiced TBD pilot reciting what he was seeing as he swung away from the ship he had attacked.

"They're all afire," he said. "But I can't tell you what ships they are. You can make out the typical Dutch-shoe bows but they're all afire amidships and the smoke is rolling back so you can't even see how long they are." Came another pilot to mention that some of the planes that had attacked Midway were just getting back. And as he spoke you could almost see the unfortunate pilots, by now probably sick of Hirohito's navy, dropping into the sea by two's and three's—a ghastly joke indeed to play on a conqueror who was coming back only for a tankful of gas and some more bombs.

By two o'clock we knew that everything had turned out just about as these conversations had led us to expect. And meanwhile the Army bombers were polishing off some heavy ships to the west and south—they mentioned battleships. They reported that they had dropped a clunk on a carrier in that vicinity which seems to verify the earlier report that there were six carriers in the push. They said their carrier seemed to be without planes—and we got the significance of that when their torpedo bombers made their last suicidal attack on our carrier line.

That, save for the finishing touches that were to come in two more days of pursuit and slaughter, was virtually the status of the battle when it was finally, as they say in the argot of this business, "broken off." Whatever else might be done to it, the Japanese fleet had been put out of action between dawn and 2:00 P.M. The drive on Midway and Hawaii was over and what was left of the invading force was speeding for Tokio at its best speed.

67

SLAUGHTER

JUNE 6, *Saturday (later)*.

There has been much discussion tonight of the attack on our carrier—regretful discussion ignoring the catastrophe that we visited upon the Jap fleet in criticism of the tactic that permitted the Japs' final smash at our carrier. It is futile, all this, as the men who do the talking seem to know. Behind the conversation most of us are prayerfully thankful that we suffered nothing more. The ack-ack that greeted the arrival of the enemy's last carrierload of planes to glory and death was about the best these tired eyes have looked upon in very nearly three years of this war. Eighteen Jap planes were shot down in the two attacks, nine of them by antiaircraft where we could see them. And this does not seem to be the proper place to note the necessity for 100-per-cent elimination of targets when dealing with bombers.

Perhaps if we hadn't been so successful in our first attack on the *Akagi*, *Kaga* and other big plane ferries that formed the warhead of Yamamoto's attack, we might not have been bothered by this belated and costly flareup. The planes that attacked us did so in all probability because they had nothing else to do. They were quite likely the complement of the carrier that the Army reported having hit. Unable to land they had expended the last of their fuel and bombs in this grand and funereal gesture.

From what we have been able to find out about it, they came through our air patrol dropping a few planes to the Grummans on the way. They met a considerable force of fighters on the edge of our fleet and that may be what determined them to attack the nearest carrier. It gave pattern to a terrific and deadly battle in which all but the immediate targets seemed never to be in any great danger.

The fight was on instantly. Protecting surface craft closed in on the carrier to give cover. In a few seconds the sky was mottled with the black puffs of the ack-ack barrage, and threading through the smoke balls came the Jap divers performing high-speed hara-kiri.

The fighters continued to beat back a considerable portion of the attack despite its motivation of despair. Heavy cruisers churned the waters about the carrier with blasts of eight-inch shell. But still some of the divers and torpedo planes came on. It all happened in so few seconds that many men in near-by ships didn't even see it. The fleet went on, unbothered by the incident. In the meantime the Japs, with nowhere to go, flew over the horizon somewhere out of sight and formed up to come back.

The ack-ack in this fight was the heaviest that had been put over a ship since the war began and we stood open-mouthed as Jap dive bombers came popping out of the black spots trailing peacock's tails of flame and heading straight into the sea.

Our fighters closed in. The Japs went back over the horizon, some to be shot down by pursuers, some to escape to the dubious alternative of death in a friendless ocean. But their wild finish was not entirely futile. They got a couple of reasonably severe hits on the carrier. The smash came too late to affect the outcome. The work of this task force was nearly done and the blasting of the carrier's deck and the withdrawal of the ship from action was no longer of much importance. But as a token of what might have happened to the rest of us and what actually had happened to the Japanese all over this area, it was a significantly impressive incident.

We left an escort with the carrier and went on our way, this time suiting our course to the fleeing Japanese.

It was two days before the Japs, running at their best speed, finally got the remnants of their fleet over the horizon and out of our ken. Whether or not some of these, or any of these, were able to get all the way home is something nobody this close to the battle is going to say.

We thought that maybe the strategists of the Japanese high command might take the people into their confidence to some extent regarding their bad guess at Midway. Admitting the loss of from five to nine capital ships, they might be better able to explain other disasters which in due course may spring from the first. But Japanese hearts are strong and Japanese hopes are still high—there's been no defeat for the Japanese at Midway if you listen to the voice of Radio Tokio. There's been no loss of the emperor's fine ships. Listen:

"Six carriers of the United States Navy, which is very deficient in carriers, were sunk in a single smashing blow." This from Japan's smoothest announcer—"Our fleet broke down the pitiful opposition of the United States fleet, bombarded the defenses of Midway and captured the islands with insignificant losses on our part. An attack has been started on Pearl Harbor and Honolulu. Honolulu is still holding out."

You don't blame these interesting and adaptable little people. They have good reason to be dizzy.

68

WE ARE STILL AMAZED

June 7, *Sunday*.

By nightfall of June 4 we were pretty sure not only that we had won a victory but that it had been a big one. However, as we began to fall asleep where we sat all over the ship, we knew also that we were still moving warily. The Japs still had most of their surface ships—even though quite a lot of them were on fire—and the remnants of the invasion fleet still made up one of the strongest battle forces ever sent on a working mission. There was no telling what might happen—although we weren't worried much.

As a matter of fact, the only person on record who appears to have had any doubt about the winner in the fight at that moment was the Japanese admiral. With his planes lying all over the Pacific, his carriers sunk or burning, and his surface line considerably smashed, he kept steaming straight on toward Midway. He'd been ordered to attack Midway and believe it or not he was only fifty miles from Midway headed straight for the zone where his annihilation could have been made complete when, most likely, somebody in Tokio heard what had already happened to him. About that time he decided to withdraw.

The United States task force planes took up the pursuit on June 5 and found two minor subdivisions of the attack force traveling close together on their way to Tokio. They worked on one carrier and one battleship and sank two heavy cruisers of the *Mogami* class. The Army in the meantime reported that flying fortresses had damaged two *Isei*-class battleships. By evening it began to look as if all the carriers brought out by the Japs had been sunk, including the one on which the Army bombers operated.

It looked as if the chase might continue all across the Pacific to the old bombing ground around Marcus Island. But Saturday morning the scouts discovered that the Japanese had found a way to increase their speed of retreat by abandoning their cripples. The ships still able to make knots had been turned loose, such as were left of them. A lot of limping craft—cruisers and destroyers—remained to meet the last of the American attacks. The line of retreat for the south had turned by this time toward Wake Island where the crocks and hulks could hope to get some protection from land-based planes. The faster ships, apparently, headed straight for Tokio and, presumably, the magnanimity of the Son of Heaven.

This morning we gave up the chase and turned our attention to the comments of home-town commentators. These strategists, taking their cue from Navy communiqués, pointed out that Hirohito probably had escaped with a lot of surface craft, that his retirement could not yet be classed as a defeat since he might be able to rearm, assemble aircraft reinforcements and come back to battle. The idea is apparently that some people are hard to convince.

It's an interesting speculation that may be worth recalling some day that we have just completed not only a battle that may turn the course of this war but what, in actual forces involved and in the actual slaughter dealt out, may yet be rated as the greatest if not the most spectacular battle in history. . . .

The battle of Jutland resulted in the bottling up of the Imperial German navy for the duration of the last war, and when fought was considered to have been the most desperate sea fight since the invention of gunpowder. But in that engagement the British lost three capital ships and the Germans two—between them equaling our lowest estimate of Japan's loss at Midway. Britain's loss of men was 3,500, the Germans' 3,000. The Japanese at Midway very likely lost 10,000 on the carriers known to have been sunk, another ten or fifteen thousand on transports, and nobody knows how many on the other ships.

I was reading a book last week about the Russian navy in the war with Japan, *The Voyage of Forgotten Men* by Frank Thiess, and until June 4, Tsushima was bright in my mind as the most magnificent of all naval battles. Yet in that battle, where Togo defeated Rojestvensky and Japan got delusions of grandeur, the fight was bitter and decisive and broken off only when most of the Russian fleet was under water. But for all that this fight is still rated by some experts as the greatest in modern sea-warfare, the Russians brought to it only five ships that might be classed as capital ships. Five or six others were recommissioned hulks whose slow speed hampered Rojestvensky's maneuvers and contributed nothing at all to the score. These matters of course are history and have nothing to do with the battle of Midway . . . but one can't help thinking of them when he listens to the radio comments and marks the callousness with which our recent performance is being treated by those most concerned.

Japan says the fight didn't amount to anything at all, that it didn't prove anything or alter the general situation in the Pacific. And some of our own communiqués seem to agree with that. I'm wondering just what a war amounts to by modern standards. How many ships have to be sunk, how many thousands of men have to be drowned before a shambles like this one will seem important?

69

VICTORY PARADE

JUNE 7, *Sunday*. At sea. Heading northwest. Bright. A little rough. Cooler.

We are moving out of the old battle zone for a rendezvous with the tanker. Everybody who has a chance to sit down—and the number runs higher than usual today—is just sitting.

The battle is apparently still in progress although we are taking no part in the proceedings. The Army reported today that a fortress had dropped a clunk on a light cruiser which sank in fifteen seconds. (It turned out to be one of our own subs which crash-dived for obvious reasons.)

Anyway Army planes probably can operate another two days before the Jap fleet gets entirely out of range. Out there somewhere also are our submarines looking after the cripples. If any targets are left to them, they should have another field day.

Official news out of Pearl today sets the score at four to five carriers sunk or damaged, three to four battleships, four cruisers and four transports also sunk or damaged.

Our unofficial count is larger and we're holding that all the carriers, two battleships and two cruisers are definitely sunk, one battleship in a sinking condition and a fourth damaged.

However, any way you read it, it adds up to a major disaster for Japan.

Later: The task-force commander's estimate of damage irrespective of any Army scores was published in the work sheet for tomorrow under date of June 6.

"Yesterday attacks by our bombers on the defeated and fleeing enemy were completed, an air action covering three full days.

"Estimate of enemy losses as a result of action by task forces

408

on Thursday: Three carriers sunk, one carrier fired and badly damaged. Of the three sunk one was the *Akagi,* one probably the *Kaga,* one was of the *Hiryu* class. The damaged carrier of the *Hiryu* class was last sighted by planes in the forenoon of Friday on a northwesterly course, still burning. Our attack groups failed to sight her on a 250-mile flight late Friday afternoon. She may have escaped or she may have been abandoned or sunk. Our attack group sighted only two small ships, probably destroyers.

"Yesterday, Saturday, our search picked up two small enemy forces bound for home. First force was two heavy cruisers and two destroyers headed southwest. It was bombed during the afternoon and hits reported on both cruisers. The second group was two cruisers and three destroyers headed west. Of these one cruiser of the *Mogami* class was wrecked and abandoned. The other cruiser received bomb hits. One destroyer was sunk, others strafed by aircraft machine-gun fire.

"Our carrier groups have done a magnificent job in spite of heavy losses suffered on Thursday forenoon in the initial attack which decided the fate of the battle of Midway. Their follow-up blows on the retreating enemy were carried out with great determination. The Japs' state of morale at the end of the battle was indicated by the abandoning to their fate of the crew of the *Mogami*-class cruiser when other ships of that group left without effecting rescue of personnel. The performance of our ships during this period leaves nothing to be desired. Our task forces have again helped to make history. Well done, to all hands."

There was no mention of the battle by Tokio's news commentators today. Admiral Nimitz issued a fairly large communiqué amplifying yesterday's but still conservative. The Japs are indignantly denying that they ever intended to use gas on anybody. Apparently there had been some loud international howl about it— which might account for the order that we carry masks at all times. (We are still carrying them, by the way, still carrying them although the Jap fleet, what remains of it, is farther away than Pearl Harbor and getting farther.)

June 8, Monday. At sea. Coolish. Misty.
Because of lights or noises or something I got up at 6:00 A.M.

after four hours of sleep. We seem to be heading for the Aleutians. A report filtered in from somewhere that the *Yorktown* had been torpedoed and sunk by a submarine soon after we last saw her. A can is also reported to be sunk.

June 9, Tuesday. At sea. Headed northwest.
We fueled today without incident. Another of our carriers is somewhere just over the horizon with a load of spare planes and pilots. The fog is thick and getting thicker. And it's quite chilly.

June 10, Wednesday. At sea. Foggy. Wet. Miserable. Rough.
We maneuvered south a bit to make possible the transfer of planes from one carrier to the other. The crew is getting into sweaters, the officers into blues.

I was beginning to wonder if I should happen to like this end of Alaska when Donald Duck set my mind at rest. At 4:30 Donald Duck announced: "This task force is now proceeding toward Pearl Harbor." For a wonder he was cheered.

June 11, Thursday. At sea. Southbound on the west side of the islands near French Frigate Shoals. Cool. Misty.
I finished three stories for the sundry censors, augmenting one I sent in by tanker when we fueled. I am writing this at midnight. No sleep in prospect.

June 12, Friday. At sea. Misty. Cool. We've been warned that there is danger from submarines about Pearl Harbor. They've been sighted by patrols. That, however, is less frightening than it might have been a week ago. We have just learned that on the night of June 5 the whole fleet steamed right through the Jap sub ring with no losses. What we didn't know didn't hurt us.

June 13, Saturday. Honolulu. Fairly cool. We arrived in Pearl Harbor at 5:35 and got ashore at 6:00. I got a quiet, almost friendly reception in the public-relations office. It makes me wonder what new trouble is being cooked.

Waldo Drake handed me some cables received during my absence, including one I should have received on May 27, if R.C.A.

had the habit of delivering messages. It orders me to come home. Had I received it I should have missed the Midway business. So right now I might be thankful if I weren't so sore about other things.

June 14, Sunday. Honolulu. Cool. Got my undelivered cables. I found out that during my absence I had been sent to Australia and then recalled. Bernie McQuaid is coming out to relieve me. . . . And I hope he likes it.

70

HOME IS THE SAILOR

June 15, *Monday*. Honolulu. Got a call from Pearl Harbor this morning. A lot of PBY pilots were waiting to be interviewed. Went out and missed breakfast.

I could spend a lot of time commenting on the sundry aspects of this case. It seems that although the admirals of the Navy sit in ivory towers and resent publicity, the kids in the lower strata share none of this lofty attitude. They want public credit for what they do. They've been led to believe that this is the American idea.

The Army had been getting all the kudos for the discovery of the Jap fleet, and the patrol sections of the Navy were indignant.

Admiral Bellinger, in charge of patrol activities, is said to have complained bitterly to Nimitz. So we were called out to do this bit of work. It was a badly handled press stunt. . . . Too much and too late. I wrote about five thousand words without half covering it. Missed luncheon.

Then I had a hell of a time getting it from Honolulu to the fleet censor's office. It was raining and of course there were no taxicabs. The drivers here are completely independent. If they feel like it they will take you where you want to go. If they don't feel like it no money will make them.

Finally I borrowed Wendell Webb's car. Missed dinner. Had a badly upset stomach all night. If I could saw it off on somebody in press relations I'd feel compensated.

June 16, Tuesday. Honolulu. Rainy. I went out to Pearl in the morning to get permission to send a cable home. And on this mission I met another example of something. Mr. Drake said that he couldn't send the telegram because my signature would reveal that I had arrived in Honolulu and that therefore the fleet had arrived. I went berserk. I wanted to know what my signature had revealed yesterday when it was attached to a wad of pap that the Navy wanted printed. He said that the order had come from the Assistant Chief of Staff, Captain Wiltse. I said that I wanted to see Captain Wiltse and that if Captain Wiltse proved to be as stupid as Mr. Drake suggested, then I'd want to see Admiral Nimitz. Waldo sent in word to Captain Wiltse and came out with word that I could send the cable. I sent it. I still don't know what idea was in Wiltse's head or Waldo's or the admiral's.

June 17, Wednesday. Honolulu. Hot. The blackout signs on now at 8 o'clock. It is still broad daylight until 9:00.

June 18, Thursday. Honolulu. Cool.

June 19, Friday. Honolulu. Warm. Our Midway stuff is still being held up.

June 20, Saturday. Honolulu. Hot. Sat around all day steaming. I'm invited to Riley Allen's for some sort of party tomorrow

June 21, Sunday. Honolulu. Hot!
After luncheon while waiting for Riley Allen to come over and get me, I got a call from the *Moana*. McQuaid had just arrived.
Tobruk fell today. Things look very tough for the British in Libya.
The Japs have made some sort of a landing in the Aleutians. McQuaid, reading between the lines, is alarmed. We, who know that a couple of carriers are loafing in Pearl Harbor, didn't feel much upset.

June 22, Monday. Honolulu. Hot. Waldo has promised me transportation home.

June 23, Tuesday. Honolulu. Hot. I go aboard tomorrow.

June 24, Wednesday. At sea. San Francisco bound. Cool.

We sailed from Honolulu at 5 o'clock aboard the ———, Capt. P. P. Powell, commanding. Wendell Webb, Jack Rice and Jonathan Rice and I are packed together in a cozy cabin on Z deck.

June 25, Thursday. At sea. All hands carry life jackets. We went up and paid our respects to the captain this morning. Dined with him tonight. He's an able citizen.

Doc Sanders is aboard this ship. So are virtually all the TBD pilots who survived Midway—all five.

June 26, Friday. At sea. Day made notable by odd accident to Mr. Webb who cut his finger on a set of weird-looking antlers (mounted) that somebody on a cruiser gave to Jack Rice. This tops all the perils of the deep in my ken.

Met a couple of officers who were dynamited off the *Yorktown* and the can that accompanied it at Midway.

June 27, Saturday. At sea. The escort cruiser lost a plane today. Everybody aboard was deeply interested in the report although one SOC wouldn't have come in for much attention a couple of weeks ago. I guess tragedies increase in poignancy in direct ratio to their futility.

We have eleven survivors of the U.S.S. *Simms* aboard—that's all the survivors there were. The destroyer was torpedoed in the Coral Sea and settled slowly enough for a large portion of her personnel to get off. The whale boat was launched and eleven men got into it. Rescue was right at hand when the ship got down to fifty feet and her depth charges blew up. Everybody was killed but the eleven in the whale boat.

June 28, Sunday. At sea. Cooler. The whole ship is upset about an article in the Washington Merry-Go-Round (Pearson and Allen) ripping up the Navy and stating in effect that the fleet was nowhere about when the battle of Midway was won by Army bombers. This of course is silly. But I gleefully pointed out to everybody that it is just the sort of publicity that the Navy's public-relations department has been asking for.

June 29, Monday. Outside San Francisco Bay. Foggy. We hung about in this muck all day tooting whistles and clanging bells. Word was passed to us about 4:00 P.M. that a sub was lurking about.

I heard a harrowing story tonight. A pretty young girl was going into the wardroom with a lot of hilarious Navy wives and pilots to an impromptu dance. An ensign nodded to her as she went in.

"Odd thing," he said. "Everybody on board except her knows that her husband didn't come back from the Midway mess. He was a TBD pilot."

June 30, Tuesday. San Francisco. We came in through fog, carefully and laboriously, and docked at 1:30.

San Francisco never looked more beautiful or, to one fresh from the battles, more fantastically unreal. We docked where once ages ago I boarded the *Taiyo Maru* for Yokohama.

It was just a year ago I came back to New York from the Middle East.

71

IN PROPER PERSPECTIVE

SEPTEMBER 30, *Wednesday*. Army Maneuver Area, Desert Center, California. Hot. . . .

. . . so the world knows now that Midway was one of the great battles of history, as significant as Trafalgar or Jutland or Tsushima and already promising more far-reaching results.

The communiqué writers were coy about it at first. We got off the transport in San Francisco—the survivors of the *Yorktown*, Hamman, and Simms and I—to find the West Coast jittery about a supposed threat to the westernmost Aleutian Island, newspapers filled with reports of bush-league bombings in the Mediterranean, radio commentators still patronizing the Navy by new assertion of the faith that it would probably turn out all right. Nobody seemed to have heard about Midway—or if they had they classed it as a nice bit of work like the raids of the Marshalls and Marcus or as a brilliant but inconclusive business like that of the Coral Sea. A lot of the wounded men who came down the planks of the transports in our convoy probably were puzzled by the silence that greeted them where they had expected bunting and brass bands. They still didn't know that so far as the nation was aware of it, they hadn't been anywhere.

When I got time I called a managing editor about this matter. He assured me that the people of the United States weren't minimizing the importance of the "engagement in the north Pacific" (sic). "But," he said, "we've got to be realistic about the Navy. We can't let wishful thinking dictate our news policies. I think the Navy will come through but we're not going to do public morale any good if we exaggerate the significance of a lot of minor battles. Nobody'll be more willing than I'll be to break out the Crack-of-Doom type when the turning point comes."

"Good God! Man," I asked him, "don't you know that the turning point has come and passed you by?"

"No," he said, "I hadn't heard of it."

However, somehow, word of this matter got about. It seems that you can't suppress word of a tremendous victory any more than you can preserve the privacy of a crushing defeat. In the Middle West it turned out that a lot of people had heard about Midway. They had put two and two together and were asking one another in awed tones if Japan had any airplane carriers left at all, if a fleet that had taken such a complete shellacking could be counted a threat to the Aleutians or any place else.

The Navy with excusable conservatism finally issued an official announcement which, in retrospect, makes you feel a bit proud of the communiqué writers however much they may exasperate you. The official score keepers took credit for the ultimate minimum of the Navy's accomplishment. The story they told was the bald truth as left when they had filtered all error due to garbled reporting, duplicate observation and human enthusiasms. The final bag, as they tallied it, was their own—without reference to what had been done by the Army Air Corps. It was strictly a naval communiqué about the accomplishment ("a poor thing but mine own") of the Navy and the Marines—a fine, gentlemanly, modest report to the people of the United States. Twenty ships had been hit, ten had been sunk—definitely. Forty-eight hundred Japanese had been blown apart or drowned.

It was conceded, with few reservations, that the Japanese fleet had been one of the biggest ever set afloat anywhere—that it had included at least the four carriers we had destroyed and from two to four battleships—that its purpose was to take the Hawaiian Islands. . . . You inferred the official belief that the war in the Pacific would then have moved to our West Coast with obviously unpleasant prospects.

Well, as things shape up, you need go no farther than the Navy communiqué to rate Midway among the important battles of the world—one of the greatest naval engagements ever fought even though no ship in either fleet fired a shot at another ship. It is only as a sort of footnote that I enter here the figures I sifted out of a lot of dizzy Army and Navy reports the night we sailed away and left the battered *Yorktown* standing glorious in the setting sun. The Japs brought from seventy-five to ninety ships into the Midway attack. They lost forty with many of the remainder so battered that they may never have reached port. Two carriers other than those listed by the Navy appear in Army reports as damaged and possibly sunk. Two battleships were definitely smashed up. Two others were claimed by the high-level bombers. Two transports appear in the composite score as sunk. And with no further evidence you can begin to tot up a loss in human life comparable to that of Gettysburg. Big carriers have a personnel of 2,500 men. Japanese battleships carry more than 1,500 apiece. Japanese transports of the size of those that came to capture Hawaii may carry as many as 5,000. . . . If Tokio were to announce tomorrow that 50,000 men had been lost in this weird shambles nobody who was there would be much surprised.

However, it isn't the number of men killed over and above the official announcements or the number of ships sunk that is significant about Midway. The main point is that it was a major engagement and that we won it . . . outnumbered and outgunned we won it after the American tradition in such things. The control of the Pacific may have passed to us as a result of it.

There came the day of the odd conference with the Navy commander from Peoria and the Army aviator—the day when the Marines were taking hold in the Solomons, when Army planes based on Guadalcanal were blasting the Japs out of their foxholes in the Owen Stanley Mountains and it appeared that the march north might have begun. This seems to be a good place to recall that bit of conversation:

" 'I suppose it breaks your heart to be out of that fight,' said the aviator. '. . . to lose your chance to help to drive the Japs back . . .'

"And the commander just shook his head.

" 'You have it wrong, boy,' he said. 'I *was* in that fight. I was in the most important part of it—the part we fought at Midway on June 4. . . .' "

The war at the moment seems to be looking up. A greater

collection of tanks than took part in the first Libyan campaign is churning up this desert in spectacular maneuver—an amazingly heartening thing to one who lived with the proceedings in Egypt in the dark days after Crete. For a country that didn't have a single decent tank a year ago we seem to have done pretty well. There are plenty of modern planes overhead to evidence that our production program hasn't been all conversation.

The outfits roaring through this dust and heat have a hard, professional look. Tomorrow or next day they'll be in battle somewhere. And all of this seems to be a long, long way from the Coral Islands and the endless Pacific and the Navy.

Yet not such a long way off. Even so remote an affair as these tank maneuvers was dependent on our performance when we rode bravely in to battle with our fly swatter and St. Christopher medal on the morning of June 4—the tank maneuvers depended on it and the Mojave county fair and the Indio date crop. If we'd lost that fight we wouldn't be holding maneuvers here. We'd be trying to hold back the East-bound Japs along Highway 66.

In the new geography Midway Island—the Navy's Midway Island, our biggest torpedo junction—is never going to be very far from the center of the United States until this war ends.

NO MYSTERY NOW

WHEN Torpedo Junction *was published in November, 1942, for reasons of security it could not be revealed that the author had been an eyewitness when Lieutenant Colonel James H. Doolittle and his squadron of volunteer fliers took off from the carrier* Hornet, *eight hundred miles from Japan's shores, to bomb Tokio on April 18, 1942. The full text of the author's diary is now released for the days from April 13 to 18, supplying the missing matter for pages 301-312. The rest, of course, is history.*

72

NO MYSTERY NOW

APRIL 13, 1942. At sea. Clear sky; rolling sea; white caps; cold.

This morning we met our pals, the U.S.S. *Hornet* and other vessels of the task force.

Commander Chappell came in to tell me this glad news after a bitter cold night, and also to spread the tidings that we are on our way to bomb Japan, possibly Tokio—most likely Tokio.

The ships are now scattered over the near-by ocean with us, so closely that all seem part of a common pattern with us, and all, as you can't help but feel after the loneliness of the past few days, part of an arrangement for common defense. This is a big force now, and in spite of all the old traditions of maneuver, a force that the Japs would hardly dare take on without twice the number of ships and at least an even break of airplanes.

News of our mission was all over the ship when I got down to the deck at 9:30. It seems that the operation orders were transmitted by semaphore, which virtually everybody aboard ship can read. I have learned that at sea in a man-of-war there is no such thing as hush-hush.

Among the odd bits of information that came to light is the fact that the *Hornet* is loaded up with North American B-25 medium bombers. These things carry a crew of five, have a top speed of about 300 miles an hour and a cruising range of more than 2,600 miles; they are powered by two 1,600 h. p. Wright Cyclone radial motors. They are army planes and very definitely not designed for carrier operation. They can take off—sometimes with effort—from a mile runway. Seeing them here, we must take it for granted that by some miracle they can also take off from a deck. But, as we figure out for ourselves after a while, no miracle could set them down again on a carrier. This expedition has all the elements of mystery as well as novelty.

If these planes can't expect to come back to the carrier, then it's obvious that they have to come down on land. And whose land? In a day or so, maybe, we shall know all about it and it may well be that any forecasts or guesses we make now will look silly in retrospect. On the other hand it may be interesting to compare today's fact with yesterday's supposition and see how closely they resemble one another. Well, anyway, this is how it appears to us at the moment:

The planes, no matter where they're going to land, will fly over Japan and drop their bombs and the roof spotters and the ARP wardens and the pursuing bombers and the ack-ack captains and the official photographers will be about three minutes figuring out their identity. U. S. planes! Big U. S. planes! Bombers! Two-engined bombers! So help us! Army bombers! And where did those things come from?

The makings of a fine incident are there. The boys will have a cabinet meeting right away and unless we are spotted on our approach (which we shall do everything possible to prevent), they will probably guess every answer but the right one. These are land planes, therefore, they must have come from land bases, therefore, Russia has permitted this outrage, therefore, Japan is at war with Russia! Could be!

Even should a carrier be seen off the Japanese coast, the mystery of the land planes is likely to remain a mystery for the reason that the Japanese know we have no suicidal impulses. If they run true to their psychological form they will figure that we'd not be taking off from a carrier in planes which we couldn't land on a carrier.

And, by devious routes, they would reach the conclusion that if we ever did set off from a carrier in such a plane it would be only with the intention of landing on Russian soil and this with the connivance of Russia. So we think that Russia's entry into our war with Japan will be in two or three days when we get going on our job.

There is, of course, the alternative that they may figure a landing place for us in China, which from our maps and a study of B-25 characteristics seems impossible. Time will correct me if I'm wrong.

The captain made one of his announcements of purpose shortly after 11 o'clock, with the aid of Donald Duck:

"I shall speak slowly and with an interval between sentences so that a repetition of what I say may be sent out over all telephones," he said. "You have probably observed that we have been joined by a very strong force. You will observe also that the carrier *Hornet* has aboard a full load of fine-looking planes. These are the very latest thing in bombers.

"You are about to take part in a very historic event. For the first time in the history of Japan, the home territory is about to be attacked. This attack will be in force and will undoubtedly have great effect.

"Before going into this action, I shall supply you with such details of our procedure as are available. From now on, our lookouts must be extremely vigilant against submarines which are likely to be in this vicinity—that is all for now."

It's odd the amount of mystery you can work up about things that you can see but can't hear. There is no end of speculation over the carrier, cruisers and cans we picked up the other day. We have a fair idea of what their inhabitants look like, even of what they are going to eat for dinner tonight, but for all that they might be people on another planet.

Where have they been? How did they pick up their load of planes without tipping off the German or Jap agents? Where did they load? Have they, perhaps, been based on Alaska? None of the answers would make any difference if we knew them. But the guess-work helps to while the time away when the sea is rolling and the wind blows free.

At 6 p. m. we were in a roaring tempest and odd noises filled the ship—not including the contribution of somebody practicing on the trombone—the usual creak of strained rivets, the bang of iron doors, plus the breathless whispering of the tumult outside, the offstage conversation of the wind, the clatter of sliding gear ... roll and pitch and smash! I've known few evenings like this.

Dinner—I suppose that, under the circumstances, I should make note of it—was fried chicken, ice cream and cake. There was no overpressure in the wardroom atmosphere. Uncertainty was there, of course, and puzzlement. You'd not expect anything else where nobody knows anything and thinks he may be dying tomorrow in some unforeseen and novel fashion. The wisdom of disclosing a new technique of attack to send 16 planes over Japan is not vigorously defended.

The executive thinks we ought to augment the performance with a hammering operation against the few and badly protected units of the Jap fleet still left in this neighborhood. And that's the way I feel about it.

April 18. Saturday.

I got up at 4:30 A. M. Went on deck at 5 o'clock to face a howling wind. Sky gray. Sea pitching. I stood it for awhile and then went down, half-frozen, to the wardroom for coffee. The place was filled with officers, but nobody was much concerned with the weird action in which we are theoretically taking part. Water is rolling down the decks, sometimes a couple of feet deep. It's hard keeping upright.

7:00. Breakfast. Ack-ack alerted. Mysterious surface craft reported to the north. May be a destroyer. After a moment's hesitation the assistant gunnery officer is allowed to eat his cakes in peace.

7:45. Report something sighted off our port bow. Object unseen by plane patrol. We verify. It's a junk or sampan, or trawler. Considerable activity aloft. I go up into the wind.

8:00. Cruiser swings out of line to port. Starts firing almost immediately. Terrific barrage with 15 six-inch guns. Shells are tossed like machine-gun bullets—eight salvos in the air at once. Flashes run around ship like lights on an electric sign.

8:10. Dive bombers attack. Trawler visible momentarily against whiteness of shell geysers. She seems to be about 600 tons.

Hornet signals: "Preparing launch airplanes." (It's obviously now or never—now that the Jap patrol has picked up and possibly reported us to Tokio.)

A cruiser chases Jap tub to horizon, slapping shells at it generously.

8:20. First bomber off the *Hornet.* Miraculous. The carrier is diving, deluging deck with white water. The big plane is just about catapulted as the ship lifts out of the sea.

9:25. Quiet on the horizon. There hasn't been a hitch. All have shot straight up in the teeth of the hurricane. A kid in the corner of the pompom section waves and clasps his hands over his head. Another kid blesses himself. The captain's mess-boy, a Chomorre from

Guam, who was on the searchlight platform with me, bowed his head as the last B-25 climbed into the gray and out of sight.

"We'll never see him again," he said surprisingly. "He'll never come back to us. We must wish him lots of luck."

When the bombers had gone—they headed toward Tokio, which was a good move in the interest of gas economy—I went below and turned on the Tokio radio. Nothing much was going on. We got no hint of anything untoward even at 12:30, by which time our planes should have completed their mission.

Got call from bridge about 1:30. We'd picked up another spitkit. As I got to the signal bridge, a cruiser standing off from formation let loose a blast at her.

The day had turned out gloriously except for the turbulence of the sea and the earsplitting wind, which, on the other hand, may not have been exceptions at all. The *Hornet* moved out a lot of SBD's to replace the departed B-25's. Several of these took the air. They hopped around in a sort of circus that didn't seem to have much purpose. Then about 3 P.M. they began to land. One nosed over on the deck of the *Hornet*. The crack washed out the plane, but apparently did little damage to the pilot and his aides. Another plane fell into the sea astern of the *Hornet*. A destroyer picked up the crew. It was difficult to see how many planes got back to the carriers, which were rolling like yachts.

2:30. Tokio announced the raid. Unidentified planes had bombed Tokio and blasted numerous schools, hospitals and shinto-temples. The quick-acting Japanese ack-ack had immediately knocked down nine of the raiding planes—but at the moment, nobody was able to say whose they were.

Such reports continued throughout the day. One bulletin—the only one which attempted to fix the nationality of the bombers—said that the capital had been raided by Chinese, American, and Russian planes. This identification was later dropped and the night report left the mystery unsolved.

The DNB (Nazi official news agency) reported that Yokohama had also been bombed. The BUP (British United Press) said that Tokio had been a target for big bombers presumed to have come from carriers operating in Japanese waters. What price our great finesse?

All through the night we continued to high-tail it directly eastward at 25 knots. It looked as if we were going to withdraw from this action. What else we shall do, if anything, nobody knows.

Today's radio broadcasts from Tokio didn't give many details of the raid other than those of yesterday which were meager enough. But they did go so far as to say that all the bombers were American. (The official Jap pictures have been developed, I guess.) They seem to have abandoned their claim to a bag of nine planes. It becomes very definite from their manner of speech and also from interrupted messages on the Japanese broadcast band that the raid caused plenty of consternation. It is quite probable that, with tons of dynamite to drop, our crews may have put some of it where it would mean more than a headline in the home-town papers.

Some more interesting broadcasts came later in the afternoon. Tokio commentators declared, positively now, that the planes were undoubtedly American . . . they could be identified by the red and white stripes on the tail and by the star marker on the wings, and besides nine of them had been shot down.

It was plain, Tokio said, that the raiders must have come from one of the following points of departures: (1) The Philippines. (It is evident from that that the Japs aren't spoiling for any war with Russia right now—otherwise in a guessing contest about the point of departure for the attack, Vladivostok would be their public guess Number 1); (2) China; (3) A secret air base in Japan proper.

The commentators noted that the attack could not have come from carriers because carrier decks aren't long enough to launch such planes as these.

The war leaders, Tojo et al, went over to visit the Son of Heaven during the afternoon and explain the bombing. Their appointment was for 4 o'clock and at that time the fires which the bombers had started in Tokio, Yokohama, Kobe, Osaka and Nagoya, were under control. These fires, the commentator cagily announced, had been caused by "the alleged bombing."

April 19, Sunday. The Pacific hereabouts is strewn with the wreckage of Japanese patrol boats. The ether is filled with strange rumblings of alarm. Tokio, just over the western horizon, appears to be afire—and Yokohama and Nagoya and Kobe. And you wonder if there is any connection between these things.

So far as we can see from where we sit (in the position of witches annoying the Japs no end) the millennium has not yet arrived. Morning will find most of Honshu island still afloat and most of tinderbox Tokio still safe from ash sifters. But it is quite apparent that the Japanese do not believe that. First one way and then another, they are a hard people to convince.

Even if you cannot see any red glow in the sky or hear the bombs and ack-ack, you do not have any trouble sensing the atmosphere of the capital.

Relays of tense-voiced announcers are pushing somewhat unintelligible comment over the beam to America. And the home-consumption radio, on the broadcast band, shudders with evidence of what has happened to local morale.

In Japanese a shrieking woman is calling for donors to the hitherto neglected blood bank. She is talking of the horrors of the bombing, shattered bodies and tenuously held lives. She speaks in the language of the hospitals, of first-degree burns and amputations, severed arteries and tourniquets, blood types, blood transfusions—an amazing program for a people supposed to care nothing about human life.

But even if she had been talking of nothing more unusual than new ways to cook rice, you would know that terror had arrived in Tokio. It is her voice, rather than the subject, that gives you the notion. She is one citizen of Japan who would not bet much on her prospects for being alive on the morrow.

The captain (long a student of the Japanese language and philosophy) translates her jeremiad and sees in it more of the things she has left unsaid.

"It is fear, of course," he says. "She thinks this is going to be something like the 1923 earthquake, only worse. But she is bewildered, too. The Japanese high command said it couldn't happen, and it happened. Japan has lost face and death would be preferable to that."

The woman goes on with her keening: "Give your blood as the men at the front are giving theirs," she demands. "Give your blood. Your lives are in danger. Tomorrow—tonight—your children may be blown to bits. Give your blood. Save them—save Japan."

"An interesting moment, gentlemen—" comments the captain.

It's amazing how much we know about this part of the ocean— how much we know of what we're doing, of what they're doing. We have obviously learned a lot since Pearl Harbor, and now, more slowly, the Japs also are learning.

The voice of one of Tokio's graduates of the University of Missouri, who had been teamed with "Tokio Rose" in English-language transmission of bedtime stories to the West Coast, comes now to advise the world in trembling English of the unspeakable outrage.

Tokio is being bombed, he says, in some surprise. Then he reads, somewhat haltingly, from what seems to be a badly written script.

"There has been no damage at all to military objectives," he says, "but several schools, hospitals and shrines have been destroyed. Thirty primary-school children were machine-gunned in the streets."

One of the officers in the close-packed group about the radio asks the senior aviator about that. He says no.

"Those planes had to be big ones to do the job at all," he says, as the agitated commentator struggles on with the story of the unimportant carnage. "You notice that none of those boys knows whose planes they are. Put it all together, and it means they came sailing over so high that nobody saw them come, and nobody has got close enough to see them yet, even though they've been dropping clunks all over the place.

"They never took a chance on coming into range of the ack-ack. Naturally, they wouldn't trade the advantage of altitude to machine-gun a lot of school kids, no matter how good the idea may have been. On the face of the evidence, I should say that the bombings had been a great success."

The announcer rises to new heights of *bushido*.

"This attack upon the civilian population—this killing of children—was quickly met," he says, chokingly. "Our patrol planes were already in the air when this armada of Chinese, American and Russian bombers came in from the sea. Our antiaircraft batteries went into action at once. Nine of the enemy bombers were shot down as they were turned about and forced to fly southward from

NO MYSTERY NOW   431

the capital. The others are being pursued by our fighters and won't
escape us."

There is a lull. Then comes another voice, rumbling something
offstage in Japanese, and the commentator resumes as if reading from
a new script:

"Nine unidentified planes have been shot down. Scores of unidentified planes have been driven from the skies over Tokio.
Damage, save for one small area on the outskirts of the city, is
slight."

The senior aviator laughs.

"More evidence that the raid was a success," he says. "We've
shot down nine planes, but we don't know whose."

The commentator, less excited now, continues.

"Japan rejoices because our emperor escaped all harm in this
cowardly attack. The prime minister, the chiefs of the victorious
forces on land and sea and in the air, immediately paid calls at the
palace to reassure His Majesty and explain what steps have been
taken to drive off such attacks as this and insure the security of
Japan."

It was only a few hours ago—last night, in fact—when this same
announcer, less worried perhaps, but no better informed, was cheering the wardroom no end with the boast of the military chiefs that
Japan could never be bombed—that the United States, powerless to
operate at long distances, has been unable to deliver a single airplane
to Russia.

"Japanese invention has produced a new air arm that will paralyze our enemies," he had boasted. "It's equal in all ways and superior in many to the English Hurricane and the American Flying
Fortress." (We had wondered about the odd combination of resemblances.) "It has made invasion of our shores by air impossible.
And in our invincible security, we ask ourselves, 'What has become
of the advertised American air power? What has become of the
British and American fleets, if any?"

The gunnery officer—as does everybody else in the wardroom—
seems to recall these things without further reminder.

"And now," he says, "they're hoping they can get themselves
out of town before Tokio burns down and their new airplane is
not working and as for the fleet—" He does not have to go on with

it. Anybody aboard could have told the Japanese where the fleet is. Their own patrol boats probably will be spreading the glad tidings, before we can get around to sinking them in the morning, that we are closer to Japan than most of the units of the Mikado's home navy—a mighty fantastic expedition, this, and it gets no less fantastic as the quavering voice of Tokio goes on into the night.

"Tokio was raided today by unidentified land planes," comes a bulletin which shows that the Japs have abandoned the theory of a Chinese-Russian-American alliance.

"The raid was quickly dispersed," it continues. "Nine of the planes were shot down, many probably damaged by our fighters. There is no damage."

An hour later the announcer declared that "a study of tail markings" led Jap experts to believe that all the raiders (including, no doubt, the unidentified nine that had been presumably shot down) were American.

They did no damage, he reiterates. They did no damage—

"Fires started by the alleged bombing in Tokio, Yokohama, Nagoya and Kobe are now under control—"

This announcement comes at about 7 o'clock, Tokio time— eight hours after a shocked propagandist announced the fall of the first bomb on old Yeddo. Even if the bulletins have unquestionably begun to tell the truth, it is evident that the "alleged bombing" was done fairly well, probably not well enough to justify the dither in which the capital's English-speaking radio personalities find themselves, but fairly well.

There comes presently the inevitable "study" of the situation by a home strategist. He turns out to be quite like any number of American experts.

"The bombers which struck Tokio were large planes, capable of carrying a heavy load," he is quoted, pompously, by some rough-voiced member of the studio staff. And that is about the last point at which he seems to make much sense.

"They came to Japan over three possible routes," he says. "The first possibility is that they came from the south—from China or the Philippines. The second is that they operated from the Aleutian islands. And the third, of course, is that they were based on a secret landing field in Japan proper." (The possibility that the bombers might have been commercial planes operated by fifth columnists is not considered by this unresourceful expert.) The suggestion of a secret air base in Japan interests our executive officer who thinks that maybe we are heading for that place to establish a secret naval base—an idea which at the moment is probably figuring in Tojo's current set of jitters.

For hours this goes on while our men-of-war continue their mysterious jaunt along this definitely unappreciative coast. We turn from the broadcast to presumably more serious concerns. For one thing, the air attack, coming as it did as a complete surprise to the Japs, has brought about a complete change in patrol strategy. The resultant confusion as we get it from the radio is something to gladden the ear. The commanders of the defense fleet have had no way of estimating our strength. They cannot guess our purpose. And they are naturally cautious about coming to see for themselves.

So, out there in the dark, they draw in their strength while we continue our strange business in what should be the most congested submarine zone in their home defense waters.

April 20. This morning, as we have learned by piecing together some bits of comment from our wild-eyed Tokio informants, Japanese planes are out in force looking for us, and with us an airplane carrier apparently half a mile long (we think it might have done better with a longer flight deck), with a displacement of probably 200,000 tons, and a crew of 3,000 men—the biggest ship since Noah's ark.

And until somebody has analyzed the long-distance photographs taken by the Japs' signal corps and discovered that the visiting bombers were three times the size of the average carrier plane, this hunt for a super-whooper-dooper will continue.

Then the searchers will give up and presumably go home to sit nervously awaiting for the next attack.

The most recent expert over the radio in Tokio says that the raiding bombers were North American B-25's, which, in view of the previous accuracy of this source, probably means that they were Messerschmitts. But if they were B-25's, then they weighed 15 tons apiece, and they had a wingspread too great to permit them to be fitted into any hangar deck on any hangar afloat.

They are generally operated from runways half a mile to a mile long, and they have a landing speed of over 100 miles an hour. Hence the search for the super-ark. Hence the nervous state of the high command and the Japanese air force over a problem that seems to justify nerves.

The noon dispatches mention that General Muto, former chief of home defenses, has been ordered to a line regiment with a possible stopover at Hara-Kiri.

Mr. Muto was asked how the bombing came about and he apparently did not know any more of the answers than anybody else. He probably realizes that he has seen the accomplishment of an epoch-making turn in aerial war technique. But there is nothing in his experience to tell him how the trick worked—and how it may be worked again tomorrow, or next week, or any day.

And, for the moment, nobody is talking.

TOO LATE TO CLASSIFY

JAPAN'S CARRIERS

Japan at the beginning of the war had nine aircraft carriers listed in Jane's *Fighting Ships*. Of these the *Kaga* and *Akagi*, converted battleships, were largest. They were similar to our *Lexington* and *Saratoga* in most respects and carried from fifty to sixty planes apiece.

Of the remaining seven, one was the *Hosyo*, an old craft, slow and unable to carry more than twenty-six planes. Three, the *Soryu*, *Hiryu*, and *Koryu*, carried from thirty to forty apiece. The *Szokaku* and *Zuikaku* carried from forty-five to fifty apiece and the *Ryujo* twenty-four to thirty. Ready to be commissioned at the time of the attack on Pearl Harbor were two other large ships. While little is known of them it is generally believed that they were made to carry sixty planes apiece.

Adding all this up they started out with a presumable eleven carriers equipped to handle a maximum of 529 planes.

As against that we had seven carriers capable of handling 580 planes and our average speed and average carrier size was considerably larger.

JAPAN'S STEEL SUPPLY
(Note to Page 106)

Señor Bourcoud was a Spanish engineer who for many years worked at metallurgical research for the Ford Motor Car Company. Along about 1925 he perfected a process for making good steel out of scrap and low-grade iron ore and started for Japan to sell it. I last saw him dancing with Admiral Togo's granddaughter at a ball in the Spanish embassy in Tokio seventeen years ago and have had cause since to wonder if he made a sale.

THE LEGEND OF THE LEIS
(Note to Page 93)

It is the beautiful superstition in Hawaii that the lei, the wreath of flowers that the natives throw about your neck in token of farewell, somehow links you with the enchanted islands. When you get out beyond the reef in your departure, you throw the lei overboard. If it floats ashore you are certain to come back.